Jules Dassin

ALSO BY PETER SHELLEY

Frances Farmer: The Life and Films of a Troubled Star
(McFarland, 2011)

*Grande Dame Guignol Cinema:
A History of Hag Horror from* Baby Jane *to* Mother
(McFarland, 2009)

JULES DASSIN
The Life and Films

Peter Shelley

McFarland & Company, Inc., Publishers
Jefferson, North Carolina, and London

LIBRARY OF CONGRESS CATALOGUING-IN-PUBLICATION DATA

Shelley, Peter.
Jules Dassin : the life and films / Peter Shelley.
    p.   cm.
Includes bibliographical references and index.

ISBN 978-0-7864-6045-8
softcover : 50# alkaline paper ∞

1. Dassin, Jules, 1911–2008. 2. Motion picture producers
and directors—United States—Biography. I. Title.
PN1998.3.D37S45   2011   791.43'0233092—dc22   [B]   2011014334

BRITISH LIBRARY CATALOGUING DATA ARE AVAILABLE

© 2011 Peter Shelley. All rights reserved

*No part of this book may be reproduced or transmitted in any form
or by any means, electronic or mechanical, including photocopying
or recording, or by any information storage and retrieval system,
without permission in writing from the publisher.*

On the cover: Filmmaker Jules Dassin (right) directs
Gina Lollobrigida and Yves Montand during the shooting of the
1958 film *La loi* (The Law) in Paris (Keystone-France/Getty Images)

Manufactured in the United States of America

*McFarland & Company, Inc., Publishers
Box 611, Jefferson, North Carolina 28640
www.mcfarlandpub.com*

Table of Contents

Acknowledgments vi
Preface 1
Introduction 5

THE FILMS 49

The Tell-Tale Heart (1941)	49	*He Who Must Die* (1957)	150
Nazi Agent (1942)	52	*Where the Hot Wind Blows* (1959)	157
The Affairs of Martha (1942)	58	*Never on Sunday* (1960)	164
Reunion in France (1942)	63	*Phaedra* (1962)	173
Young Ideas (1943)	70	*Topkapi* (1964)	185
The Canterville Ghost (1944)	77	*10:30 P.M. Summer* (1966)	195
A Letter for Evie (1946)	86	*Survival 1967* (1968)	203
Two Smart People (1946)	95	*Up Tight!* (1968)	205
Brute Force (1947)	101	*Promise at Dawn* (1970)	217
The Naked City (1948)	112	*The Rehearsal* (1974)	223
Thieves' Highway (1949)	122	*A Dream of Passion* (1978)	227
Night and the City (1950)	132	*Circle of Two* (1980)	234
Rififi (1955)	141		

Bibliography 243
Index 249

Acknowledgments

I offer overall thanks to the invaluable Barry Lowe, who has helped me with this book and my previous two. I also offer thanks for technical support from Herb Kane and Stewart South, financial and moral support from Kath Perry, and additional moral support from Kate Buchanan, Brian Edgeware, Boze Hadleigh, Chris Lewis, Desire Loveridge, Anne-Louise Luccarini, and Hugh Monroe.

Preface

The writing of this book has been a journey of discovery. Although I had heard of Jules Dassin, the only one of his films I had actually seen was *Reunion in France*, and that was more because Joan Crawford was in it rather than the fact of him directing it. Yes, I knew he was also the director of several notable film noir titles, and that he had been blacklisted during the activities of the House Un-American Activities Committee (aka House Committee on Un-American Activities) in the 1940s and 1950s, but I really didn't know if that meant that a great talent had been stymied (since I didn't know the context of his career or the quality of his work). I agreed to write the book on faith, and my faith has been happily rewarded when I came to watch Dassin's catalogue and could acknowledge that he was talented, that being blacklisted had effectively ended his promising career in Hollywood, and that his move to Europe had allowed him to continue filmmaking and receive continued praise for doing so.

While one doesn't necessarily have to hold totally positive feelings towards a subject in order to provide a critical assessment and evaluation (in fact, it's easier to write about something you dislike), I was relieved to find that Dassin's work pleased me in many ways. The films from his early Hollywood period, which Dassin himself later disregarded as "awful" and "shit," actually have value, since they display examples of visual innovation, comic invention, and the director's ability to get good performances from his actors. (In their book *Tender Comrades*, Patrick McGilligan and Paul Buhle quote Marsha Hunt, who appeared in two of Dassin's films and one of his stage comedies, as saying that he was a superb comedy director.) Dassin seemed to refute F. Scott Fitzgerald's claim that there are no second acts in American lives by reinventing himself as a director in exile, and his later European films are also noteworthy for the nine appearances by the actress Melina Mercouri (in a working relationship that rivaled that of Ingmar Bergman and Liv Ullmann, and Woody Allen and Mia Farrow). In his *Biographical Dictionary of Film*, David Thomson comments ambiguously on the Dassin-Mercouri teaming: "[They] made some of the most entertainingly bad films of the sixties and seventies; pictures that outstrip their own deficiencies and end up being riotously enjoyable as one waits to see how far pretentiousness will stretch."

Dassin is also a unique blacklisted director in the sense that while he did manage to continue to find work once he was blackballed, the quality of his filmmaking suffered. I make this argument based on an assessment of all his films, and deduce that Dassin benefited from being a Hollywood studio director because, despite the so-called interference and control the studios exercised on his films, a discipline was imposed on his work which is lacking in his later independent titles. I count *Night and the City* as his best picture; it is the culmination of his working in the studio system and benefits from being such.

Although Dassin would achieve moments of brilliance in his later work, like the robbery set piece of *Rififi*, and enjoyed box office and critical success with *Never on Sunday*, these and the rest of his second-career titles all suffer from what can be read as self-indulgence and what has been described as pretentiousness. However, it is reasonable to assume that if Dassin had testified before HUAC rather than having been named he would have likely been an unfriendly witness and therefore officially blacklisted from Hollywood anyway. So either way, we lost the potential of what might have been, and have to settle for what was.

Perhaps the most interesting aspect of his films is the fact that Dassin, whether deliberately or not, seemed to be drawn to narratives that explored the themes of duplicity, betrayal and subversion that prefigured the way he was viewed by HUAC and its sympathizers, and which led to his banishment from Hollywood. (An argument could be made that since drama is based on conflict, any conflict requires duplicity, betrayal and thematic subversion, although I can think of successful scenarios of conflict that operate without these attributes.) In his *Time* magazine essay on Dassin (April 6, 2008), Richard Corliss commented that informers, toxic whisperers and people who just can't keep a secret are everywhere in his films, as well as erotic sadists. Corliss claims that "it is likely that Dassin saw similarities between the wielders of the whips and his own bosses in Hollywood, or was finding objective correlatives for his own victimization by the blacklist."

While some may find my interpretation of Dassin's themes (or even Corliss' claims) in the films a projected stretch, I make no apology for them, since any evaluation and assessment is ultimately subjective, as is the nature of my notes in the film chapters within this book. I have recorded what I have seen—things another viewer may not—but I have noted them because I think they make the film in question (and the director) interesting, which I see as the aim of the book.

There exists no English language biography or work of film appreciation on Dassin; this book is an attempt to fill that void. A brief biographical chapter is provided to give context to his life and work, which also includes the stage plays he directed. This chapter is brief simply because there were limited biographical sources to access and few recorded interviews with the director. However, from what I have found I applied the rule that any statement of fact must be supported by common agreement in the accessed sources, with variations recorded as such. Each of Dassin's feature films warrants its own chapter. I have viewed all of the available titles to accurately describe the content and to give my critical evaluation and assessment. The only Dassin title I could not access was the documentary *Survival 67*, for which I have collected whatever material I could find. For another title, *Where the Hot Wind Blows* (1959), I have viewed a dubbed version (the only available copy). Since some of Dassin's later films were released in Europe before the United States, I have used their first release date in chronologically ordering chapters. The classification of a film as an "A" or "B" title can be contentious, and differs depending on the source, especially in regards to Dassin's MGM films. As a rule I have used the running time of 75 minutes as a guide, so that if a film runs less than 75 minutes I consider it a "B"; if more, an "A."

I have made observations on the films in terms of narrative, filmmaking technique and style, and performance, as well as pointing out the recurrence of the themes and motifs I consider to be the director's hallmark. I do not have the slavish agenda of a biased fan, so I do not hesitant to point out elements that are disappointing or downright bad; nor do I hesitate to praise things I consider worthy.

Films are listed by their English titles so *Du rififi chez les hommes* appears as *Rififi*,

Celui qui doit mourir is *He Who Must Die*, and *La Loi/La Legge* is *Where the Hot Wind Blows*. An interesting title note is that *Up Tight!* was listed in the film's credits as *Uptight*.

Each chapter has a cast and crew filmography taken from the film. Listings are supplemented by information on the Internet Movie Database and Turner Classic Movies website to include uncredited cast and crew members.

As more than half of the titles are not available commercially, I have accessed prints from auctions and collectors; therefore, I have not judged the quality of photography too harshly in these sometimes less than ideal copies. The chapters also provide a plot synopsis, make mention of any songs, the filming dates of the production, any location sites, the release or screening date, any publicity taglines, period and contemporary reviews, and information about video or DVD availability. In my chapter notes I also give the history of the producers and provide any known behind-the-scenes information. Acronyms are used as abbreviated references to repeated sources, such as TCM for Turner Classic Movies, and HUAC for the House Un-American Activities Committee. To supplement chapters I have attempted to provide imagery to complement the text, including portraits of Dassin, and stills, lobby cards and posters where possible.

Introduction

Jules Dassin was born Julius Moses Dassin in Middletown, Connecticut, on December 18, 1911. He was the son of poor Jewish immigrants with a family of eight children. Some sources say his father, Samuel, was Austrian, others that Samuel came from Odessa; however, all agree that he was a barber. Sources also differ about the nationality of Dassin's mother, Berthe Vogel. Some say she was French, others Polish. Dassin's grandfather had supposedly been a wigmaker for the Odessa Opera, and the family shared a love of classical music. They moved to Harlem in New York, hoping for a better life, and Jules went to school in the Bronx at Morris High School. Like his older brother, Jules was required to work various jobs to help the family, but it is said that this work made it impossible for him to graduate. However, in his interview with Dassin in *Films Illustrated*, Tony Crawley says that Jules did graduate, and that he even took a graduation trip to Europe. In his interview with Dassin in *Films & Filming*, Gordon Gow claims that the European trip began in 1934 and evolved into a two-year study of European dramatic centers.

An interest in the theater saw Jules attending acting lessons at Eva La Gallienne's Civic Repertory Theatre Company; and he joined the New York Yiddish Proletarian Theatre company, called ARTEF (an acronym for Arbeter Teater Farband—Workers Theatrical Alliance), in 1936. After learning the language, Dassin appeared in several Second Avenue plays, including *Recruits*, by Lipe Resnick, *First Prize or 200,000*, by Sholem Aleichem, and plays by Moshe Kulbak. Dassin also worked as a director for the company, and extended this ability to being a social director at the Catskill Mountains Jewish holiday camps for five years, where he was responsible for Sunday's Get Together nights and Monday's Camp Fire evening. At the Catskills he met his future wife, Beatrice Launer, a Hungarian violinist who took part in the events and whom he married in 1933.

Dassin became involved in the Federal Theatre Project, an initiative of President Franklin Delano Roosevelt's "New Deal" to provide jobs for actors, directors and writers during the Great Depression. He played the role of a young beaver in the children's musical *Revolt of the Beavers*. When the Group Theatre was formed by Lee Strasberg, Harold Clurman and Cheryl Crawford in 1931, Dassin attended their productions, and he joined the Communist Party after seeing the Group Theatre play *Waiting for Lefty* in 1935. (In his audio commentary for *Night and the City*, Glenn Erickson states that Dassin joined the party in 1937.) Dassin would withdraw his membership in 1939, when he recognized the disparity between the Party's radical alignment with the Soviet Union and the American people's acceptance (the Party's Soviet connection would become a sore point when the Russians changed from allies to enemies in World War II). Dassin claims in the book *Tender Comrades*, by Patrick McGilligan and Paul Bule, that he had been threatened with expulsion many times over disagreements with the Party on different issues.

Dassin and his wife had their first child on November 17, 1938, a son they called Joseph. Jules started writing for radio, including penning sketches for Kate Smith's popular CBS show and an adaptation of the Gogol novel *The Overcoat*. Broadway producer Martin Gabel hired Dassin to direct *Medicine Show*, a play by Oscar Saul and H.R. Hays, on Broadway, which starred John Randolph, Dorothy McGuire and Norman Lloyd. The production ran for 35 performances at the New Yorker Theatre at 254 West 54th Street, from April 12 to May 11, 1940, and was described by Brooks Atkinson in *The New York Times* (April 13, 1940) as "a completely absorbing presentation ... well-staged for the most part and more illuminating than most things the theater offers." This success led to Dassin being offered a six-month contract with RKO Studios at $200 a week as an apprentice director—an offer he accepted. (In his 2004 Los Angeles County Museum of Art interview, Dassin says he was paid $250 a week, and that his agent told him he could have gotten him more.) The year 1940 also saw the birth of Dassin's second child, Richelle.

At RKO Dassin observed the production of two Carole Lombard vehicles. The drama *They Knew What They Wanted* (1940) filmed from June 10 to July 31, 1940, was directed by Garson Kanin and co-starred Charles Laughton, whom Dassin would later direct in the comedy *The Canterville Ghost* (1944). The other Lombard film he observed in production was the romantic comedy *Mr. and Mrs. Smith* (1941), directed by Alfred Hitchcock from September 5 to December 4, 1940 (and thought to be one of Hitchcock's most atypical films). Hitchcock's own claim, made later in life, that he never wanted to make the film (and only did it as a favor to friend Carole Lombard) is refuted by Donald Spoto in his books on the director, *The Dark Side of Genius* and *Spellbound by Beauty*. Spoto advises that the RKO archives tell of Hitchcock's enthusiasm for the project, based on (1) his desire to work with Lombard; (2) an interest in doing an American comedy about Americans (as opposed to the English stories and characters in *Rebecca* and non–American settings in *Foreign Correspondent*); and (3) an eagerness to work at RKO to avoid his unfulfilling relationship with his contracted producer David O. Selznick.

Dassin told Gordon Gow how he was impressed by Hitchcock's placement of the camera, and by his extraordinary knowledge of what the lens contained without ever looking through the camera. Dassin also spoke of Hitchcock's generosity, saying that after each take he would turn to Dassin and ask, "All right, for you?" (though some might interpret this as Hitchcock indulging his own impish sense of humor, since one can't imagine him doing a re-take to please an observer). Dassin would tell Tony Crawley that Hitchcock's parting words to him were, "Never make a film with animals or children or Charles Laughton." Hitchcock had directed Laughton in the crime adventure *Jamaica Inn* (1939), and would work with him again in the legal drama *The Paradine Case* (1947). Of course, Dassin would go on to work with both Laughton, a child (Margaret O'Brien), a stag and dogs—all in the same film. Dassin told Crawley, "You can imagine the exchange of telegrams that followed between Hitch and me." Interestingly, Harry Stradling was the director of photography for both these films, and he would photograph Dassin's feature debut, *Nazi Agent* (1942). Dassin would also tell Gordon Gow how he learned to work with actors from Garson Kanin, and particularly how to create and sustain an atmosphere on the set to enable the actors to give their best performances.

His RKO contract up, Dassin was fired and about to go back to New York, when he was hired by MGM. Gordon Gow quotes Dassin as saying, "Everyone seemed to think I was a nephew of Louis B. Mayer, and I had never met Louis B. Mayer." The Melina Mercouri Foundation biography of Dassin claims he directed two shorts, one about the Polish pianist Artur (aka Arthur) Rubinstein and the other about black American opera singer Marian Anderson. However, the biography later claims that in 1951 Dassin made the documentary episode "Trio" as part of the NBC television series *Meet the Masters*, which is believed to have aired on February 24, 1952. This episode was about Rubinstein, Jascha Heifetz and Gregor Piatigorsky. Marian Anderson is also said to have been a guest performer on the series, so perhaps her episode was the "short" that Dassin directed.

Dassin then made the short film *The Tell-Tale Heart* (1941), starring Joseph Schildkraut and Roman Bohnen, an adaptation of the Edgar Allan Poe story which was screened at the movie theater next to the MGM lot in Culver City in October that year. Both Tony Crawley and Gordon Gow quote Dassin as stating that the film was only screened as an emergency replacement for a lost newsreel—after three months when nobody would look at it—and it then became an immediate success and won several prizes. This success led to Dassin being given a seven-year contract at MGM. In November and December he directed *Nazi Agent* (1942), a spy drama starring Conrad Veidt in a double role. In February and March he made the comedy *The Affairs of Martha* (1942), which starred Marsha Hunt and Richard Carlson, and from June to September he directed the World War II romance *Reunion in France* (1942), with Joan Crawford and John Wayne.

Collage still for *Nazi Agent* (1942). Clockwise from upper left: Dorothy Tree (Miss Harper) and Conrad Veidt (Otto Becker); Jules Dassin (right) looks into the camera with an unidentified cameraman; an unidentified man threatens Conrad Veidt (Otto Becker). Conrad Veidt (as Baron Hugo Von Detner).

In January and February 1943 Dassin directed the college comedy *Young Ideas* (1942), which starred Mary Astor, Herbert Marshall, and Susan Peters. From August to December 1943 he was called in to replace Norman Z. McLeod as director of *The Canterville Ghost* (1944), a very loose adaptation of the Oscar Wilde short story, which starred Charles Laughton, Robert Young and Margaret O'Brien. (In his audio commentary on *Night and the City*, Glenn Erickson claims that this film was the only one of Dassin's MGM titles that was a box office success.) Laughton was perfectly acceptable to Dassin, after they had become friends on *They Knew What They Wanted*.

Additionally, Dassin was said to have been one of the founding members of the Actors Laboratory (aka the Lab), a workshop and theater for actors, with one class for beginners and one for professionals (which Laughton attended, as well as Roman Bohnen from Dassin's *The Tell-Tale Heart*). However, in *Tender Comrades*, Jeff Corey says that Dassin simply taught classes.

Tender Comrades states that the Lab was announced in May 1941, with the executive board being comprised of Virginia Farmer, J. Edward Bromberg, and Roman Bohnen. Jeff Corey told Patrick McGilligan that the Hollywood studios also sent actors who were under contract to study at the Lab, including a young Marilyn Monroe. The studios kept their players away after the 1947 HUAC hearings; and after the IRS revoked their tax-exempt status in 1948, and Lab people were being subpoenaed, audiences dropped and sources of revenue dried up, so that the doors closed forever in 1950.

In his memoir *A Terrible Liar*, Hume Cronyn says that the heart of the Lab was made up of former members of the now-disbanded Group Theater, including Morris Carnovksy, Bohnen, Art Smith, Phil Brown, and new recruits like Anthony Quinn, Larry Parks and Vincent Price. They were actors with a theater background who found working in films unfulfilling. A lease was held on a small shabby space in Hollywood just off Sunset Boulevard and immediately behind the landmark Schwab's Drug Store. Rent had to be paid for the space by the small nonprofit company, and the struggle between commercial concerns (like attracting an audience) and producing art often divided the loosely knit collection of supporters who had a hunger for theater but also a political bias to the left (which became evident from policy discussions and the choice of plays). A case in point was a proposed production of Jean-Paul Sartre's one-act existential French play *No Exit* which John Huston wanted to direct after finding conditions in New York unsatisfactory. There were objections made to the production of any play by Sartre because of his shifting political attitudes. Once a darling of the Communist Party, the writer had now become anathema. Cronyn expressed his disagreement, but Huston could not be accommodated. The director would go on to do the play in New York at the Biltmore Theatre from November 26 to December 21, 1946.

Plays that were approved for production included Ben Jonson's *Volpone*; a USO play called *Declaration*, directed by Daniel Mann; the James Thurber/Elliott Nugent comedy *The Male Animal*, about teachers suspected of being communists, which featured Cronyn and which toured military installations in California in May 1944; and a series of Tennessee Williams one-acts. One of these was called *Portrait of a Madonna*, which is said to have been a kind of first draft of his later full-length play *A Streetcar Named Desire*. *Portrait of a Madonna* was produced at the Las Palmas Theatre in Los Angeles, with Jessica Tandy playing the title role of Miss Lucretia Collins, and her husband, Cronyn, directing (though apparently Tandy thought she was miscast in the role of a lonely spinster suffering the bedevilment of violent sexual fantasies and the illusions of social ostracism, in spite of the

Jules Dassin and actress Lenore Ulric on the set of *Two Smart People* (1946).

triumph she enjoyed with it). Sources differ as to whether this January production and its revival in July were in 1946 or 1947. Cronyn cites a letter dated January 16, 1947, from Joe L. Mankiewicz to Darryl F. Zanuck which describes Tandy in the production, and later in his book Cronyn gives the date as Summer 1946.

Dassin had cast Hume Cronyn in his next film, the home-front comedy-drama *A Letter for Evie* (1946), which he made from May to July 1945, and which also starred Marsha Hunt and Spring Byington from *The Affairs of Martha*, and John Carroll. On July 17, 1945, Dassin's third child was born, a daughter named Julie. From September to November 1945 he made his last film for MGM, the crime drama *Two Smart People* (1946), with Lucille Ball, John Hodiak, and Lloyd Nolan. Dassin had been discontented at MGM because of his perceived lack of control in the process of making a film—"It was just plain unhappiness and embarrassment." He claimed he never met the writers of the screenplays which he worked on, and that his producers had more say in editing than he. Dassin would also say that the studios were so powerful that even the big directors of the time did not have the legal right of final cut on their own films. In his book *Report on Blacklisting*, John Cogley writes that Dassin and others circulated a petition at MGM to halt production on a film with whose political content they disagreed. Cogley does not name the picture, but the action taken when the director was presumably still under contract was not seen as contentious (as it may have been viewed in later years when Dassin was suspected of being a political subversive).

Dassin asked Louis B. Mayer, who Dassin describes in *Tender Comrades* as "an evil man," to let him out of his contract, but Mayer said no. Dassin told Mayer that he would stop work and be on his own "one man strike." He took a break for a year (thirteen months, according to Dassin's *Cine-Parade* interview), which he spent reading at a house on the beach. Mayer kept Dassin on his payroll since Mayer knew that the director would soon become bored and want to work again.

When Dassin came back to MGM, Mayer invited him into his office, where Dassin sat in front of a group of MGM executive producers. He claimed that Mayer wanted to make an example of him, to show how he treated "a rebel" director. Mayer told the men in the room the story of his two-year-old horse named Pater that he had purchased as a foal for $50,000, despite the trainer telling Mayer that the horse cost too much and didn't have much pedigree. The horse kept winning races, and he became Mayer's favorite in his stable of horses. Mayer wants to enter the horse into the Kentucky Derby. His trainer says he can't win there, but Mayer enters him. However, when the horse was tried out in a local race before the Derby, it would suddenly stop cold and come in last. This happened four times. The trainer realizes the reason why the horse is behaving like this—it has developed "the biggest balls he has ever seen on a horse," and when it runs, they bang so hard against him it has to stop. So Mayer had the horse gelded, and Pater began to win races again. In response to the story, Dassin said, "Not my balls, you son of a bitch." (In the *Cine-Parade* interview with Dassin on the DVD of *Night and the City*, Dassin adds that he treated Mayer to a stream of his best New York obscenities). At this, Mayer yelled back, "Get out of here, you dirty red." (Mayer considered Dassin "a pinko" Communist but tolerated him at MGM because he was deemed talented.) Dassin tells the story to explain how he got out of his MGM contract, which presumably had not expired.

Dassin's interview on the DVD of *Night and the City* also gives more detail as to why Mayer did not want to release the director from his contract. Dassin had done a comedy where all the characters were rich, respectable, and upper class (this is presumably referring to *Young Ideas*), and Mayer told him that people who can make films about the upper class are rare. Mayer also feared that if he released Dassin he would simply sign with another studio—at which the director promised in writing he would not do this, since he wanted to return to New York and work in the theater. (It's interesting that Dassin did not immediately live up to his promise to Mayer.) In his *Cine-Parade* interview Dassin also tells the story of how David O. Selznick had wanted him to direct the next film he was to produce after *Gone with the Wind* (1939). Selznick had originally wanted to reteam with that film's main director, Victor Fleming, but after they had a fight, Selznick hired the inexperienced Dassin to show that it's not the director who makes the film, it's the producer. This project did not materialize, with Dassin presumably refusing to work under these terms, and Selznick moving on to make his next film, *Rebecca*, with Hitchcock, a more experienced director.

Dassin forged a relationship with independent producer Mark Hellinger, declining to bind himself to another long-term contract. From February to April 1947 Dassin made the prison drama *Brute Force* (1947) at Universal International for Hellinger, which starred Burt Lancaster, Hume Cronyn (from *A Letter for Evie*) and Rohman Bohnen (from *The Tell-Tale Heart*). Hellinger had been an associate producer and producer at Warner Bros. since 1939, though he moved to Universal Pictures as an independent producer, where he had made the crime drama *The Killers* (1946) and the postwar melodrama *Swell Guy* (1947). Ironically, the director of *Swell Guy*, Frank Tuttle, would become a friendly witness at the HUAC hearings on May 24, 1951, where he would name Dassin as a communist. In his book *Only Victims*, Robert Vaughan claims that Tuttle had been named by Edward

Dmytryk on April 25, 1951, that Tuttle also named himself as a communist when he named Dassin, and that he added that he thought Dassin had left the party.

Dassin again worked with Hellinger and Universal Pictures on the crime drama *The Naked City* (1948), filmed from June to September 1947 on location in New York City. The film starred Barry Fitzgerald, Howard Duff (from *Brute Force*), Dorothy Hart, Don Taylor, and Ted de Corsia. However, the professional relationship with Hellinger ended when the producer died in December 1947 before the film was released. Dassin went to Broadway, where he directed two plays. *Joy to the World* ran from March 18, 1948, to July 3, 1948, at the Plymouth Theatre. A comedy by Allan Scott, it starred Marsha Hunt (from *The Affairs of Martha* and *A Letter for Evie*) as the liberal girlfriend of a Hollywood production manager fight-

Publicity portrait of producer Mark Hellinger. Hellinger made two films with Jules Dassin, *Brute Force* (1947) and *The Naked City* (1948) (Photofest).

A shirtless Jules Dassin on location in New York for *The Naked City* (1948) (Photofest).

ing the chairman of the board to make "fine pictures" rather than escapist entertainments. In *The New York Times* of March 19, 1948, Brooks Atkinson called the production "a knockabout Hollywood comedy, staged like a comic horse-race.... Dassin has directed it lickety-split," and said Hunt "supplies the spiritual influence painlessly."

Magdalena ran from September 20, 1948, to December 4, 1948, at the Ziegfeld Theatre. A musical by Heitor Villa-Lobos, with lyrics by Robert Wright and George Forrest, and book by Frederick Hazlitt Brennan and Homer Curran, it had a huge cast. In *The New York Times* of September 21, Atkinson wrote that it was "one of the most overpoweringly dull musical dramas of all time. Watching the slow process of the plot is like being hit over the head with a sledge hammer repeatedly all evening. It hurts." He also described the direction as "ponderous." Dassin left New York in November to make his next film, the film noir *Thieves' Highway* at 20th Century–Fox, which starred Richard Conte, Valentina Cortesa, Lee J. Cobb and Barbara Lawrence. Although the director had agreed to the casting of women in *Brute Force* on Mark Hellinger's suggestion (so as to appease Universal), Dassin was less happy with the interference of producer Darryl F. Zanuck at Fox, who inserted new shots and scenes into *Thieves' Highway*. However, the director's future with Fox had become problematic in light of HUAC.

The special investigating committee of the United States House of Representatives had been established in 1938, aimed mostly at German-American involvement in Nazi and Ku Klux Klan activities. It also looked into the possibility that the American Communist Party had infiltrated projects like the Federal Theatre Project (in which Dassin had been involved) and the Federal Writers Project, and carried out a brief investigation into the wartime internment of Japanese-Americans living on the West Coast. In 1945 the committee began to investigate suspected threats of subversion or propaganda "that attacked the form of government guaranteed by the constitution." In 1947 they held hearings into alleged communist propaganda and influence in Hollywood, summoning artists to appear who were members of, or in sympathy with, the Communist Party (those who were not members but were sympathetic were referred to as "fellow travelers"), or who were involved with liberal or humanitarian political causes.

The documentary *Blacklist: Hollywood on Trial* claims that the committee's investigation had been invited by conservatives in Hollywood, who were fearful of the new wave of filmmakers who had emerged in the late 1940s and who were making message pictures like the social drama *Gentleman's Agreement* (1947). This argument is weakened by the fact that the film would be not released until after the first round of open hearings in October 1947. However, another claim made in the documentary, which seems more reasonable, is that no communist propaganda could have been inserted into a production's screenplay (if such an intention was ever present) because the studio heads held strict control over content. Other factors that are said to have led to the committee's interest in Hollywood include the idea of blaming communists for post-war union activities, President Harry Truman ordering anti-communist loyalty oaths to be signed by all federal employees, and Congress discussing legislation to outlaw membership in the Communist Party. This fearmongering is said to have resulted from the collapse of the alliance between the Soviet Union and the Western democracies (an alliance that had helped defeat the fascist states of Germany, Italy and Japan), and the worry over the "Iron Curtain" that was thought to have fallen over Europe after the war.

Closed hearings were held in May 1947, where witnesses like Robert Taylor, Adolphe Menjou, Gary Cooper, Ronald Reagan, Walt Disney, and Louis. B Mayer gave testimony supporting the idea that communists were trying to take over Hollywood with the help of duped, indoctrinated liberals. Some of the witnesses were known as "friendly" because they offered names of communists or communist sympathizers. This resulted in subpoenas being issued for 19 witnesses to give testimony at open hearings in October. A collection of celebrities, including Humphrey Bogart, Lauren Bacall, John Huston, Danny Kaye and Marsha Hunt, followed those called to Washington to testify and observed the proceedings for two days, their group known as the Committee for the First Amendment. However, this Committee's impact waned once Bogart recanted his support. (Huston's role is explored by way of a fictional counterpart, George Bissinger, in the 1973 film *The Way We Were*). Later declaring his original expression as "ill-advised," Bogart was no doubt fearful of how the activity would jeopardize his career. At the hearing, only 11 testified (Playwright Bertolt Brecht is said to have been the eleventh, who denied being a communist then swiftly left the country to avoid any prosecution). They were Alvah Bessie, Herbert J. Biberman, Lester Cole, Edward Dmytryk, Ring Lardner, Jr., John Howard Lawson, Albert Maltz (screenwriter of *The Naked City*), and Dalton Trumbo.

The 10 were considered "unfriendly witnesses" because they refused to cooperate with the committee, and were charged with contempt. They had defended themselves by invoking their constitutional First Amendment right to freedom of speech and the right to peacefully assemble, and their Fifth Amendment right to not incriminate themselves. But by refusing to answer questions posed by the committee, the men were considered "guilty by suspicion," a phrase that would become the title of a 1990 film about HUAC. In November, Hollywood studio heads met at the Waldorf Astoria Hotel in New York and agreed to discharge the Ten (and the other 9) until they were acquitted or purged the contempt charge by declaring under oath that they were no longer communists. Sam Goldwyn was one of the few studio heads who refused to fire people, and Darryl F. Zanuck said he would only do so if ordered to by his board of directors (who so ordered). The "Hollywood Ten" lodged an appeal with the Supreme Court, which had two liberal judges recently replaced by Truman with two conservatives ones, which prefigured the Court's eventual decision to refuse to consider the appeals on April 10, 1950. (While awaiting the Supreme Court decision, Communist Party leaders had been jailed for supposedly plotting to overthrow the government, a plot line used for the 1951 film *I Was a Communist for the FBI*).

The Hollywood studios, in a remarkably insensitive reaction to the ordeals of the Ten, exploited the supposed post-war anti-communist doxa by producing crude genre films in much the same way they had done by making anti–Nazi films during the war (though it is a relief to read in Dorothy B. Jones essay "Communism in the Movies: A Study of Film Content" that none of these titles were box office successes or even considered good films). Some of the red-baiting titles they produced were *The Iron Curtain* (1948), *The Red Menace* (1949), *Walk a Crooked Mile* (1949), *The Woman on Pier 13* (aka *I Married a Communist*, 1949), and *I Was a Communist for the FBI* (which was inexplicably nominated for the Best Documentary Academy Award!). *The Iron Curtain* told the true story of spies in the Soviet embassy in Canada during World War II and the defection of cipher clerk Igor Gouzenko.

The Red Menace uses the symbolism of the far-reaching tentacles of an octopus to present the paranoid idea of people who attempt to leave the Party being victimized, because the Party is so evil it can never let you go. One subplot features a poet styled to resemble the playwright Clifford Odets whose work is seen to deviate from the accepted party line and who is expelled from the Party. Repeatedly stopped from keeping a job (because the Party ensures that his employers know he was a Party member), his isolation leads him to suicide by jumping out a window (after he learns that his girlfriend is to be disciplined for being seen with him). The idea that one could be in trouble by associating with someone who *wasn't* in the Party was a twist on the fear of being seen with someone who was thought to be a communist. The narrative is also interesting in featuring a black journalist who also rejects the hypocrisy of the party line once his father parallels the journalist's blind faith in the Party to a form of slavery, with the journalist's resultant discipline presumably occurring off-screen. *The Woman on Pier 13* includes a terrifying scene of a Party member thought to have informed to the FBI being tied up by Party gangsters and thrown into the river to drown.

This type of propaganda would continue with *The Whip Hand* (1951), *The Atomic City* (1952), *The Thief* (1952), *Big Jim McLain* (1952), *Invasion USA* (1952), *My Son John* (1952), *Walk East on Beacon!* (1952), *Pickup on South Street* (1953), the television series "I Led 3 Lives" (1953–1956), *Prisoner of War* (1954), and *Trial* (1955). *The Whip Hand* is especially interesting since it plays like a horror movie, with its scenario of a Nazi scientist employed by the communists to experiment with germ welfare in the ghost town of Lake Winnoga. It seems fitting that at the film's climax the scientist, who had used supposed volunteer members and Party traitors as guinea pigs to be inflicted with incurable diseases and deformities, is set upon by his Frankenstein-ian victims. *The Atomic City* has the son of a Los Alamos physician kidnapped by "spies" who want the formula for the H-bomb, but the word communism was never mentioned in the screenplay. *The Thief* focuses on a Washington physicist who copies documents from the Atomic Energy Commission to sell to agents in Cairo (also never named as communists).

Big Jim McLain purports to be based on HUAC documents about the investigation of communists in Honolulu, although the narrative sees accused communists walking free after claiming their rights under the Fifth Amendment both in Washington and in Hawaii. That John Wayne should want to produce a red-baiting title isn't surprising given his known political conservatism (and although he had worked with Dassin on *Reunion in France*, it was at a time before the director was under political suspicion). However, what is surprising is how unfocused the film's screenplay is, seemingly wasting time on lame attempts at humor and a sappy romance between Wayne and Nancy Olson (perhaps to compensate for the mild activism that the presented communists engage in). The film garnered additional notoriety when it was later re-edited for the German market so that Wayne could substitute marijuana smugglers for communists. *Invasion USA* has a hypnotist induce a group of people at a bar to imagine that America has been invaded by the Soviets.

My Son John sees the mother of an accused communist swear on a bible that he isn't one, and the father hitting his son on the head with the bible because he knows swearing on one is meaningless to a communist. John eventually admits to be "intimate" with a woman involved in a red spy ring, which causes his mother to have a nervous breakdown (adding to the ham served up by Helen Hayes' theatrical performance). John is assassinated, presumably by loyalists who perhaps guessed that he had recorded a five-minute speech to be delivered at the college that had planned to honor him with a doctorate, during which he denounces his former beliefs. It's telling and unintentionally amusing that as the communist John, Robert Walker is the most likeable character of this turgid melodrama, which also features scenes of cloying sentimentality and attempts at folksy comic relief. The film is remarkable for the way director Leo McCarey tries to conceal the absence of

Walker in its second half, since the actor died during production, and features a howler of a line when an F.B.I. agent tells John, "Use whatever free will you have left and get over here now!"

One of the subplots of the labyrinthian *Walk East on Beacon!*, which was produced with the cooperation of the F.B.I., involves an Albert Einstein–type mathematician, who has developed plans for space satellites, being blackmailed and eventually kidnapped by Bostonian communists. The film's most ludicrous scene comes when the F.B.I. use a school of lip-readers to de-code—in vocal unison—silent film footage of communist conspirators. *Trial* has an attorney's co-counsel in a murder trial conceal his communism until a rally reveals financial support is to be provided by the "All People's Party." Served a subpoena by a state committee on loyalty and subversion, the attorney discovers that his assistant had also been a fellow traveler, and that the communists had taken a percentage cut from the rally's proceeds. When it appears that the attorney is about to get his Mexican client, accused of murdering a white woman, acquitted, the co-counselor takes over, supposedly planning to purposely lose the case so that the Mexican's conviction and execution will stir up race hatred. The attorney delivers a last-minute speech to the sentencing judge, calling himself a communist front and saving the Mexican boy, who is instead sent to state industrial school since he is a minor. The communist co-counsel is held in contempt of court for attempting to make the judge lose his temper (he calls the black judge an "Uncle Tom") and imprisoned for thirty days. The man who had served the subpoena now tells the attorney that his appearance before the committee has been postponed indefinitely because they are only interested in people who won't fight back.

With the complicity of the studio heads, the 10 were blacklisted in the industry, fined, and served prison sentences. The length of the sentences varies according to sources. *Blacklist: Hollywood on Trial* claims that eight of the ten served nine months, and the other two (said to be Herbert Biberman and Edward Dmytryk in the book *Tender Comrades*) served six months; whereas *Tender Comrades* claims the longer jail term was one year. Dmytryk is said to have issued a statement while in prison stating that his membership in the Party was a mistake, which allowed him to testify in the second round of hearings held in 1951. There he was a friendly witness to the committee and named 24 names (including Dassin) after refusing to do so in 1947. (The blacklist drama *One of the Hollywood Ten* [2000] presents Dmytryk's predicament.) *Blacklist: The Hollywood Ten* makes the claim that it was the friendly testimony of actor Larry Parks in 1951 that set the precedent, since he was the first to name names, although reluctantly. Additionally, the political climate of the country had changed between the two rounds of hearings because America had entered the Korean War on June 25, 1950, where they were fighting the communist troops of North Korea. The later 1953 execution of accused communist spies Julius and Ethel Rosenberg also made an impact.

In the 1950s the blacklist would extend to all walks of life in America, jeopardizing the livelihood of school teachers, ministers, civil servants, members of the armed forces, and auto workers because of their alleged political sympathies or affiliations, with Senator Joseph McCarthy the head of the Senate Subcommittee on Investigations, which was particularly interested in alleged communists and fellow travelers in government and the army. (The film *Guilty by Suspicion* shows how a school teacher might lose her job, apart from the fact that her husband was considered a communist, because she had been photographed having attended what was considered a subversive rally for the elimination of the atomic bomb.) Dalton Trumbo, one of "The Hollywood Ten," would write that it was "a time of evil." People could be accused on the basis of rumor, hearsay and innuendo, and denied the opportunity to face their accusers or be shown any supporting evidence for the claims made against them. Those convicted lost friends, possessions, were insulted, and had things written on the walls of their houses. For the approximately 250 blacklisted screenwriters, directors and actors, what was lost was the work they might have created or produced.

In Hollywood in June 1950 a pamphlet called *Red Channels: The Report of Communist Influence in Radio and Television* would be published by the right-wing journal *Counterattack*. It would list the association with purported communist committees of over one hundred and fifty actors, writers, musicians, journalists, and others in the entertainment industry. In the documentary *None Without Sin*, actors Lee Grant and Madeleine Sherwood describe how they came to appear in *Red Channels* and be blacklisted by voicing dissent at the workings of HUAC. *Blacklist: The Hollywood Ten* states that Grant's return to film work after sixteen years was in the racial drama *In the Heat of the Night* (1967), though the Internet Movie Database lists some film credits for the actress after she was blacklisted in 1951 and before this title. Actress Beatrice Straight is said to have been blacklisted simply for appearing in a featured role (for which she won a Tony award) as Elizabeth Proctor in Arthur Miller's allegorical play *The Crucible* on Broadway in 1953.

Additionally, the documentary *Trumbo* makes the case that the deaths of actors John Garfield (who was never a communist but was called repeatedly to testify and refused to name names) and Mady Christians, and the later deaths of screenwriters Hugo Butler and Samuel Ornitz, were a direct result of being blacklisted. The made-for-TV movie *Fear on Trial* (1975) highlights the case of John Henry Faulk, a blacklisted radio and television performer who fought back proactively. After not working for five years, Faulk successfully sued Aware Inc. for libel in 1962. The company was the writer of a bulletin that accused artists of being communists and offered a clearance service to advertisers, sponsors and television networks. (Ironically, Faulk would see none of the three-and-a-half-million dollars he was awarded, after an appeal decision lowered the amount, and legal fees and accumulated debts had been deducted). However, the case is considered landmark for helping to break the blacklist.

Red Channels was updated regularly and used as a means to deny employment, with the only way one could be removed from the publication being to testify in front of HUAC as a "friendly" witness, which meant identifying oneself as a member of the Communist Party and "purging" (i.e., naming names of other members). If you refused to cooperate under the First Amendment, you could be jailed. If you refused to cooperate under the Fifth Amendment, you were not jailed but blacklisted. Some agreed to cooperate because their need to work was based on having a family to support, which was judged as more important than betraying friends. In the interview on the DVD of *Rififi*, and in *Tender Comrades*, Dassin lists director Robert Rossen as an example of a man who initially refused to cooperate and explained why to his children, but then changed his mind and did cooperate—and had to explain *that* to his children. Dassin claims that the children's problem with accepting their father's actions led to many years of trouble afterwards.

Rossen was one of the original Hollywood 19 that was whittled down to 10, but was not called to the stand in 1947. In 1951 he refused to cooperate but, when blacklisted, named fifty names in 1953. In *Trumbo* we also hear how Dalton Trumbo's daughter Mitzi was victimized at school because of her father. Some blacklisted writers, like Trumbo, would continue to write screenplays that were produced with pseudonyms or using "fronts" (i.e., having a real, non-political person pretend to have done the work). (The idea that suspected communists would use false names is particularly ironic since it was believed that some did the same thing in their communist cells anyway.) The latter phenomenon was explored in the Martin Ritt comedy-drama *The Front* (1976), which starred Woody Allen as a restaurant cashier and penny-ante bookie who fronts for three blacklisted writers, and who is eventually called before HUAC and imprisoned for contempt for refusing to inform. The film is also notable for being made by blacklisted participants: the director, the screenwriter Walter Bernstein, and the actors Zero Mostel, Herschel Bernardi, Lloyd Gough, and Joshua Shelley.

Bernstein also wrote the screenplay for the thriller *The House on Carroll Street* (1988), which told of how in 1951 a blacklisted female assistant picture editor for *Life* magazine takes a job as a reader for a wealthy widow and stumbles across a plan to smuggle Nazi war criminals into America, a plan connected to the aide of one of the senators that had charged her with contempt. Ironically, it is the F.B.I. agent who has had the heroine under surveillance who becomes her ally, repeatedly saving her from death and getting to bed her in the process. Thankfully, the narrative posits Nazi concentration camp doctors, and those that wish to use their expertise, as worse criminals than liberal political activists (the screenplay never suggests that the heroine is a communist—her crime being her refusal to name names of other associates).

Dassin's fear of being named by the committee as a subversive in light of his past associations, and being blacklisted, is discussed in the director's interviews on the DVDs of *Night and the City* and *Rififi*, the audio commentary by Glenn Erickson on *Night and the City*, and in the books *Tender Comrades* and Twentieth Century's Fox, George F. Custen's book on Zanuck. Dassin says that he had been under suspicion by HUAC for some time, with Erickson claiming that Zanuck was one of the few studio heads who would not support the blacklist. Erickson says Zanuck set up a project for Dassin, *The Journey of Simon McKeever*, a book by Maltz about a man who has arthritis and hitchhikes from San Francisco to Los Angeles to find a doctor, having adventures along the way. John Huston was prepared to write the screenplay, and Walter Huston would star. (In *Tender Comrades*, Dassin says that he brought to project to Zanuck, with filming to take place in San Francisco, where *Thieves' Highway* had been shot.) Erickson claims that Zanuck wanted to show that he could employ a blacklisted writer as long as the Fox New York Board of Directors were not made aware of his hiring practices. However, Albert Maltz decided to hold a press conference, announcing in *The Hollywood Reporter* that the blacklist had been broken, and this attention made the board order the film be cancelled.

Apparently Fox's chairman, Spyros Skouras, had told Dassin that he was going to "step on his neck," and Dassin says that Zanuck told him he would never work in Hollywood again. Although this appeared to be a threat, it was actually more a concern and led Zanuck to effectively "save" the director temporarily by instigating *Night and the City* as his next title. By making the film in London at Fox's subsidiary studio, 20th Century–Fox Limited, Dassin would be out of the country and seemingly away from the HUAC threat. *Night and the City* starred Gene Tierney and Richard Widmark. (Dassin said that he had such admiration for Richard Widmark's range as an actor that he wanted to do *Hamlet* on stage together, a project that never materialized). Dassin began shooting in July 1949 and returned to America when the production finished in October. (In *Tender Comrades*, Dassin claims that he was at the Peekskill riots where mobs attacked the attendees of a concert by Paul Robeson. As the first cancelled concert was dated August 27, and the second successful concert date was September 4, it would seem that the director was still out of the country at these times.)

Dassin maintained that he could not get film work for five years after 1949 because of the blacklist, although he was not listed in *Red Channels*. In an interview on the DVD of *Rififi*, Dassin says that he earned income for stories he sold to Fox. In *Tender Comrades* he also said that to stay alive he lived on the money that others didn't have, and he played cards in a fashion he called "exile magic." Since nobody had any money to lose, the players just redistributed the pot all over again. What is intriguing is that in June 1950 it is said that Dassin started shooting the Technicolor comedy *Half Angel*, starring Loretta Young and Joseph Cotten, for Fox, a claim supported by Joe Morella and Edward Z. Epstein in their biography of Young, *An Extraordinary Life*. A return to comedy might have seemed a surprise for Dassin (as would be working for Fox, given Spyros Skouras' animosity); however, given his current trouble in finding work, he may have had little choice. The treatment's protagonist was a split personality sleepwalker, a prim and engaged nurse who turned into a femme fatale (Princess Felicity, "the girl with the magic lips") at night, pursuing an attorney under a subconscious impulse, a man whom she had supposedly loved from childhood. The character's duplicity recalls those of others in the director's filmography, which is perhaps the reason Dassin would have been drawn to the project, with the screenplay even including a court hearing where the heroine is subpoenaed and must defend her identity when she charges the attorney with disorderly conduct for accosting her in the daytime. Dassin was supposedly fired two weeks into production, according to a *Hollywood Reporter* news item dated July 10.

Joseph Cotten receives the amorous attentions of the sleepwalking seductress played by Loretta Young in a still for *Half Angel* (1950). It is said that Young used her star power to have Jules Dassin fired as the director of the film.

It is said that he was fired at Young's request, since she had director approval, because Dassin did not agree with her interpretation of her role. One has to wonder whether the politically conservative Young was influenced by the talk of Dassin being an alleged political subversive. Perhaps another reason for the differences between director and actress may have been Young's concerns, at the age of thirty-seven, about appearing desirable. (The superficial differences between the looks of Young's nurse and her alter ego indicate that she wasn't about to let herself look too dowdy, no matter how Young herself claims she differentiated the psyches of the characters in her book *The Things I Had to Learn*.) Dassin was replaced by Richard Sale, a screenwriter who had directed two "B"s at Republic before joining Fox to make the musical western *A Ticket to Tomahawk* (1950) and the showbusiness musical *I'll Get By* (1950). It is not known how much (if any) of Dassin's work remains in the film, which is a minor, though occasionally amusing, effort featuring the repeated use of the song "Sophisticated Lady" whenever the femme fatale takes over, some slapstick effects, and a rather tepid conclusion.

Dassin travelled to Paris and Rome. In 1951 he was to direct a film in Rome called *The Little World of Don Camillo*, based on the communist novel by Giovanni Guareschi about a mayor and a priest, but Dassin had to abandon this plan over artistic differences with the producer, Giuseppe Amato. (The film went into production in September 1951 as *Don Camillo* [1952] and was directed by Julien Duvivier.) Dassin attended the Cannes film festival where he learned that Dmytryk and Tuttle had named him. (In *Tender Comrades* Dassin says he also might have read it in a newspaper.) He returned to America. In *Tender Comrades* Dassin also tells how he ran into Tuttle before he was to appear before HUAC. It was raining and there were no taxis to be had. Tuttle was a diabetic and he had an attack, so Dassin carried him on his back to his hotel in the rain. The next thing Dassin heard, the man had named him (which Dassin laughs at). In *One of the Hollywood Ten* it is claimed that Dassin was offered the job of directing the independent social drama *Salt of the Earth* (1954), but was unavailable, perhaps because he was then in Europe. (The film would be directed by Herbert Biberman, another of *The Hollywood Ten*.)

In the *Rififi* DVD interview, Dassin says that it was 1951 and not 1953 (as claimed by Glenn Erickson) when the offer came to direct the film *L'ennemi public no. 1* (aka *Public Enemy No. 1*), starring Fernandel. Dassin says that a week before shooting was to begin, Zsa Zsa Gabor told him that she couldn't do the film. Apparently she had been told that if she did, she wouldn't be allowed to work in Hollywood again. Dassin claims that a message came from Roy Brewer, who was head of the Hollywood technicians union The International Alliance of Theatrical and Stage Employees, and the head of The Motion Picture Alliance for the Preservation of American Ideals. Brewer had the power to turn men out of jobs in their own country and keep them unemployed abroad. In *Report on Blacklisting* John Cogley quotes Brewer in response to Gabor supposedly asking him whether she should make the film with Dassin: "I made it clear that I wasn't telling her whether she should go into the picture or not, but I did answer her question."

The message had been relayed to the film's French producer, Jacques Bar, that if he employed the director the picture would never received an American release, and neither would any film the producer subsequently made. Therefore, Dassin was fired by Bar. The movie would go into production in Rome in April 1953—with Gabor—and was directed by Henri Verneuil. The French press labeled the incident "l'affaire Dassin" and immediately made him an honorary member of the French director's union. Erickson claims that the director was fired two days before shooting was to begin, and that a May 1953 article in

Variety reported on the letter from Brewer. Erickson also claims that it was Gabor who, perhaps unwittingly, instigated the incident, since she had told Brewer of Dassin's hiring. The Mercouri Foundation biography claims that he had an offer from Universal to direct a film under a fake director's name, since it was impossible for him to sign a contract using his own, but this was a proposition he refused.

Dassin denies that he fled from HUAC, and says he returned to the States so that he could be questioned because he *wanted* to be, although Tony Crawley claims in his *Films Illustrated* article that the director returned from Europe to work on the Bette Davis musical revue *Two's Company*. Dassin says (rather naively) he had all the heroic answers necessary, since presumably he wasn't going to cooperate, but he wasn't immediately called. (In the film *Guilty by Suspicion*, an actor in a Monogram western that the director figure briefly works on boasts that he gave testimony without being called.) In *Tender Comrades* Dassin is asked what he would have said if he was called. He replied, "All the cliché things: What right did they have? What horrible people they were! That I had the right to be what I wanted to be." When told that's pretty much what John Howard Lawson tried to say (Lawson was a screenwriter and head of the Hollywood Communist Party, who became one of the Hollywood Ten and was blacklisted), Dassin answered, "I was going to say it prettily."

Dassin thought the Davis revue "silly and idiotic," and never knew why she wanted to do it, but he admired her for ignoring the pressure not to work with someone who was unofficially blacklisted. Davis had said, "I'm not going to listen to this nonsense. I'll work with anybody I care to work with." In his *Cineaste* interview, Dassin would claim that he was asked to work with Davis because it was thought she needed special handling by someone who'd come from Hollywood. Produced by James Russo and Michael Ellis, the show had words by Ogden Nash and Sammy Cahn, and music by Vernon Duke, and the dances and musical numbers would be directed by Jerome Robbins, the legendary director of the theater shows *On the Town*, *Call Me Madam* and later *West Side Story*. A showbusiness-themed evening tailored for the limited musical comedy talents of its star, who had not appeared on Broadway for two decades, the revue featured twenty-two original sketches by Charles Sherman and Peter DeVries. There were takeoffs of Davis herself and Tallulah Bankhead breaking up the premiere of a Davis film, parodies of Arthur Miller and Noel Coward, Davis as Sadie Thompson from Somerset Maugham's play *Rain*, a black-toothed hillbilly choir leader on a television variety show, an amorous American actress in Rome, and a blues singer. Dassin agreed to direct on two conditions: he wanted to tour the show in ten American cities instead of opening in Boston and Philadelphia before going to New York, and he wanted his name in lights. This latter point was not an ego trip (though perhaps there *was* some ego involved) but rather to prove that he could still work and defy the American Legion, who had promised to organize groups to protest against a Hollywood "communist." (His name appeared in lights, and no protests materialized.)

When rehearsals began, Dassin's subpoena to appear in Washington arrived, but when he told the server he couldn't come, this was accepted. The server followed the company from town to town (in her biography of Davis, *The Girl Who Walked Home Alone*, Charlotte Chandler claims that Davis's pal and script doctor John Murray Anderson was brought in to restage the revue during out-of-town tryouts.) In his book *Dance with Demons*, Greg Lawrence quotes an interview with Dassin dated November 24, 1998, in which Dassin says he and musical director Robbins had a "love-hate" relationship. Things presumably were not helped by both of them finding Davis temperamental and self-conscious about what she was asked to do. Tryouts began in Detroit on October 19, where Davis collapsed and was revived by her husband Gary Merrill. She supposedly commented to the audience, "Well, you can't say I didn't fall for you."

The show moved to Pittsburgh before arriving in Boston. There Anderson is said to have recast roles, eliminated sketches and added new ones, rearranged musical sequences and collected new song contributions and additional sketch material. The New York supporting cast included David Burns, Nora Kaye, Tina Louise and Himan Sherman, who would win the Tony Award for Best Featured Actor in a Musical. The opening was scheduled for December 4 but postponed because of Davis' illness, since she suffered exhaustion from the challenge of an eight-shows-a-week schedule. Dassin finally agreed to go and appear before HUAC the day after the New York opening on December 15, 1952, at the Alvin Theatre, where the show would play until March 8, 1953. In *The New York Times* on December 16, 1952, Brooks Atkinson wrote, "Good things only come at intervals in a handsome production that has mediocre spots all through the evening and that does not make use of Davis' best talents." Of Davis, he wrote, "No one should be surprised to discover that her severe performing is on the elementary side—colorless and monotonous. She has never had a chance to learn the sharp techniques of music hall acting."

Before he could leave, Dassin received a telegram saying all hearings had been called off. (In the *Cineaste* interview, Dassin claims that the election of General Dwight D. Eisenhower affected the workings of HUAC.) That was the end of the subpoena, but Dassin's name remained on the informal blacklist, which made it difficult for him to find work in Hollywood. He went back to France. Dassin would say that he wasn't bitter about leaving Hollywood: "In many ways, I was happy about it. I made a life that pleases me; and my kids have made a life that pleases me, because I came to Europe. It worked out." Dassin spent five years in Europe with no passport. In Paris he was offered a job by a producer named Romain Pines (in *Tender Comrades*, Dassin forgets what the title of the film was to be or what the material was). It was to be a French-Italian coproduction, but without a passport things would be difficult for the director. The producer went to the Quai d'Orsay to get travel papers, and a titer de voyage was obtained; but Dassin was not allowed into Italy, so the production with him as director could not go ahead.

The French "l'affaire Dassin" had extended to Rome, according to Erickson, and Dassin was considered an "undesirable." This led to his intention to film the Giovanni Verga book *Mastro Don Gesualdo* to be blocked. (The novel would eventually be made into a movie for television in Italy in 1964.) The director went to the American Embassy for help but was turned away by Ambassador Claire Boothe Luce. Dassin obtained help from the writer Vitaliano Brancati, who was going to co-write the screenplay. Brancati managed to have the foreign minister rule that Dassin could stay, but by this time the film's producer no longer wanted the undesirable director. This pattern was repeated, with different variations, for over five years. Erickson quotes an interview conducted by *L.A. Times* writer John Halliwell in 1968 wherein Dassin claims that pressure from Hollywood union bosses stopped him from making an unnamed film in 1952 (which could be the Verga film). A second offer came, as reported in *Tender Comrades*—to do a film of the novel *Zorba the Greek* by Nikos Kazantzakis. Dassin wanted to cast the Russian actor Nikolai Cherkasov as the title character, but as the producer disagreed, the offer was withdrawn. (The film would be made by director Michael Cacoyannis in 1964 with the Mexican Anthony Quinn.)

Dassin's blacklisted friends in Paris had survived by writing television between 1951 and 1953, and in *Tender Comrades* John Barry tells how he suggested to Dassin that he try to do a series about Captain Valiant set in the desert. Dassin apparently replied, "In spite of the fact that I am desperate, I can't do that." A third film offer, however, came from the French and broke his string of bad luck. This was *Rififi* (1955, aka *Du rififi chez les hommes*), based on the book by Auguste Le Breton. One unverified source claims that the film was originally to be made by Frenchman Jean-Pierre Melville, and that Dassin had asked permission to take over. Dassin's film starred Jean Servais, Carl Mohner, Robert Manuel and Dassin himself (billed as Perlo Vita) as the gang members in a jewelry store heist drama. Despite the director's difficulty in making it in the winter of 1954, particularly as he was still learning the language, the film turned out to be a huge success. In his article for *Picture Post*, Arden Winch would write that it was the most successful French film of all time to that date. *Rififi* won Dassin the shared Best Director award at the Cannes Film Festival in 1955, which Tony Crawley says was partly due to Otto Preminger being one of the jurors (Preminger was a noted foe of the blacklist). In the interview on the DVD of *Rififi*, Dassin tells the story of seeing Gene Kelly at Cannes and hiding from him to spare him the perceived embarrassment of being seen with a blacklisted person. Apparently when he was hiding, the director felt a strong grip on his arm. It was Kelly, who brought him out of hiding and walked with Dassin in front of photographers so they would be seen together. The director also tells how at Cannes he saw the film's producer, Henri Berard, gambling in a casino and asked for some money so he could do the same. Dassin chose to bet on the number 18, since it was the day production began, and he won enough money to live on afterwards for a long time.

Dassin's Cannes triumph effectively put an end to the blacklist for him, at least in regard to working in Europe, though at this time he was still being shunned in America. Erickson claims that when *Rififi* played in the United States in 1956, it seemed that Dassin had either been forgotten or the press decided to ignore him, and reviewers wrote about him as if he were a foreigner. In *Tender Comrades* Dassin says that someone from the American Embassy was assigned to talk to him at Cannes, and it looked as though he would get his American passport. However, it didn't happen, with Dassin claiming that he had embarrassed Americans when he was represented by the French flag. He also says that he was offered large sums of money by American companies to have the film released in America without his name as director, but he refused. In Melina Mercouri's autobiography, *I Was Born Greek*, she claims that the other condition demanded of Dassin for the film to obtain an American release was that he sign a declaration repenting youthful indiscretions and stating he was duped into subversive associations—something else he refused. When *Rififi* was finally released in the States, it was by small distributors who did not belong to the associations of the majors, and who could only provide limited engagements. Dassin claims it was the first film that appeared with a blacklisted person's name on it, as opposed to the belief that the historical epic *Spartacus* (1960) was the first, which featured Dalton Trumbo as screenwriter. (Trumbo had won the Best Original Story Academy Award for the romantic comedy *Roman Holiday* [1953] under one fronted name, and a second under another fronted name for the animal drama *The Brave One* [1956]. In *Spartacus* and his later screenplay for the prison drama *Papillon* [1973], Trumbo created treatments that explored the issue of naming names.) Where *Rififi* was shown, Dassin points out that there were no protests, which he claims proves that the American public didn't care about or want the blacklist. They just wanted good movies.

However, his meeting at Cannes with actress Melina Mercouri, who was apparently nominated as Best Actress for her film debut as the free-living bouzouki café singer in the title role of the Greek romantic drama *Stella* (1955), changed the course of Dassin's future. Mercouri's meeting with the director on May 18, 1955, and their subsequent romance and film collaboration, was thought of by her as fate because 18 was her lucky number, and both of them were born on the 18th of the month. (Dassin's wife, Beatrice, was also born on an 18th). Mercouri had been a theater actress in her native Greece, and she had also worked in Paris. She was married at the time to Pan Characopos, though she writes in her autobiography, *I Was Born Greek*, that their married relationship ended a few months after they wed, and that from then on they led separate lives. Mercouri tells how she met Dassin after a screening of *Stella*, where she says he jumped over seats, "leapfrogging the backs like a mountain goat," to be introduced to her by her film's director, Michael Cacoyannis.

Mercouri writes that, knowing Dassin was on the Hollywood blacklist, she had expected to find a man who was sad and bitter, with the mark and bearing of a victim. Rather, she found him to be a gay, optimistic, dancing spirit. The actress laughed at Dassin's improvisation in which he half-played and half-danced the manner in which Americans from different parts of the country paid court to a lady. When the couple went to a sidewalk café, a famous (unnamed) American screen star left so abruptly that he spilled his orange juice on the table, so afraid was he that he would be photographed with Dassin.

In *Tender Comrades*, Norma Barzman says that her husband Ben had brought Dassin's next project to him via Joe Belfort, one of the executives at Fox-Europe. It was to be a film based on the Nikos Kazantzakis novel *Christ Recrucified* (aka *The Greek Passion*). Dassin had wanted to make a picture in Greece and would claim in the interview in *Cineaste* that he was the first foreigner to make a film there. Dassin worked on the screenplay with Ben, although Norma claims that all Dassin contributed were quotations from the New Testament. Dassin told Mercouri that there was a part for her in the film—that of Katerina (in spite of the co-screenwriter's objection to the casting of the thirty-four-year-old as the supposedly eighteen-year-old girl, a part Barzman had suggested Brigitte Bardot play), and that he hoped to go to Greece when he could arrange travel papers.

On the evening of the Cannes awards ceremony, Betsy Blair, who had also been nominated for Best Actress for her performance as the "dog" high school chemistry teacher in the domestic drama *Marty* (1955), was one of the few Americans unafraid to be seen with Dassin. (Blair herself had been blacklisted but was cast in *Marty* thanks to the influence of her husband, Gene Kelly.) When the jury announced that no Best Actress award would be given, Dassin (who had already received an award) comforted the crying Mercouri, telling her, "Does the prize mean that much? You're worth much more than that." In his 2004 LACMA interview, Dassin says that he introduced himself to the actress on the night of the awards, and in response to his comment, she said, "You got the prize. Screw off!"

When Mercouri returned to Athens, two letters from Dassin awaited her, reporting on the progress of the film. Her father, being a deputy in the Greek parliament, assisted the director in getting him his travel papers so he could make the film in Greece. Dassin went with his art director, Alexander Traunner, and Mercouri acted as guide for the location village. A problem arose with the film's producer, who had misgivings about the commercial value of the project. After seven months in Paris, the problem was resolved, and Dassin returned to Greece to meet with Kazantzakis and Mercouri. In the meantime, she had seen all of the director's previous films and was particularly impressed by the fact that in two of them the protagonists were Greek (Nick Garcos in *Thieves' Highway*, and Gregorius and Kristo in *Night and the City*). When Dassin and Mercouri arrived at the novelist's home in Antibes, they learned that he was dying of leukemia (he would succumb October 26, 1957). Kazantzakis knew of Dassin's wish to make a film of *Zorba the Greek*, and Mercouri says that the writer adopted Dassin as a Cretan, naming him Dassinaki (since most Cretan names end in a-k-i).

The Greeks would not allow the film to be shot in Greece because of their antipathy towards Kazantzakis, who loudly complained how he thought they had turned over their country to foreign control and foreign money. The writer suggested Crete as an alternative, since Cretans adored Kazantakis. When Dassin came to Athens again to meet with Mercouri, it was without his wife and children. Together they looked for locations for the film. Because Yugoslavia offered interesting conditions, the remnants of a Turkish village in Montenegro was considered. In Crete they visited Heraklion and Chania, looking for a physical setting where the people had Greek faces (and could also act). They finally found the village of Krista, built on a mountain slope above the plains of eastern Crete. Since the inhabitants worked in fields and olive groves, many of them couldn't read, so Mercouri read the story to them over three nights in the schoolyard so that they could understand the details of what Dassin wanted to do. However, the Cretans refused to play the Turkish cavalrymen in the film, so the director cast young Texas cowboys from an American military base on weekend leave, and hid them behind massive Turkish moustaches. The clerical authorities also refused permission to film in the village church, so a new church was built. A road also had to be built to grant access to the mountaintop location used for the Sarakina campsite.

Along with Mercouri, Dassin cast Jean Servais and Carl Mohner from *Rififi*, as well as Gert Froebe, Pierre Vaneck and Fernand Ledoux. Dassin and Mercouri spent three days in Mykanos before returning to Paris. In her book *The Red and the Blacklist: The Intimate Memoir of a Hollywood Expatriate*, Norma Barzaman says that Dassin left his wife to be with Melina when he came back to Paris to edit the film. In the spring of 1957, *He Who Must Die* represented France at Cannes. After the film was screened on May 7, the president of the jury, Jean Cocteau, embraced the couple, which shocked the festival officials, who saw his act as inappropriate to the discipline of a jury member. Dassin would say at Cannes he (and Ben Barzman, according to Norma) had not been invited to the American reception for the film; but when this was reported in the press, an invitation was sent. After they were both invited, Dassin agreed to attend, but Norma writes that as they proceeded down the receiving line, backs were turned to them and American stars held up champagne glasses to cover their faces while the director and writer were nearby. Obviously, these stars did not want to be photographed or seen to associate with blacklisted individuals. The Melina Mercouri Foundation biography says the film was a bit hit in Europe. In *I Was Born Greek*, Mercouri herself says that it was initially a commercial failure, but it later made a profit when it opened in New York in December 1958. In *5001 Nights at the Movies*, Pauline Kael wrote that the film was very popular at American art houses, supporting Mercouri's claim that the major companies had refused to distribute the film. Glenn Erickson states that when it was shopped around for an American release, all invitations were turned down because the agents were supposedly still afraid of their clients' association with the blacklisted director. Glenn Erickson also quotes an interview in *The New York Times* conducted by Murray Shumack in which Dassin blamed Hollywood right-wingers.

In *I Was Born Greek*, Mercouri says Dassin divided his time between her and his children. Dassin's son Joseph was more able to understand the situation because he was older. It also helped that he had worked on *He Who Must Die* and had played a small role. Dassin's two daughters were not so solicitous and refused to meet Mercouri. However, the antagonism of Dassin's youngest daughter, Julie, lessened after she encountered Mercouri emerging sweating and gasping for breath from a clothes closet where she had been hiding so as not to encroach upon the child's time with her father.

Money was tight for the couple, but things improved thanks to another blacklisted director in exile, Joseph Losey. He cast Mercouri as the lead in her first English language feature, the Regency romance *The Gypsy and the Gentleman* (1958), which was filmed in England. In his book *Conversations with Losey*, Michel Climent commented that Dassin frequented the set, which Losey claimed adversely affected Mercouri's performance. Climent also says that Losey claims Dassin stood behind the camera until Losey asked him not to because it was "destroying me and destroying her."

Dassin was hired for another film by producer Jacques Bar, who had previously fired him as the director of *Public Enemy No. 1* in 1951. It was based on the novel *The Law*, by Roger Vailland, which had won the Prix Goncourt, a French prize for literature (which would be mentioned in the film's credits). Five days before filming was to begin, the director learned that the producer had not secured funding. Dassin was told that the money could be obtained if Gina Lollobrigida replaced the twenty-year-old Claudia Cardinale, the former Tunisian model who had made her film debut in a supporting role in the French film *Goha* (1958) and who been cast in the role of the fifteen-year-old lead. Dassin rewrote the script in four days to accommodate the thirty-year-old Lollobrigida, since he knew that without her the film would be cancelled and the waiting crew would lose their jobs. Filming would take place from June to September 1958 in France and Italy, and the picture would star, along with Lollobrigida, Pierre Brasseur, Marcello Mastroianni, Mercouri and Yves Montand. Mercouri says that all of Dassin's children were with him during production, meaning that all three had finally accepted Melina being in the director's life.

After the United States Supreme Court ruled that it was illegal to deprive American citizens of their passports, Dassin was finally able to travel easily. He received a request from United Artists to come to New York to discuss a contract. So Dassin and Mercouri left their home in Lausanne and travelled together to New York. An agreement was reached for the director to make four films in Europe. The couple then traveled on to Hollywood, where a screening of *He Who Must Die* was to take place. The morning of the screening they received word that some of the invited celebrities had the flu and could not attend. By the evening there was an epidemic, and eventually only three Hollywood people turned up. They were Richard Brooks, Gene Kelly, and Walter Wanger.

United Artists gave Dassin an office in Paris, and Dassin used the money they had paid him for the four-picture deal to rent a furnished apartment. However, he became worried when someone sent them a copy of *Variety* which reported the UA deal and how the American Legion again threatened that any film made by him would be met with picketing. Although the company claimed to be unconcerned, it seemed a coincidence that all the director's proposed projects were subsequently rejected. These included *Sundays and Cybile*, based on the novel by Bernard Eschasseriaux (and made as *Les dimanches de Ville d'Avray* in 1962 by Serge Bourguignon), and *The Longest Day* (1962), based on the book by Cornelius Ryan (and made by 20th Century–Fox and credited to four directors— Ken Annakin, Andrew Marton, Bernhard Wicki, and Darryl F. Zanuck).

Dassin stopped suggesting projects, and it appeared to be the end of the United

Artists deal. Some French producers made offers to rehash *Rififi*; while other offers failed to include Mercouri, so they were rejected because Dassin did not want to make a film without her (though he encouraged Mercouri to make pictures with other people). The director's reasoning was that he could cope with her being away for ten weeks, but that he being away from her for a year to make a film without her would end their relationship, since it could not survive such a long separation. Mercouri writes that she agreed with him because she would be jealous if he made a film with another actress, or even with male actors and not her, because she would have been shut out of his private working world. With neither of them working, Dassin and Mercouri spent time with friends, including a new one, the author Françoise Sagan, and the director's children. It was at this time that the idea of *Never on Sunday* came to Dassin, although Mercouri says the character he would play in the film seemed to partly come from how he used to hate going to nightclubs with Sagan because the loud music (and her way of speaking quietly, with a cigarette in her mouth) made it impossible to hear the funny stories she would tell. As a result, Mercouri says, Dassin became a "dreary, suffering companion." She quotes the director on the proposed film:

> It's about a man who tries to make people think as he does. He's a guy who can walk into the happiest environment and by the time he leaves, succeeds in making everyone miserable. He screws everything up. He meets a woman. She's Greek. And he's an American. Wherever he goes, he tries to impose the American way of life. He's not a bad guy. He's just dangerously naïve. He's a boy scout. She's so happy, he can't stand it. He doesn't think she should be happy.

They decided to make the film in Greece, in the Port of Piraeus. The story was originally called *The Happy Whore*, and changed to *Never on Sunday* at the suggestion of their friend, the screenwriter and producer Harry Kurnitz. The problem was to find a producer who would back the film. Although it was to be another low-budget production, Dassin could not interest anyone. He even approached the Greek shipping magnate Aristotle Onassis, who had never (and would never) produced a film, but he too said no. Dassin went to England and Italy. Mercouri went to Greece. But neither was successful. In Greece, Mercouri learned that Dassin had been offered a job by United Artists. A film was to be produced by Abby Mann for Burt Lancaster and Ingrid Bergman, and Lancaster wanted to work with his *Brute Force* director again. Apparently, the company was not intimidated by the American Legion threat after all. Dassin was unsure, and Mercouri advised him to reject it, partly based on her not being in the film. Dassin agreed with her and rejected it. It is not known what this film project was, and it appears that is was never made. However, in Kate Burford's book *Burt Lancaster: An American Life*, she claims that United Artists had wanted Dassin to direct the prison biography *Birdman of Alcatraz* (1962), to star Lancaster; but that film would be directed by John Frankenheimer.

Dassin tried United Artists again, and met with Charles Smadja, the head of the European unit, in Athens. Smadja liked the idea of *Never on Sunday* and naturally asked to see a script, but Dassin hadn't written it yet. When Smadja asked the name of the whore, which the director had yet to come up with, Dassin thought of Ilya Lopert, a man that worked at UA, and feminized it as "Illya." When he was asked if he could at least tell how the story begins, Dassin improvised. "Men are working on the docks of Piraeus. A girl comes running down a pier. She undresses as she goes. Stark naked, she dives into the water. In a matter of seconds every man on the docks leaps into the water to join her." Smadja loved it, but approval was only given for partial funding as a loan (in his 2004 interview at the Los Angeles County Museum of Art, Dassin says the loan was for $60,000). Dassin had to submit a script, and if that was approved, the rest of the money would come. He also had to begin production within a month. Dassin and Mercouri moved into an apartment on Mount Lycabetos and made it their home and office, and the director wrote the screenplay in ten days to meet the UA deadline. To save the time of mailing the script, Dassin delivered it in person, and the director read Smadja the script. Although Smadja was meant to have it signed off by the UA New York office, he approved it himself. To cover themselves, Mercouri's husband, Pan, got a bank to guarantee the completion of the film.

A friend helped Mercouri set up a production company, Melina Films, and permission was sought to shoot in streets and public places. Dassin went to the Perema ship repair yard to obtain clearance to shoot there. The director wanted the esteemed Greek theater actor Titos Wandis to be in the film, and Dassin persuaded him to take the role in spite of the actor's doubts about how the character he would play had no lines. The director also wanted to cast the tragedienne Despo in a comic part as another whore and also overcame the actress' reluctance. The only part still vacant was that of the American, Homer Thrace. Dassin had written it for someone like Jack Lemmon or Henry Fonda, but their salary demands were beyond the $120,000 budget. (In *The United Artists Story*, Ronald Bergan reported that the budget was $100,000. Both *Time* magazine and the TCM website claim the budget was $125,000; and in his *Films Illustrated* article, Tony Crawley writes it was $150,000.) In his book on Anthony Perkins, *Split Image*, Charles Winecoff claims that Perkins had been the first choice for the part, but that he too was beyond the production's price range. Mercouri suggested that Dassin play the part, but Dassin was uncertain. He tried Van Johnson, who turned him down over money, and also some actors in Rome. Finally, Dassin agreed to do it.

Jules Dassin cast himself as the male lead in the comedy *Never on Sunday* (1960).

Keeping the opening scene for the film that he had concocted for Smadja, Dassin put a call out for twenty strong swimmers, and hundreds of men crowded into the apartment office. A small, frail man wearing glasses was aggressive in wanting to be cast, and Dassin thought of a way to use him in the film that would get one of its biggest laughs. He would take off his glasses, pocket them, jump into the bay, surface, put on his glasses again, and swim out of the shot. The film would be shot from March to April in 1960, and Charles Smadja was the first to see the finished product. Harry Kurnitz and Richelle Dassin came to the screening and were asked to laugh out loud wherever they could to influence Smadja, but he didn't need to be influenced, as he liked it. Another screening was held for United Artists vice-president Arnold Picker, who was suspiciously silent during the entire film. However, afterwards, he told Dassin and Mercouri, "I love it. It will make a lot of money."

The film was Greece's entry at Cannes, and it helped that the title song had become a hit before the picture had been seen in public. (The music's publishing rights had been sold by United Artists to Eddy Barclay, who had the song recorded in French and played on the radio in record time.) For some reason Greece had no official reception organized, so Dassin asked United Artists for money to finance an after-screening party, to which they agreed. The screening went well, with the audience laughing all the way through it, but apparently the party was a greater success, continuing long into the next morning. Seven hundred people attended, with the Ambassador Room transformed into a Greek taverna. Bouzukis were played, glasses and plates were smashed, and black-tied and begowned celebrities, dignitaries and diplomats danced on a floor of broken glass. Stories and photographs of the party appeared in newspapers all over the world, and served to launch the film with a bang. And Mercouri would be awarded the Cannes Best Actress prize.

Never on Sunday was a great commercial success, so much so that tourism in Athens supposedly skyrocketed. Dassin says that when it was running in Paris he ran into Jack Lemmon. The director asked United Artists if they would give him the money to remake the film with Lemmon in the role Dassin had played, and they said yes. He told the actor that it would be three weeks work for a lot of money. He and Lemmon went and saw the film together, and afterwards Lemmon purportedly told Dassin, "You're so terrible that it's charming. Let it alone."

The fact of Dassin being nominated for the Best Director Academy Award suggested that perhaps his blacklisting was over, although he did not win. Glenn Erickson claims that the director was still considered an "undesirable" in Hollywood, in spite of the nomination, since the blacklist still existed to stop certain people from working. (While some maintain that the blacklist had officially ended by 1961, some people who had been blacklisted would never be able to work in Hollywood again.) In 1967 the newspaper *Variety* reported that the American IRS wanted $946,000 from Dassin for the profits from *Never on Sunday*, in spite of the American government having been instrumental in denying the director a passport.

Dassin directed a play starring Mercouri at the Théâtre des Variétés in Paris—*Flora*, by Fabio Mauri and Franco Brusati. (This production goes strangely unmentioned in Mercouri's autobiography.) Unlike before the success of *Never on Sunday*, when Dassin had trouble finding producers willing to back his projects, he had little difficulty now. Except now they wanted him to make another film with Mercouri playing the same kind of character. An American even suggested a title—*Illya Goes to New York*—and an opening shot. Illya arrives at New York Harbor, carrying a bird cage. She walks down a gangplank. She waves. The camera pans over to see a dozen whores from Piraeus who follow her down the gangplank. But Dassin wasn't interested in repeating himself. At least, not yet. He was more interested in doing a Greek tragedy, and was drawn to the character of Phaedra from the Euripides play *Hippolytus*, first produced in 428 B.C., about a woman who seduces her stepson, although Phaedra's story also appears in many other plays, novels and operas. (Euripides also wrote the play *Medea*, which was featured in the screenplay of *Never on Sunday*.) Dassin wanted the story updated to the twentieth century by

Greek novelist and playwright Margarita Liberaki, making Phaedra the wife of a Greek shipping magnate.

When the script was finished, Dassin and Mercouri spotted Anthony Perkins at the circus. Ironically, Perkins had played the Hippolytus role to Sophia Loren's Phaedra in the melodrama *Desire Under the Elms* (1958), the film adaptation of the Eugene O'Neill play which had updated the Euripides story to a 19th century New England farm. Perkins

Jules Dassin and Melina Mercouri arrive from Paris on November 16, 1960, for the London premiere of the comedy in which they co-star, *Never on Sunday* (1960).

was in Paris filming a supporting role in the United Artists romance *Goodbye Again* (1961, aka *Aimez-vous Brahms*) with director Anatole Litvak, the first movie he made after his seminal role as Norman Bates in Alfred Hitchcock's horror classic *Psycho* (1960). The film was based on a novel by Françoise Sagan, a friend of Dassin and Mercouri; and since neither Dassin nor Mercouri knew Perkins, they had Françoise take them to lunch at the Studios de Boulogne-Billancourt so that they could be introduced to him. The couple invited the actor to their home for dinner, and he agreed to do the film—once Dassin agreed to Perkins' condition that he be supplied with fresh milk daily. The picture would also star Raf Vallone, with Charles Winecoff in *Split Image* claiming that filming occurred from July to October 1961. United Artists worked to make the release a success, sending Mercouri on a publicity tour through Europe and the United States, though this did not translate into results at the box office.

From January 1962 Dassin directed the play *Isle of Children* by Robert L. Joseph for a New York season. Produced by Lester Osterman, Jr., in association with Shirley Bernstein, it had four weeks of rehearsal and four weeks of out-of-town tryouts before opening on Broadway. However, it would only play for eleven performances at the Cort Theatre from March 16 to 24, 1962, with a cast that included the fifteen-year-old Patty Duke as the child who is dying from an incurable heart disease, and Noel Willman and Norma Crane as her parents. In *The New York Times* (March 17), Howard Taubman wrote, "Occupied for a good many years as a film director, Mr. Dassin brings to the theater a feeling for order and power. He has managed to give *Isle of Children* intensities that mitigate its talkativeness." The play would later be made into a film by Don Taylor, *Echoes of a Summer* (1976), in Canada, starring Richard Harris, Lois Nettleton and Jodie Foster in the role Duke had done in the play.

Jules Dassin and Melina Mercouri on the set of *Phaedra* (1962).

Dassin's wife had agreed to a divorce—after he had been away from her and with Mercouri for seven years—so Mercouri asked her husband for one too. (Mercouri writes in *I Was Born Greek* that she had assured Dassin's children that she and the director would not have a child together, which helped them accept her and to consider their relationship with their father unthreatened by peer rivals. This is an assurance that the actress kept, since she would never bear children.)

Dassin worked on a new screenplay about Socrates, the Greek philosopher, in the age of the general Pericles—a project that never came to fruition. Rather, over Mercouri's objections as to what she saw as the director's attraction to commercialism, he received approval from United Artists to make another heist drama in the vein of *Rififi*. It was based on the 1962 novel *The Light of Day* by Eric Ambler, and was to be filmed on location in Istanbul, Turkey. The film was called *Topkapi* (1964) and would star Mercouri, Maximilian Schell, Peter Ustinov, Robert Morley, and Akim Tamiroff. As Dassin's first color title, it is said to have done for Turkish tourism what *Never on Sunday* did for Greece, since Turkey was considered an undiscovered and out of the way place. Reportedly six weeks after the release of the film (presumably in America), a similar, real-life heist took place at the American Museum of Natural History in New York when three men stole twenty-two priceless gems, including the famous Star of India and the De Long Ruby. The jewels were recovered within forty-eight hours, with the men admitting that they had seen *Topkapi* prior to the robbery.

Mercouri writes that the Greeks had accepted Dassin as one of them because he had pioneered the way for foreign companies to make films there and in the process spend money in the country. She says that since Greeks found it hard to pronounce his first name, they called him "Zyl" instead. Supposedly once at a football stadium thousands of people waived to him and chanted "Zyl-Zyl." Dassin was apparently frightened of large crowds, so once when people came running toward Mercouri to ask for autographs, he shouted to her to refuse because if she stopped a crowd would gather. However, Mercouri did stop to sign autographs, and the crowd grew until the couple thought they would be crushed to death. In response, Dassin began flailing with his fists to open a passage, and those that were with the couple managed to form a protective wedge around them and push their way forward so that they could be free. Mercouri writes of a similar incident when they were lifted onto the shoulders of people marching to the British embassy to demonstrate for the independence of Cyprus, which was located across the road from the hotel where the couple had been staying. With Mercouri and Dassin on shoulders, the chant began, "Free Cyprus—Melina and Zyl are with us," but Mercouri tells how Dassin was more concerned with trying to pull down Mercouri's awry skirts.

Dassin had been approached by Kermit Bloomgarden, a New York producer who wanted him to make *Never on Sunday* into a Broadway musical, with Mercouri repeating her film role and Dassin to direct (although the idea of Dassin repeating *his* film role was not suggested; the role would be played by Orson Bean). He initially said no, but then became interested in 1965 when Manos Hadjidakis agreed to write new songs, and the writer of the show *Man of La Mancha*, Joe Darion, agreed to do the lyrics. Another reason for Dassin's change of mind is that he wanted to make a film in America on the situation of black people with an all-black cast, and that meant that there would be no part for Mercouri. By having her do the show, Dassin hoped that she would not feel so abandoned by him. In the summer, work began on the stage show in a house on the edge of the sea in Spetsai. However, work was put aside the day that a rowboat owned by Cecile de Rothschild sailed into the island carrying Greta Garbo.

Since Cecile was a friend of Mercouri's, she asked if she could meet Garbo. Dassin insisted to the legendary actress that he had met her before, allegedly saying, "I command you to remember me," but she refused to indicate whether she remembered him or not. Matters weren't helped by the fact of Garbo being more interested in Mercouri, for whom Garbo removed her sunglasses so that Mercouri could see her beautiful blue eyes. A party was given for Garbo in a garden taverna, and Dassin seemed to forgive Garbo's toying with him after Mercouri saw her whispering in his ear. Plates were smashed in the Greek tradition, bouzouki music played, and Greek songs were sung for her. Garbo cried and asked the group to sing a song by Mikis Theodorakis called "Kaimos"—repeatedly, as her boat took her away.

Before the couple were due to go to New York, they were married in Lausanne, after having lived together unmarried for ten years. (The date of their marriage is unknown.) They had also made Dassin's next film, *10:30 P.M. Summer* (1966), in Spain in the winter of 1965. An adaptation of a novel by Marguerite Duras, the film also starred Romy Schneider and Peter Finch. The title gets no behind-the-scenes stories in Mercouri's book; the only mention: "Everybody called it a disaster." In her book *Finch, Bloody Finch*, Elaine Bundy claims that Peter Finch was unwell during the shooting. When he dined with Mercouri and Dassin one evening at their Paris apartment, he supposedly collapsed after experiencing severe abdominal pains. The doctor who attended diagnosed him with hepatitis, and warned the actor (who had a prodigious thirst for alcohol) not to drink again for one year, since his liver would not tolerate it. Bundy says that Finch stayed in bed at the Dassins' for a month, with Mercouri nursing him, before he felt well enough to leave for London.

In Trader Faulkner's biography of Finch, he claims that the actor caught hepatitis by drinking the water in Spain, and that his attack occurred on the final day of dubbing the film at the Dassin house in the Rue Weber. Faulkner says Finch was a house guest for forty days, and was "acutely embarrassed by the situation." In regards to *10:30 P.M. Summer*,

Peter Finch (left) and Jules Dassin on the set of *10:30 P.M. Summer* (1966).

apparently the actor had an ambition to make a film with a good screenplay and a top European director, which is why he had accepted the role. However, he commented that the result was "murky and confused," and that the only value of the experience was the friendship he forged with Mercouri and Dassin. While Mercouri's nursing perhaps helped save his life, Finch did not extend the friendship with Dassin to working with him again.

In his book on Joseph Losey, *A Revenge on Life*, David Caute claims that Dassin and producer Anatole Litvak had originally asked Losey to direct the film, since it was a project he had long been interested in. Losey apparently went to Spain with Dassin in November 1964, but in January 1965 dropped out of the project. Caute quotes Losey as saying that Dassin had been repeatedly offended by him while they were in Spain. "Your condescending attitude, your tolerating me, your insults" all confirmed Losey's prediction that he could not work with Dassin. Apparently Dassin and Losey had a checkered past: Losey thought Dassin had interfered with the making of *The Gypsy and the Gentleman*, although Dassin had supposedly helped Losey financially, and even attended the Parisian premiere of Losey's film *The Servant* (1963) in April 1964.

Bloomgarden arranged for the couple to live in a New York apartment that overlooked Central Park. Dassin wanted to cast as many Greeks as possible for the show so brought Despo and Titos Wandis from Athens, both of whom had been in the film. A reception was held by the Greek consul in New York and by the Greek ambassador in Washington. Mercouri writes that, along with the agonies she endured following a program of calisthenics, athletics, and acrobatics by choreographer Onna White to get her in shape to perform eight shows a week, the work on the project was not going well. Dassin was frustrated by the abbreviated rehearsal time he had with the actors (since they were always needed by the musical director, the choreographer, the composer or the costume fitter), and he was rarely able to get the ensemble together at the same time. However, Mercouri says that the bigger problem was that Dassin was not a good collaborator, as had been suggested by Jerome Robbins regarding their show *Two's Company*.

The new show, now named *Illya Darling*, opened in Philadelphia—to the approval of audiences and critics—and the word from New York was that pre-opening ticket sales were good. However, Dassin was not satisfied. He wrote new scenes and new dialogue, and requested new songs. He complained that the show was not Greek enough, that it was too heavy and the characters too thin. He disliked the orchestrations, perhaps because they were not done by a Greek, and asked Hadjidakis to redo them, which led to trouble. New scenes would be rehearsed and put into the show the same night, which confused some of the actors who had learned the old scenes, and changes kept occurring as the show moved to Toronto and Detroit. Dassin knew that the work was not going well, and he looked for another director to replace him but couldn't find one. In Detroit he fell ill, but the show staggered on. What surprised Mercouri was that audiences still loved it, though what wasn't a surprise was that a large percentage of the audiences were Greeks who were obviously attracted to the material.

When the company came to New York, the alleged advance pre-sales amounted to something near two million dollars. Everyone took this as an omen of success—except Dassin, who dreaded the critical drubbing he thought the show deserved. After a preview on March 22 at the Mark Hellinger Theatre, the show opened on April 11—to bad reviews. On April 12, 1967, Walter Kerr in *The New York Times* wrote, "I think they've made a mistake. They've left the show in Detroit or wherever it was last warming up, and brought in the publicity stills.... Inadvertently and unluckily makes movies seem better than ever."

Poster for production of *Illya Darling*, the stage musical adaptation of Jules Dassin's film *Never on Sunday*.

Time magazine (April 21) dubbed it "Gloomy Sunday" and wrote, "A 15-watt musical with one trace of Greek fire—Melina Mercouri. She plays furiously across the footlights to keep audiences from realizing that there is nothing behind them. Flaccidly adapted by Jules Dassin ... the Greeks had a word for shows like this—katastrophē." In spite of the reviews, however, the show would run for 320 performances—until January 13, 1968.

In his book *Second Act Trouble: Behind the Scenes at Broadway's Big Musical Bombs*, Steve Suskin quotes from Lehman Engel's autobiography *This Bright Day* on Engel's experience as the aborted musical director of the show. Suskin's chapter is entitled "The One-Eyed Prostitute," and he says Engel offers a "cautionary tale of working with international star-producers and their international director librettist-producer husbands." Engel says that he had known Dassin twenty-five years earlier, although it seems they had not worked together before, and when he had learned of the director's intention to turn his film into a stage show, had cautioned him that he foresaw it to be a difficult thing to do. Engel claims that the show needed a subplot, since Mercouri seemed to be in practically every frame of the original, to give both the performer and the audience some relief. Though Dassin agreed that the idea had value, he did not use it, and the actress was in every scene in the show. (In his book *Open a New Window: The Broadway Musical of the 1960s*, Ethan Mordden writes that Dassin cut a song which was performed by Nikos Kourkoulos as Illya's Greek boyfriend, and the male chorus in the Philadelphia try-out, because it shifted focus away from Mercouri.)

Engel claims that time was wasted in production meetings on eating, dancing, and singing. He was concerned about how all the songs sounded the same, but Engel was even more concerned with two of Dassin's ideas that he thought impracticable. First, Dassin wanted Mercouri at the start of the show to dive into the orchestra pit (as she had done in the film into the Aegean Sea), followed by a number of men. This dangerous stunt would have required the pit be cleared, and then more time would have been needed for the players to be reseated with their chairs and music stands. (Apparently this stunt was not attempted in the eventual production.) Second, Dassin wanted to fly four bazouki players, on a platform festooned with flowers, to play the show's overture.

The director also objected to the simple vocal arrangements Engel had written for the chorus of male singers and dancers, which had been approved by the composer. Dassin preferred only unison or two-part singing, but kept changing his mind so that from one day to the next the choice was different. Money was wasted on overtime for one hour a day for rehearsals. After the Philadelphia opening, all rehearsals had to include the scenery, which meant paying a full stage crew, which was an unheard of extravagance in the theater. Dassin became dissatisfied with the lyrics by Joe Darion and wanted to send for a Greek poet who spoke no English. Schedules were seldom made for the next day until after the cast had been dismissed, so that they all had to be telephoned. The orchestrator did not get the songs early enough to work on them. The costume designer complained that the cast had not been selected for each scene so that they could be measured, since Dassin changed the ensemble scene almost daily. Engel complained that he could not train a chorus with shifting personnel, shifting arrangements, missing lyrics, and unfinished songs. He never knew who to take orders from since Hadjidakis and Dassin gave conflicting orders. The composer wanted slow arrangements and the director wanted fast ones.

Nearly all the principals suffered from laryngitis. After two weeks of rehearsals, the ensemble was still confused, not knowing what songs to sing or which lyrics were being used. Dassin promised more rehearsal time that was never delivered since plans were changed. The part of the leading man was too unimportant, and the show had no second act. And as Engels had predicted, there was too much Mercouri, in spite of her charm. Things began to look up when orchestra rehearsals began, but when Dassin arrived in Philadelphia he announced that he was not going to use the lighting that Jean Rosenthal had cued, because he wanted to do his own lighting. When the show opened on January 16, Engel says it was terrible, but the song "Never on Sunday" was given an encore because it was the only song that the audience bought.

Engel gave an interview in the *Philadelphia Bulletin* in which he said that the show would be his last. "I have better things to do than run bad shows," he was quoted as saying. Rehearsals in Toronto often nearly came to a standstill because of the many changes the composer wanted and the language problem that caused his inarticulateness. The show opened to bad reviews, and Dassin had Engel removed and replaced by his assistant, Karen Gustafson. Apparently the director and Mercouri had been upset by the *Philadelphia Bulletin* piece, particularly with the line about "grotesque, middle aged women who star in some of the big shows of today." Engel would claim that he had not intended it personally, but rather commented on the growing trend in the American Musical Theater. Not wanting to quit the show because of the work he had put into it, Engel agreed to be bought out of his contract. He claims that all he foresaw as wrong with it was wrong when it opened in New York, and it only played for an extended run because of the audiences' attraction to Mercouri (in spite of the bad reviews).

Dassin and Mercouri moved to a hotel in Greenwich Village, where Dassin was visited by black writers to discuss his new film, although Mercouri writes that she sensed the anger these men had towards the director. Although they knew Dassin's history, what he had struggled against, and who he was, the difference between them that remained was the color of the skin. Other writers also visited. John Steinbeck, Tennessee Williams, and Edward Albee attended baseball games with the couple. But their happiness was soon shattered when they heard on April 21 about the military coup in Greece. Mercouri recognized the irony of playing in *Illya Darling*, which presented a Greece that was free and gay when the real Greece was ruled by force and torture. She was angry that pictures of her celebrating her success in New York were used as propaganda by the junta, who hailed her as "Our Melina." Mercouri considered asking Bloomgarden if she could make a curtain speech, telling the audience that the free Greece seen in the play no longer existed; however, Dassin persuaded her to wait. He planned to go to Lausanne for a few days and would go on to London to visit Mercouri's father, a former member of Parliament who has declared himself an enemy of the regime and worked to fight the junta. Before he left, Dassin asked Manos Hadjidakis to write a song about freedom, which he did, and it was planned for Mercouri to appear on a national television show to present the song.

Six days after Dassin had left he was seen in a photograph at Athens airport. Mercouri had not expected him to go to Greece. When she finally was able to speak to him on the telephone, she writes that she wanted to howl her anger at him, but before she could he told her that he had gone there to try and get friends out of the country. Dassin was unafraid of being detained because he was an American citizen, but was angered at the spin the propaganda had put on his visit, claiming that he had come to make a new film. He told her he would contact her again from London; however, three days later Dassin was back in New York. He told how people's behavior recalled his treatment when he was blacklisted: people were afraid to be seen with him. He had learned that many of their Greek friends were in prison or hiding. Dassin said he had visited Mercouri's father in

Introduction

London, where he was suffering from an illness that would kill him a few months later. However, even being sick had not stopped his activism against the junta; traveling all over Europe, he created committees, organized public meetings, sought help from the democratic parties, and pleaded before the Council of Europe. He was buried in London, since he had told his family that he would only return to Greece when Greece was free.

There arose a problem with the song Manos Hadjidakis had promised. Mercouri writes that he had lost his courage and refused to write it. He stopped communicating with the couple, and gave an interview to a newspaper criticizing Mercouri's anti-junta stance and activities. Then he went back to Greece and was photographed with one of the colonels, making the composer's alliances apparent. Mercouri's mother, who had been with the couple in New York, decided to go back to Greece. Before she was to leave, the actress did a radio interview, which had been organized so that she could talk about her career. Mercouri had wanted to speak out against the junta, but her mother convinced her not to, as she was afraid of the repercussions it would have for her back in Greece, in spite of the protection Mercouri's brother might afford her (he was an admiral of the navy). However, when the interview took place, with her mother in the room, and Mercouri was asked if she was enjoying doing the show, she couldn't control herself: "I hate playing Illya. I hate it.... Because it's a lie. There is no happiness in Greece today. It's a country in chains." When asked if she was making a statement against the colonels, her mother cried out, "No," but Mercouri said yes. Asked if American tourists should go to Greece in the summer, she looked at Dassin, who smiled at her, and answered, "If you can sail the Greek islands, knowing that some of them are prisons where people are tortured, then go to Greece. If you want your dollars to support a fascist regime, then go to Greece." The interviewer stopped and said that he would like to return with a television crew and camera to interview her, which would be broadcast nationally. Mercouri agreed.

When the crew returned with their camera, Mercouri had had time to reflect on her previous response. She thought of how she had worked to bring tourists to Greece, of the tours she had made, the foreign artists (like Dassin) who had been persuaded to work in Greece. How she had been sent to Stockholm by the Minister of Tourism, and, as a result, how thousands of Swedish tourists had come to Greece. How when she had come to New York the tourist office in New York had printed posters which read "Melina Is Here," with a picture of herself and the Acropolis. And how at a government reception before the coup she was introduced as an unofficial ambassadress at large. When she was asked again if American tourists should go to Greece that summer, Mercouri knew that if she gave the same answer as before it would keep her away from her country for a long time. She began to cry, and she felt ashamed at telling people to stay away from Greece. But after a moment, she composed herself and repeated the same comments, speaking from her heart.

The interview appeared on the NBC news, and was repeated a number of times that evening. Congratulatory telephone calls flooded the house, but upon reaching the theater, she heard a dissenting voice threatening her life. After the show there were hundreds of telegrams, all hostile. Letters arrived at their home—some poems of love, others filled with hate and vicious threats, replete with images of sexual torture and perversion. A phone call came from the Greek representative in New York, saying, "Bravo, Melina. Thank you. Please keep it up." But soon this same man would claim that "the actress Melina Mercouri and her Jew husband were being financially supported by the American Communist Party." Mercouri was flooded with requests to appear on radio and television, and to give interviews to newspapers and national magazines. She agreed because she wanted the help of the

American people to restore democracy in Greece, although she was aware of the curiosity value the story had, given her current run in *Illya Darling*. They began to receive money in the mail, to be given to the families of the junta's prisoners. Mercouri accepted speaking requests at universities and high schools.

Naturally, Mercouri leaned on Dassin, but also their press agent, Jim Proctor. Proctor arranged a schedule of speaking engagements, and Dassin organized a team of speech writers. Together they created committees from New York to California in defense of Greek democracy. Dassin took a crash course in modern Greek history and became a research source that anyone could call upon. Then suddenly Dassin's focus changed. When the threat of war between Egypt and Israel pushed Greece off the headlines, Dassin told Mercouri, "If there is war, I will go to Israel." She told him, "Don't be silly, you're too old to carry a gun," to which he replied, "I'm not too old to carry a camera." They had taken a house in Long Island for the summer. Before she left for the theater, Dassin had received a telephone call from Paris. He told her it was nothing; she went to do the show, and he went to the airport to board a plane for Paris on the way to Israel. Mercouri told her producer to bring him back or this would be her last performance. Dassin was found in Paris and flew back to New York. Mercouri writes that Dassin told her, "I knew you would try to stop me, so I left without telling you. I came back only to apologize. Now I tell you, I'm going to Israel." And then he flew back. Dassin's daughter Ricky stayed with Mercouri, and in spite of missing her husband, Mercouri didn't miss a performance of *Illya Darling*. She also kept on making speeches against the Greek colonels.

When Mercouri's father died, Dassin flew in for the London funeral, although she could not be released from the show. On July 12, Mercouri was declared an enemy of the Greek people by the Greek Minister of the Interior and was deprived of her citizenship. In his *Films Illustrated* article, Tony Crawley claims that the Greeks also confiscated the house Dassin had supposedly built for Mercouri, "overlooking the Acropolis," where they had lived until 1967 for six months of every year. It is also thought the couple was forbidden to return to Greece. Mercouri felt abandoned and alone, living in a foreign country with no passport, which meant she could be sent back to Greece to face the repercussions of her criticism of the new regime. In response, Mercouri made the statement "I was born Greek and I shall die Greek," and people took up her cause. Shops in New York sold lapel buttons with the slogan "Melina is a Greek." *Look* magazine did an article about her fight, which apparently was read into the Congressional Record. The actress Irene Pappas called a press conference in Rome and protested the theft of Mercouri's nationality. Telegrams and letters of support from all over the world were delivered in huge canvas bags. Dassin returned to New York after six weeks, when presumably he had done the interviews for his documentary *Survival 67* (1968) about the six-day war.

In spite of the apparent renewed sympathy for Mercouri, threatening letters still arrived. The show's company was concerned for her safety, and orders were given not to permit any unknown person backstage. Tony Crawley claims that Dassin had hired seventeen bodyguards for her, although Mercouri writes that she only had one. In August a stranger came to see her, and Dassin interceded. The stranger was a young man who had brought her a tape from Athens from Mikis Theodorakis. He was the composer of *Zorba the Greek*, whose music was now banned in Greece. On the tape Theodorakis whispered, suggesting that he had recorded it in a hiding place, and sang a song to the accompaniment of his drumming fingers. Mercouri would sing this song countless times for audiences all over America and Europe, as an anthem of resistance. The night the tape was delivered, the radio reported the capture and imprisonment of the composer. Dassin and Mercouri organized a campaign amongst artists and composers across Europe and America to save Theodorakis, with Simone Signoret in Paris and Betsy Blair in London joining the plea. Mercouri asked Bloomgarden again if she could make a curtain speech to the audience of the show, and this time he agreed. She urged them to wire the State Department and plead its intervention. When Mercouri sang the song *Zorba the Greek* the audience all rose in tribute to the man who was locked in a junta prison.

Some people who were considered friends warned that artists who meddle in politics could destroy their careers, to which Mercouri replied with the first English word she had learned: "Bullshit." At the Venice Film Festival, the writer Albert Moravia presided over the jury, and he wrote a petition requesting the Italian Minister of Foreign Affairs have a Red Cross inspector go to Athens to investigate the conditions under which the composer was detained. The petition had been signed by all the members and film people attending the festival. Another petition came from France, signed by Jean-Luc Godard, Yves Montand, and Simone Signoret, among others. In the United States, Arthur Miller forbade the performance of any of his plays in Greece, and Edward Albee organized a petition which had been signed by people like Leonard Bernstein, Betsy Blair, Irene Pappas, Edna O'Brien, and Vanessa Redgrave, who all agreed not to participate in the Athens festival.

On August 25, King Constantine of Greece went to the United States for a luncheon at the United Nations in New York. Given his seeming alliance with the colonels, Mercouri and Dassin organized a demonstration. Jim Proctor alerted the press of the couple's intention. They were interviewed by print and television media until the King arrived, who was whisked into the building to avoid the fracas. *The New York Times* the next day bore the headline "Melina Upstages Greek King at U.N." It was rumored that the King was seeking increased military aid for Greece, after the American government had reduced arms when the junta had taken control. His next stop was to see President Lyndon Johnson in Washington. The couple organized another demonstration, which was held in the park that faced the White House, and people wore the "Melina is a Greek" badges. Mercouri gave a speech, but the couple didn't see the King. They wondered if their activism was making any difference, since they realized that the junta must have secured American support to stay in power. The press showed photographs of junta chiefs being entertained at luncheons on the American flagship of the Sixth Fleet, and American corporations traded with the craven junta.

On December 12 the young man brought more tapes from Mikis Theodorakis, with new songs seemingly recorded under the same conditions. The couple spent the night organizing a television program built around the songs, but the next morning the news came that the King had supposedly called on the army and the people of Greece to fight against the junta. The press wanted a comment from Mercouri. Dassin wanted her to express their suspicion of the Kings's alliance, a King who might have crushed the junta when he had the chance six months ago but didn't. Mercouri decided to voice her support of the King, figuring that he only now moved to act because he had the help of the Americans. However, the next day would show the ineffectiveness of the King when he fled to Rome, his revolt a miserable failure. The junta had preempted him, knowing the details of his planned coup in advance and disempowering the monarch, without any casualties. The King left the country to avoid becoming another prisoner, although Mercouri and Dassin thought that if this had occurred, it might have spurred Johnson into action. With the titular head of the state ousted, it seemed that foreign powers now had to recognize the junta as the official government of Greece. Claiming that Greece was still a monarchy, a regent to the King was named, who announced Colonel George Papadopoulos as the new Prime Minister.

Dassin went to Paris to edit *Survival 67*. He had been delegated to visit Andreas Papandreou, the former Greek minister who had been released from prison and who had formed the resistance movement called PAK (Pan Hellenic Liberation Movement). Meanwhile, in New York two FBI agents came to warn Mercouri at the theater that an attempt would be made on her life, although they didn't tell her how they knew this. There had been a crazy man who had pushed his way backstage to see her, but hadn't threatened to harm her. Could this be who the FBI was afraid of? Police were positioned in the wings and plain clothesmen were placed in the audience, but Mercouri became distracted by her fear during her big number "Piraeus, My Love," thinking that in the spotlight she was an easy target. Consequently, that performance was not her best, and the audience's tepid applause recognized this. The police added men to the bodyguard that Dassin had engaged, who Mercouri says rode in her car to the theater with her while the bodyguard drove a car behind. After six weeks of this coverage and no attempted murder, she was told that she was costing the city of New York too much money, and she agreed that the police detail should cease (though they agreed to make occasional checks with her).

When Dassin returned, the bodyguard was let go after two weeks—on Mercouri's request, since his battery of guns frightened her more than the phantom person he was supposedly protecting her from. She felt better anyway, with her husband with her, and they enjoyed going to a restaurant in Greenwich Village without armed guards. The run of *Illya Darling* came to a close in New York, and now it toured the country. In Chicago, Mercouri appeared with Andreas Papandreou to make a speech, although the police had been alerted to search for bombs. When the speakers arrived at the theater they faced a picket line of Greek-Americans who shouted obscenities and curses. Mercouri was also asked to address a luncheon in Washington given by the Women's National Democratic Club, consisting of an audience of seven hundred people. Her speech included her objection to an opinion that had been expressed by Dean Acheson, the former Secretary of State, in a published letter in *The Washington Post*. Acheson had written that what Greeks needed was authoritarian rule, but Mercouri stated that he was wrong—Greeks had invented democracy, knew the meaning of it, and would embrace it in the future to be free again.

In March 1968, Mercouri started a tour of Europe, to cover eighteen cities in less than six weeks, to plead the cause of free Greece. She would give speeches in theaters, banquet halls, university auditoriums, and sing with exiled musicians from Mikis Theodorakis' orchestra and give interviews. There were more threats and more applause. Dassin would stay in New York to work on his film about black political activism, which acquired a renewed urgency after the assassination of Martin Luther King in April. Arrangements had been made for the simultaneous placing of wreaths—with the words of Lord Byron on them: "I dreamed that Greece may yet be free"—on the statues of Byron in London by Mercouri and a member of Parliament in Athens. In Athens the member was arrested and held while the wreath was removed. In London, Mercouri was not arrested, and the wreath was left. In Stockholm for May Day fifty-thousand people filled the stadium where Mercouri sang Mikis' song "Metapo," meaning liberty or death, under an enormous Greek flag. In Essen news came of Mercouri being excommunicated from the Greek church, and eight thousand Greeks there sang "Metapo" for her, then a chorus of "We want guns." In Berlin there was a demonstration against her at her hotel; in response Mercouri blew kisses from her balcony. In Amsterdam the International Greek Aid Fund was created, and its creator, Van der Stoel, led the fight for Greece to be removed from the Council of Europe. Although this would prove unsuccessful, Greece would resign from the Council when they learned that the issue of their expulsion was to be voted on. In Brussels three busloads of hoodlums stormed the university where Mercouri was to speak, but they were stopped and Mercouri spoke as planned. In Paris Mercouri's press conference was interrupted by cries of "Those who are in Greek prisons deserve to be there," but the criers were shouted down and the conference continued.

Before Mercouri left to go back to America (where she had been offered a film, to be directed by Norman Jewison—the 1969 comedy *Gaily Gaily*), she witnessed an uprising in France. Although it was crushed, it was still a sign that people cared about democracy for Greece.

Dassin's film about blacks would be called *Up Tight!* (1968) and was partly shot on location in Cleveland, Ohio, in May and June (in *Tender Comrades* Dassin says that filming was taking place when Robert F. Kennedy was shot on June 5). It had no stars, but its all-black cast was headlined by Raymond St. Jacques, Ruby Dee, Frank Silvera, Roscoe Lee Browne, and Julian Mayfield. Dassin went to Los Angeles to continue *Up Tight!*, and Mercouri was there to make her film, although *Gaily, Gaily* would also be shot on location in Chicago and Milwaukee, Wisconsin. (In her book, Mercouri writes that her first meeting with Jewison did not go well when she told him that her main interest in the film was to

Jules Dassin, on location for the film *Up Tight!* (1968), is visited by Melina Mercouri (seated).

make money to buy bombs.) Working during the week, the couple saw each other on weekends.

In his *Films & Filming* article, Gordon Gow would say that Dassin's film was a difficult and a brave one to make as a return to American cinema after his time in Europe. Gow would also write that he considered the director an international filmmaker in the fullest sense, with all his journeying, but Dassin denied the title of cosmopolite. "I think I'm deeply American. I felt it more than ever when I made the film." Dassin also said:

> I would make films only in America now. Coming back was a very strong emotional experience, working again there; getting close to what is going on. There is such ferment, such promise, such strife, such hope, that I would like to be in it and part of it and make films about it. Also, the American director today has finally (although it still has to be fought for) achieved a freedom, a liberty that he didn't have before. Now the American director can function as the author of a film in the European sense. Now he can insist on cutting his own film. And all that is, of course, a great advance from the way things used to be. There is a new sense of cinema in America, more sophisticated than it has ever been before.

Asked about making another film in Greece, Dassin replied, "Of course I would adore it ... not only to make another film in that beautiful country—but because it would mean that those bastards are out and it's free again."

In August there was an unsuccessful attempt to assassinate Papadopoulos by an army officer in Greece; but pressure from the Vatican and the heads of governments stopped the colonels from executing him, and he was imprisoned instead. In 1969 Mercouri went back to Europe to attend hearings before the Council of Europe in Strasbourg and heard testimony from witnesses who had been tortured in junta prisons. In Rome she gave speeches to workers and received promises from the Italians to supply financial help for the cause, although Mercouri writes that there was conflict between the differing Greek resistance organizations. In Paris she met with friends who had escaped Greek prisons, and was asked by a Greek from the Soviet embassy in Paris to tour Russia the way she had toured Europe on a speaking tour. Mercouri agreed to the tour on the condition that she not be censored in the press or in public meetings, but she would never hear from the man who made the offer, or the embassy, again. In London she joined a hunger strike outside the Greek embassy when it was announced that Alexos Panagoulis, the army officer who had attempted to assassinate Papadopoulos, would be executed, and the action, covered by BBC television cameras, successfully stopped the execution.

Back in Lausanne, Dassin was engaged to make his next film in France, despite his quoted hopes of wanting to work in America again. Based on the book by Romain Gary, the biographical drama *Promise at Dawn* (1970) starred Mercouri and Assaf Dayan, the son of the Prime Minister of Israel. Mercouri writes that the casting director had employed dozens of Greek refugees as extras in France, despite the fact that they had no work permits. During filming Dassin was charged by the Greeks with smuggling bombs and manuals on the manufacture of explosives into Greece. When asked if the charges were true, Dassin is purported to have said, "If I sent bombs, I would not admit it. If I did not send bombs, I'd be ashamed to say so." He was to be tried in absentia, and if found guilty could be condemned to death. In Genoa, Italy, to make a speech, the couple were acknowledged by Greek sailors from a merchant marine ship docked in the harbor, signaling the sign of victory. However, not all Greeks were their friends. An explosive device was found under the speaker's rostrum before it was due to go off, and safely disposed of by the police. It was said to have had enough force to potentially destroy the theater and kill the two hundred attendees. When news of the planted bomb spread, thousands came to demonstrate, and

François Raffoul, Melina Mercouri and Jules Dassin on location for *Promise at Dawn* (1970).

Mercouri made her speech. When Mikis Theodorakis was freed after three-and-a-half years of prison and exile, Mercouri and Dassin met his plane in Orly.

In January 1971, Mercouri wrote of Dassin's hopes to film a story of prisoners of the junta that would eventually be realized in his later title *The Rehearsal* (1974), a theatrical recreation of the November 1973 revolt of the Athens Polytechnic students whose demonstration was crushed by the Greek military. In spite of considering it one his best films, Dassin was disappointed that it could not immediately get an American release because it was considered untimely after the collapse of the junta, which allowed the couple to return to Greece. The film would eventually be seen in 2001, although by then it was considered a period curiosity. In the *Films Illustrated* article, Tony Crawley says that Dassin had hoped to make a film of the 1972 novel by John Gardner, *The Sunlight Dialogues*, but it was a project that he shelved and was never made by anyone else.

Dassin's family suffered a loss with the death of Dassin's newborn grandson, Joshua, who had been born two-and-a-half months before term on September 12, 1973, and then died five days later. The child was the son of Joseph and his first wife, Yvette Maryse Massiera, who he had married on January 18, 1966. The couple separated as a result of the loss of the baby, although they did not officially divorce until May 5, 1977.

After making an appearance in *The Rehearsal*, Mercouri become actively involved in the establishment and promotion of the Pan-Hellenic Socialist Party (PASOK) in Greece. She was a member of the party's central committee and a rapporteu for the Culture Section. In the Greek elections of 1974 Mercouri was the party candidate for the Piraeus B constituency. Mercouri didn't win enough votes to secure her a seat in Parliament, but she tried again in 1977 and was successful. The actress also worked on fourteen episodes of a television program called *Dialogues*, which focused on social issues. However, only two episodes were broadcast, and Mercouri failed to have the ban from the National Broadcasting Organization lifted by appealing to Parliament. In spite of this obstacle, Mercouri would go on to make two more episodes for the series.

Dassin would work in the theater in Athens, although the exact dates of the productions are unknown. The plays he directed include *The Threepenny Opera*, by Kurt Weill and Bertolt Brecht, in 1975; *An Evening with Bertolt Brecht* in 1977; and *Sweet Bird of Youth*, by Tennessee Williams, in the winter of 1979 to 1980, all with Mercouri. He also did *Who's Afraid of Virginia Wolf*, by Edward Albee; *A Month in the Country*, by Ivan Tourgenev; *Heartbreak House*, by George Bernard Shaw; *Extremities*, by William Mastrosimone; *The Road to Mecca*, by Athol Fugard; *Anatol*, by Arthur Schnitzler; *The Seagull*, by Anton Chekhov; and *Death of a Salesman*, by Arthur Miller. In his article for *Film Criticism*, Andrew Horton says that Dassin also directed Mercouri in a production of *Medea* in 1976 (although the Mercouri biography on the Foundation website claims that the director was Minos Volanakis), and worked on several film scripts (though none of them were completed or financed). The director, however, would not succeed in making another film until *A Dream of Passion* (1978), which co-starred Mercouri with American actress Ellen Burstyn, and would be filmed in Greece. It went to Cannes, and Dassin was nominated for the Golden Palm.

In his article for *Films Illustrated*, Tony Crawley says Dassin had begun to write a novel when the film offer came out of the blue (after years of regularly refusing everything Hollywood offered) to make *Circle of Two* in Canada. Crawley quotes Dassin as saying, "I could easily have made the disaster or other sort of vogue film but I won't do anything I don't care about." The film would co-star Richard Burton and Tatum O'Neal, and was filmed from August 27 to November 3, 1979. It would prove to be the last that the director would ever make, because it was such a bad experience for him. However, in 1980 Dassin was approached by producer Allan Carr, who had made the phenomenally successful musical *Grease* (1978)—but also the phenomenally disastrous musical *Can't Stop the Music* (1980)—and who was at one time Melina Mercouri's manager. Carr wanted Dassin to make a film about Edith Piaf, to star Bette Midler. Crawley says that Dassin told Carr he had never seen Midler perform, but he had seen Piaf in Paris and knew her. To entertain Carr's idea, Dassin saw Midler's film *The Rose* (1979), for which she had been nominated for the Best Actress Academy Award, and found her remarkable. The idea did not seem as misguided as he first thought, but it was a project that never came to fruition.

Jules Dassin on the set of *Circle of Two* (1980).

Mercouri performed the part of Clytemnestea in *Oriesteia*, staged by Karolos Koun's Art Theatre in Epidaurus in the summer of 1980, but that year tragedy struck the couple's family. Dassin's son Joseph suffered a heart attack at the age of forty-two and died on August 20, 1980, while on vacation in Tahiti. Joe left behind a wife, Christine Delvaux (whom he had married as his second wife on January 14, 1978), and two sons, Jonathan aged one, and Julien, aged only four months. Joseph had appeared in Dassin's *He Who Must Die*, *Where the Hot Wind Blows*, and *Topkapi*, as well as narrating the French version of *Survival 1967*, and was his father's second assistant director on *Topkapi*. Joseph had made other film appearances, and as Joe Dassin was known as a pop singer in France and Canada, and had recorded sixteen albums. Joseph's body was interred in the Beth Olam Mausoleum of the Hollywood Forever Cemetery in California. With his filmmaking career over, it seemed Dassin's focus now turned to his family.

In 1981 Mercouri was appointed Minister of Culture when PASOK won the October elections, the first woman ever to hold the post and one she would hold for eight years. In this time she would campaign for the return of the Parthenon Marbles, worked on the preservation of the Acropolis monuments, and held an international competition for the design of the new Acropolis Museum. Mercouri commissioned a study for the integration of all the archaeological sites of Athens because she wanted to create a traffic-free park where residents and visitors could learn about and enjoy the history of Athens. She introduced free access to museums and archaeological sites for Greek citizens to aid education, and organized a series of exhibitions of Greek cultural heritage and contemporary Greek art over five continents. Mercouri supported the restoration of important buildings, like the Schlieman Mansion Weiler building in Athens, to protect Greece's architectural heritage, and helped to complete the Athens Hall of Music. She established annual literary prizes and Municipal Regional Theaters, and contributed to the creation and operation of Municipal Conservatories.

In 1983 Dassin was interviewed by Patrick McGilligan for the book he would write with Paul Buhle, *Tender Comrades*, which was published in 1999. In the same year Mercouri organized a meeting of the Culture Ministers of the ten European Union Member States in Zappeion, to participate in a joint action to increase cultural awareness, which resulted in the EEC Ministers of Culture sessions. In 1984 it is said that Dassin and Mercouri both appeared in a West German documentary about their lives by Christine Kerr entitled *Keine Zufällige Geschichte* (aka *Not by Coincidence*). The film has not received a commercial release and was not readily available for the author of this book to see. In 1985, Mercouri enabled Athens to be chosen as the first capital of the established Cultural Capitals of Europe, an institution she established. Mercouri supported Athens' bid for the 1996 Olympic Games, since it would commemorate the centennial of the first modern Olympic Games of 1896, although ultimately no games would be held in 1986.

In *Tender Comrades* Walter Bernstein tells Paul Buhle that in 1988 Dassin attended the Barcelona Film Festival as part of a panel to discuss the blacklist, after a screening of *The Front*. Others on the panel were Bernstein, John Berry, and Rosaura Revueltas, the Mexican actress who had played the heroine in *Salt of the Earth*. When the panel heard that Edward Dmytryk was also to be at the Festival, although attending separately (as some of his movies were being shown), they made it clear that they wanted nothing to do with him and were assured that they would not see or meet the director. However, after the film was screened, Dmytryk was sitting in the front row of the hall facing the panel on the dais. Before the panel began, Dmytryk apparently grabbed the microphone, apologized for his naming names, and then began to attack John Berry. Bernstein says that he had to physically restrain Berry from going down to throttle Dmytryk (Dmytryk had named Berry as a communist at the same time he named Dassin). Dassin then stood up and announced, "This is not why we came here," and the panel all left the stage.

In his book *Odd Man Out: A Memoir of the Hollywood Ten*, Dmytryk's memory of the July 1988 event is different. He claims that another member of the panel was Daniel Taradash, best known for winning the Academy Award for his screenplay of the war romance *From Here to Eternity* (1953), and who had not been blacklisted because he was not a communist or a communist sympathizer; while the panel's moderator was the Spanish film scholar Ruben Gubern. Dmytryk says that he was miked as he sat in the front row of the audience, but when the panelists saw him they asked him to excuse himself from the discussion. Dmytryk claims that he moved further back into the audience, and the panelists then began attacking him for naming names. Dmytryk does not say that he apologized for his actions, as Bernstein claims, but he does say he had to endure lies from Dassin, such as Dassin saying, "If my memory serves me correctly, I took care of Dmytryk's children while he was in jail." Dmytryk disputes this claim made by Dassin, as he says he had not seen Dassin since early 1948 when he lived in Europe—before he went to jail and before his wife had their first child. Dmytryk says that he was only friends with Dassin prior to 1948 because he had worked with his wife, Jean Porter, during his MGM period (she had an uncredited part in *Young Ideas*). Dmytryk doesn't say how the event ended, only that his wife was very offended by Dassin's remarks, but neither does he say that the panel all left the stage upon seeing him, as Bernstein also claims.

It is not known whether Mercouri attended the Barcelona event, although she remained busy in Greece. That year she worked on the cooperation of Eastern Europe and the European Union to open up borders, despite the strong reservations of the European partners. The initiative that Mercouri began would be implemented in 1989 with the celebration of a Month of Culture in Eastern countries. While being supportive of his wife's work, Dassin would also receive honorary awards, including the Legion of Honor, the Order of Arts and Letters, and an honorary doctorate degree by the Greek University. The Greek State granted him honorary Greek citizenship in 1988 for all his contributions and the love he had shown for Greece, although in his *Tender Comrades* interview with Patrick McGilligan Dassin said that he had previously refused the offers of citizenship in Greece and France because "I am an American, and that I will stay." In 1988, Dassin was interviewed by Barry Norman for the British television series *Talking Pictures*. Although this interview is not available on DVD, it can be viewed, according to the British Film Institute website, at the B.F.I. National Library in London.

In 1989, although PASOK lost the November elections, Mercouri was elected as a national Parliamentarian, and remained a member of PASOK's Executive Bureau. In 1990 she was a candidate for the city of Athens at the municipal elections but lost. Mercouri returned to the stage in 1992 to again play Clytemnestra in the opera *Pylades*, which was directed by Dionysis Fotopoulos at the Athens Hall of Music (which she had helped to create). In the 1993 elections, Mercouri returned as Minister of Culture, although she would only serve a short term due to the illness from cancer that would kill her. However, in this time she instigated the creation of a park in the Aegean to safeguard and enhance the environment of the Aegean islands, and created a new system of post-training of teachers so that cultural references could be included in all subjects, using the slogan "Education through Enjoyment."

On March 6, 1994, Mercouri died in New York at the Memorial Sloan-Kettering Cancer Center where she had gone for treatment for lung cancer. A state funeral was held for her in Greece, where she was given Prime Minister's honors on March 10 at the First Cemetery of Athens. Mercouri was 73 when she died, and Dassin was 82. After her death,

Jules Dassin, with dog, and Melina Mercouri, photographed on holiday in London.

Dassin established the Melina Mercouri Foundation to continue the work Mercouri had started in promoting and disseminating Greek culture in Greece and abroad, as well to archive the life and work of the actress. This archive included press clippings from 1951; 13,000 photographs; films, documentaries, and recordings; and speeches made between 1982 and 1994. The Foundation's Honorary Committee would include such people as Sir Peter Brook, Jacques Cousteau, Julie Christie, Sean Connery, Costa Gavras, Sir Ian McKellen, Paul Newman, Nana Mouskouri, Peter Ustinov, and Joanne Woodward. The projects that would require continued support were the reunification of the Parthenon Marbles, the Acropolis Restoration Project, the new Acropolis Museum, and the Unesco Melina Mercouri International Prize for scientists and artists. The Foundation renamed the Melina Mercouri scholarship as the Melina Mercouri—Jules Dassin scholarship, which awarded money to Greeks for pursuing a Ph.D. in Literature or Theater Studies. In May 2000 Dassin submitted a memorandum he had written to the British House of Commons requesting the return of the Parthenon Marbles, and the Foundation followed this with an exhibition that toured Athens, Brussells, Cyprus, Paris, Strasbourg, and Frankfurt from 2002 to 2006 called "The Reunification of the Parthenon Marbles—a Cultural Imperative." Additionally, the Foundation sells CD-Roms and Video-CDs on Mercouri and the Parthenon Promenades.

In 2000 Dassin went to New York for a screening of *Rififi*, which was organized to celebrate the 2001 Criterion Collection DVD release of the film. There he was interviewed by Masha Leon of *The Jewish Daily Forward*, although her article would not be published until after his death. Dassin would also give an interview as a special feature for the DVD, and would be interviewed by telephone by Michael Sragow for an article that was published for the website Salon.com on August 24, 2000. In 2002 Dassin was interviewed for the British television series *Film Genre* in an episode entitled "Heist." In 2004 Dassin attended the Los Angeles County Museum of Art for an interview that was filmed and is included on the 2007 Criterion Collection DVD of *The Naked City*. In the interview the director said that he had gone back to the 20th Century–Fox lot to see the restoration work done on *Night and the City* by Sean Bolston and his team. He was interviewed for the Criterion Collection DVD releases of *Night and the City* and *Thieves' Highway*, which were both released in 2005.

Dassin also appeared in the documentary *Buzz* (2005) by director Spiro N. Taraviras, which was about the screenwriter A. E. Bezzerides who had written *Thieves' Highway*. The film was screened exclusively at Laemmle's Fairfax Cinemas in Los Angeles on August 25, 2006, but to date has not received a DVD release. Dassin was also interviewed for Fay Efrosini Lellios' documentary on Bezzerides, *The Long Haul of A. I. Bezzerides* (2005), which was previewed on the Criterion Collection DVD of *Thieves' Highway* but as yet has not received a commercial or full-length DVD release. Additionally, Dassin would be interviewed for an appearance on the Carlos Benpar–directed Spanish biographical documentary *Filmmakers in Action* (2005), and the Greek television series *Otan giortazoun oi theoi*, which was broadcast in July 2007.

In 2006 the Foundation curated an exhibition called The Grand Promenade, organized by the National Museum of Contemporary Art so that the public could have pedestrian walkways in close proximity to the archeological sites and monuments of Athens. The project aimed to complete permanent premises in 2008. The same year, the Foundation established the annual Melina Mercouri Theater Award, to be given to the best young actress of the past theatrical season. This award was to coincide with the Dimitris Horn Award, which was given to the best actor. The Mercouri award winner was also to be given a broach that belonged to the deceased actress, while the winning actor was to receive a cross that belonged to Horn.

Jules Dassin died on March 31, 2008, at the Hygeia Hospital in Athens, Greece, of complications from influenza. He was 96 years old, and he was survived by his two daughters, Richelle and Julie, and his three grandchildren. The Athens News Agency reported that his burial was held at the synagogue in the Israelite sector of the 3rd Athens cemetery, and the service was attended by relatives, friends, politicians, actors and intellectuals. At the end of the service his body was taken to the 1st Athens cemetery where he was buried next to his beloved Melina Mercouri, in accordance with his wishes. Attorney Christos Zouraris was the executor of his will, and the Melina Mercouri Foundation reported that in it Dassin bequeathed five-hundred-thousand euros to the continuation of the Melina Mercouri–Jules Dasin scholarship award for postgraduate students. He also bequeathed a hundred-thousand euros to the Athens branch of Doctors Without Frontiers; all his books on theater and cinema to the Theatre Museum; and one work of art to the Benaki Museum.

On February 22, 2009, Dasin was included in the In Memoriam section of the 2009 81st Academy Awards show. From March 27 to April 7, 2009, the New York Film Forum gave a retrospective of Dassin's films, screening *Night and the City*, *The Naked City*, *Thieves' Highway*, *Reunion in France*, *Nazi Agent*, *Up Tight!*, *He Who Must Die*, *Brute Force*, *Rififi*, *Topkapi*, *Never on Sunday*, *10:30 P.M. Summer*, *The Rehearsal*, *Phaedra*, and *A Dream of Passion*. This was both a tribute to a recently deceased director and, given that 15 of his 25 titles were screened, an acknowledgment of the perceived relevance of the work to today's film scholars.

THE FILMS

The Tell-Tale Heart (1941)

[aka *Edgar Allan Poe's The Tell-Tale Heart*]
MGM

Credits: Director: Jules Dassin; Screenplay: Doane Hoag, based on the short story by Edgar Allan Poe; Photography: Paul Vogel; Music: Sol Krandel; Editor: Adrienne Fazan; Art Director: Richard Duce; B&W, 19.40 minutes.

Cast: Joseph Schildkraut (Young Man); Roman Bohnen (Old Man). Uncredited: Oscar O'Shea (First Deputy Sheriff); Will Wright (Second Deputy Sheriff).

VHS/DVD: Included as a Special Feature on the DVD *The Complete Thin Man Collection*, released by Warner Home Video on August 2, 2005.

Synopsis

A twenty-nine-year-old man shares lodgings with an older man, who is abusive towards him. After the young man strangles the older man during a rainstorm one night, the young man continues to hear what he imagines is the sound of a heart beating. When two sheriffs come to the house to enquire about the older man, the sound of the beating heart that the young man hears forces him to reveal how he has buried the older man under the floor. The sheriffs remove the wooden floorboards to find the corpse of the old man, and take the young man away.

Notes

This short is Dassin's film debut and an atmospheric psychological study with stylistic touches that prefigure film noir. If the music is too much at times, Dassin also uses silence pleasingly, as well as dolly and zoom camerawork, and jump-cut edits. Performances are equally stylized and non-naturalistic, which adds to the fantasy aspect of the tale.

The narrative opens with a quote from Romans, 11.5: "The law is written in their hearts, their conscience also bearing witness." This idea will be aligned to Edgar Allan Poe's notion of how the young man hears what he believes is the sound of the beating heart of the old man he has murdered, although this idea is never verbalized as such. The slow dolly into an extreme close-up of the young man's ear as he hears the sound of the old man's feet climbing the wooden staircase to the house is an introduction to Dassin's focus on sound in the film and also the young man's sensitivity to sound. Seeing the young man in the first shot also establishes him as the treatment's protagonist, although when he later commits murder, he will become a protagonist with moral ambiguity. The young man is also photographed with diagonal shadows across his face and body to express his entrapment in the house. The circumstances of his situation are left unexplained, with this lack of detail extending to the fact that characters remain nameless. The old man is seen in shadowed long shot at the doorway behind the strands of the loom which the young man works at. The old man's left eye lacking an eyeball, described by Poe as resembling that of a vulture's (a pale blue eye with a film over it), presents him as a grotesque. The wardrobe is equally schematic in having the old man dressed in black, and the young man in white or grey.

Dassin stops the music when the young man walks to the old man at the door, to receive a slap from him. This act of violence perhaps justifies the young man's later murder, but it also establishes the old man as the treatment's antagonist (which differs from the old man in the Poe story, who the young man says had never wronged him). Dassin's fade to black for a scene transition at this point is particularly interesting because the close-up of the young man suggests that he is thinking of killing the old man. A close-up of the young man's hand on a doorknob—a horror movie convention—receives a fresh touch via the moving light of the lantern he holds. This movement also suggests the young man's nervousness and fear at his intention. We get the old man's point of view of the young man holding the lantern, with the light shining onto the old man's face, and Dassin allows the old man a moment of vulnerabil-

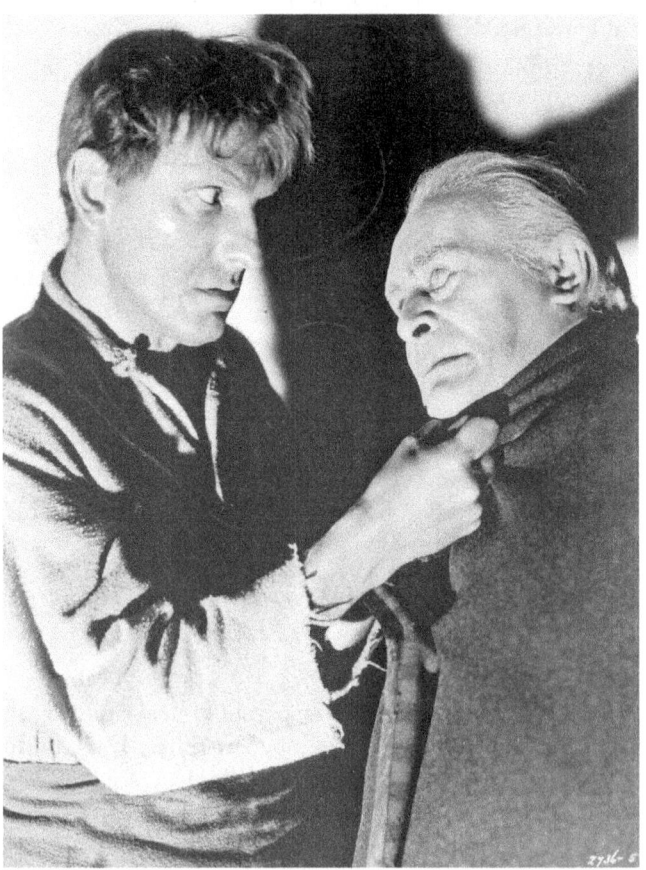

This publicity still shows the Young Man (Joseph Schildkraut) taking revenge on the Old Man (Roman Bohnen) in *The Tell-Tale Heart* (1941) (Photofest).

ity before his defensive tirade, causing the audience to momentarily switch empathy to someone who is about to be murdered. It is the young man's superior strength that defeats the old man, though it is a sad commentary on the young man that violence and murder is the only way he can reclaim his independence. The irony of the tale is that this reclaiming is a falsehood, since one psychological entrapment gives way to another when he is tormented by his own guilt. Or is it that the old man doesn't lose his control over the young man when the beating of his heart continues to disempower his victim?

The murder is not shown but rather suggested by the pulling down of a wall tapestry and the bed coverings, presumably by the old man during his struggle. These actions prefigure the way the shower curtain is pulled from its connections in the shower scene from *Psycho* (1960). An odd touch is that the young man first hears the old man's beating heart as he leans over the body—*after* (we presume) the old man is dead. Poe had the young man hearing the old man's beating heart before he killed him, which makes more sense. What makes the presentation here even odder is that Dassin doesn't attach any great trauma to the moment. We simply observe it, with the young man perplexed but not anguished. The Poe story had told us that the young man was driven mad by the sight of the old man's diseased eye, but the young man here is not shown as such. It is later, when the sound returns, that Dassin attaches the anguish, employing jump-cuts as the young man hears noises coming from a ticking clock, a dripping faucet, and water dripping into a pail outside a window. This behavior is only mad in the context of his perception of the sound, and reads as a normal reaction to hearing a noise that cannot be identified or stopped.

The sheriffs arrive at the film's climax (though the treatment changes Poe's three men to two), and Dassin stays on the young man's revealing behavior rather than the sheriffs' reaction to it. A rambling speech about where the old man's whereabouts makes the lie apparent, and the narrative scores its one laugh from his question "Why are you looking at me?" after the young man slowly takes a chair and sits on it in an almost balletic fashion. Dassin uses stylized acting and staging for the big reveal, as if the action has been timed to the sound of the beating heart on the soundtrack, and thankfully spares us the sight of the corpse under the floor. The conclusion offers narrative irony because the young man's relief over the sound of the heart finally stopping comes with his being taken away, presumably to jail, by the sheriffs. Dassin has the three actors walk into the camera for the final shot, so that he ends on a close-up of Joseph Schildkraut as the young man.

In his autobiography *My Father and I*, Joseph Schildkraut says that the film won the Academy Award for Best Short Subject, but this claim is unverified. He also says he learned of the part from Michael Kanin, the brother of Garson Kanin, whom Dassin had observed making *They Knew What They Wanted*. Poe's tale had been previously filmed as a British short in 1934 by director Brian Desmond Hurst for DuWorld Pictures, with a seemingly inappropriate alternative title *Bucket of Blood*. This short's treatment had included additional characters not in the original story—the Girl, and the Doctor—presumably to extend the film's running time to 55 minutes. Viennese Schildkraut was actually age 45 at the time of filming, though he passes for a 29-year-old "Young Man." In real life, Roman Bohnen, who played the Old Man, was only two years older than Schildkraut. Schildkraut had been a silent movie matinee idol and had won the Best Supporting Actor Academy Award for *The Life of Emile Zola* (1937). *The Tell-Tale Heart* was an early role for character actor Bohnen, a former member of the Group Theatre who, like Dassin, would see his Hollywood career ended by the blacklist.

Release

October 25, 1941.

Reviews

"Possibly the very first movie to be influenced by *Citizen Kane* (which came out less than six months before).... Positively a-swill in Wellesian tropes: the crouching camera, the chiaroscuro lighting, the mood-deepening use of silences and sound effects."—Richard Corliss, *Time* magazine, April 6, 2008

"A solid enjoyable horror short ... Dassin treats [the story] with his characteristic sweaty intensity and slow-burning suspense, making the Poe classic feel new again."—Ed Howard, *Only the Cinema*, February 21, 2009

"Dassin proved his mettle as a director with this chilling short adaptation of a Poe story. Adopting something of the expressionistic style of early German cinema, with harsh lighting and exaggerated use of shadows to create atmosphere, this haunting film presages Dassin's later film noir masterpieces."—James Travers, *Filmsdefrance.com*

"A small masterpiece of accelerating tension.... A first encounter with the talent of a man who might not please me always, but would excite and command my attention very often."—Gordon Gow, *Films and Filming*

Nazi Agent (1942)

[aka *Salute to Courage*; *House of Spies*; *Out of the Past*]
MGM

Credits: Director: Jules Dassin; Producer: Irving Asher; Screenplay: Paul Gangelin, John Meehan, Jr., based on an idea by Lothar Mendes; Photography: Harry Stradling; Editor: Frank E. Hull; Music: Lennie Hayton; Art Director: Cedric Gibbons; Set Decorations: Edwin B. Willis; Costumes: Shoup; Hair for Miss Ayars: Sydney Guilaroff; Makeup: Jack Dawn; Sound: Douglas Shearer. B&W, 83 minutes. Filmed November to December 16, 1941.

Song: "Columbia, Gem of the Ocean" (David T. Shaw).

Cast: Conrad Veidt (Otto Becker/Baron Hugo Von Detner); Ann Ayars (Kaaren De Relle); Frank Reicher (Fritz); Dorothy Tree (Miss Harper); Ivan Simpson (Professor Jim Sterling); William Tannen (Ludwig); Martin Kosleck (Kurt Richten); Marc Lawrence (Joe Aiello); Sidney Blackmer (Arnold Milbar, aka Frederick Williams); Moroni Olsen (Brennet); Pierre Watkin (Grover Blaine McHenry). Uncredited: Ernie Alexander (Sailor); Rudolph Anders (Cab Driver); Jessie Arnold (Landlady); Polly Bailey (Fat Woman); William Bailey (Cigar Store Clerk); Roy Barcroft (Chief Petty Officer); Barbara Bedford; Arthur Belasco (Detective); Margaret Bert (Mrs. Dennis); Walter Byron (Officer); Baldwin Cooke (Waiter); Hal Cooke (Clerk); Clyde Courtright (Doorman); Stuart Crawford (Commentator's Voice); Jack Daley (Reporter); Mark Daniels (Cab Driver); Cliff Danielson; Drew Demorest (Reporter); Joe Gilbert (Submarine Radioman); Bernadene Hayes (Rosie); Edward Hearn (Reporter); Robert Homans (1st Captain); Wilbur Mack (Reporter); George Magrill (Thug); Frank Marlowe (Sailor); James Millican (Operator); Roper Moore (Messenger); George Noisom (Bellboy); William Post, Jr. (Harry's Voice); Christian Rub (Mohr); Tim Ryan (Officer); Charles Sherlock (Detective); Russell Simpson (2nd Captain); Harry Stafford (Elderly Man); Hermine Sterler (Mrs. Mohr); Tom Stevenson (Head Waiter); Brick Sullivan (Radio Operator); Ray Teal (Officer Graves); Philip Van Zandt (Thug); Roland Varno (Bauer); Duke York (Sailor); Jeff York (Keeler); Joe Yule (Barney).

VHS/DVD: Not available in either format.

Synopsis

The German consul to New York, Baron Hugo Von Detner, is a Nazi agent involved in acts of sabotage on American soil. He visits his twin brother, stamp and bookseller Otto Becker, and blackmails him into allowing the shop to be used as a message exchange site for German agents. Otto writes a letter about the setup to his friend, Professor Jim Sterling, but his brother intercepts the letter and plans to kill Otto. In the struggle, Hugo is shot, and Otto assumes his identity to fool Hugo's waiting henchmen. Otto is believed to be Hugo by Hugo's assistant, Kurt Richten, although Hugo's butler, Fritz, realizes the deception but agrees to keep the secret. Otto informs on two agents to the police, but deflects suspicion away from Kaaren De Relle, an operative with mixed loyalties, (Otto is sympathetic to her own trapped situation). Otto learns about the new action to blow up the ship *Farrington* when it passes through the Panama Canal, and again informs the police. The plan is thwarted and Otto delivers the names of all the agents except for Kaaren. Gestapo thug Joe Aiello is thought to be the informant and is arrested by the F.B.I. after he is shot by two agents. When Otto's shop assistant (and German spy) Miss Harper notices that Otto's canary sings only when "Hugo" enters the room, she realizes the deception and tells Richten. After the F.B.I close the consul, Richten confronts Otto, and they make an agreement whereby Otto will go back to Germany with him as the betraying Hugo, leaving Kaaren unharmed. As his ship leaves the dock, Otto's last glimpse of the country where he had sought refuge is the Statue of Liberty.

Notes

Dassin's graduation from short to "A" movie resulted in a violent spy drama with occasional visual interest and a theme of the entrapped man. Although the treatment disappoints in the way it develops as an expression of wartime patriotism (the American entry into World War II occurred during filming), the initial scenario of a duplicitous protagonist with ambiguous morality is fascinating in terms of the director's later blacklisting.

Producer Irving Asher had started producing for Warner Bros. in 1929, and had moved to England to work for Warners there. His own British production company had made the war thriller *The Spy in Black* (1939), with Conrad Veidt. Asher returned to America to produce the MGM western *Billy the Kid* (1941), and his last title was the biographical drama *Blossoms in the Dust* (1941).

The film begins with a zoom into a radio microphone stand, which dissolves to the image of a train derailment, for the acts-of-sabotage montage. This montage is enhanced by a spider web pattern at the front of the screen, and ends in a close-up of the back of

Hugo's head. Dassin generates some mystery by filming Hugo standing with his back to the camera, so that the reveal of his face only comes later, in his scene with Otto. Conrad Veidt is almost unrecognizable as Otto, who has grayish loose hair, a beard and spectacles, and smokes a pipe. Otto's canary is used as a device to make him seem gentle and likable, and will also become an important plot point (in the way that it only sings when he is near). Dassin dollies into a close-up reaction shot of Otto seeing Hugo, finally giving us the delayed view of Hugo's face so that we can compare his appearance to that of his twin brother. Hugo's darker, slicked-back hair and unshaven face creates the impression that Hugo is younger than Otto, since Otto is styled to look like an old man. Later we will see that Hugo smokes cigarettes, but the most interesting aspect of Hugo's appearance is his monocle, which adds a touch of perversity to his character.

Dassin shows the brothers shaking hands in profile, presumably to accommodate the split screen effect necessary when one actor plays twins; while various over-the-shoulder shots indicate the obvious use of body doubles.

Otto uses a forged passport to enter America, revealing the first sign of the character's moral ambiguity. The following exchange reveals more about Otto's character (and ends with a patronizing—and amusing—retort):

> OTTO: I did enter the country illegally. I might have stayed on the border for a year waiting for a quota number. I might never have got one. I couldn't wait to become an American. To start life over again.
> HUGO: How touching.

The notion of Otto's rebirth as an American receives an ironic twist when Otto is reborn as Hugo—with Otto having to commit murder in order for this to happen. Unintentional as the act may have been, it still adds the element of opportunism to his character, and demonstrates that Otto is both physically and morally stronger than his brother. Otto's new life as a salesman has been undermined by the betrayal of Miss Harper, though one has to wonder why Otto would have stayed in New York when he surely would have been aware that Hugo was consul there, since Hugo is shown to be enough of a celebrity to attract the media. Otto's illegal entry to America comes full circle when we see him, as the new Hugo, allowing a German couple to apply for American citizenship without fear of recrimination.

Dassin reveals the fight between the brothers via an extreme long shot, with a cut-in to a gun (presumably in Hugo's hand), and the survivor identified as Otto from his shadow on the wall. Otto taking his brother's identity is portrayed by a close-up of him looking at himself in a mirror and moving

Conrad Veidt as Otto Becker, one of the twin brothers he plays in *Nazi Agent* (1942).

to cut off his beard, and then a dissolve which reveals Otto as Hugo. The narrative development of Otto becoming Hugo is both obvious and welcome, and additionally prefigures Dassin's future perceived duplicity as a suspected undesirable.

Otto placing Hugo's corpse in a closed box conveniently circumvents the potential problem of Hugo's henchmen making a direct comparison, while the nails they hammer into the box both seals Otto's fate and underlines the carelessness that will lead to their ultimate downfall. Otto's presence in the boat when the box is thrown into the sea is both a private tribute to his brother and the finalization of the plan to get rid of incriminating evidence.

Hugo having a card that gives his address as the Park Regent Hotel is another contrivance to aid Otto in his deception, and Otto's entrance to the hotel is the first real test for him. Dassin uses silence to add to the suspense of the scene, with the tension arising from Otto's role-playing and the fear that he will be discovered. Otto's exchange with the hotel clerk, while hardly witty, furthers the suspense:

> OTTO: My key.
> CLERK: You must have it.
> OTTO: If I had it, I wouldn't ask for it.

Otto's entrance into his room is accompanied by the sound of piano music, which suggests that there is someone else there. This device mirrors the use of the singing canary in Otto's shop room. Our introduction to Kaaren as the piano player creates the false impression that she's a femme fatale—complete with shimmery dress. Kaaren's "enthusiasm" for being a spy is also misleading (via the recorded conversation she plays), as later we will learn that Kaaren is not the Nazi idealist we expect her to be.

The issue of Otto not knowing Hugo's safe combination is the next test of Otto's duplicity, with Otto conveniently observing Richten opening the safe as a way to learn the combination. This point receives a later payoff when we see Otto speedily open the safe, as witnessed by Richten. The next testing point comes when Milbar at the Colonial Restaurant tells a waiter that he has met Hugo before and hopes that he remembers him. The hope, naturally, gives Otto an out (although Milbar sending his card—presumably with his name on it—to Hugo's table lessens the threat). Otto becoming an informant creates more moral ambiguity (on top of murder and the deception of pretending to be his brother). By being saboteurs, the Nazi agents are positioned in the treatment as antagonists, so it is ironic that Otto's betrayal of them should be considered questionable. But questionable it is, since Otto doesn't have the foresight to realize that someone else may be accused of being the informant.

Fritz leaving a glass of milk for Otto is the expression of his awareness of Otto's deceit, with milk representing Otto's comparative innocence in counterpoint to Hugo's presumed intake of alcohol. Fritz as a threat to Otto is nullified by his admission of his dislike for Hugo, which in narrative terms is a little disappointing. Thankfully, Fritz will only exist in the progressive narrative as a confidant and not an active party fighting the agents, with Fritz' loyalty capped at the film's end by his willingness to accompany Otto to Germany on what is a suicide mission. Otto makes an interesting point to Fritz about why he killed Hugo. When Fritz urges Otto to discontinue his deception, Otto tells him that if he doesn't try to stop the agents, then he would have only killed Hugo in self-defense. This attaches more nobility to Otto's character, even if it is aligned with the propagandistic agenda of the screenplay.

The next plot point concerning Otto's deception is his attitude towards Kaaren and her awareness of a change in Hugo. Making her a reluctant spy gives Otto the opportunity to empathize with her, and allows her to speak to him in a way that she would not have otherwise spoken to Hugo. There is a suggestion that Kaaren is a potential love interest for Otto, exemplified by the scene in which they take a moonlit drive and listen to

This publicity still shows the Nazi spies operating in New York: Martin Kosleck, Conrad Veidt, and Dorothy Tree in *Nazi Agent* (1942).

Mendelssohn—a Jewish composer banned by the Nazis—on the radio. However, this idea is undercut by the casting, since Veidt is not a conventionally romantic actor, and his formal German doesn't match with the equally unromantic Ann Ayars as Kaaren, who uses an American accent for what we presume is a European character.

As the narrative tension changes focus from Otto's deception to Otto's dangerous activities as the informant, Dassin's visual style becomes more conventional. The burning of Kaaren's information card, removed from the rest that Otto gives to the F.B.I., though shown in close-up, lacks resonance. The confrontation scene between Richten and Otto, when Richten uncovers Otto's deception (thanks to the singing canary), features the shadow of Venetian blinds on a wall, with blocking that would seem to allow Otto to easily escape from Richten. Presumably, because Otto is such a noble creature, he would not stoop to such an act of cowardice. Also, his escape would not guarantee the safety of Kaaren, for whom he is willing to die.

Otto's sense of patriotism is expressed in the following exchange:

> RICHTEN: I hope you don't think that anything you have done could put an end to our work here.
>
> OTTO: No, I don't. But I am only one of a hundred and thirty million Americans who together with all the good people of the world are rising to crush you and everything you stand for, once and for all.

The boos of the crowd that greet Otto at the shipping dock creates a strong aural effect, and also prefigures the rejection that Dassin would come to feel in his blacklisting and exit from America. For the film's final scene, Veidt appears with his back to the camera again, though here he admires the Statue of Liberty as the ship passes by, the ultimate symbol of tolerance. Dassin lays on an orchestral arrangement of the song "Columbia, Gem of the Ocean" to end the film with the knowledge that Otto is a hero—and more importantly, an American hero. It's an odd ending for the protagonist, since he is going back to Germany still pretending to be Hugo, where he knows he will be punished as an informant. Otto remains trapped by his act of murder, by his lies, by his being outsmarted by Richten, by his feelings for Kaaren, and perhaps by simply being a German in America during World War II. He is ultimately more a pathetic figure, who has caused his own destruction through poor choices, than the heroic one the treatment would have us believe. It's a sad and rather frightening morality tale (and a subtle warning for immigrants—especially those who come with a twin sibling).

German born Conrad Veidt was age 49 at the time of filming. He had worked in silent films in Germany as an actor, producer and director. At six-foot-three-inches tall, Viedt was cast as the somnambulist killer in the German classic horror title *The Cabinet of Dr. Caligari* (1920). He moved to England to escape the Nazis in the 1930s, though ironically there (and in Hollywood) he would be cast in a series of roles as German officers. Veidt memorably played Nazis in *Escape* (1940), *A Woman's Face* (1941), *All Through the Night* (1941), and, in his next and probably most famous film, *Casablanca* (1942). He would die in 1943 of a heart attack, apparently while playing golf.

In their book *Tender Comrades: A Backstory of the Hollywood Blacklist*, Patrick McGilligan and Paul Buhle quote Dassin about his meeting Veidt for the first time. Dassin remembered as a youth watching Veidt "in awe" in his German films, and when Dassin was introduced to Veidt at the MGM executive office, Veidt took one look at the twenty-nine-year-old Dassin, said "Nien," then turned and left the room. Dassin says Veidt's initial lack of confidence in him may have come from the fact that Dassin looked younger than his age. Fortunately, the film's director of photography was Harry Stradling, which helped smooth things over during production because Veidt had worked with Stradling in Europe.

Release

Premiered January 21, 1942, wide release in March 1942, with the taglines "The Girl and the Gestapo! Hidden enemies! It's thrilling!!" and "The Man who Double-Crossed Hitler!"

Reviews

"Tautly intriguing and sometimes hair-raising ... a good tight script, subdued direction and a cool performance by Conrad Veidt give to the film a quiet distinction."—Bosley Crowther, *The New York Times*, June 13, 1942

"Modest suspenser with a plot twist similar to *The Great Impersonator* and *Dead Ringer*."— John Walker, *Halliwell's Film & Video Guide 2000*

"A solid, lush-looking wartime programmer."—Dennis Schwartz, *Ozus' World Movie Reviews*, July 8, 2005

"Slow moving, rather arid tale that could have been much better."—Leonard Maltin, *1997 Movie & Video Guide*

"One of those wild ones about identical twins. Bad brother was a Nazi swine and good brother an anti-swine who—oh, you guessed. Ann Ayars was the girl for whom two Veidts didn't make a wrong."—John Douglas Eames, *The MGM Story*

The Affairs of Martha (1942)

[aka *Once Upon a Thursday*]
MGM

Credits: Director: Jules Dassin; Producer: Irving Starr; Screenplay: Isobel Lennart, Lee Gold; Photography: Charles Lawton; Music: Bronislau Kaper; Editor: Ralph Winters; Art Director: Cedric Gibbons; Set Decorations: Edwin B. Willis; Gowns: Howard Shoup; Hair: Sydney Guilaroff; Sound: Douglas Shearer. B&W, 66 minutes. Filmed February 23 to March 21, 1942.

Cast: Marsha Hunt (Martha Lindstrom); Richard Carlson (Jeff Sommerfield); Marjorie Main (Mrs. McKissick); Virginia Weidler (Miranda Sommerfield); Spring Byington (Mrs. Sophie Sommerfield); Allyn Joslyn (Joel Archer, aka Larfcardio Wufflecooler); Frances Drake (Sylvia Norwood); Barry Nelson (Danny O'Brien); Melville Cooper (Dr. Clarence Sommerfield); Inez Cooper (Mrs. Jacell); Sara Haden (Mrs. Justin I. Peacock); Margaret Hamilton (Guinevere); Ernest Truex (Llewellyn Castle); Cecil Cunningham (Mrs. Llewellyn Castle); William B. Davidson (Homer Jacell); Aubrey Mather (Justin I. Peacock); Grady Sutton (Justin I. Peacock, Jr.). Uncredited: Leonard Carey (Butler); Edgar Dearing (Motorcycle Cop); Gloria Gaye, Mae

Roberts, Virginia Tallent (Castles' Daughters); Jody Gilbert (Hadwig); Raymond Hatton (Patrolling Beach Cleaner); Ralph McCullough (Postman); Buddy Messinger (Butcher Boy); Robin Raymond (Juanita); William Tannen (Mechanic); Ralph Volkie (Garbage Man); Dave Willock (Milkman).

VHS/DVD: Unavailable in either format.

Synopsis

The quiet of Rock Bay Long Island is disturbed by news of an unidentified maid having written a forthcoming book which exposes the secrets of her household. The author is Martha Lindstrom, one of the maids of the Sommerfields, who is also secretly married to Jeff Sommerfield. An anthropologist, Jeff returns home from the Arctic with a mathematician fiancée, Sylvia Norwood. Martha hasn't divorced Jeff, as he had requested, because she is still in love with him, although she must fend off the advances of her publisher, Joel Archer, and the local handyman, Danny O'Brien. Jeff works out that Martha is the author of the book and demands that she finalize the divorce so he can marry Sylvia. However, Jeff becomes jealous of the other men in Martha's life and begins to question his true feelings about her. Jeff's father, Clarence, and his sister Miranda, talk him out of marrying Sylvia, though Sylvia dodges Jeff's attempt to break their engagement. Jeff stops Sylvia from announcing the engagement at a party by lambasting Joel, who admits to being the publisher of the maid's book; and Joel outs Martha as the book's author. When Martha runs away with Joel, Jeff reveals his marriage to her and catches up with Martha to admit his love for her.

Notes

Dassin's step down from "A" to "B" movie status resulted in a mildly amusing lightweight comedy about deception and the seeming betrayal of loyalty (continuing his previous themes). These themes again prefigure Dassin's future political troubles, and add an unintentional resonance to what is otherwise a minor entertainment. Although the music score often overplays its supposedly humorous commentary, the director provides occasional visual interest, aided by a group supporting players with comedic skill. The casting of Marsha Hunt in the leading role dilutes the majority of the dark motivations and behavior of her character; although, ironically, the picture failed to make a star of the actress. While photographed and styled attractively, and given a drunk scene to play, Hunt lacks that all-important leading lady quality, appearing to be more suited to comic rather than romantic roles.

The film opens with a street sign which reads "Quiet. Do Not Blow Your Horn." A car horn sounds, then a "Shhh" by the narrator (which presumably is Richard Carlson's Jeff). This joke is repeated with the sound of a crashing wave, then a bird singing, and finally receives the capper when a horse-drawn carriage enters the scene with the horse's shoes muffled by coverings.

Though filmed in 1942, the picture makes no mention of the war, and there is not a man in uniform in sight.

The comment made by Mrs. McKissick in regards to Miranda's appetite is one of the script's few genuine witticisms:

That kid's been feudin' with me since the day she was born. Looked right up at me from her cradle. "Kitchee koo," I said, and she spit up her breakfast. Been eatin' double to make up for it ever since.

The meeting of all the maids has the suggestion of unionization, with mention of a strike as a possible reaction to the suspicion of their employers. Although the maids don't question each other as to who wrote the book, the liberal speech made by Martha about their right to write such a book makes it clear to the audience that *she* is the author. The maids' meeting is juxtaposed with a meeting of the women of all the households, who voice their feeling of betrayal by the author, and who suggest that they dismiss their staff. This idea is proposed in the same way the strike had been proposed by one of the maids, although dismissal would seem to be a more severe reaction to the crisis. However, like the strike, the idea of dismissal is rejected, since the women acknowledge how hard it is to get good servants. This idea then places an overriding value on the maids in a universe where it seems that the maids are needed more by the women than the maids need the employment.

The screenplay allows for a visual joke after Miranda tells Sophie, "Our two [maids] are probably out in the kitchen right now, sifting plans," and Dassin cuts to Martha sifting flour for gravy. Martha is presented as the less competent of the two Sommerfield maids, since she is covered in food when she is required to prepare dinner, in contrast to Mrs. McKissick's experienced confidence. This incompetence extends to her motivation for writing the book, which she admits is done to impress Jeff, an ambitious attempt to raise her station in life. The treatment puts a negative connotation on Martha's ambition, since the book is publicized as an expose, which will eventually be revealed to be just spin.

Martha's naivety, enhanced by the guileless performance of Hunt, allows for the character to have three romantic interests, who are all shown to be flawed men. Danny appears to be a womanizer who loiters at the Sommerfield kitchen, teases Martha by repeatedly untying her apron strings, and spies on her. (The narrative is actually full of characters spying or eavesdropping on others.) Danny's unsuitability extends to a volatile temper, since he instigates the fist fight between himself and Jeff. Jeff's marriage to Martha is described as being "accidental" and "a mistake." As an anthropologist who wears spectacles, he cuts a less-than-romantic figure, which makes his attachment to Sylvia all the more perplexing. Although her being a mathematician supports an argument that their union is based on intellectualism, Frances Drake's glamour counteracts this notion by presenting her as a vamp. Sylvia's affected voice may be intended to identify her as an educated woman, but it also suggests that she is not to be trusted, and the scene where Jeff fails to break off their engagement highlights both Jeff's weakness and Sylvia's power over him.

Joel Archer appears to be the most honest of the three romantic interests, although he is seen to be far more worldly than Martha and therefore the worst match. Additionally, his motives are clouded by his wanting her to finish writing the book that his company is publishing. When Martha goes to Joel's office we see maids cleaning steps and scrubbing the floor outside the office door. They provide another parallel to Martha's station as a maid, since they are portrayed as being of a lower class. The closest we will come to seeing Martha performing similar duties is when she later cleans windows, although this action is used for a comic payoff when she gets to insult Sylvia and uses a southern accent on the pretence of being an ignorant servant. (This scene ends in an extended shot of Hunt mugging behind a face she has drawn in the window soap.)

Martha's book is also paralleled with Jeff writing his own book about anthropology.

A publicity still showing the cast of *The Affairs of Martha* (1942). From left, Spring Byington, Barry Nelson, Virginia Weidler at bottom of frame, Frances Drake, Marjorie Main, Marsha Hunt, and Richard Carlson.

Although this plot point is dropped soon after it arises, it does align the characters via a shared literary interest.

Martha failing to obtain the divorce—as agreed to by Jeff—is evidence of her deceptive nature. She defends this inaction by saying that she could not get time off work to go to Reno (the haven of quickie divorces of the time).

The fist fight between Danny and Jeff displays Dassin's use of violence in his films, as does Martha's later slap of Jeff when he accuses her of blackmail. However, the screenplay adds a comic element to the fight, with Martha catching a lamp that falls during the struggle, and the scene ending with her tripping and pulling a tablecloth out from under a vase of flowers, which smashes onto the floor.

Dassin intriguingly stages the scene of Jeff trying to breaking his engagement by showing both Jeff and Sylvia reflected in the mirror where she sits. This reflection represents both Jeff's duplicity in being engaged when he is already married to Martha, and Sylvia's duplicity in not listening to what he is saying to her.

The engagement party scene begins with an odd touch, when we see how Mrs. McKissick wears a maid's uniform—something she had stated at the earlier maids' meeting that she refused to do. The crowd going into dinner quiets down when they hear Joel telling Miranda that he is a publisher, and all eyes are on him as they eat in silence. The screenplay uses the device of Jeff talking about the issue of Martha's book to delay and avoid Sylvia's announcement of their engagement, in spite of our knowledge that such an engagement is impossible given his marital status. Joel naming Martha as the author can be read as a betrayal of her confidence, with the idea of naming names aligned with the future HUAC hearings. Martha's exposure results in her dropping a tray of squib onto Jeff (and thankfully not onto Sylvia), and Jeff's admission to Sylvia about his marriage to Martha in front of the crowd signals his cruel embarrassment of a woman (Sylvia) he supposedly cared for. Sylvia's humiliation is doubled by Jeff's added admission of wanting to be with Martha and not her. The final use of a motorcycle cop to stop Joel driving away with Martha thankfully suggests that Joel will not be prosecuted, with the reunion of Martha and Jeff symbolized by their kiss. The reunion also puts the publication of Martha's book in doubt, since her position as the benign subversive has been dependent upon Jeff's approval of her worth as a woman.

Notes on the Turner Classic Movies website say that a news item in the *Hollywood Reporter* advised that the film was originally to be directed by S. Sylvan Simon. He had just finished the MGM musical comedy *Rio Rita* (1942) and would be reassigned to the mystery *Grand Central Murder* (1942) instead. Producer Irving Starr had made his last films at MGM, although they had been "A" titles: the boxing comedy *Sunday Punch* (1942) and the mystery *Fingers at the Window* (1942). *The Affairs of Martha* is the first produced screenplay for both Isobel Lennart and Lee Gold. Lennart would go on to be nominated for Academy Awards for her screenplays for *Love Me or Leave Me* (1955) and *The Sundowners* (1960).

Beginning at Paramount Studios, Marsha Hunt moved to MGM in 1939, where she worked in supporting roles in "A" and "B" features and a short. She was memorable as the spectacled bookworm Mary Bennet in the historical drama *Pride and Prejudice* (1940), and played leading roles in the crime dramas *The Penalty* (1941) and *I'll Wait for You* (1941), which also co-starred Virginia Weidler. Hunt supported Greer Garson again (as she had done in *Pride and Prejudice*) in the social drama *Blossoms in the Dust* (1941), and played a supporting part in the musical comedy *Panama Hattie* (1942). She was back playing leads in two "B" titles, the spy drama *Joe Smith, American* (1942) and the crime drama *Kid Glove Killer* (1942), before making *The Affairs of Martha*. Hunt would go on to work with Dassin again in the home-front comedy *A Letter for Evie* (1946), which also co-starred Spring Byington. Dassin would also work with both Richard Carlson and Allyn Joslyn again in *Young Ideas* (1943).

Release

June 21, 1942, with the taglines "That Pretty Maid Tells All!" and "It Happens on the Maid's Night Out!"

Reviews

"Fairly amusing comedy with an ingratiating cast."—John Walker, *Halliwell's Film & Video Guide 2000*

"Deftly directed by Jules Dassin, [the film] was given a surprisingly big buildup by MGM, including a preferred slot in the studio's annual coming-attractions trailer; the extra 'push' paid off at the box-office in spades."—Hal Erickson, *All Movie Guide*

"An entertaining, enjoyable domestic comedy.... Dassin's direction is deft and stylish, and he is helped by the efforts of a large, hard-working and agreeable ensemble of players, headed by the pleasantly unassuming, mildly vivacious Hunt."—George Aachen, *Memorable Films of the Forties*

"Excellent cast in a better than average B film offering an amusing plot.... Very funny in spots and humorous throughout."—Jay Robert Nash and Stanley Ralph Ross, *The Motion Picture Guide*

"Jules Dassin directed a large and effective cast."—John Douglas Eames, *The MGM Story*

Reunion in France (1942)

[aka *Reunion*; *Mademoiselle France*]
MGM

Credits: Director: Jules Dassin; Producer: Joseph L. Mankiewicz; Screenplay: Jan Lustig, Marvin Borowsky, Marc Connelly, based on the original story by Ladislas Bus-Fekete; Photography: Robert Planck; Music: Franz Waxman; Editor: Elmo Veron; Sound: Douglas Shearer; Art Director: Cedric Gibbons; Set Decorator: Edwin B. Willis; Special Effects: Warren Newcombe; Gowns: Irene. B&W, 100 minutes. Filmed June 30, 1942 to September 15, 1942.

Cast: Joan Crawford (Michele "Mike" de la Becque); John Wayne (Pat Talbot); Philip Dorn (Robert Cortot); Reginald Owen (Schultz, aka Pinkum); Albert Basserman (General Hugo Schroeder); John Carradine (Ulrich Windler); Ann Ayars (Juliette); J. Edward Bromberg (French Gendarme Durand); Moroni Olsen (Paul Grebeau, aka General Grovedale); Henry Daniell (Emile Fleuron, aka Major Robley); Howard da Silva (Anton Stregel); Charles Arnt (Honoré); Morris Ankrum (Martin); Edith Evanson (Genevieve); Ernest Dorian (Captain); Margaret Laurence (Clothilde); Odette Myrtil (Mme. Montanol); Peter Whitney (Soldier). Uncredited: Harry Adams (Mons. Clemens); George Aldwin (Pilot); Martha Bamattre (Newsstand Woman); Muriel Barr (Girl in Café); Felix Basch (Pawnbroker); Barbara Bedford (Mme. Vigouroux); Trude Berliner, Louise Colombet, Greta Meyer, Philip Van Zandf (Customers); Joseph E. Bernard (R.R. Mechanic); Rodney Bieber, John Considine (Little Boys); Wilda Bieber (Little Girl); Oliver Blake (Hypolite); Basil Bookasta (Delivery Boy); Elfriede Borodin (Saleslady); Frederic Brunn, David Clarke, Carl Ekberg, Hans Fuerberg, Paul Kruger, Otto Reichow (Soldiers), George Calliga (Mons. Bertheil); Ann Codee (Rosalie); James Craven, Hans von Morhart, Crane Whitley (Officers); Jean Del Val, Fred Farrell (Porters); Guy D'Ennery (Station Master); Ray De Ravenne (Bartender); Kay Deslys (Wife); Bobby Dillon, Peter Leeds (Boys); Ludwig Donath (Hotel Desk Clerk); Claudia Drake, Leatice Joy Gilbert (Girls); William Edmunds (Horse and Buggy Taxicab Driver); Amo Frey (Guide); Joel Friedkin (Frenchman); Ava Gardner (Marie); Jody Gilbert (Brunhilde); Larry Grenier (Mons. De Brun); Eddie Hall (German Officer Dancing in the Nightclub); Stuart Hall, Allen Shute (RAF Pilots); Bert Hicks; Sheldon Jett (Tourist); Greta Keller (Baroness von Steinkamp); Henry Kolker (General Bartholomew); Eddie Lee, Tommy Lee (Japanese Men); Adolf E. Licho (Hawker); Louis Mercier (Conductor); John Meredith (RAF Navigator); Adolph Milar (Gestapo Agent); Sandra Morgan (Mme. Berthil); Lotte Palfi Andor (Unpleasant German Customer); Edward Rickard (Chauffeur); Henry Rowland (Sentry); Natalie Schafer (Frau Amy Schroeder); Harry Semels (R.R. Mechanic); Lester Sharpe (Warden); Arthur Space

(Henker); Walter O. Stahl (Baron "Pookie" von Steinkamp); Robert R. Stephenson (Emile); Hermine Sterler; Christine Steward; Norma Thelan (Girl in Café); George Travell (Jeannot); Lisl Valetti (German Customer); Michael Visaroff (Vigouroux); Wilhelm von Brincken (Major); Paul Weigel (Old Man); Jacqueline White (Danielle); Gayne Whitman (Maitre d'hotel); Buck Woods (Jazz Singer in Nightclub); Jack Zeller.

Songs: "La Marseillaise" (Claude Joseph Rouget de Lisle), played under opening credits; "Frère Jacques" (Traditional), sung by woman with a baby in the air-raid shelter; "Concerto for Violin in D Minor, 2nd Movement" (Felix Mendelssohn—Bartholdy), played by George Travell; "I'll Be Glad When You're Dead (You Rascal You)" (Spo-De-Odee), sung by Buck Woods. Top of Form

VHS/DVD: DVD released May 22, 2007, by Warner Home Video as part of *The John Wayne Collection*.

Synopsis

In May 1940, Paris fears a Nazi occupation. Socialite Michele de la Becque asks her fiancé, automotive designer Robert Cortot, to come with her to the South of France, but Robert refuses. Michele learns of Paris falling to the Nazis and comes home to find her

Michele de la Becque (Joan Crawford) shakes the hand of Honoré (Charles Arnt) as she looks at Robert Cortot (Philip Dorn) in *Reunion in France* (1942).

house occupied, with her belongings moved to the servants' quarters. She sees that Robert has been untouched by the invasion, and learns that this is because he seems to be a collaborator. Penniliess, Michele takes a job as a fitter's assistant at the Montanot fashion house, where she used to be a customer. One night on the way home, she meets RAF Eagle Squadron flyer Patrick Talbot, an escapee from a concentration camp. Michele lets him stay in her quarters while she arranges money and forged papers. When the Germans have a party at her house, Michele and Pat are caught together by the drunken Captain. He and Pat fight, but Michele pretends she is attracted to the Captain so that Pat can be taken safely away by Jeannot.

Robert agrees to help Michele and her "chauffeur," Pat, get out of France, although Robert learns of Pat's true identity. When a car comes for Michele at night with two men in Nazi uniforms (who are actually British agents), she believes that Robert has betrayed her. Pat is picked up in another car by the British agent who has been acting as the Gestapo Schultz, and at the Melun checkpoint the agents outsmart the Nazi officers and get through. The wounded Schultz tells Michele that Robert is a leader in the French underground before he dies, and a plane arrives at the airfield to take her and Pat to London. The Nazis question Robert about Michele and Pat, but Michele's return moves suspicion away from him. Michele has decided to join Robert in the fight against the Nazis, and they admire a French plane which writes "Courage" in the sky.

Notes

Dassin's return to "A" filmmaking resulted in a wartime romance with a literate and witty screenplay that repeats the themes of betrayal, treason, and duplicitous characters. It is also the director's first opportunity to work with a genuine movie star—Joan Crawford, whose mythology the treatment exploits.

Unfortunately, the narrative's initial focus on character interplay and the rapid pacing dwindles when the labyrinthine mechanics of a chase is introduced at the climax, and the patriotic elements overwhelm the material. Dassin provides occasional visual interest, which includes a montage of the Nazis conquering Europe early in the film, but his work here is more noteworthy for performance and mood, and a minimal use of violence.

"La Marseillaise" is played under the opening credits in a military arrangement, as animated scenes of ruined buildings are shown. A title card reads, "The ninth night of the ninth month of a war too uneventful to be taken seriously, and too far away to worry about," which will prove to be the initial sentiment of Michele, and also an American audience at a time before the Americans entered World War II. (This rationalizes Pat being an American in the RAF.) Michele reveals herself to be a "spoiled and selfish" aristocrat when she displays her disinterest in the patriotic speech made at the dinner she attends (being more interested in her romance with Robert). Michele's indifference extends to when she visits the Montanot couturier to arrange her holiday wardrobe, and it is said of her, "Mademoiselle seems annoyed at the war," and, "It's a wonder she doesn't forbid it." These comments will come back to haunt her via the staff's reaction to Michele later working at Montanot, although she (perhaps in line with Crawford's manufactured elegance and glamorous wardrobe) retains the hauteur and manner of the aristocracy.

Newsreel footage is intercut with scenes of Crawford reacting for the montage of the

Nazi invasion, culminating in the newspaper headline "Paris Falls." Seeing the real Hitler at the Eiffel Tower adds a gothic resonance to the montage, and an authenticity that the resultant film lacks. However, Dassin uses an unidentified French building to express Paris' defeat. The montage begins with a pan to the top of the building where the French flag flies, and ends with a Nazi flag having replaced it as the camera pans down the building to show it covered in black cloth and swastikas. The wind that blows pieces of paper around the empty courtyard expresses the Nazi aridity, and it is appropriate that Michele's return has her walking through the courtyard to allow us to see the sad spectacle.

Her confrontation with the Captain inhabiting her house provides some amusing banter. When a soldier tells the Captain that Michele has ignored his warnings to stop, the Captain says, "You should have shot her." Michele replies to the soldier, "Why didn't you? My back was turned to you all the way." The Captain asks Michele to sit down; when she declines, he tells her, "Then permit me. My leg." She comments, "A severe wound, I hope," and he replies, "I was bitten by a Belgian sheep dog. We found them infinitely better equipped than the soldiers."

A painting of Michele in Robert's house is of the young Crawford, and the fact that his house remains untouched by the Nazis is the first clue that he may be a collaborator. The men whom Robert has a meeting with remain unseen, but are revealed to be Nazis by their hats left outside the room. Robert as a possible collaborator is Dassin's signature duplicitous man, and he will be shown to be doubly deceptive since he only pretends to be a collaborator. Michele is equally duplicitous when she pretends to be Robert's fiancée in order to help herself (and Pat) get out of Paris, although Michele's transition from socialite to patriot is more character development than deception. The treatment's other duplicitous characters include the British agents who pose as Nazi officers, and Pat, who deceives Michele during his first contact with her, pretends to be her chauffeur, and fails to confide the mechanics of their escape to her.

The dinner at the Atlanta Hotel climaxes in a high-angled shot of the candlelit tables, which are arranged in the shape of a swastika. (This touch is perhaps a little heavy-handed, but the treatment scores other points via the supposed stupidity of the Germans, the silliness of their names, and the fatness of their women.) Gestapo agent Windler's spying on Martin (something Michele later comments on by noting that Windler also peeks through keyholes) is shown by Windler's cigarette smoke blowing over Martin, while Martin's arrest is given a nice spin in the way Windler stubs his cigarette out on the carpet, and Martin, as a good servant, picks it up.

Michele becoming a fitter's assistant (although we never see her do such work) recalls the youthful Crawford persona of her being a shop girl, though here the rags to riches scenario is reversed. The only scene in which Crawford acts as an employee is when Frau Schroeder demands the coat whose furred shoulder pads hide money that is to be given to Pat, although Michele's defiance can be read as just an extension of her aristocratic hauteur. This scene is perhaps one of the two best in the film, given the suspense that it incorporates, with the over-the-top playing of Natalie Schafer appropriately coming across as juvenile German entitlement.

When Jeannot plays the forbidden Mendelsson on his violin, the French Durand and the German Stregel misidentifies the music as Wagner—another example of the ignorance of the Nazis and their collaborators. Their incorrect assumption and gullibility continues in the way they fail to capture Pat when he makes a supposed romantic advance on Michele in the street, and her resistance is described by Durand as the French game of love. The mirror in Michele's purse used by her to see if she and Pat are still being followed is the perfect symbol for the acts of duplicity of both the watched and the watchers.

The narrative's convenience of Michele breaking her engagement with Robert, setting her free to become a romantic interest for Pat, is undermined by Michele's continued resistance to him. While she may entertain the idea, her continued return to Robert, even when it is merely to scold him, prefigures the resolution of their relationship. John Wayne's intonation makes Pat even more American than Crawford's American-accented Michele.

The extended scene in which the Captain interrupts Michele and Pat in her room, and which continues into the street, is perhaps the film's best, due to the suspense generated and the way Crawford is photographed. The scene features an odd moment of staging before the Captain enters, when Michele approaches Pat and kisses him after he expresses his shame over her hiding him, particularly since she finds him hiding among her dresses. Her kiss, then, is her attempt to restore his confidence and lessen his feeling of emasculation, an idea given more resonance in light of Wayne's real-life exemption from serving in World War II. The first physical violence in the film occurs when the Captain spits at Pat after learning he is an American, and Pat responds by punching him. Michele takes the Captain into the street, and this moment between them is wonderful. He tells her, "I can't be seen on the street in this condition. I am drunk." To this she replies (in a diplomatic lie), "If you hadn't told me, I'd never have guessed it." When he kisses her, the Captain tells her, "You let me kiss you as if it was some sort of penance." The Captain has the idea that her aristocratic pedigree aligns her with him as a Nazi world-conqueror, with his delusion as false as her justification for passionately kissing him, since she does so at the same time that she signals Jeannot to take Pat away. In this scene Crawford's perfect, porcelain-skinned face is contrasted with Ernest Dorian's sweaty, tanned, imperfect countenance, while Michele's duplicity stands as counterpoint to the Captain's brazen display of lust for her.

Not all the scenes are so convincing, however. For instance, a long shot of Michele's car on the deserted Champs-Elysees, with Pat acting as the chauffeur, features an apparent painted backdrop of the Arc de Triomphe. And a nightclub featuring an all-black jazz band is simply unbelievable, given the Nazis' view of black people. Even more unbelievable is the benign reaction of the Germans in the audience, who seem to be so ignorant of the English language that they fail to realize the song being performed, "I'll Be Glad When You're Dead (You Rascal You)," is anti–Nazi.

For the scene in which Robert says goodbye to Michele, who thinks he has betrayed her, Dassin casts the shadows of leaves across their faces. In his *Cine-Parade* interview on the DVD for *Night and the City*, Dassin tells the story of how the slight shadow brought him into Mayer's office, where Mayer said, "The whole world pays to see Joan Crawford. I want to see her! No shadows."

The fight at the Melun checkpoint offers more violence, greater in intensity than the simple punch landed by Pat on the Captain, with the violence topped by the shooting and killing of Schultz. Thankfully, this death is presented with some restraint, and Schultz firing at the Nazi jeep following him only has Schultz hitting the jeep's tires and not any soldiers.

The searchlights in the background of the landing field create an expectation of bombing and an air fight, though neither materializes. The lights do upstage the foreground talk, and we are spared a *Casablanca*-style goodbye between Pat and Michele. The comparatively benign (and perhaps stupid) Nazi general Schroeder, who had been previously charmed by Michele, inadvertently rescues Robert from suspicion, while he and Michele being called Nazi traitors and spat at by children outside his house when the Nazis leave them is a

General Grovedale (Moroni Olsen) introduces himself as a British officer masquerading as a Nazi to Michele de la Becque (Joan Crawford), as Pat Talbot (John Wayne) and another British masquerader, Major Robley (Henry Daniell), look on in this still for *Reunion in France* (1942).

poignant expression of their situation as secret underground subversives. The spitting recalls the Captain's spitting at Pat, while the plane writing "courage" in the sky, meant for the French people in general, is advice that Michele and Robert can take personally.

Thirty-seven-year-old Dutch-born Philip Dorn had come to American after having been a matinee idol in Holland and Germany before World War II. He worked at Universal Pictures from 1940, then joined MGM as a supporting player. *Reunion in France* was his one and only leading role in an "A" MGM title.

Thirty-five-year-old John Wayne had begun his film career playing uncredited silent bit parts at MGM. After having toiled in routine titles at various studios in the 1930s, he finally achieved stardom as the Ringo Kid in the John Ford western *Stagecoach* (1939). *Reunion in France* was Wayne's return to MGM, and he would go on to co-star with Philip Dorn in the Republic western *The Fighting Kentuckian* (1949).

Reunion in France is also noteworthy for featuring one of Ava Gardner's early bit roles. Here she has one line, as Marie, a salesgirl at Montanot. She would also be cast in Dassin's next film, *Young Ideas* (1943), although she had no lines.

Producer Joseph L Mankiewicz had previously produced the Crawford vehicles *The Gorgeous Hussy* (1936), *Love on the Run* (1936), *The Bride Wore Red* (1937), *Mannequin* (1937), *The Shining Hour* (1938), and *Strange Cargo* (1940). In their book *Tender Comrades: A Backstory of the Hollywood Blacklist*, Patrick McGilligan and Paul Buhle quote Dassin as saying that Mankiewicz was supposed to direct *Reunion in France* but changed his mind, something which isn't mentioned in the Mankiewicz biography *People Will Talk*, by Kenneth L. Geist.

Reunion in France is generally thought to be the beginning of the end of the thirty-seven-year-old Crawford's run at MGM, since she would only make one more film for them, the spy drama *Above Suspicion* (1943), before her contract was cancelled prematurely by mutual agreement. In *Conversations with Joan Crawford*, Roy Newquist quoted Crawford as saying, "If there is afterlife, and I am to be punished for my sins, this is one of the pictures they'll make me see over and over again." Crawford says it was a "silly script," and that she and John Wayne were mismatched, but at least she had a nice collection of gowns to wear. In Shaun Considine's book *Bette and Joan: The Divine Feud*, Considine says Wayne was used as "bait" to make Crawford appear in the film, though Wayne plays what is ostensibly a supporting role, with Philip Dorn getting more screen time with Crawford. The TCM site quotes *The Hollywood Reporter* claiming that Alan Ladd was originally sought for Wayne's role (presumably since Ladd had just become a star thanks to his breakout performance in the film noir *This Gun for Hire* [1942], though Ladd chose to make the Paramount spy drama *Lucky Jordan* (1942) instead.

Crawford's attraction to the married Wayne (Josephine Saenz was his wife at the time) is also written about in various Wayne biographies, as well as *Joan Crawford: The Essential Biography*, by Lawrence J. Quirk and William Schoell. The authors claim that Crawford wanted to sleep with Wayne, who rebuffed her advances. She is quoted as saying, "That lousy movie! Just because I wanted to get Wayne in the sack! And the only thing he could play was cowboys. We hit it off like filet mignon and ketchup!" Crawford's alleged sexual appetite (in spite of her marrying Phillip Terry on July 12 during filming) also (according to Considine) focused on Philip Dorn, who, after he purportedly rejected her, was knocked out of the two-shot they were sharing in a scene. Considine maintains that Dassin raged at Crawford in response and "threatened to punch her out," to which she dared him with "Go ahead!" This tale is called an exaggeration by the Quirk-Schoell biography, since they say Crawford was too much of a professional to behave in such a way, although they admit that she and Dassin did not get along well.

In the book *Tender Comrades*, Patrick McGilligan and Paul Buhle quote Dassin on the pre-production of the film, where hours were spent discussing Crawford's wardrobe in what was supposed to be a story conference addressing the director's concerns over the script's perceived weaknesses. In Roger Clarke's 2002 interview with Dassin for *The Independent*, the director was more specific, stating that the talk was about Crawford's hats. Dassin related:

> Finally, I got a word in and said I thought the script was bad. One of the executives took me over to a window overlooking the parking lot and said, "Which one is your car?" I had this little old car at the time. And he pointed to his car, a big new thing. And he said, "That's my car and that's your car, and I say the script is good."

Clarke also quotes Dassin on his being fired from the film on the first day of rehearsal. After he had said "Cut" to Crawford to finish a scene with her and John Wayne, Wayne supposedly took him aside and told the director, "Never say cut to Miss Crawford. You just give a hand sign." Thinking this nonsense, Dassin said "Cut" again, and Crawford walked off the set. Louis B. Mayer called Dassin into his office and fired him. That night Crawford rang Dassin at his house and asked him to come to dinner, which he did. There the following exchange supposedly took place:

> CRAWFORD: Mr. Dassin, do you think I'm a bad actress?
> DASSIN: No, I don't.
> CRAWFORD: Don't ever say cut to me again. Just do this.

Crawford drew two fluttering fingers across her brow, "like a diva having a neuralgia attack. So that's what I did." This anecdote is also told by Dassin in his *Cine-Parade* interview for the *Night and the City* DVD, though the director says the person who told him not to say cut to Crawford was the assistant director and not Wayne. Dassin also elaborates that he originally called "cut" because the scene played was not good. He told Crawford, "When you're in character, and it's part of you, I love it. When you act the grand lady, it's fake." According to this version, the exchange between Crawford and Dassin at her house was more civilized, with Crawford telling Dassin, "Let's try it again tomorrow. Under the condition you don't say 'cut.' Make this gesture [Dassin runs his finger over his right eyebrow] and I'll know we have to redo it." Dassin also says that Crawford had a sixth sense because she could tell if he had made the gesture even if she had her back to him.

Release

December 25, 1942, with the taglines, "WHAT A THRILL! Startling drama of a stranded Yankee flyer and a Parisian beauty!" "The Picture Of The Hour! France In Open Revolt! Leaping From The Headlines! The Underground Of Paris!" and "Paris Fights Back! Thrilling Romance of the Underground Revolt!"

Reviews

"Starting out with some promise, it falls apart at the halfway point. Attempts to generate a hot triangular romance with Crawford the pivot prove very tepid.... Direction lacks smoothness in pace and dwells too long on many minor incidents."—*Variety*, December 1, 1942

"A shallowest drama made out of the pith and substance of an ironic tragedy ... a stale melodramatic exercise for a very popular star.... Miss Crawford as usual makes an elegant mannequin for a series of ensembles that probably will excite more female comment than the picture itself."—*The New York Times*, March 5, 1943

"A Joan Crawford version of the fall of France.... Philip Dorn, who has his first starring role in this picture, shows that he deserves a better one."—*Time*, January 4, 1943

"Miss Crawford isn't making all the sacrifices implied in the script.... Dressing like a refugee is certainly not in her contract."—*New York Herald Tribune*

"Forever threatening to lapse into self-parody ... one could never be quite sure whether the results were intentional or not."—Charles Higham and Joel Greenberg, *Hollywood in the Forties*

Young Ideas (1943)

[aka *Faculty Row*; *The Professor Takes a Wife* (working title)]
MGM

Credits: Director: Jules Dassin; Producer: Robert Sisk; Screenplay: Ian McLellan Hunter, Bill Noble; Photography: Charles Lawton; Music: George Bassman; Editor: Ralph E. Winters; Sound: Douglas Shearer; Art Direction: Cedric Gibbons; Set Decoration: Edwin B. Willis; Costumes: Irene. B&W, 77 minutes. Filmed January to February 1943.

Cast: Susan Peters (Susan Evans); Herbert Marshall (Michael Kingsley); Mary Astor (Josephine, aka Jo Evans); Elliott Reid (Jeff Evans); Richard Carlson (Tom Farrell); Allyn Joslyn (Adam Trent); Dorothy Morris, Frances Rafferty (Co-Eds); George Dolenz (Pepe); Emory Parnell (Judge Canute J. Kelly). Uncredited: Ed Agresti (Boulevardier); Fred Aldrich (Peanut Vendor); Charles Arnt (Station Master); Polly Bailey (Old Woman); Carlos Barbe, William Bishop (French Lieutenants); Paul E. Burns (Gardener-Caretaker); Budd Buster (Elderly Driver); Lois Collier, Ava Gardner, Marilyn Harris, Noel Neill, Roberta Smith (Co-Eds); Marcel De la Brosse (Artist); Arthur Dulac (Gendarme); John Estes, Myron Healey (Students); William Farmer (Mr. Williams); Frank Faylen (Reporter); Harry Holman (Harry, Court Clerk); Edward Kilroy (Faculty Member); Harry Lamont (Flower Vendor); Ellen Lowe, Ann O'Neal (Secretaries); Ken Lundy (Intellectual Student); Alex Novinsky (Old Bicyclist); Daniel Ocko (Waiter); Robert Emmett O'Connor (Train Conductor); June Pickerell (Older Secretary); Jean Porter (Southern Co-Ed); Rod Rogers (Bill); Shimen Ruskin (Book Clerk); Almira Sessions (Club Woman).

Songs: "Tiger Rag" (Original Dixieland Jazz Band), performed by Joe Sweet and His Reet Beaters.

VHS/DVD: Unavailable in either format.

Synopsis

Josephine Evans, the author of the popular though scandalous book *As I Knew Paris*, leaves a lecture tour because she has fallen in love and married Michael Kingsley, the chemistry professor at Digby College in Pennsylvania. Her agent, Adam Trent, enlists the aid of Josephine's children, Susan and Jeff, to find her. They decide to break up their mother's marriage because they think Michael unsuitable (he doesn't want Josephine to continue her writing career). Enrolling as students at the college, Susan decides to break college rules by dating her theater professor, Tom Farrell, while Jeff poisons Michael against Josephine by telling him that her book about a woman with many lovers is autobiographical. Michael becomes jealous of Pepe, a French delivery boy and mature-aged student who likes to have tea and speak French with Josephine.

Michael returns early from a meeting of the Society of American Chemists and sees a man, Adam, kissing Josephine. Adam had been summoned by Jeff and Susan to entice Josephine with a magazine editing job back in New York. The group goes to an out-of-bounds roadhouse called The Pink Tiger, where Adam engages Michael in a drinking contest. Michael wins, although he drunkenly plays the bass in the club band. Reprimanded by his dean, Michael confronts Josephine about her lifestyle, and she leaves him to file for divorce. Susan has second thoughts about the plan, but Jeff tells Tom that the women in the book are based on Susan, which puts her romance with Tom in jeopardy. However, after Tom and Susan reconcile, she conspires with the repentant Jeff to reconcile their mother and Michael. They convince the New York judge in the court case to deny the divorce, and Josephine and Michael reunite. When they deduce what the children have done, they spank them, although Josephine stops spanking Susan when Tom reveals that she and he are newlyweds.

Notes

This college comedy features another witty screenplay which also includes themes of betrayal, duplicity and subversion; increased visual ingenuity by Dassin; and a climax and conclusion marked by violence. The film displays the director's increasing ability to create comic material, and is supplemented by good performances, with a spectacled Herbert Marshall, in particular, on display in a rare funny performance. While the music score often overplays the intended humor of a scene, Dassin succeeds at times in demonstrating the humanity of those at the center of a seemingly farcical situation. The treatment is also interesting in its reversal of convention in relation to the behavior of older people in love, as opposed to younger people, though the disapproving reaction of the younger couple can be rationalized as more immaturity than an expression of what is generally socially unacceptable.

The film opens with a clever montage detailing the success of Josephine's book—and displaying Dassin's mastery of this technique. Piles of books are juxtaposed with New York skyscrapers, and people read the volume over the shoulders of others. The montage continues with a series of numbered book editions; review quotes (like "timely and important" and "spiced with rowdy wit"); and a handful of brief scenes. These show a woman in a negligee reading the book and eating chocolates; a cab-driver reading the book and ignoring a potential passenger, who eventually takes the book and walks away, reading it; and three girls reading the book at the same time. The montage ends with a telegram delivery boy reading the book as he enters Adam's office, which features a portrait of Josephine on the wall with the title of the book.

The following exchange between Susan, Jeff and Adam offers the first witticism of the screenplay:

> SUSAN: Where was her last lecture?
> ADAM: A little college town. Digby, Pennsylvania.
> JEFF: Have you ever been there?
> ADAM: Don't let's get insulting.

The business of Susan handling a letter opener in the scene receives a payoff when she leaves and hands it to Jeff, who takes it and faces the blade towards himself, as if he is going to stab himself. The impudence of Susan and Jeff is expressed by them opening the door to Josephine's cabin without knocking, although Jeff's line, "It's your past catching up with you," serves as both a description of themselves as her children and a prefiguring of the problems Josephine's past will cause with Michael. When Jeff learns that Michael is a professor of chemistry, he responds with, "Some fella who goes around with his clothes smelling of rotten eggs?" The scene ends with Josephine admitting her marriage by touching her cheek with her finger, which allows her wedding ring to be seen. This moment comes with the following exchange:

> JOSEPHINE: For the last ten days I have been living with Michael as a respectable married woman.
> SUSAN: You didn't.
> JOSEPHINE: I did.
> JEFF: No.
> JOSEPHINE: Yes.
> SUSAN: Mother, you ought to be ashamed of yourself.

Why Josephine needs to be ashamed is unclear, although the scene is given a button by a drumbeat on the soundtrack and Josephine's shocked reaction to Susan's line.

A pan of the interior of Michael's living room is accompanied by Susan's line, "This looks like the set from that play of Freddy's. You know, the one about the two old ladies that murder their borders." Jeff replies with, "They hid the bodies under here." This judgment of Michael as being out of date is aligned with him as a conservative character, which makes him seem an uncharacteristic choice for the woman of the world Josephine. Later, during their confrontation, Josephine will remind him of the impetuousness that made her agree to marry him—an expression of the "young ideas" of the title (although the title can also be applied to the ideas that the comparatively youthful Susan and Jeff have). Susan equating the room with the play *Arsenic and Old Lace* also represents her interest in the theater, which is explored further in her relationship with Tom.

A funny exchange between Josephine and Michael acknowledges the possible negative aspects of the independent thought of her children, no doubt an extension of her own personality, and also prefigures their scheming against Michael:

> JOSEPHINE: Susan and Jeff may be a little difficult to know at first but you will make an effort to like them, won't you?
> MICHAEL: Is an effort required?

The narrative doesn't explain what has happened to Josephine's first husband, the father of Susan and Jeff, so that there is the inference that she has had them illegitimately during her time in Paris. This lack of a father figure does not allow them to warm to Michael as a replacement, since he presents as an authority figure (being a college teacher), and may also explain their selfish feeling of entitlement to interfere in their mother's marriage. Jeff, in particular, is the more obnoxious of the two, as the instigator of the plot to break up the marriage, although he does score a laugh in his impersonation of Michael's voice and manner. Their motives are rationalized by what they see as Michael trying to subvert Josephine's creativity by demanding that she give up writing, although Michael's rationale is that she has no financial need to continue with it, since he can give her the security she had been working to provide. This idea of artistry for financial gain, rather than as a creative outlet, presents Michael's pragmatic thinking—like the scientist that he is. However, the use of Josephine's book as a moral weapon against Michael (and later Tom) shows the power that art possesses.

When Michael talks to Susan and Jeff (honoring Josephine's request to make an effort with them), he commits a faux pas by opening, "Speaking man to man." Jeff responds with, "Let's keep it heart to heart so she [Susan] can be in it too." While Michael's comment may be viewed as misogynistic, he is correct in focusing on Jeff as the more troublesome of the two.

Susan's plan to date Tom gives her the amusing line, "My first class is contemporary playwrights. Here that probably means Shakespeare," while her laughing at Tom as he lectures to his class is underscored by the alarm that sounds on the soundtrack. This alarm will later be revealed by Jeff to be that of a fire engine summoned by his action in physics class, though initially it seems to be only a response to the continued laughing of Tom's students (an un-sourced sound effect, much like the drum sound in reaction to Josephine earlier). Susan making a bet with other co-eds that she can get a date from Tom, co-eds that she has only just met, is more evidence of her calculated behavior, and Dassin cleverly reveals her victory. In a two-shot, to the left of the screen we see the co-eds counting their money, assuming that they have won, when Susan and Tom appear on the right of the screen, and Tom says, "That's a date."

Michael's reaction to reading Josephine's book is expressed by the cover image coming to life, with a woman seen at a second story window and a group of working men admiring her. The men go up the stairs (in fast-motion) to what we presume is the door to her room, she disappears from view, and then one of the men appears at her window to draw down the shade. Dassin zooms in on the woman after the men go up the stairs so we can recognize her as Josephine. Michael buying every copy of her book from a bookshop which has a window display of them is presented with no dialogue, so that just the music conveys Michael's concern. When he comes home, we see Josephine wearing the same outfit she wore in the book cover scene, as she speaks French with Pepe.

Herbert Marshall gives a funny shocked reaction to Pepe's impersonation of the noises a horse makes in his French story, a device that will be repeated later when Pepe makes other animal noises. This device also paints Pepe as a foolish and unromantic character, which lessens his real threat to Michael, although Michael doesn't see that. Michael believing the lie that Josephine is a tramp may represent his lack of faith in her present behavior, but it is also a sign that he really doesn't know her well enough.

Susan's date with Tom offers an amusing exchange when she meets him:

> Tom: Would you mind walking a few steps behind me?
> Susan: Well, I'll walk in the opposite direction, if that's your attitude.
> Tom: It's because of the rules.

Susan's change of heart over using Tom comes after she decides to help him rewrite his play, which, funnily enough, has a Frenchman character. Her change will also cause her to abandon the plan with Jeff to sabotage their mother's marriage. In spite of her final

Michael Kingsley (Herbert Marshall) tries to stop his wife, Josephine Evans (Mary Astor), from divorcing him in front of Judge Canute J. Kelly (Emory Parnell) in *Young Ideas* (1943).

deception before the Judge (done to save her mother's marriage), Susan is presented as the more humane of the two children. Susan's reneging on the plan ironically only stiffens Jeff's resolve, since this is what motivates him to bring in Adam (and also causes him to attempt to sabotage Susan's romance with Tom). It will take violence to stop Jeff, even though, like Susan, he ultimately prevaricates again to sway the Judge.

In Michael's first questioning of Josephine, she claims that she wrote her book with a political objective, with the intention of making sure that what she saw happen in Paris didn't also happen in America. Interestingly, she comments that the details of the book are unimportant, although it is those very details that Michael objects to, saying that a lot of the incidents "belong in a cheap magazine." The idea of Michael buying up all the town's copies of the book to stop others from reading it gets a laugh from Josephine's line, "We won't make any money if we buy all the copies ourselves." It is worth noting that she refers to "we" and not "I," since Josephine is generous enough to include her husband in any profit the book makes, though clearly they have differing views on the product's quality.

Michael's entrance to The Pink Tiger causes the jitterbugging co-eds to stop dancing, and it isn't much of a surprise when we learn that Michael doesn't drink. The drinking competition starts clunkily, with Michael's scientific explanation disproving Adam's claim of a greater alcohol tolerance. However, Dassin cleverly reveals Michael's inebriation by first showing the returned jitterbugging co-eds, Michael's empty chair, and finally Michael himself playing a bass guitar. The sequence offers some real-life resonance when Michael attempts to demonstrate that he can walk a straight line, photographed in long shot—actor Herbert Marshall was rarely photographed in long shot because of his wooden leg.

The confrontation between Michael and Josephine begins with her funny "Michael, what you know about me wouldn't stuff an olive." The scene is handled with surprising delicacy of feeling and tender playing by Mary Astor, ending with Josephine saying, "I'm not going to explain anything; that's not my definition of trust."

Adam's overt duplicity is expressed by his encouraging Josephine to file for divorce, and this information is what leads to Michael punching Adam (Adam's admission to Michael is a mixture of boldness and stupidity). The punch is the film's first act of physical violence, and it's followed in the same scene by Tom kicking Jeff. What makes the latter duplicitous is that Susan sets up Jeff for the attack, no doubt as payback for his betrayal of her. Thankfully, Jeff's falling into the fireplace occurs off-screen, expressed by a noise on the soundtrack, and the attack offers some comic relief with the following exchange:

> ADAM: What are you doing in the fireplace?
> JEFF: I am imitating a burning log.

This "imitation" also serves as payback for Jeff's earlier imitation of Michael, with Jeff's acceptance of the predicament prefiguring his—and Susan's—acceptance of their spankings at the film's conclusion. For their final deceit, Susan and Jeff dress to look younger than their real ages. She wears pigtails, and he wears a Mickey Mouse sweater and ears. However, this section of the film strains believability with the idea that a judge would allow his opinion to be influenced even before the hearing—particularly by the tale he is told. Michael and Josephine get a funny double-take at the Judge's question, "What has this got to do with who takes the hot bath?" and the case is dismissed on the condition that "from now on she promises to leave some hot water for her husband." At this, Josephine, obviously thinking the Judge crazy, remarks, "If it'd make you happy." The

In *Young Ideas* (1943), Jeff Evans (Elliott Reid, left) and his sister, Susan Evans (Susan Peters), show her boyfriend Tom Farrell (Richard Carlson) how they dress younger than their real ages in a plan to stop their parents from divorcing.

expectation of seeing the attacks upon Susan and Jeff at the end (no pun intended) is not met when they are chased off-screen; however, it is fulfilled when we see them alternately spanked by Josephine and Michael in different parts of the courthouse corridor. This act of double violence, although intended to be funny, is an interesting continuation of Dassin's thematic use of violence in his films. At least Tom's announcement of "Stop beating my wife" allows Josephine to stop spanking her daughter so that she can kiss her new son-in-law, although Jeff does not receive a similar reprieve. However, there is something in Tom's attitude that suggests that he would like to spank Susan himself. His kissing Josephine on the mouth seems inappropriate, although perhaps it matches her personality and the reverse expectations of behavior raised by the treatment.

The way the screenplay made its way to Hollywood is rather unique. Bill Noble was a student at the University of Washington and submitted the script over the transom as part of his application to MGM's junior writing department. Noble was even included in the script rewrite by a more experienced comedy writer, though the resultant screenplay would be Noble's only produced work.

Producer Robert Sisk had come to MGM to make his prior title, the "B" political drama *A Stranger in Town* (1943), which had also starred Richard Carlson. Herbert Marshall's last title for MGM was the Shirley Temple vehicle *Kathleen* (1941), her first for MGM. Mary Astor had won the Best Supporting Actress Academy Award playing the temperamental pianist Sandra Kovak and out-acting Bette Davis in the Warner Bros.

melodrama *The Great Lie* (1941), and had played the endlessly lying, fake-school-girlish Brigid O'Shaughnessy in the classic Warner Bros. detective drama *The Maltese Falcon* (1941). She had come to MGM under a new five-year contract to make *Young Ideas*, and the role would be the first of many mothers-of-grown children roles she would play—as a woman aged thirty eight. The twenty-three-year-old fawnlike beauty Susan Peters had earned a Best Supporting Actress Academy Award nomination for MGM's Ronald Colman/Greer Garson romance *Random Harvest* (1942), but her Hollywood career effectively ended when she became paralyzed and wheel-chair bound in 1945 after a duck-hunting accident (she made only one more film).

Release

August 2, 1943.

Reviews

"A lightly concocted and amusing affair, and as such, is in tune for diverting entertainment."—*Variety*, July 30, 1943

"Dismal."—Leonard Maltin, *1997 Movie & Video Guide*

"An amusing little film, lacking in any real weight, but entertaining nevertheless. It has several clever moments and the players take it in the intended spirit."—Jay Robert Nash and Stanley Ralph Ross, *The Motion Picture Guide*

"Predictable light concoction with practiced players."—John Walker, *Halliwell's Film and Video Guide 2000*

"A deliberately 'small' MGM feature designed as a trial balloon for up-and-coming director Dassin ... the film nonetheless satisfies within its own modest limits."—Hal Erickson, *AllMovie.com*

The Canterville Ghost (1944)

MGM

Credits: Director: Jules Dassin: Producer: Arthur L. Field; Screenplay: Edwin Harvey Blum, based on "The Canterville Ghost" by Oscar Wilde; Photography: Robert Planck; Editor: Chester W. Schaeffer; Music: George Bassman; Dance Direction: Jack Donohue; Sound: Douglas Shearer; Art Direction: Cedric Gibbons; Set Decoration: Edwin B. Willis; Costumes: Irene; Men's Costumes: Valles; Makeup: Jack Dawn. B&W, 96 minutes. Filmed at Busch Gardens, Pasadena, California, from August 21 to December 6, 1943.

Songs: "Bless 'Em All" (by Fred Godfrey, Jimmy Hughes, Frank Lake, Albert Stillman), sung a cappella by the soldiers; "Gertie from Bizerte" (James Cavanaugh, Walter Kent, Robert C. Haring), sung a cappella by the soldiers, reprised a cappella by Charles Laughton and Robert Young.

Cast: Charles Laughton (Sir Simon de Canterville); Robert Young (Cuffy Williams);

Margaret O'Brien (Lady Jessica de Canterville); William Gargan (Sergeant Benson); Reginald Owen (Lord Canterville); "Rags" Ragland (Big Harry Wallers); Una O'Connor (Mrs. Umney); Donald Stuart (Sir Valentine Williams); Elisabeth Risdon (Mrs. Polverdine); Frank Faylen (Lieutenant John Kane); Lumsden Hare (Mr. Potts); Mike Mazurki (Metropolus); William Moss (Hector); Bobby Readick (Eddie); Marc Cramer (Bugsy McDougle); William Tannen (Jordan); Peter Lawford (Anthony de Canterville). Uncredited: Harry Allen (Mr. Cawthorne); Jimmy Aubrey (Chimney Sweep); Frank Benson, Herbert Clifton (Men at Party), Margaret Bert (Woman Wanting to Dance); Colin Campbell (Vicar); Fred Coby (Ranger); Aina Constant (Factory Girl); Syd Dawson, Charlie Hall (Bold Sir Guy's Squires); Vernon Dowling (Officer); Elspeth Dudgeon (Aged Woman); Tay Dunn (Comb Playing Ranger); Brandon Hurst (Mr. Peabody); Charles Irwin (Marshall of the Hunt); Tor Johnson (Bold Sir Guy); Colin Kenny, Gordon Richards, Tom Stevenson (Noblemen); Guy Kingsford (British Tommy); Jack Lambert (Trigger); Greg McClure (Sergeant); Mary McLeod, Viola Moore (Girls at Party); Patsy O'Byrne (Servant); Frances Raeburn (Eleanor); Brent Richards (Arthur); John Rogers (Sir Simon's Squire); Robert Schuler (Stanley); Roy Seager (Roly Poly Man); Will Stanton (Stone Mason); Anna Marie Stewart (Buxom Lass); Herberta Williams (Matron).

VHS/DVD: DVD released by Warner Bros. Archive Collection circa December 2009.

Synopsis

In 1634, in England, Sir Simon de Canterville agrees to take his wounded brother Anthony's place in a duel with Sir Valentine Williams, but runs away when Sir Valentine has his cousin, Sir Guy, replace him. When Simon is found hiding in an alcove of the Canterville castle, his father has him walled up alive for his cowardice, condemned to walk the castle's halls until a kinsman commits a brave deed while wearing Simon's signet ring. In 1943, the now-deserted Canterville castle accommodates a platoon of American soldiers who are attached to British commandoes. After the castle's owner, six-year-old Lady Jessica de Canterville, tells the men about Simon, the ghost appears before them, attempting to frighten them. However, one of the soldiers, Cuffy Williams, conceives a plan to chase the ghost away. When cleaning the castle the next day, Cuffy meets Jessica, and together they find Simon. Jessica sees that Cuffy has the same Canterville birthmark as Simon, and Simon gives Cuffy his signet ring, hoping that his descendant can wear it in battle and free Simon from his curse.

Simon shows Cuffy the castle's portrait gallery, explaining that all Cantervilles have been cowards, but Cuffy assures him that he is not. The platoon is assigned to blow up a German refinery, and Simon brings Cuffy the signet ring Cuffy has forgotten to take with him. When the machine-gunner Trigger is killed by an oncoming motorcycle patrol, Cuffy is unsettled by Trigger's blood and cannot man the counterattack. When the platoon returns to Canterville, Cuffy is informed that he is to be transferred, and he is left out of the platoon's drill in the woods. Jessica sees a parachute falling to the ground and she leads him to where it has landed. It carries a blockbuster mine, which, if exploded, will wipe out the platoon. Cuffy overcomes his fear when Jessica kicks the mine to show how she is not afraid, which starts the bomb's timer. With Simon, Cuffy chains the mine to his jeep and drives it into a ravine before it explodes. Saving the platoon, Cuffy is recognized as a hero, and his act of bravery allows Simon to disappear into peaceful serenity—marked by a newly erected graveyard headstone.

Notes

If this comic fantasy ultimately reads as bland, forgettable, and having the irksome patriotism of wartime entertainment (not to mention an overdone music score), Dassin is able to redeem it somewhat. The special visual effects, comic touches, and Charles Laughton's comparatively restrained and touching performance all reap the benefits of Dassin's work here, even if the film is less successful than his prior efforts. While the treatment lacks the recurring themes of duplicity and betrayal from Dassin's previous titles, parallels can still be made between the condemned, haunted and subversive figure of Simon Canterville and the blacklisted director. It also features more screen violence, which is hardly surprising given it is set during World War II, and adds some surprising perversity and cruelty. Additionally, the screenplay's loose adaptation of the Oscar Wilde short story repeats Wilde's comparison of American and English behavior, with 1940s jargon and cultural references mixed in.

The film opens on a *Book of Famous Ghosts of England*. A narrator reading the text skips over a page, showing that the Canterville ghost takes on a variety of forms and guises, and displaying illustrations of same. This beginning introduces a gothic tone to the proceedings that will be lost when the narrative updates to 1943, in spite of the use of a ghost as a potential horror antagonist. The 1634 stag hunt, with the stag pursued by a pack of dogs and horsemen, prefigures Dassin being hunted by the HUAC and its sympathizers, and ultimately trapped by those that wish him harm. The fact that hunting a stag is con-

Sir Valentine Williams (Donald Stuart) challenges Anthony de Canterville (Peter Lawford) to a duel for marrying Eleanor (Frances Raeburn), the woman Sir Valentine was engaged to in *The Canterville Ghost* (1944).

sidered a sport adds irony to the parallel of the Communist witch-hunt. Thankfully, we don't see the stag killed, since attention is diverted to Anthony de Canterville (Peter Lawford wearing a blonde period wig) and Sir Valentine.

The narrative turnabout of Sir Valentine replacing himself with Sir Guy for the duel, as Anthony has replaced himself with Simon, is a clever plot twist, and also immediately deflates the arrogance and perceived superiority of Simon over Sir Valentine. Simon's helmet opening and closing as he rides towards the advancing Sir Guy is a broad comic touch in a treatment that will employ other bits of broad comedy, and the humiliation of Simon's retreat is enhanced when he's seen to trip as he alights from his horse. Simon hiding behind the castle alcove curtain is revealed by his dog, and the walling up of the alcove is pure grand guignol, as Simon is effectively buried alive. An amusing dialogue exchange attempts to dilute the horror, as Lord Canterville and Sir Valentine wait for the stonemasons to complete their task:

> LORD CANTERVILLE: Have we not had enough of this playacting, Sir Valentine?
> SIR VALENTINE: One never leaves the theater, m'lord, until the curtain has fallen.

However, Lord Canterville's attitude changes in the face of Sir Valentine voicing his regret, with Canterville answering, "I heard no sound," in response to Simon calling "Father," followed by Sir Valentine's "It was only meant in jest." Laughton effectively conveys Simon's horrifying entrapment, and Dassin dollies in for a close-up of the back of the actor's head, which shows us the all-important Canterville birthmark. This close-up then becomes another of the opening book's illustrations.

The narration tells us that three hundred years have passed, which would make the year 1934, ten years shy of the film's 1944 setting.

Dassin employs thunder and lightning to heighten the scene in which a blood stain appears on the carpet, and the sequence is capped by the funny fainting of Una O'Connor's Mrs. Umney. Simon's ghost first appears as a shadow on the wall, and his entrance is intercut with shots of Harry being frightened by a falling sword (how's that for phallic imagery?) and counting to twelve (since we have been told that the ghost appears at midnight). Simon's presence is expressed by the sounds of rattling chains, moaning and laughing, and more thunder and lightning. A white light appears and moves down a stairway before Simon appears (or, rather, only half-appears, since he is shown out of focus when in haunting mode). We may ask why Simon is chained, since he was not originally chained in the alcove, but this is explained by his series of guises, which includes a hangman's noose around his neck. This latter guise is paralleled by the way Eddie reaches behind him in fear and unintentionally holds up Harry's dog-tags as a noose.

Another visual effect utilized to depict Simon's ghost is smoke coming through a keyhole, which turns into his headless apparition. The smoke effect is reversed when Simon is scared away by Cuffy in a sheet and gas mask. The idea that Simon can be scared by a human pretending (badly) to be a ghost demonstrates Simon's cowardice and gullibility. Cuffy donning the ghost disguise shows his initiative, creating an expectation of heroism that will be played with in the narrative. It also allows us to see the birthmark that reveals him to be a Canterville descendant before Jessica sees it and points it out to Simon.

The scene between Laughton and O'Brien shows how the actor uses tenderness to heighten the tone of her acting. It is telling that Robert Young's Cuffy lacks the same tone in his encounters with little Margaret O'Brien, and that her solo scenes lack the sense of truth that Laughton's contribution inspires, so that she comes across as no more than a coached and cloying child star.

The first in a series of homoerotic moments occurs when Harry, fearful of ghosts, jumps into bed with the Sergeant, with both men in their underwear. At this the Sergeant asks Harry, "What am I, your mother?" The scene where the men of the platoon attack and strip Cuffy of his trousers is more homoeroticism, although the attack feels like a violent rape (in spite of the incident being somewhat rationalized by Cuffy's pretentiousness as a long-lost Duke of Canterville). The arrival of Jessica and Mrs. Polverdine causes the attack to cease, with the presence of the women used for comic payoff when Cuffy unintentionally exposes himself to Mrs. Polverdine.

The dance sequence continues the treatment's broad comedy via the encounter between Harry and the Woman Wanting to Dance. She amusingly stumbles over her words before asking a man who holds a tray (presumably a waiter) to ask Harry to ask her to dance. The man asks Harry, "Oh, would you like to dance?" and Harry responds by dancing with the man. The later dancing of two soldiers will show that the idea of two men dancing together is more acceptable for soldiers than in normal society, although Harry's faux pas still scores a laugh in spite of its predictability.

Sergeant Benson's repeated mimicry of Simon as the apparition with the hanging noose is eventually paid off when the Sergeant demonstrates to a crowd of men how Simon walked through a wall. Naturally, the Sergeant cannot duplicate the trick, and his smashing into the door gets the expected laugh from the crowd.

The staid music being played at the dance, representing British reserve and good taste, is supplanted by the soldiers taking over instruments to make some up-tempo boogie woogie. This leads to two men jitterbugging with each other. The fact that they don't ask the women present to jitterbug can be excused by the idea that the British ladies do not know how, though this doesn't stop Jessica being taught by one of the men. There is something disturbing about the sight of Margaret O'Brien jitterbugging with a grown man, since the jitterbug's movements have a decidedly sexual connotation. Such a scene recalls the pedophilic appeal of Shirley Temple when she was a child star in the 1930s. This interpretation is admittedly a postmodern one, since it is apparent that the intention of the filmmakers was innocent playfulness and not deliberate perversity. However, it still gives one pause.

The platoon's attack on the refinery is the only scene in the film in which the musical score complements the action, and the subsequent fight between the motorcycle patrol and Cuffy at the machine gun creates an expectation that is not met. While we have been warned of the Canterville curse of cowardice, and in spite of Simon bringing the forgotten signet ring, Cuffy's fear, which makes him unable to take over as the machine gunner, comes as a surprise, since the conventional narrative would have him taking over and slaughtering everyone. Rather, his horror at Trigger's blood on the gun seems to paralyze him, and he is ungallantly pushed aside so that another soldier can do the slaughtering. This scene of carnage continues Dassin's taste for violence, even though the idea that one machine gunner can manage to take out a whole platoon may seem a stretch.

The plot point of Cuffy being left out of the drill in the woods conveniently allows him the opportunity to attend to the parachute. However, the treatment pleasingly delays Cuffy's heroics, creating an expectation that he will fail again. Although he ultimately succeeds, Dassin is wise enough to mix in doubt and some comic touches, which adds dimension to what could otherwise have been a one-dimensional scene of stoic heroics.

French movie card for *The Canterville Ghost* (1944).

Dassin begins the scene by photographing Cuffy with shadows of branches cast over him as he tells Jessica he is a coward, although the fact that the shadow is over his midsection and not his face may suggest that he is wrong. Duffy initially runs away from the mine, before finally trying to chain it to his jeep, with the chain recalling Simon's mock chains. Although Duffy becomes aware of the mine's threat to the platoon, it takes Simon and Jessica's presence—and her kicking the mine (which starts it ticking)—to persuade him to complete the chaining.

The tension is not dissipated by the comic touches of the chase, with soldiers jumping out of the way of the jeep, and a tree branch knocking Simon onto the mine. Tension is increased when the chain breaks and Cuffy must re-attach it, though comedy returns when Cuffy and Simon jump from the jeep and the un-manned vehicle drives in a circle to face them. The mine's explosion is delayed, with Simon counting over the twenty-second assumed detonation time, raising the expectation that it is a dud. However, when the explosion finally occurs, another expectation is created in that we think Duffy has been killed—before we hear him and Simon singing as they approach the castle. The fact that the mine has bombed the castle shows the circular route Cuffy had taken to avoid harming the platoon, although he has damaged property that we presume his Canterville descendency gives him some ownership of. We question why Simon is still with Cuffy, since we assume that Cuffy's action can be seen as an act of bravery that will free the ghost. However, the narrative requires that Simon must remind his father (in a moment of pathos for Laughton) before he can be rewarded with the white light around his figure that makes him disappear (complete with angelic choir on the soundtrack). The treatment ends on a comic note (if we discount Duffy and Jessica's final moment at Simon's headstone), with the Lieutenant's shocked silence following the platoon's witnessing of Simon's disappearance.

Dassin had been called in to replace director Norman Z. McLeod, who had already begun work on the film. (In his *Cineaste* interview, Dassin claims that he had originally been offered the project but had turned it down because he didn't like the script, and McLeod took over.) The extent of McLeod's contribution differs according to sources, with some proposing that none of what he shot remains in the final cut. TCM quotes *The Hollywood Reporter* and production charts to report that McLeod left after completing thirty-eight days of filming. Charles Higham's book *Charles Laughton: An Intimate Biography* says that the director left after only seven days. As to whether McLeod bowed out voluntarily or was fired is also a matter of controversy. Higham says he was fired at Laughton's insistence; the actor's unhappiness with the director was compounded by Laughton's distaste for the script, which he thought was a travesty of Wilde's original story. *The Hollywood Reporter* claimed that McLeod left because of a "difference of opinion," which may imply that McLeod had some choice in the matter.

Dassin says in *Cineaste* that he was told by Louis B. Mayer to take over the film after two weeks. Dassin told Mayer that he still didn't like the script, and since McLeod was a friend of his, he wouldn't take it away from him. Supposedly, McLeod then appeared on bended knee and said, "Please, take it away from me, please." Dassin claims McLeod couldn't work with Laughton. Describing Laughton as "a very special kind of person," Dassin would say that he hit it off with the actor "after I found out his secrets"(!). The agreement was that Dassin could re-shoot whatever had been done that he didn't like, but that promise was never kept; the film had to be finished quickly because Laughton had to be free for other commitments. So for Dassin, the end result "was kind of a bastard film." McLeod also took his director of photography, William Daniels, with him when he left.

McLeod had been a director known for comedies, having worked with the Marx Brothers on *Monkey Business* (1931) and *Horse Feathers* (1932); W.C. Fields in the episode "Road Hogs" of the comic anthology *If I Had a Million* (1932) (Laughton also appeared in this film but was not directed by McLeod), *Alice in Wonderland* (1933), and *It's a Gift* (1934); Cary Grant on the similarly ghostly comic fantasy *Topper* (1936); and other comic performers like Mary Boland, Charles Ruggles, Gracie Allen, George Burns, Harold Lloyd, Red Skelton, and Marjorie Main. Ironically, McLeod had been in the U.S. army in World War I as a fighter pilot, which may have informed the army component of *The Canterville Ghost*, since Dassin had not served. McLeod's departure from the film affected his subsequent career, since he would not work again until 1945, when he would make the boxing musical comedy *The Kid from Brooklyn* (1946), with Danny Kaye, for Sam Goldwyn Productions.

TCM states that the rights to the property had been purchased in 1939 as a proposed vehicle for Margaret Sullivan and James Stewart, though these actors would seem to be miscast as Jessica (who is actually fifteen in the original short story) and Simon de Canterville, respectively. Robert Young's character of Cuffy does not appear in the short story, which presents a more romantic relationship between Jessica and the ghost. The new adaptation was designed to accommodate the secondary teaming of Young and Margaret O'Brien. They had previously appeared together in MGM's World War II drama *Journey for Margaret* (1942), O'Brien's credited film debut and the role that resulted in her changing her name from Angela to Margaret. That film too had been another troubled production that had also undergone a change of director when W.S. Van Dyke replaced Herbert Kline after two weeks of shooting. *The Canterville Ghost* would be a career boost for O'Brien, since she had only been cast in less effective parts since *Journey for Margaret*, although she managed a credible French accent for her supporting role in the historical romance *Jane Eyre* (1944).

O'Brien would go on to receive a greater showcase in the Vincente Minnelli historical musical *Meet Me in St. Louis* (1944), for which she would win a special juvenile Academy Award for Outstanding Child Actress of 1944. She was top-billed in the musical *Music for Millions* (1944), the comedy *Three Wise Fools* (1946), *The Unfinished Dance* (1947), *Tenth Avenue Angel* (1948), *Big City* (1948), and the family drama *The Secret Garden* (1949). After leaving MGM, O'Brien attempted to continue her stardom as a teenager in Columbia Pictures' *Her First Romance* (1951) and the independent *Glory* (1956) after a screen absence of four years. However, the perilous transition from child star to adult lead did not happen for her, and O'Brien was reduced to working mostly in television and in the occasional supporting film role.

Charles Higham says that Laughton was kind and considerate to the "gifted and sensitive" Dassin, though Higham also calls Dassin "inexperienced" and McLeod "mediocre." Higham says Laughton helped with "valuable suggestions behind the set when nobody was looking." Higham also claims that Laughton improvised moments, which Dassin presumably allowed, such as a "grotesque dance among the Canterville graves and whooping through the great hall of the mansion clanging his chains" (both moments unnoticed by this author). Higham also says that Laughton admired O'Brien's "expert, impeccably calculated, crowd-pleasing delivery of lines." In his book *Charles Laughton: A Difficult Actor*, Simon Callow supports Higham's claims by writing, "Laughton was cooperative and full of good, discreetly delivered suggestions. He took time and trouble with Dassin, and evidently taught him a great deal."

Callow points out that Laughton being able to have the director removed indicates the power he held at this time in his career, a power acknowledged by the executives at MGM who saw him as more indispensable to the production than McLeod. McLeod had actually come to MGM to make the romantic comedy *Remember?* (1939), after having worked for the most part at Paramount studios since 1930. For MGM, McLeod had also made the legal melodrama *The Trial of Mary Dugan* (1941), which starred Robert Young; the show business musical *Lady Be Good* (1941), also with Young; the musical comedy *Panama Hattie* (1942), which starred Rags Ragland; the western *Jackass Mail* (1942); and the home front comedy *Swing Shift Maisie* (1943). Laughton, on the other hand, had made the film version of his stage drama *Payment Deferred* (1932), the historical biography *The Barretts of Wimpole Street* (1934), the historical adventure *Mutiny on the Bounty* (1935), the World War II drama *Stand by for Action* (1942), and the World War II domestic drama *The Man from Down Under* (1943). Callow also points out that McLeod may have initially seemed an ideal director for the material, since Laughton had previously been happy to work with comedy directors. But not this time.

In his book *The Charles Laughton Story*, Kurt Singer writes about how difficult Laughton was during production, in spite of his playing a character more benign than his previous screen monsters (Nero, Dr. Moreau, Henry VIII, Captain William Bligh, and Quasimodo). Singer says Laughton confounded the director, who "gave up" trying to control the actor. Singer does not identify the film's director, so it is unknown whether this confounded filmmaker was McLeod or Dassin. Although Laughton's insistence on using Wilde's original text in his speeches is acceptable, some of the actor's behavior seems less so. Refusing to wear a wig ("Whoever saw a ghost with a wig on?"), Laughton let his hair grow for three months for a special coiffeur and appeared on the set with a moustache that looked like cat's whiskers (which the make-up man objected to because it grew upward and not downward). The actor also used masseurs and Turkish steam baths to lose weight (though apparently the studio had no problem with this).

Andrew Horton's 1984 *Film Criticism* article on Dassin makes some amusing errors and observations. He names McLeod as "McCloud," and claims that Dassin had little freedom on *The Canterville Ghost*, despite the film "coming under his control after McCloud was let go." Horton says that Dassin "nonetheless manages a few brilliant comic moments, such as the scene where GI's try to drink tea from china cups," but that the director was "limited by a predictable script which aimed no higher than to show Robert Young falling in love with a six-year-old British girl." Although he is right about the comedy of the tea-drinking scene, surely that can be credited to the screenplay as much as Dassin; and the plot does *not* have Robert Young fall in love with the Margaret O'Brien character. While the Young character surely has warm feelings towards her, the idea of a mature man falling in love with a child would never have been allowed by the censors of a 1940s Hollywood film.

The Canterville Ghost was the first picture produced by Arthur L. Field, who would go on to make only two more films, both for MGM—the teenage comedy *Twice Blessed* (1945) and the "B" movie crime drama *Dangerous Partners* (1945).

The Canterville Ghost is the last film Robert Young made under his MGM contract, which had begun in 1931. After this he freelanced. Young's persona of the affable nice guy fit his role of Cuffy perfectly, with Cuffy's moments of hesitant weakness recalling the change-of-pace roles Young essayed as the spy Robert Marvin in Alfred Hitchcock's spy drama *Secret Agent* (1936) and the Nazi Fritz Marberg in the war drama *The Mortal Storm* (1940). His willingness to acquiesce to the dominance of a bigger star is demonstrated here in his playing with the portly British-born Laughton and the diminutive, weepy O'Brien. It would be six years before Young would return to MGM again (to play a leading role in the 1949 historical melodrama *That Forsyte Woman*.

The Canterville Ghost would be remade as a French feature in 1962, and adapted for an Indian film in 2008. Various made-for-television adaptations came in 1962, 1974, 1985, 1986, 1996, 1997, 2001, and 2005.

Release

July 28, 1944 with the tagline "It puts you in the best of spirits!"

Reviews

"Entertaining comedy-drama, with the accent on comedy despite the mystery-chiller emphasis in the title. Tight scripting, nimble direction and excellent casting are about equally responsible for the satisfactory results."—*Variety*

"A genial whimsy.... A good one-half of this fable is charmingly fantastic fun and toys with the supernatural in a delightfully impudent way. But a ghost, once raised, becomes a problem with which all scenarists cannot cope.... Laughton gives a lively and whimsical show of chicken-hearted pomposity in an over-stuffed costume."—Bosley Crowther, *The New York Times*, July 29, 1944

"Fantasy, like realism, pays off only when it is created with fingers instead of thumbs. The best of this film is Laughton's broad hamming of the hammy ghost and some friendly moments between Miss O'Brien and Mr. Young."—*Time* magazine, August 14, 1944

"In this heavy whimsy ... Laughton is atrociously coy and florid.... Dassin clearly lacks the requisite light, comic tone; was some executive punishing him?"—Pauline Kael, *5001 Nights at the Movies*

"An accomplished comedy ... directed by Dassin with great spirit and attack.... Laughton makes the ghostly Canterville a touching, and pleasantly grotesque figure of fun."—Charles Higham, *Charles Laughton: An Intimate Biography*

"The performance [of Laughton] remains unfulfilled and there is a not wholly inappropriate air of a slightly tetchy uncle forced somewhat against his will to dress up for the children's amusement. However, his scenes with O'Brien are affecting, endowed with the father-daughter tenderness which came from somewhere deep inside him."—Simon Callow, *Charles Laughton: A Difficult Actor*

A Letter for Evie (1946)

MGM

Credits: Director: Jules Dassin: Producer: William H. Wright; Screenplay: De Vallon Scott, Alan Friedman, based on the story "The Adventure of a Ready Letter Writer" by Blanche Brace; Photography: Karl Freund. Editor: Chester W. Schaeffer; Music: George Bassman; Sound: Douglas Shearer; Art Direction: Cedric Gibbons; Set Decoration: Edwin B. Willis; Costumes: Irene. B&W, 89 minutes. Filmed May to July 1945.

Songs: "All the Things You Are" (Jerome Kern, Oscar Hammerstein II), played over opening credits and repeatedly as the film's theme; "Here Comes the Bride" (Richard Wagner), whistled by Supply Sergeant; "The Trolley Song" (Hugh Martin, Ralph Blane), heard over the radio.

Cast: Marsha Hunt (Evie O'Connor); John Carroll (Edgar "Wolf" Larsen); Hume Cronyn (Johnny Phineas McPherson); Spring Byington (Mrs. McPherson); Pamela Britton (Barney Lee); Norman Lloyd (DeWitt Pyncheon); Percival Vivian (Mr. McPherson); Donald Curtis (Captain Budlow); Esther Howard (Mrs. Edgewaters); Robin Raymond (Eloise Edgewaters); Therese Lyon (Mrs. Jackson); Lynn Whitney (Miss Jenkins). Uncredited: Ernie Adams, Garry Owen (Firemen); Bob Alden (Sailor); Fred Aldrich, Peter Seal, Harry Wilson (Uncles); Carmen Beretta (Mother); Margaret Bert; John Brohn, Leonard Fisher (Musicians); Lulamae Bohrman (Dowager); Lennie Bremen (Mail Sergeant); Don Brodie, Harry Rose (Barkers); Lane Chandler (Army Captain); Bob Brown, Dick Crockett, Fred Fisher, Michael Kirby (Soldiers); Bryn Davis, Marjorie Henderson, Mercedes Mockaitis, Alix Nagy, Margaret White (Girls); Marcel De La Brosse (Priest); Harry Depp, Art Miles, Forbes Murray (Straphangers); Patrick Desmond, William "Bill" Phillips, Charles Sullivan (Sergeants); Dolores Day (Barbara); Evelyn Dockson (Mrs. Clancy); Aminta Dyne (Gypsy Woman); Frank Evers, Walter Pietila (Soldier Wire Walkers); Sam Finn (Gambler); Ray Flynn (Lieutenant Colonel); Diane Garrett, Beverly Haney, Zaz Vorka (Showgirls); Mona Gutierrez, Sonny Lamont, Harry Woolman (Wire Walkers); Tom Kennedy (Driver); Bertha Lelchuk; Carl LeViness; Jimmy Magill (M.P.); Sharon McManus (Little Girl with Kitten); Cameron Mitchell (Joe); Howard Mitchell; Amira Moustafa, Jean Wayne (French Girls); Ottola Nesmith, Geraldine Wall (Graylaides); Paul Newlan, Lee Phelps (Policemen); Robert Emmett O'Connor (Mr. Clancy); Vic Parkas (Sailor Wire Walker); George Peters (Lieutenant); Albert Petit (Photographer); Rose Plumer; Jack Riley (Fat Man); Rod Rogers (Supply Sergeant); Edgar Sherrod, Walter Soderling (Old Men); Doris Stone; Henry Sylvester; Ray Teal (Cab Driver); Arthur Walsh (Freckles).

VHS/DVD: Not available in either format.

Synopsis

Disinterested in the affections of her office manager, DeWitt Pyncheon, of the Trojan Shirt Company in Brooklyn, New York, Secretary Evie O'Connor writes a letter to an unknown soldier and places it in a size sixteen-and-a-half shirt that is destined for an army camp. She does this after learning that many of her co-workers have found romance via this method. The letter is found by Private Edgar "Wolf" Larsen at the Texas army camp. Wolf, a notorious womanizer, reads it to fellow soldier Johnny Phineas McPherson, then throws it away, since he senses that Evie is more the marrying kind than fun. Johnny, however, retrieves the letter and writes back to her, since he wants a girl to write to. They continue to correspond, and Johnny sends Evie a picture of Wolf, since he knows he is more her type, after she sends Johnny her picture. When the platoon is given furlough to New York, Johnny visits Evie, posing as Wolf, who he says cannot meet her because he was sent on a special assignment overseas.

Evie agrees to go out with Johnny, and he falls in love with her. When borrowing Johnny's toothpaste, Wolf sees the letters Johnny has written and Evie's picture. When Johnny next visits Evie, Wolf appears, pretending to be the Johnny of the letters to irritate his pal. Johnny pretends to drink rubbing alcohol so as to seduce Evie's roommate, Barney Lee, and to prevent Evie getting close to Wolf. The scheme works, and when the men leave, Johnny attacks Wolf, who promises not to pursue Evie. However, Wolf does go back to Evie's, and Johnny sets a smoke pot on fire in the building. Wolf knocks his head and, while semi-conscious, proposes marriage to Evie. However, the next day Wolf and Johnny are sent overseas to the war. Johnny is wounded in battle and Wolf marries a French woman. Not hearing from Johnny, Evie visits his parents in St. Thomas, Connecticut, where she sees a photograph of the two men and learns which one is which. Leaving the New York hospital where he recuperated, Johnny goes to Evie, giving her his own dog tags and Purple Heart medal, pretending that her Johnny is deceased. Touched by his bravery, Evie tells him she knows he is really Johnny, and they kiss.

Notes

This mix of home-front comedy and drama presents a narrative with the uneasy undercurrent of romantic manipulation, and again allows Dassin to explore his themes of subversion, duplicity and betrayal. Providing the occasional interesting visual flourish (and a montage sequence that uses World War II newsreel footage), the director once again displays his talent for comic staging and performance, in spite of the de rigueur MGM overdone music score. Apart from its wartime setting (although only one battle sequence is shown), a brutal fistfight represents another expression of Dassin's taste for violent behavior. The screenplay is also interesting in its variation of the plot of the 1897 French play *Cyrano de Bergerac* by Edmond Rostand, the tale of the ugly man who writes beautiful poetry and uses the guise of another to win the woman he loves.

The opening credits feature animated little birds at the opposing corners of the screen, one holding a letter and the others waiting in anticipation. The dreamy song "All the Things You Are" (introduced in the 1944 MGM show business musical comedy *Broadway Rhythm* over the credits tells us that romance will feature in this narrative (if the birds aren't clue enough). The (one-sided) office romance between Evie and her boss DeWitt is a subversive element in the idea that office romances cross the line between professional and personal behavior, even though Evie is an unenthusiastic participant. Dassin introduces the first of three instances of Evie kissing a man and opening her eyes in reaction. Her kiss with DeWitt gets a funny payoff when he stands in front of a framed halibut, recalling the comment that Miss Jenkins had made that kissing him would be the same as kissing the halibut.

The entrance of Bill the Soldier into the all-female typing pool has the women react by stopping typing all at once, and his encounter with Barbara shows Evie how Miss Jenkins' idea of leaving a note in one of the company's shirts can result in finding a handsome love. Dassin provides a cute button to this moment in the way Barbara drags her coat behind her unawares, the coat having been put in her hand by another typist, as she and Bill walk to the elevator.

The script is peppered with witticisms, an early example of which is the following exchange:

Evie O'Connor (Marsha Hunt) is more interested in Edgar "Wolf" Larsen (John Carroll) than Johnny Phineas McPherson (Hume Cronyn) in this publicity portrait from *A Letter for Evie* (1946).

> JOHNNY: I thought that from now on you and women were going to be strangers?
> WOLF: Some of my best friends are strangers.

Wolf taking a coke from Bobby, who has just bought it from a machine, and pocketing the pack of cigarettes he is offered by Johnny demonstrate Wolf's careless selfishness (as does Wolf taking the coin Johnny tosses in the air to pay Bobby in an attempt to compensate one while still using the other). However, the idea of Wolf retrieving Johnny's pack from his pocket only to find Evie's letter is business that moves the plot along.

The screenplay references the film *Wuthering Heights* several times. After Evie mentions the picture, Johnny suggests that he and Evie go to a revival, but the date is interrupted by Wolf's arrival. At one point Evie writes, "Sometimes I feel just like Cathy, the heroine [of *Wuthering Heights*]. On the surface, I lead a very conventional life. Underneath it I like to do all the 'wild impulsive things she did,'" but this doesn't really match our impression of Evie. However, these lines in Evie's letter do allow for a differentiation between Wolf and Johnny, since Wolf replies "What she do?" while Johnny tells him that the film is his favorite. This makes it clear that Johnny is more suited to Evie than Wolf, who assesses her from the letter as being "nice and lonesome," which he calls "a dangerous combination," and rejects her by throwing away the letter. The issue of fate, described by Evie as "kismet," is something that will arise repeatedly in the narrative—something that Wolf scoffs at but Johnny believes in, although Johnny rationalizes his writing lies to Evie by supposing they are fated never to meet.

The more problematic issue is that of Johnny's action of writing to Evie while pretending to be Wolf. Since Evie has placed the letter in a particular sized shirt, this is assumed to be her type, a size that the diminutive Johnny can't measure up to. However, it wouldn't be that hard for Johnny to explain how he accessed the letter, and it's hardly an insult to her that he wants to write to her. The deeper issue is that Johnny feels he is unattractive and not (superficially) suited for Evie. While the treatment repeats the idea that he is short (he will be called a "little soldier" by a carnival barker), Johnny is hardly bad looking. In fact, Hume Cronyn has a sensual feminine mouth, and at five-feet-six is the same height as Marsha Hunt's Evie, although he will initially photograph as shorter than she. Rather, Cronyn is only short (as most men would be) in comparison with John Carroll's Wolf, since Carroll was six-feet-five-inches tall.

Johnny writing to Evie without the appropriate explanation then makes him a duplicitous character, and this action creates the narrative expectation that he will be found out and punished by Evie rejecting him. By making Johnny the narrative protagonist, after the screenplay had initially presented Evie as such, the issue of his deceit colors the notion of his romance. We want him to succeed because we see that he is more deserving of Evie's love; but because he goes about it in the wrong way, this undercuts his likeability. Rather, he is considered foolish, and an anti-hero, which seems to be a radical idea for a romantic comedy.

Evie and Barney Lee have a funny exchange which references an earlier MGM feature:

> EVIE: He [DeWitt] kissed me one day and I didn't hear any music.
> BARNEY: Music? What did you expect to hear, "The Trolley Song?"

This exchange also sets up the joke for the next time Evie is kissed—when she *does* hear "The Trolley Song."

The scene between Evie and Barney features an ill-advised checkered dress worn by Evie which makes her meld into the set decoration of their apartment, though perhaps it is a deliberate indication of Evie being a home girl.

Johnny sending a photo of Wolf compounds Johnny's deceit, and Wolf's vanity is underscored by the twelve photos he has of himself, in various outfits and poses, for Johnny to choose from. The photos confirm Wolf's shallowness, since he tells Johnny that he had them made up in a studio. Consequently, the athletic poses of Wolf as a boxer, a race car driver, a horseman, a lifeguard, and a lumberjack are as false as Johnny's portrayal of himself to Evie.

Dassin uses superimposed images for a transition sequence that shows Evie and Johnny exchanging letters over a period of time. Behind the image of Evie reading a letter, an aerial long-shot is followed by soldiers marching and then Johnny reading a letter among the marching platoon. Johnny tells her that "All the Things You Are" is his favorite song, and his playing a record of it dissolves to rippling water in a pond, and the pond dissolves to Evie's record player as she listens to the song.

Johnny's initial fear of meeting Evie when the platoon gets furloughed changes after he decides to go to her; however, it is interesting that the letter he writes to her to introduce himself as Wolf is late, and he is forced to introduce himself in person. The uncomfortable introduction is initially avoided when Evie tells Barney how she had not been there when Johnny first arrived, with Dassin expressing Evie's panic by showing her dropped grocery bag and panning to her shoes on the floor as she enters the room and changes clothes in preparation for Johnny's anticipated return. The close-ups during the introduction are telling, showing Evie's disappointment at the sight of Johnny followed by a slow reaction shot of Cronyn. We see the transition on his face from excitement at meeting her to an awareness of, and embarrassment at, Evie's disappointment. Cronyn's delicate acting indicates that perhaps Johnny might have considered telling her the truth, but he changes his mind out of fear of her rejection, which speaks of his low self-esteem.

The Walk-the-Wire-and-Kiss-a-Girl act at the carnival might seem an odd setting for Johnny and Evie's outing, although we have to remember that Evie is not out on a "romantic" date with Johnny. This is underlined by her wanting Johnny to succeed on the wire and kiss the girl, since the girl poses no romantic threat. However, Johnny's initial reluctance to kiss her betrays his true agenda. The crowd's reaction to Johnny is interesting, as they laugh at his reluctance and then cheer when Johnny eventually does kiss the girl (after Evie's encouragement). The passion of Johnny's kiss shows his romantic intensity, with the barker's comment somewhat undermining Johnny's achievement of walking the wire and kissing the girl: "There, gentlemen. It can be done—the little soldier did it."

The scene with the Gypsy Woman at the Gypsyland Café has Evie holding Johnny's hand as she listens with pleasure to the tea-cup reading of "An early marriage, four children, and a happy and long life," although Evie undercuts the reading by telling Johnny that she thinks they're fun but she doesn't believe them. Johnny's physical prowess after the wire walk is shown in the way he steps onto the top of a parked taxi in order to rescue the kitten at the top of the Café sign, with the applause from the gathering crowd acting as further psychological approbation.

Homoeroticism is evident in the scene where Wolf tells the other soldiers, who sit around him in their underwear, about his date, with the sexual tension dispersed by the comic end of the story (the girl's four brothers were waiting at her home).

The kitten returns in the plot after Johnny brings it to Evie on their second "date," telling her he has bought it from the Little Girl seen in the rescue scene. The treatment of the kitten will be used to differentiate character, since Evie and Johnny are kind to it, and Wolf and Barney are shown to be unkind to it.

The extended scene where Wolf appears is perhaps the best in the film, since it features multiple examples of duplicity and allows Dassin some farcical staging. Before the men arrive, Barney appears in a frilly white dress to counter the suggestion that she, as a baseball player, cannot be feminine. (The fact of her having a man's name is presumably supposed to add to her perceived androgyny.) Barney's intention to seduce Johnny is acceptable to Evie, since Evie is not romantically interested in him. Johnny is continuing to be duplicitous by deceiving Evie, and his pretence of being drunk and wanting to seduce Barney is only kept up to undermine Wolf's attempts to seduce Evie. Wolf is duplicitous since he claims to be the Johnny that the real Johnny has pretended to be (the fictional Johnny of Evie's letters). The only person who is not acting duplicitously in the scene is Evie.

Johnny falling over the couch in order to stop Evie and Wolf from kissing begins the physical comedy of the scene, and shows his willingness to injure himself for Evie, although the greater pain comes from Barney's pursuit of Johnny on the patio. To witness a woman pursue a man who we know is not interested in her is to see a woman humiliated, and the moment is only redeemed by the performances of Pamela Britton and Hume Cronyn.

Barney's retreat in the face of Johnny's perceived advance is surprising. When he says, "You're my type of girl—feminine, strictly feminine," she merely gives a dismissive snort. The moment when he kisses her and she hits him in response is made funny by the playing, as is Johnny's chase after her. The appearance of Mrs. Jackson adds to the farce, with her disapproval of Johnny's supposed drunkenness upping the humor. However much we appreciate Dassin's expert comic staging, the light tone of the scene changes when Johnny attacks Wolf in the street. Johnny's repeated punching of Wolf turns the assault into a beating. Perhaps because it is the only overt physical violence in the film, it becomes all the more disturbing in its severity.

After a bugle player sounds at dawn on the film's camp set, Dassin uses newsreel footage for the montage of Johnny and Wolf's platoon shipping out, providing air and battle footage for the mission. The screen goes dark after an explosion goes off in front of a soldier who has fallen to the ground, which we will learn later represents Johnny, and Dassin then cuts to Johnny, wounded by shrapnel in his right leg, in a hospital in France.

Given that Wolf has been corresponding with Evie, it seems odd that he should ask Johnny to write to her to tell her that Wolf has married a French girl, rather than telling her himself. His line, "Tell her I was captured by the free French," is undercut by the non-stop talk of the French Girl with him (who we assume is his new wife). The scenes after the wounding of Johnny change the tone of the film, moving it into dramatic territory, with Evie's trip to visit Johnny's parents grounded by the earnest performance of Spring Byington as Mrs. McPherson, although Dassin adds the comic touch of both she and Evie crying into handkerchiefs at the same time in the same shot.

It is the two photos on the McPhersons' mantelpiece that reveal the deception to Evie. Dassin shows Evie and Mrs. McPherson looking diagonally across each other at the two different photos when they speak of Johnny, then looking at each other, and finally straight ahead when they speak of Wolf. Even Mrs. McPherson's line "He looks so dignified in his uniform" remains ambiguous until Evie asks for clarity with, "Who?" At this, Mrs. McPherson replies, "Why, Johnny, of course," which helps Evie identify Johnny in the uniformed photo on the mantel as the man who had told her he was Wolf.

When Johnny finally goes to Evie, Dassin shoots Evie in close-up, with her controlled fury at Johnny's deceit indicated by Hunt's cold stare, showing that she now knows something that he doesn't. This may be considered duplicity on Evie's behalf (the first and only time in the narrative), but the screenplay's willingness to have her wait and see what Johnny says is a pleasing surprise. Johnny now using a cane reveals his injury and a different kind of vulnerability, and Dassin, oddly enough, shows Cronyn and Hunt as the same height for the first time. The idea that Johnny should give Evie his own dog tags and the Purple Heart he has won, with the information that her Johnny is now dead, is more duplicity from him and a kind of emotional suicide (he has given up trying to win her).

The expected blow-up from Evie doesn't happen, with her being so touched by his heroism that she pins the medal onto him and says, "It belongs to you, Johnny." Even the expected embrace—first a hug, then a kiss—is used for a comic payoff when Evie hears an angelic chorus of "All the Things You Are" as the music that she yearns for when kissed. Dassin photographs the final kiss with Hunt in close-up and the back of Cronyn's head, perhaps a final indication that Hunt is the bigger box office name.

The film is said to be a remake of the Metro Pictures silent comedy drama *Don't Write Letters* (1922), which is based on the same November 13, 1920, *Saturday Evening Post* short story by Blanche Brace but which features different character names. John Douglas Eames' book *The MGM Story* describes it as a "B" movie, although for the purposes of this book it is considered an "A." The TCM website quotes *The Hollywood Reporter* as saying that Les White was the original director of photography for the film; but it is not known how much (if any) of his work remains in the film (the title does not even appear on his filmography). *A Letter for Evie* was only the second picture for producer William H. Wright at MGM, whose prior title was the "B" comedy drama *Blonde Fever* (1945). He had previously been an associate producer for David O. Selznick on the comedy drama *The Young at Heart* (1938), and for three "B" titles at Paramount Pictures.

A Letter for Evie was Dassin's second film with Marsha Hunt; she starred in his previous *The Affairs of Martha* (1942). Since that earlier film she had continued at MGM, scoring leading roles in the musical romance *Seven Sweethearts* (1942), and the World War II dramas *Pilot #5* (1943) and *None Shall Escape* (1944); for Columbia Pictures). *A Letter for Evie* was Hunt's last film for MGM, though she would have subsequent leading roles in the historical drama *Carnegie Hall* (1947) for United Artists, the drama *The Inside Story* (1948) for Republic Pictures, and the "B" detective drama *Mary Ryan, Detective* (1950) for Columbia Pictures. Although Hunt's association with Dassin extended to her Broadway debut in the comic play *Joy to the World*, directed by him at the Plymouth Theatre, which ran from March 18 to July 3, 1948, her Hollywood film career was stalled by the blacklist.

According to Patrick McGilligan and Paul Buhle in their book *Tender Comrades*, it was in June 1950 that Hunt's name appeared in the broadcasting pamphlet *Red Channels* as a "patriotically suspect citizen." The pamphlet listed the leftist petitions she had signed, the anti–HUAC gatherings she had attended (such as the October 1947 flight to Washington as one of the members of the Committee for the First Amendment), and other political activities in which she had participated. She was never a Communist and had not been subpoenaed by HUAC, but Hunt was still considered unemployable in Hollywood. She would manage to work in television nonetheless, and play leading roles in independent productions like the comic mystery *Actors and Sin* (1952); the crime thriller *Diplomatic Passport* (1954), filmed in England; and the drama *No Place to Hide* (1956), her last leading role. She finally returned to a major studio in a supporting role with Warner Bros.' aviation drama *Bombers B-52* (1957).

McGilligan and Buhle quote Hunt on the troubled that occurred during the production of Stanley Kramer's domestic comedy *The Happy Time* (1952) in which Hunt had a supporting role. She was told that protests had been made about her casting, and that she was required to sign a statement to the effect that she was not a Communist. She did prepare a statement—not denying that she was a Communist "but expressing my pride and affection for my country's form of government," and supporting the flight to Washington, which was now considered by others to have been "ill-advised" and "masterminded by Communists." This was accepted by Kramer. Kramer's executive producer, George Glass, himself a cooperative witness before HUAC who had named names, wanted her to take out a full-page add in *Variety* swearing her hatred of, and unswerving opposition to, Communist doctrine. Hunt refused, telling Glass, "If any of those shadowy groups wants to step forward and accuse me of some wrong, I will answer an accusation.... Let somebody call me a Communist or charge me with subversive activities. Then I can answer. But I'm not gonna fight shadows." Despite this refusal, she was allowed to remain in the film. Hunt says, amusedly, that this was hardly the environment within which to make a comedy, let alone one that presented a supposedly buoyant and idealized family. She would survive thanks to being married to the novelist and screenwriter Robert Presnell, Jr., who was not blacklisted, and by touring in stock theater around the country.

The Canadian born Hume Cronyn had made his film debut in Alfred Hitchcock's suspense drama *Shadow of a Doubt* (1943), and had earned an Academy Award nomination as Best Supporting Actor for MGM's World War II drama *The Seventh Cross* (1944). Apart from *Shadow of a Doubt* and his other Hitchcock title, the World War II sea drama *Lifeboat* (1944), Cronyn was working exclusively for MGM. In his autobiography, *A Terrible Liar*, Cronyn recalls the wire-walking sequence of *A Letter for Evie*, which he did himself. Cronyn says learning to do the walk, and being trained by a professional walker, did not come easily for him, and his body was covered in a mass of yellow, green and blue bruises that resulted from his many falls into the sawdust pit six feet below the wire and wire rips, in spite of the metal jockstrap he wore for the scene. The actor would go on to work with Dassin again on the prison drama *Brute Force* (1947).

Although he was an American, born in New Orleans, Louisiana, John Carroll had the appearance of a Latin lover. He had started his career at MGM in 1929 playing uncredited bit parts, and scored a leading role in RKO's "B" historical comedy drama *Hi, Gaucho!* (1935), playing an Argentinean bandit. Carroll continued at RKO (though an uncredited role in Paramount's 1936 prison drama *The Accusing Finger* may have had him cross paths with star Marsha Hunt), played Zorro for Republic's adventure western *Zorro Rides Again* (1937) and a faux Zorro in the western *Rose of the Rio Grande* (1938), and jumped into "A" films with a supporting role in Howard Hawks' aviation drama *Only Angels Have Wings* (1939). He returned to MGM for the Maisie series' jungle comedy drama *Congo Maisie* (1940), and continued in supporting roles, apart from the title role in the "B" northwest comedy drama *Pierre of the Plains* (1942). Carroll had what is considered his best known role playing opposite John Wayne in Republic's World War II aviation drama *Flying Tigers* (1942). He was the singing lead in the Republic show business musical *Hit Parade of 1943* (1943), and his film appearance prior to *A Letter for Evie* was as the lead in the "B" romantic comedy *Bedside Manner* (1945).

After *A Letter for Evie*, Carroll's career would improve, as he would go on to play leading roles for Republic Pictures. These include the legal drama *The Flame* (1947), the westerns *Old Los Angeles* (1948), *Surrender* (1950), and *Belle Le Grand* (1951), the religious drama *Angel in Exile* (1948), the legal drama *I, Jane Doe* (1948), the adventure *The Avengers* (1950), and the comedies *Hit Parade of 1951* (1950) and *Geraldine* (1953). Carroll ended the 1950s in 20th Century–Fox's comedy *Reluctant Bride* (1955), which he also produced; the Columbia western *Decision at Sundown* (1957); and *Plunderers of Painted Flats* (1959), his last western for Republic in a leading role.

Release

June 27, 1946

Reviews

"A frequently gay and pleasant little piece ... the film provides a number of delightful moments, chiefly through the shenanigans of Hume Cronyn, one of Hollywood's better comedians."—*The New York Times*, June 28, 1946

"Predictable comedy with longueurs."—John Walker, *Halliwell's Film & Video Guide 2000*

"A harmless, easy-going 'B' picture, and ably abetted by a good comic cast."—Jay A. Steinberg, *Turner Classic Movies* article

"In consequential romancer."—Leonard Maltin, *1997 Movie & Video Guide*

"A programmer [that] was just a pale imitation of the Broadway hit *Dear Ruth*."—James Robert Parish and Ronald L. Bowers, *The MGM Stock Company: The Golden Era*

Two Smart People (1946)

[aka *Time for Two*]
MGM

Credits: Director: Jules Dassin; Producer: Ralph Wheelwright; Screenplay: Ethel Hill, Leslie Charteris, based on a story by Ralph Wheelwright and Allan Kenward; Photography: Karl Freund; Editor: Chester W. Schaeffer; Music: George Bassman; Sound: Douglas Shearer; Art Direction: Cedric Gibbons; Set Decorations: Edwin B. Willis, Keogh Gleason; Costumes: Irene; Men's Costumes: Valles; Hair: Sydney Guilaroff; Makeup: Jack Dawn. B&W, 93 minutes. Filmed September to November 1945.

Songs: "Dangerous" (Peligrosa) (Ralph Blane, George Bassman), sung by guitarist at Mexican Hotel; "How About You?" (Burton Lane, Ralph Freed), played in Del Vista Hotel; "Darktown Strutters Ball" (Shelton Brooks), played on riverboat.

Cast: Lucille Ball (Ricki Woodner); John Hodiak (Ace Connors); Lloyd Nolan (Bob Simms); Hugo Haas (Senor Rodriguez); Lenore Ulric (Senora Maria Ynez); Elisha Cook, Jr. (Fly Feletti); Lloyd Corrigan (Dwight Chandwick); Vladmir Sokoloff (Jacques Dufour); David Cota (Jose); Clarence Muse (Porter). Uncredited: Gloria Anderson (Grecian Girl on Riverboat); Jean Andren, Bess Flowers (Policewomen); George Calliga (Stewart); Gabriel Canzona (Monkey Man); Harold DeGarro (Stilt Walker); Harry Depp (Spectator); Helen Dickson, Maria Dodd, Mary Emory (Women); Phil Dunham (Drunk); Margaret Jackson (Bystander); Bobby Johnson (Waiter); Frank Johnson (Fat Man at Andre's); Erwin Kalser (Franz); Paul Kruger (Cop); Lorenzo Lopez (Gardener); James Magill (Reveler); George Magrill (Renif Taxi Driver); Cleo Morgan (Cleopatra); Leo Mostovoy (Headwaiter at Andre's); Fred Nurney (Victoire); John Piffle (Jolly Fat Man); Tom Quinn (Sheik on Riverboat); Emil Rameau (Riverboat Waiter); William McKeever Riley (Pete); William Tannen (Clerk); Fred "Snowflake" Toones (Clarence); Peter Virgo (Indian Attendant); Constance Weiler (Hat Check Girl); Lynn Whitney (Swedish Girl); Marek Windheim (Captain); Shelley Winters (Princess).

VHS/DVD: Not available in either format.

Synopsis

Ace Connors has stolen $500,000 in government bonds and has hidden them in the binding of his favorite book, The Art of Fine Cooking. He meets with businessman Dwight Chandwick at the Del Vista Beverly Hills Hotel to discuss an oil investment, where he also meets Ricki Woodner, a woman who has smuggled oil paintings out of Europe. When Ricki sours Chandwick on Ace's deal, Ace, in turn, scares Chandwick away from her, claiming her paintings are fake. Ace receives a telegram that he is to serve five years in Sing Sing if he voluntarily goes to New York for trial. Detective Bob Simms arrives to ensure that Ace goes to New York, agreeing to escort him on a five-day whirlwind trip to New Orleans. Ace's partner, Fly Feletti, suggests to Ricki that she get the bonds and split them with him. She catches the same train as Ace and Bob, and they begin a romance, although they recognize each other as criminals. Feletti appears on the train and blackmails Ricki into becoming his partner, threatening to give her location to the Hot Springs police, who are looking for her for a past scam.

Ace buys Ricki a miniature-booted pin from a curio shop in El Paso on a train stop, and they spend a romantic evening in a Mexico hotel. However, when Ace finds the pin in his belongings, he deduces that Ricki has been looking for the bonds and that she is not to be trusted. In New Orleans, Ace, Ricki, and Bob hire costumes for Mardi Gras, and Ace leaves the cookbook at the costume store. The couple gives Bob the slip and plan to run away together to South America on a ship. Agreeing to give the bonds back to Bob, Ace tells Ricki where they are. Losing Ace in the crowd, Ricki goes with Ferelli to get the book. At the store, Ricki takes the book and gives Feletti the slip, but he confronts Ace and Bob when they arrive. Feletti shoots Bob, and, at gunpoint, takes Ace to look for Ricki. The wounded Bob catches up with Ace and Feletti at Ace's hotel room, which Ricki has left, and Bob shoots Feletti dead. Bob handcuffs Ace, who surrenders, believing that Ricki has abandoned him, and he and Bob go to catch a train to New York. Ricki appears to give Bob the cookbook; however, Bob shows them that he had already found the bonds in the book when Ace had "lost his poise" that night in the Mexican hotel. Ricki splits the miniature boots from the pin to give Ace half, and tells him she is going back to Hot Springs to face her own past.

Notes

This crime drama is an interesting vehicle for Dassin as a transition from comedies to film noir titles, although we can assume that the transition was more coincidence than planned. The mood of dread and foreboding that permeates this treatment, and the low-key performances, help create what can be read as a film noir, in spite of a lot of the action occurring in the daytime. The late introduction of the Mardi Gras carnival into the narrative adds irony to the doomed predicament of the characters, and the crowd scenes are used in the dramatic conflict with a wonderful payoff at the climax. The score being limited only to source music in the first third of the film (this initial minimalism matching the emotional bleakness of the characters and tone) creates a promising expectation that regrettably goes unfulfilled when George Bassman's score takes over and overplays in the manner of Dassin's previous titles. Dassin provides noteworthy visual touches to the film, as well as many comic flourishes. The treatment repeats what was becoming a trademark interest of the director—protagonists of a duplicitous nature—with a bitter romance constantly struggling against the cynicism of swindlers; while the level of violence is here limited to one punch, a non-fatal gunshot and a shooting murder.

The opening credits feature an animated couple in period dress who court, retreat and end up together when Dassin's name appears. This struggle prefigures that of Ace and Ricki in the narrative, who must overcome their fear and mistrust of each other to come together, although only momentarily at the end of the film. Lucille Ball's Ricki wearing a black dress with a bejeweled jacket and hat presents her like a cross between an Aztec warrior and a film noir femme fatale. This obfuscates the subsequent issue of whether or not she is a duplicitous character, particularly since there is some ambiguity in regards to the authenticity of the painting she shows Chandwick. However, what *is* immediately apparent is that Ball gives Ricki a certain oddball quality; while not overtly comic, it may be a tactic to sabotage Ace's proposed oil venture, as shown in this exchange:

> RICKI: Eleven wildcat wells out of twelve are failures. Isn't that amazing?
> CHANDWICK: Are you certain of that?
> RICKI: Well, I oughta be. My father wanted it engraved on his tombstone, but we talked him out of it.

Ricki will later be confirmed as a duplicitous character through her initial interest in stealing the bonds, when Feletti talks of her past scam, and when she lies to Feletti about her intention to help him. What redeems Ricki, however, is her love for Ace, since after she falls for him she doesn't betray him. Equally, Ace is a duplicitous character via only his past (and when he plays Ricki in regards to the painting). After that, he doesn't deceive her because he has fallen in love with her (and his deception of Bob at the climax is relatively minor).

Dassin uses the cigarette-smoke-revealing-a-character's-presence trick he employed in *Reunion in France* for Feletti's scene with Ace, although we have seen someone hiding near Ace's door before the smoke. Dassin adds some comic business by having Ricki fall into Bob's train compartment as a result of the train lurching. Ricki's toast "to crime" reads as odd, but while Ace's acceptance of it is believable, Bob's is not.

Fly Feletti (Elisha Cook, Jr.) is not pleased to hear how his partner in crime, Ace Connors (John Hodiak), is to be escorted by Detective Bob Simms (Lloyd Nolan) to New York to stand trial for stealing government bonds in *Two Smart People* (1946).

The kiss that plays against the idea of Ace and Ricki as "strictly a business merger" is initially interrupted by a train whistle that repeats and continues as they embrace. The scene ends on an amusing note when an older lady smiles as she sees the kiss, turns to her husband, who smiles at her, and she winces in response.

The narrative's change of tone to encompass the blossoming romance between Ace and Ricki becomes apparent in the scene where they listen and react silently to the singing guitarist at the Mexican hotel. Dassin cuts quickly away from Ricki in a long shot, dressed in a white sheath, but Ball's emotional demeanor during the song suggests that Ricki has depths of emotion beneath her shallow swindler surface persona. Their walk in the desert receives an erotic payoff when they kiss while standing in front of two erectile cacti.

The issue of Ricki's duplicity is raised again when Feletti appears in Mexico. Clearly he is following her, but as with his previous appearance on the train, doubt remains as to whether she is in cahoots with him. This ambiguity is confirmed when he has to blackmail her into agreeing to steal the bonds. A bird pin on Ricki's white Grecian goddess gown is positioned oddly—on her lower waist, with the bird pointing towards her crotch, a detail Dassin's initial quick long shot did not reveal. It is interesting that this should become apparent only when Feletti appears to blackmail her.

The Mardi Gras sequence was singled out by *The New York Times* reviewer as enlivening the film, and Dassin uses the large crowds celebrating to counterpoint the climactic chase. A street float with people dancing with mannequins reads as odd, though it will receive a payoff in the murder of Feletti. Ace as a pirate and Ricki as a princess is a schematic representation of their characters, although the princess gown is too hippy to be flattering to Ball, which may explain the look of anguish on her face when she is first seen in it. Feletti gets a noirish introduction to the scene when the camera pans from Ace and Ricki dancing to him emerging behind two beast-headed men; and his costume as a harlequin is equally schematic, since he will ultimately become a pathetic rather than heroic figure.

Ace's speech about how the Mardi Gras carnival is Shrove Tuesday, which leads to the fasting and penance of Lent, and that the word "carnivale" means farewell to the flesh, describes how the good times are coming to an end. The narrative uses the repeated joke of the searching Bob finding other couples dressed as a pirate and a princess, and this is paid off later when Ace finds yet another princess (the young Shelley Winters in an uncredited bit part) after he loses Ricki.

The business of Ricki taking the cookbook, unseen by Feletti, finally confirms that she is *not* his partner, while Feletti lighting a match on the mannequin that holds the book in which the bonds are hidden (unbeknownst to him) is clever and funny. The final showdown is enhanced by the revelers outside the shop, while Ace threatening Bob with the gun is the film's first real violence (after he and Feletti both had previous occasion to make armed threats). Bob advancing on Ace is a frightening moment, because it seems to be forcing Ace to shoot someone he doesn't want to shoot, although Bob will later turn out to be just as deceitful as Ace and Ricki.

The chase among the revelers returns to the mannequins, this time as one is tossed in the air from a blanket. The corpse of Feletti is mistaken for another mannequin when he falls into a blanket after being shot by Bob.

The final shot of the film appears to have been a re-shoot, since the back of someone we assume to be Ball is seen watching the train to New York depart—via a process screen. Equally odd, just before this, Ball backs out of the frame when Ace and Bob board the train after the expected reconciliation kiss.

It's hard to see the symbolism of the miniature-boot pin as hopeful, since we know Ricki is probably going to face prison, the same as Ace. This avoidance of the standard happy ending effectively matches the treatment's noirish tone.

Two Smart People is the first credited picture for producer Ralph Wheelwright, who also co-wrote the original story. However, the only other film that Wheelwright ever produced, the MGM domestic drama *Tenth Avenue Angel* (1948), had actually been made prior to *Two Smart People*, but its release was held back for nearly two years. Wheelwright was also the author of the stories for MGM's war sea drama *Thunder Afloat* (1939) and the social drama *Blossoms in the Dust* (1941). He would go on to write the stories for the MGM domestic drama *These Wilder Years* (1956) and the Universal Pictures Lon Chaney biopic *Man of a Thousand Faces* (1957), which would earn him a shared nomination for the 1958 Best Writing Story and Screenplay Written Directly for the Screen Academy Award.

A publicity portrait of Lucille Ball and John Hodiak, the stars of the crime romance *Two Smart People* (1946).

Lucille Ball had begun her film career playing bit parts at 20th Century–Fox from 1933, and continued the same at Columbia Pictures and RKO. She scored a supporting role in the RKO Astaire/Rogers musical *Follow the Fleet* (1936), and after playing a few leads in RKO shorts, she had a break-out supporting role in the show business comedy *Stage Door* (1937). Ball graduated to leading roles in "B" titles at RKO, like the crime comedy *Go Chase Yourself* (1938), the show business comedies *The Affairs of Annabel* (1938) and its sequel *Annabel Takes a Tour* (1938), the romantic road comedy *Next Time I Marry* (1938), the drama *Beauty for the Asking* (1939), the crime drama *Twelve Crowded Hours* (1939), the drama *Panama Lady* (1939), the jungle drama *Five Came Back* (1939), and the comedy drama *You Can't Fool Your Wife* (1940). She also played the lead in a few RKO "A"s—the musical comedy *Too Many Girls* (1940), the romantic comedy *A Girl, a Guy, and a Gob* (1941), the historical western *Valley of the Sun* (1942), the melodrama *The Big Street* (1942), and the military romantic comedy *Seven Days' Leave* (1942).

It was Ball's singing in pictures like *That Girl from Paris* (1936), *Too Many Girls*, and *The Big Street* that led her to sign at MGM in 1942 as a musical comedy performer, though she would only stay for four years. At MGM she starred in the musicals *Du Barry Was a Lady* (1943); *Best Foot Forward* (1943), for which she played herself; *Meet the People* (1944); and *Ziegfeld Follies* (1946), in which she memorably cracked a whip to tame a pack of exotic catwomen in the musical number "Here's to the Girls." Ball also supported Spencer Tracy and Katharine Hepburn in the comedy *Without Love* (1945). Ball's title prior to *Two Smart People* had been as the film noir *The Dark Corner* (1946), on loan-out to 20th Century–Fox. After leaving MGM, she would freelance in film, and her starring role in the 1948 radio comedy show *My Favorite Husband* led to CBS television asking her to repeat the part of a scatterbrained wife in her own sitcom. Ball would find her greatest fame with *I Love Lucy*, a series she owned the rights to and held creative control over, and which reportedly made her the richest woman in television.

Gruff, masculine John Hodiak had signed with MGM in 1942, and after a bit part in the Maisie series homefront comedy *Swing Shift Maisie* (1943), he graduated to supporting roles in the "B" political comedy drama *A Stranger in Town* (1943) and the musical *I Dood It* (1943). He was cast as the lead in Alfred Hitchcock's World War II sea drama *Lifeboat* (1944), made for 20th Century–Fox. After another Maisie series comedy, *Maisie Goes to Reno* (1944), he continued playing leading roles in the domestic drama *Marriage Is a Private Affair* (1944), and (on loan-out to Fox) the homefront comedy drama *Sunday Dinner for a Soldier* (1944) and the World War II drama *A Bell for Adano* (1945). Hodiak returned to MGM for the historical musical *The Harvey Girls* (1946) before making *Two Smart People*.

He would continue at MGM, supporting the leading men that had returned from serving in World War II and playing leads himself in some films, which included the crime melodrama *The Arnelo Affair* (1947), the World War II drama *Battleground* (1949), the western *Ambush* (1950), the crime romance *A Lady Without Passport* (1950), the drama *Night into Morning* (1951), and the newspaper drama *The Sellout* (1952). After leaving when his contract expired, Hodiak played leading roles in independent and Columbia Pictures titles, and even returned to MGM for a supporting role in the legal drama *Trial* (1955). This last film was released in the same month as his premature death at the age of forty-one. A heart problem had made Hodiak unfit to serve in World War II (simultaneously giving him the opportunity to inherit those roles that MGM's roster of serving leading men had abandoned), but it was this same problem that would resurface to kill him.

Character Bob Simms' combination of tough guy earnestness and duplicity was a mark of Lloyd Nolan, who positioned himself on either side of the law with ease, playing gangsters, cops and detectives. He had started his career at Warner Bros. in 1935; and after a stint at Columbia Pictures, where he scored some "B" leads, he settled at Paramount, where he played the lead in the "A" gangster romance *King of Gamblers* (1937) and supporting roles in other "A" titles. Nolan played the lead in "B"s like the crime dramas *The Tip-Off Girls* (1938), *Hunted Men* (1938), *Prison Farm* (1938) and *King of Alcatraz* (1938), and starred in the "A" *Ambush* (1939), the musical *St. Louis Blues* (1939), and the political melodrama *The Magnificent Fraud* (1939). He scored a leading role for 20th Century–Fox's "B" legal mystery *The Man Who Wouldn't Talk* (1940), and followed it with leads in the police comedy drama *Pier 13* (1940), the aviation drama *Charter Pilot* (1940), Republic's "B" gangster drama *Gangs of Chicago* (1940), the newspaper drama *Behind the News* (1940), and Universal's "B" mystery *Mr. Dynamite* (1941).

The crime comedy *The Golden Fleecing* (1940) was his first role at MGM, though a supporting one. Nolan's lead in Fox's detective comedy drama *Michael Shayne: Private Detective* (1940) would turn into a recurring role for him, resulting in six other titles within two years. In one of them, *The Man Who Wouldn't Die* (1942), he would even sing two songs. In the meantime, Nolan returned as the lead for Paramount's "B" gangster comedy *Buy Me That Town* (1941), Warner's "B" drama *Steel Against the Sky* (1941), Fox's "A" baseball comedy *It Happened in Flatbush* (1942) and the World War II island drama *Manila Calling* (1942). He returned to MGM as the lead in the "B" western *Apache Trail* (1942) and took the lead in Fox's World War II drama *Guadalcanal Diary* (1943). His film immediately prior to *Two Smart People* had been Fox's spy drama *The House on 92nd Street* (1945).

After *Two Smart People*, Nolan supported in MGM's film noir *Lady in the Lake* (1947), and took the lead in the Lassie title *The Sun Comes Up* (1949) and the independent youth drama *Bad Boy* (1949). Nolan supported Lucille Ball again in RKO's football drama *Easy Living* (1949). He won the 1956 Best Actor Emmy for playing Capt. Queeg in the *Ford Star Jubilee* television broadcast of "The Caine Mutiny Court-Martial," the role Humphrey Bogart had played in the legal drama *The Caine Mutiny* (1954). Nolan would get his own crime drama television series, *Special Agent 7*, which was broadcast in 1958, and though his leading man days had ended, he enjoyed late career success supporting Diahann Carroll in her television series *Julia* from 1968 to 1971.

Release

November 1946, with the taglines, "Adult: Heartbeats and Gunplay! A Thrill Romance!" and, "Romance and danger at the Mardi Gras!"

Reviews

"A flippantly-treated melodrama.... Dassin's direction often fumbles what could have been bright situations."—*Variety*, June 4, 1946

"Except for a colorful and lively series of Mardi Gras sequences in New Orleans introduced quite late in the picture, [this is an] otherwise dreadfully boring hodgepodge.... The principals are painfully defeated by the script at almost every turn ... also suffers from a lack of competent direction."—*The New York Times*, February 15, 1947

"A real dog."—Lucille Ball, *Love, Lucy*

"Neither comedy nor drama, this film only succeeds if you're a diehard fan who can suspend disbelief in the mundane plot twists."—Michael Karol, *Lucy A to Z: The Lucille Ball Encyclopedia*

"A much-maligned film, which is far from deserving its poor reputation ... direction is both stylish and polished ... the acting engrossing."—George Aachen, *Memorable Films of the Forties*

•••

Brute Force (1947)

Universal International/Mark Hellinger Productions, Inc.

Credits: Director: Jules Dassin; Producer: Mark Hellinger; Associate Producer: Jules Buck; Screenplay: Richard Brooks, from a story by Robert Patterson; Photography: William Daniels; Special Photography: David S. Horsley; Editor: Edward Curtiss; Music: Miklos Rozsa; Art Direction: Bernard Herzbrun, John F. DeCuir; Sound: Charles Felstead, Robert Pritchard; Technical Advisor: Jacques Gordon; Set Decoration: Russell A. Gausman, Charles Wyrick; Gowns: Rosemary Odell; Hair: Carmen Dirigo; Makeup: Bud Westmore. B&W, 98 minutes. Filmed February to April 1947. Background footage shot at the Sacramento River in Northern California.

Cast: Burt Lancaster (Joe Collins); Hume Cronyn (Capt. Munsey); Charles Bickford (Gallagher); Yvonne De Carlo (Gina Ferrara); Ann Blyth (Ruth); Ella Raines (Cora Lister); Anita Colby (Flossie); Sam Levene (Louie Miller); Jeff Corey ("Freshman" Stack); John Hoyt (Spencer); Jack Overman (Kid Coy); Roman Bohnen (Warden A.J. Barnes); Sir Lancelot (Calypso); Vince Barnett (Mugsy); Jay C. Flippen (Hodges); Richard Gaines (McCallum); Frank Puglia (Ferrara); James Bell (Crenshaw); Howard Duff (Robert "Soldier" Becker); Art Smith (Dr. Walters); Whit Bissell (Tom Lister). Uncredited: Bobby Barber (Jack); Guy Beach (Convict Foreman); Ralph Brooks (Convict); Paul Bryar (Harry); Howland Chamberlain (Joe's Lawyer); Eddy Chandler (Chappie); Edmund Cobb (Bradley); Gino Corrado (Italian Father); William Cozzo, Rex Dale, Billy Wayne (Prisoners); Virginia Farmer (Sadie); Al Ferguson, Howard M. Mitchell, Jerry Salvail, Peter Virgo (Guards); Alex Frazer (Chaplain); Chuck Hamilton, Frank O'Connor (Prison Guards); John Harmon (Roberts); Herbert Haywood (Chef); Al Hill, Will Lee, Larry McGrath (Convicts in Chow Line); Lee Kendall (Shorty); Rex Lease (Hearse Driver); Jack S. Lee (Sergeant); Kenneth MacDonald (Cell Check Guard); Hal Malone (Young Inmate); Frank Marlowe (Prisoner); Francis McDonald (Regan); Don McGill (Max); Charles McGraw (Andy); Edmond O'Brien (Inmate); William H. O'Brien (Convict); Blanche Obronska (Young Girl); James O'Rear (Wilson); Kenneth Patterson (Bronski); Charles Perry (Prisoner in Yard); Carl Rhodes (Strella); Sam Rizhallah (Convict Son); Wally Rose (Peary); Gene Roth (Hoffman); Ruth Sanderson (Miss Lawrence); Tom Steele (Tom); Glenn Strange (Tompkins); Ray Teal (Jackson); Kippee Valez (Visitor); Dale Van Sickel, Bud Wolfe (Guards in Machine Shop); Crane Whitley (Armed Guard in Drainpipe); Harry Wilson (Tyrone).

VHS/DVD: DVD released by Image Entertainment July 6, 1999. Criterion Collection edition released April 17, 2007.

Synopsis

Joe Collins is released from solitary confinement (there for carrying a shiv that was planted on him) and sent back into the Westgate Penitentiary cell R-17 that he shares with five other men. The inmates help Joe murder fellow inmate Wilson, who is the stoolpigeon of Captain Munsey, by forcing him into the machine shop die stamper. After Tom Lister refuses to be Munsey's new informer, Munsey lies to Tom that his wife Cora is divorcing him, and Tom hangs himself. After the Warden revokes all privileges, Joe plans an escape with his cellmates through the drainpipe where they are assigned to work. The editor of the Westgate News, Gallagher, joins the group of escapees after his upcoming parole hearing is cancelled.

Dr. Walters treats Louie, who has been beaten by Munsey, and tells Joe that Munsey has learned of the escape plan via an informer. Joe believes the informer is Freshman and ties him to the front of the handcar that the inmates use in their escape. Freshman is shot by the waiting guards, and a riot ensues in the prison courtyard when the announcement is made that Munsey has been named the new warden. Joe is also shot but manages to climb up to the observation tower and release the gate lever, although Gallagher fails to drive a truck through the gate. Before Joe dies, he fights with Munsey and throws him off the tower, where Munsey is killed by the mob below. The escape by the other inmates is foiled by guards armed with tear gas. Afterwards, Dr. Walters wonders why the men attempted such a foolish endeavor, saying, "Nobody escapes. Nobody ever really escapes."

Notes

A rather straightforward prison drama with the fatalism of film noir, this film lacks some of the visual invention of Dassin's previous efforts, although he does utilize many long takes in scenes. Given that matters here are of a more serious nature here, it is not a surprise that Dassin's gift for comedy is hardly utilized; while the humorless screenplay allows for multiple expressions of violence, including two set pieces. The treatment features the director's favored themes of duplicity, deceit and betrayal, which were explored in his previous titles, as well as the suggestion of misogyny. Perhaps the most interesting character, played by Hume Cronyn in his second outing with the director, is the Nietzsche-styled superman prison captain, who is presented as a Hitler-ite figure. However, Dassin again falters in his use of music, since the score (in which Rozsa repeats cues from his famous score for *Double Indemnity*) tends to overwhelm the material, particularly in flashbacks, turning memory into melodramatic hokum.

The film begins with rain on the prison under the opening credits, rain being a common film noir motif; while the fateful rhythmic pulsing of the tower light is equated with the film noir flashing neon from a sign outside a hotel. Other film noir motifs seen in the film are shadowy lighting, the black hearse that carries out the corpse of Frank McLain in the film's opening scene, and the use of clocks to reinforce the grim determinism and existential despair. The six men in cell R-17 are introduced via a roll call, though the treatment avoids claustrophobia, in spite of six men sharing one cell, in the size of the prison and the use of flashbacks as a standard form of "opening out" a limited environment.

These flashbacks recall producer Hellinger's journalistic vignettes about the foibles of life, which apparently Dassin objected to using but which the producer insisted on. The fact that the men are named in the role call, as opposed to being identified by their inmate numbers (as in other prison films), is an attempt to humanize and personalize them, and make them the narrative's protagonists. The cellmates as protagonists stand in counterpoint to the narrative's authority figures as thematic antagonists—the weak-willed warden, the sardonic alcoholic doctor, and the hypocritical brutal captain of the guard.

The singing of Calypso as a kind of Greek chorus commenting on the action is an arch device, aligned with film noir narrative, that is thankfully dropped for the bulk of the narrative (though it returns for the ending).

Munsey's power, and the fear of it, is expressed by the reaction he receives when he enters the mess hall, with the crowd going silent. Cronyn's comparative shortness is used to emphasize Munsey's Napoleonic complex, with his stopping a guard from striking Tom (who walks into him) only later explained by Munsey's attempt to make Tom another informer. Munsey's hypocritical duplicity is also apparent in the way he pats inmates on the shoulder as he works the hall. It is interesting that at one point he shrugs off his stoolpigeon—perhaps because he has no further use for him. This can be interpreted by Munsey not wanting to be seen talking to Wilson, since it makes their collusion apparent, and perhaps (as with Wilson's ultimate demise) explains why Munsey calls Wilson careless.

The scene in which McCallum badgers the warden about his liberal treatment of the

French movie card for *Brute Force* (1947).

inmates ends with Dassin filming the Warden with a wide-angle lens. The warden stands alone and fearful as he tells Dr. Walters, "I've been warden here for such a long time I wouldn't know where to go ... what to do." His ineffectual disempowerment prefigures losing his job later in the narrative.

The murder of Wilson is prefigured by the inmates hammering and a riot that is created as a distraction. The use of blowtorches to threaten Wilson offers a horror movie sensibility, with the flames prefiguring those around Munsey in the tower at the climax. Although Wilson walking backwards to be crushed in the steam hammer is perhaps unbelievable, the powerful silence after his death redeems it.

Joe has an exchange with Gallagher, which presents their comparative attitudes toward prison life:

> JOE: I don't care about everybody else.
> GALLAGHER: That's cemetery talk.
> JOE: Why not. We're buried, ain't we? Only thing is we ain't dead.

The idea of Gallagher being the top dog of the prison inmates is efficiently expressed in the way he takes a cigarette from inside Joe's shirt without asking—and without Joe reacting. Gallagher displays his cynicism regarding Joe's pipedream of escape when he comments, "It's been all set every Tuesday for twelve years, and twelve years from now it'll still be next Tuesday."

The treatment's use of flashback to convey the characters' backstories (another film noir motif) begins with that of Spencer, who gazes at the calendar on the wall of the cell, which features a dark-haired mysterious woman (the portrait is said to have been a composite picture of Ann Blyth, Yvonne De Carlo and Ella Raines painted by John Decker), a device Dassin will repeat for each flashback. In this flashback, Dassin employs narration and silent action in what is perhaps the best of the four in the screenplay, even though he uses cigarette smoke to convey Flossie's presence before a pan reveals her standing there, a device he used previously in *Reunion in France* and *Two Smart People*. Though Flossie may be a femme fatale, Spencer is equally duplicitous (by playing at an illegal casino), and her betrayal of him is shown as both shocking and funny. This first flashback also presents a man who takes the rap for a woman, a film noir motif (and one that will be repeated). This theme also presents the inmates as victims of circumstances rather than psychotic aggressors (like Munsey), and therefore reinforces the idea that they are undeserving of their imprisonment and deserving of escape.

Tom looking at the woman on the calendar introduces *his* flashback, with Dassin dissolving from the painting of the woman to a close-up of Ella Raines, so that the parallel is made in both visual and literary terms. This memory is presented via dialogue that tells how Tom stole money to buy a mink coat for his wife Cora in order to "save their marriage." Cora's refusal to part with the coat, even after she learns it has come from stolen money, presents her as a kind of femme fatale, so again the man takes the rap for a woman's avarice. Dassin provides the comic touch of the couple reacting in shock to a knock at their door to conclude the flashback, a sound that is matched by the guards clanging on Spencer's cell door to announce Munsey's entrance.

The subsequent scene is the first presentation of Munsey's duplicity, since we do not know whether he is lying about withholding Cora's letters to Spencer or not. The fact the he would read the letters shows Munsey's disregard for privacy, even if it is prison policy (which it may well be, since Munsey speaks of having to censor mail). However, we can tell that Munsey wants to manipulate the inmate, and we get a sense of his possible homosexuality in his misogynous attitude towards Cora (and women in general).

Although we don't know why the door to his cell is opened, or by whom, Dassin spares us the sight of the hanged Tom by showing the hanging via a shadow (much as he had spared us the sight of Wilson being crushed).

A rare humorous exchange occurs between Louie Miller, who works for the *Westgate News*, and Mugsy, who works in the kitchen:

> LOUIE: I just got a pip of an assignment. I gotta write a story provin' how good the chow is round here.
> MUGSY: *Time* magazine will make you Man of the Year.

The kitchen scene offers another mild laugh when Louie asks Hodges to smell a soup being cooked, and says, "Now you know what happened to Rin Tin Tin."

Joe's plan to escape can be viewed as a duplicitous action on behalf of the inmates. However, given the barbaric conditions under which they live, we don't consider them to be as duplicitous as Munsey.

The woman on the calendar is again employed to introduce the third flashback, that of Soldier, which uses dialogue and Miklos Rozsa's sentimental music score. This flashback reads as perhaps the worst, due to the poor playing of the actors, although the idea of a daughter shooting her own father during wartime is an interesting one. And again the man takes the rap for it.

Dassin dissolves from Joe's line "There are ears all over this drum, and they all belong to one guy" to a shot of Munsey as he listens to the warden and Dr. Walters. Munsey's confrontation with the doctor allows us to see Munsey's delusional self. He tells the doctor that he walks alone and unarmed among the inmates, who respect him, but we have already seen how he walks among them while accompanied by a Gestapo-type guard. Dr. Walters says to Munsey, "Where else would you find so many helpless flies to stick pins into," and receives a slap from Munsey for it, prefiguring Munsey's beating of Louie. The slap is also evidence of Munsey's opportunistic sadism, since the doctor is drunk. Munsey's remark about how he sees himself as being superior to other men because of his cleverness and imagination is underscored by the action of Munsey cleaning up the Warden's desk before he sits in the warden's chair, reveal both Munsey's control-freak nature and envious appropriation. Dr. Walters accuses Munsey of behaving worse than the inmates, saying, "Not cleverness. Not imagination. Just force. Brute force that makes leaders and destroys them." While the lines reference the film's title, it also prefigures Munsey's demise.

The screenplay introduces the fourth and final flashback after Joe wakes from a nightmare, again uses the woman on the calendar to let us enter his memory. Like the other men, Joe has committed a crime to benefit a woman, though the woman's "sickness" of being in a wheelchair makes her more a pathetic figure than a femme fatale. The relationship between these two recalls that between Humphrey Bogart's Roy "Mad Dog" Earle and Joan Leslie's lame Velma in *High Sierra*. As Ruth, Ann Blyth brings some pathos to her performance, although Lancaster's pained, even embarrassed, stoicism works against the romantic ambition of his lines. (Here the actor lacks the grinning self-confidence of his forthcoming roles.) It is telling that it is Joe who takes the calendar with him when he leaves the cell on the day of the attempted escape, but it's disappointing that we don't get flashback backstories for the two other men of the cell, Coy and Freshman. The latter would have been most interesting, since he is thought to have betrayed the others at the film's climax.

A guard uses his black club to come between Louie and the mechanic Andy in a rather Freudian sexual way. Andy and Louie's fake laughter at the guard's stupid joke arises from relief that they have not been caught hiding the Molotov cocktails to be used during the escape.

The scene of Munsey in his office is perhaps the most interesting in the film, even better than the movie's celebrated climax. Munsey's smug self-portrait on the wall and his playing of Wagner (sources differ as to what the music is—some say the "Overture" from *Tannhäuser*, others "Liebestod" from *Tristan und Isolde*) further suggests him as a Hitlerite figure, with the beautiful music used to counterpoint the ugliness of his beating of Louie. Munsey's slap of Louie, and then strapping Louie into a chair to make him helpless and vulnerable, continue his dominance, and Munsey pulling the window shades down before he attacks is a nice ominous touch. Dassin doesn't show us the beating, keeping it off-screen (as he does with the killings of Wilson and Tom). Rather he shows the guard and the warden sitting outside the office, listening to the beating. The prim flower bed that Dassin shows in a cut-away to cover Louie's beating can be seen as a suggestion of Munsey's homosexuality, as can the long rifle barrel that Munsey was lovingly cleaning when Louie was brought in.

One can also infer that Louie is Jewish (from Sam Levene's casting) and interpret

Captain Munsey (Hume Cronyn) applies some *Brute Force* (1947) in an attempt to obtain information from prisoner Louie Miller (Sam Levene) as guard Jackson (Ray Teal) looks on.

Munsey's attack upon him as of a Nazi upon a Jew as much as an expression of Munsey as a fascist figure. Munsey is positioned as the bad apple of the prison officers. All the violence we see in the narrative comes from him, directly or indirectly, and the only violence the inmates express towards each other (the murder of Wilson and the setting up of Freshman to be killed) also springs from Munsey's actions. (This notion of the moral civility of the inmates extends to their applauding in thanks after a film screening at the prison.) The beating of Louie would seem futile (and thus wholly sadistic) since Munsey already knows about the escape plan; but Louie's refusal to inform prefigures the refusal of accused subversives to name names to HUAC. It is interesting that Munsey's attack should be upon a man who has a small frame like himself; but also revealing is the fact that Munsey is dressed in a singlet for the scene, and sexualizes the beating with a phallic-shaped rubber hose into a homoerotic rape.

The drainpipe work site is the representation of the lower depths—a filthy and miserable underworld populated by banished individuals who must suffer performing a pointless task in the way prisoners in German concentration camps were made to perform pointless tasks so that they would die of exhaustion.

Dr. Walters informing Joe about Louie's beating shows his momentary duplicity, although his allegiance to the inmates is not surprising given his contempt for Munsey. However, the important plot point that this act makes is that Munsey wants the escape attempt to happen because it will allow him to assume command of the prison.

Joe identifies Munsey's informer by asking each of the inmates what position he wants to take during the escape in which the Freshman is caught out because he asks to go last, while all the others leave it up to Joe. There is an ambiguity about this assumption of Freshman's guilt, since nothing we have previously heard Freshman say suggests that he is a betraying character, and also because we do not know what he could hope to gain by the betrayal. Joe's realization is expressed by Dassin's close-up of Lancaster's face, perhaps the only close-up provided in the entire film. Dassin cuts away from Joe as he advances on Freshman, delaying the act of revenge by re-focusing on the warden being forced to resign by the state bureaucrat McCallum. The warden's loudspeaker announcement of his resignation, and the assumption of Munsey, is met by a collective moan by the inmate mob in the courtyard. Their chant of "Yarrrgh" to Munsey standing in the watchtower recalls the "Sieg Heil" of Nazis to Hitler seen in news footage of Nuremburg rallies (though here it is anything but supportive).

The revenge upon Freshman—being tied to the front of the handcar so that he is the first to emerge from the drainpipe rather than the last—is a resonant and horrifying image, more powerful than the off-screen deaths of Wilson and Tom, and an ironic Judas-as-Christ on the crucifix metaphor. Coy's bloodied face after being shot adds gore to the violence, while Gallagher's escape attempt in the crashed truck that blocks the gate from opening—an exit that Joe sacrificed everything to open—adds a touch of irony. The pain of the escape plan failing is assuaged by the murder of Munsey, who is seen surrounded by flames in the observation tower as he mercilessly machine guns anyone he can in the courtyard with the phallic weapon. While Joe punching Munsey to knock him out is only half-seen, Joe lifting the unconscious Munsey over his head to throw him down to the courtyard mob is just as horrifying—and resonant—as the death of Freshman, with Joe recalling Frankenstein's Monster (*Frankenstein* being a Universal film title). What could only have made the image more gruesome was if Munsey had been conscious and resisting. We don't know if it is the fall or the mob setting upon him that kills Munsey, but their hunger to destroy not only the person who was machine-gunning them but also the man whose past sadism bedeviled their lives is both gothic and understandable.

The aftermath of the escape attempt as a coda is symbolized by Dassin's pan over the prison cells, where we see the miserable faces of inmates that recall the stunned look of German concentration camp survivors in newsreel footage. We see that R17 is now empty, so that Calypso's singing and Dr. Walters' final comment are unnecessary moralizing; we know that whenever men are in a desperate situation they will resist and try to escape it. Dr. Walters walking toward the camera inside Calypso's cell, as if he is now an inmate, is effective, and the film's last shot of what is a miniature model of Westgate, seen in long shot seen from across the river, recalls real-life island prisons like Alcatraz as much as it makes apparent the gap between prison and normal society.

In his article in *Films & Filming*, Gordon Gow calls *Brute Force* "a contrast to the norm ... shock cinema." In *Film Criticism*, Andrew Horton says, "More than another prison break film.... [*Brute Force*] still commands attention ... because of the unsentimental honesty with which Dassin portrayed the inmates, their pasts, and the violence which was so much a part of their lives." In an interview on the DVD of *Brute Force*, Paul Mason, a criminologist specializing in media representation of prison at Cardiff University in Wales, comments that *Brute Force* was a reemergence of the classic prison film genre for the 1940s. The 1930s had seen titles like *I Am a Fugitive from a Chain Gang* (1932), *Each Dawn I Die* (1939), *Numbered Men* (1930), and *Invisible Stripes* (1939), but the genre had been co-opted into prisoner-of-war films during World War II. Like the prison films of the 1930s, which used prison as an allegory for ordinary people oppressed by the political system during the Great Depression, *Brute Force*, claims Mason, is an allegory for the bigger problems in society. He goes on to say that the treatment's presentation of prison is a plea for reform, since the environment shapes and changes inmates only for the worse. The men, like Gallagher, who hope that their good behavior can be rewarded by parole are disappointed, and this shows that prison as a place for rehabilitation is a myth. The film claims that prison provides a reversal of fortune for all associated with it—inmates *and* those who watch over them.

In his interview with Patrick McGilligan and Paul Buhle in their book *Tender Comrades*, Dassin dismisses the film as a "really dumb picture. I remember saying, but all these prisoners are such nice sweet guys—they're all so lovely—what are they doing in jail! Hellinger says we have to get women into the story. Oy! And yet Hellinger let me begin to learn." In his *Films & Filming* article, "Style and Instinct," Gordon Gow writes of Lancaster's invaluable "unstressed ease of mobility," and that the film "provoked in many a resistance, perhaps a self-protective reaction, but today it is noted with respect by film historians."

In Kate Burford's book *Burt Lancaster: An American Life*, she claims that the screenplay was based on an article written by a former convict; and Dassin is quoted as saying that the film was a welcome exercise in "making a film about people locked in at a time when I had achieved liberation" (from a "slave contract" at MGM). Burford also quotes Dassin saying of Lancaster, "He was a gay marvelous boy," and reports that the two men made a daily entrance onto the set with the diminutive director perched on the star's shoulders. Burford also quotes Yvonne De Carlo, who claims she had an affair with the recently married Lancaster during filming. In her book *Femme Noir: Bad Girls of Film*, however, Karen Burroughs Hannsberry claims rather that De Carlo became involved with Howard Duff; and although they became engaged to be married, De Carlo soon broke it off. The film was only Lancaster's second, his debut being in the Mark Hellinger production *The Killers* (1946).

Though it is not known how Dassin and Mark Hellinger met, an article on the TCM website claims that Hellinger had wanted to make a prison movie for ten years, which suggests that he was the instigating party. Hellinger was famous as a syndicated Broadway columnist for *The New York Daily News*, and later *The New York Daily Mirror*, who had been brought to Hollywood by Warner Bros. (allegedly to provide authenticity to their gangster titles). Previous to this, the play he had co-written, *Night Court*, was made into a film at MGM in 1932, and he would go on to write the screenplay for Warners' Kay Francis melodrama *Comet Over Broadway* (1938).

Hellinger became an associate producer in 1939, and worked on various "B"s, including the newspaper crime drama *The Adventures of Jane Arden* (1939), the aviation drama *Woman in the Wind* (1939), the football comedy *The Cowboy's Quarterback* (1939), the boxing comedy *Kid Nightingale* (1939), and the spy drama *British Intelligence* (1940). Hellinger was also the uncredited producer of the "A" teenage gangster drama *Hell's Kitchen* (1939). His first credited full-fledged producing job was on the comedy drama *It All Came True* (1940), though he continued as associate producer on the drama *Torrid Zone* (1940), the gangster drama *Brother Orchid* (1940), the drama *They Drive by Night* (1940), the gangster drama *High Sierra* (1941, on which he had supposedly been responsible for the casting of Humphrey Bogart), the newspaper romantic comedy *Affectionately Yours* (1941), and the drama *Manpower* (1941).

Hellinger moved briefly to 20th Century-Fox to produce the college football comedy *Rise and Shine* (1941) and the drama *Moontide* (1942) before returning to Warners to produce the show business variety *Thank Your Lucky Stars* (1943), the drama *Between Two Worlds* (1944), the homefront comedy *The Doughgirls* (1944), the fantasy comedy *The Horn Blows at Midnight* (1945), and the suspense drama *The Two Mrs. Carrolls* (1947 but filmed in 1945). However, he left Warners when he was given the opportunity to become an independent producer at Universal Pictures, where he made the crime drama *The Killers* (1946) and the postwar life melodrama *Swell Guy* (1946), which featured Ann Blyth. Hellinger would go on to produce Dassin's next title as well, *The Naked City* (1948).

Associate producer Jules Buck had been an assistant to Hellinger on *The Killers*. *Brute Force* was his first producing position, and he would go on to be the associate producer of the crime drama *The Naked City*.

Since his last title with Dassin, *A Letter for Evie*, Hume Cronyn had played supporting roles in three films for MGM: the religious drama *The Green Years* (1946), the crime romance *The Postman Always Rings Twice* (1946), and the World War II drama *The Beginning or the End* (1947). He writes in his autobiography about *Brute Force* and the climactic fight between Joe and Munsey:

> Burt, who had at one time been a circus acrobat, was in magnificent physical condition and weighed about two hundred pounds. He could in reality have picked me up with one hand and wrung me out like a washrag. As a concession to the casting and the totally unbelievable match, it was agreed that before the struggle began, Burt's character should be shot and wounded. Even so, Julie [Dassin] staged one of the most murderously filthy fights ever photographed, so filled with kicks to the groin, eye gouging [a still exists of Munsey gouging Joe's eye] and karate chops that when the scene was cut together, it was considered altogether too violent for the public and portions of it were eliminated.

Cronyn tells how Dassin wanted him to do the fall after Lancaster had hurled him over the parapet of the burning tower, rather than use a stunt double. This meant a free-fall of about twenty feet, down to a specially built platform piled with mattresses and surrounded by padded railings to stop him bouncing. The stunt was done in one take, filmed by multiple cameras. Cronyn landed "on his butt, climbed down from the scaffolding and went home." The actor admits that he wanted to do it because he saw it as *his* part and he wanted to play all of it, rather than hand part of it over to a stuntman. Cronyn also attributes his decision to "sheer vanity, since I was young, in good physical shape, athletic and cocky."

Cronyn also writes about the part of Munsey under the shorthand heading "Devil and Angel," since he believes, "When playing a devil, look for the angel in him." To counterpoint the "primary colors" of Munsey, he made him soft-spoken, a lover of classical music, and inoffensive in demeanor. Cronyn comments that he feared that his playing of Munsey's attack on Louie—very calmly and methodically—while the music came from the record player might have produced derisive laughter. The actor tells how for some years he would be followed down the streets by kids who would chant, "Yah, yah, yah, Captain Munsey!" repeating the prisoners' catcalls. Cronyn comments, "In a perverse fashion, it did say something about the impression left by the character." However, after *Brute Force*, he was under real pressure to play every other miserable sadistic character that came along. "If Granny was to be pushed down the stairs in her wheelchair [he turned down the part of Tommy Udo in the 1947 crime drama *Kiss of Death*], or some child raped in the bushes, the script would come to me." Cronyn would avoid the specter of repetition by asking to be released from his MGM contract, and go on to enjoy a long career as a supporting player in films.

Brute Force marked the debut of Howard Duff, Radio's Sam Spade (he played "Soldier" in the film), who would go on to appear in *The Naked City*. In her book *Bad Boys: The Actors of Film Noir*, Karen Burroughs Hannsberry claims that in 1946 Duff had been directed by Dassin in a stage play entitled *Birthday*; however, this information cannot be confirmed in other sources.

The opening credits say the film is also the debut of Art Smith (Dr. Walters) and Whit Bissell (Tom). In the case of Smith, this is incorrect, since he had made his debut with the independent social drama *Native Land* in 1942. While he had appeared uncredited in nine titles, he had been credited for supporting roles in Warner Bros.' World War II drama *Edge of Darkness* (1943) and Columbia Pictures' World War II drama *None Shall Escape* (1944). It is also partly incorrect for Bissell, who had appeared uncredited in nine prior titles, beginning with the Warners historical adventure *The Sea Hawk* (1940). Like Dassin, Art Smith, Jeff Corey, Howland Chamberlain (who would go on to appear uncredited in Dassin's 1949 drama *Thieves Highway*) and Roman Bohnen would all be blacklisted by HUAC, with the news of the blacklist said to have caused the heart attack that killed Bohnen in 1949.

Release

June 30, 1947, with the taglines, "MEN CAGED ON THE INSIDE … driven by the thought of their women on the loose!" "HUMAN DYNAMITE! Told the Raw, Ruthless 'KILLERS' Way!" "Raw! Rough! Ruthless!" "Man hate! Woman love!" and "Mark Hellinger's POWER PACKED PICTURE!"

Reviews

"Dassin's steel-springed direction keeps the whole thing appropriately taut."—*The New York Times*, July 17, 1947

"A showmanly mixture of gangster melodramatics, sociological exposition, and sex."—*Variety*

"A crudely powerful prison picture.... This is the kind of movie that's often called a man's picture; that is, fast, action-packed, pseudo-realistic."—Pauline Kael, *5001 Nights at the Movies*

"A prison movie with a vengeance! ... Hume Cronyn was monstrously effective as the sadistic Wagner-loving prison captain.... The virile direction was by Jules Dassin."—Clive Hirschhorn, *The Universal Story*

"Tingling, hard-bitten prison film with its few clichés punched across solidly."—Leonard Maltin, *1997 Movie & Video Guide*

The Naked City (1948)

[aka *Homicide*]
Universal International/Hellinger Productions

Credits: Director: Jules Dassin; Producer/Narrator: Mark Hellinger; Associate Producer: Jules Buck; Screenplay: Albert Matz, Malvin Wald, from a story by Mr. Wald; Photography: William Daniels; Editor: Paul Weatherwax; Music: Miklos Rozsa, Frank Skinner; Art Direction: John F. DeCuir; Sound: Leslie I. Carey, Vernon W. Kramer; Set Decoration: Russell A. Gausman, Oliver Emert; Gowns: Grace Houston; Hair: Carmen Dirigo; Makeup: Bud Westmore. B&W, 96 minutes. Filmed June to September 1947 on location in New York City.

Song: "Goodbye Johnny Boy" (author unknown), sung throughout the film by Barry Fitzgerald.

Cast: Barry Fitzgerald (Lieutenant Daniel Muldoon); Howard Duff (Frank Niles); Dorothy Hart (Ruth Morrison); Don Taylor (Detective Jimmy Halloran); Frank Conroy (Captain Donohue); Ted De Corsia (Willy Garzah); House Jameson (Dr. Lawrence Stoneman); Anne Sargeant (Mrs. Halloran); Adelaide Klein (Mrs. Batory); Grover Burgess (Mr. Batory); Tom Pedi (Detective Perelli); Enid Markey (Mrs. Edgar Hylton). Uncredited: Jean Adair (Little Old Lady); Celia Adler (Dress Shop Proprietress); Janie Alexander (Little Girl); Joyce Allen, Amelia Romano (Shopgirls); Beverly Bayne (Mrs. Stoneman): Ralph Brooks (Detective); Harris Brown (Harvey); Ralph Bunker (Medical Examiner Hoffman); Walter Burke (Peter Backalis); Alexander Campbell (Policeman): Retta Coleman (Crippled Girl); G. Pat Collins (Charles Meade); Curt Conway (Detective Nick); Russ Conway (Ambulance Doctor); Grace Coppin (Miss Livingston); William Cottrell (Bisbee); Harold Crane; Sarah Cunningham (Nurse); Johnny Dale (Mr. Stillman); Denise Doyle, Maureen Latorella, Judith Suzanne Locker, Diana Pat Marlow, Norma Jane Marlow, Margaret McAndrew, Marsha McClelland, Carole Selvester, Mildred Stronger (Girl Children); Paul Ford (Henry Fowler); Andre D. Foster (Jeweler); Kathleen Freeman (Stout Girl on Elevated Train); Pearl Gaines (Mrs. Hylton's Maid); Earle Gilbert (Banker); Bruce Gordon (Cop at Williamsburg Bridge); Raymond Greenleaf (City Editor); William E. Green; James Gregory (Patrolman Albert Hicks); Chuck Hamilton (Cop); Robert H. Harris (Druggist); Stevie Harris (Billy Halloran); Bern Hoffman, Joseph Karney (Wrestlers); Cavada Humphrey, Blanche Obronska (Mothers); Edwin Jerome, Judson

Laire (Publishers); Reggie Jouvain, Charles Latorella, John Joseph Mulligan, Clifford Sales (Boy Children); Nicholas Joy (Mr. McCormick); Kermit Kegley (Qualen); Albert Kelley (Newsboy); David Kerman, George Sherwood, Lee Shumway, Victor Zimmerman (Patrolmen); Joe Kerr (Ned Harvey); Perc Launders (Police Photographer); Marion Leeds (Nurse); George Lynn (Det. Fredericks); John Marley (Managing Editor); John McQuade (Detective Dace Constantino); Carl Milletaire (Young Man); Virginia Mullen (Martha Swenson); Arthur O'Connell (Sgt. Shaeffer); David Opatoshu (Sgt. Dave Miller); Nehemiah Persoff (Smiling Man Departing Subway); Molly Picon (Soda-Selling Shopkeeper); John Randolph (Police Dispatcher); Anthony Rivers (Ed Garzah); Richard W. Shankland (Blind Man); Gregg Sherwood; Ralph Simone (Old Gentleman); Hester Sondergaard (Miss Owens); Elliott Sullivan (Wrestler's Trainer); Charles P. Thompson (Ticket Taker); Mervin Williams (Records Clerk).

VHS/DVD: DVD released by Image Entertainment on June 29, 1999. Criterion Collection DVD released on March 20, 2007.

Synopsis

Former dress model and playgirl Jean Dexter is killed by Willie Garzah and Peter Backalis in her bathtub. When Backalis gets drunk after the murder, Willie strikes him unconscious and drops his body into the East River to drown. Homicide Lieutenant Daniel Muldoon is assigned to investigate Jean's death, which a medical examination

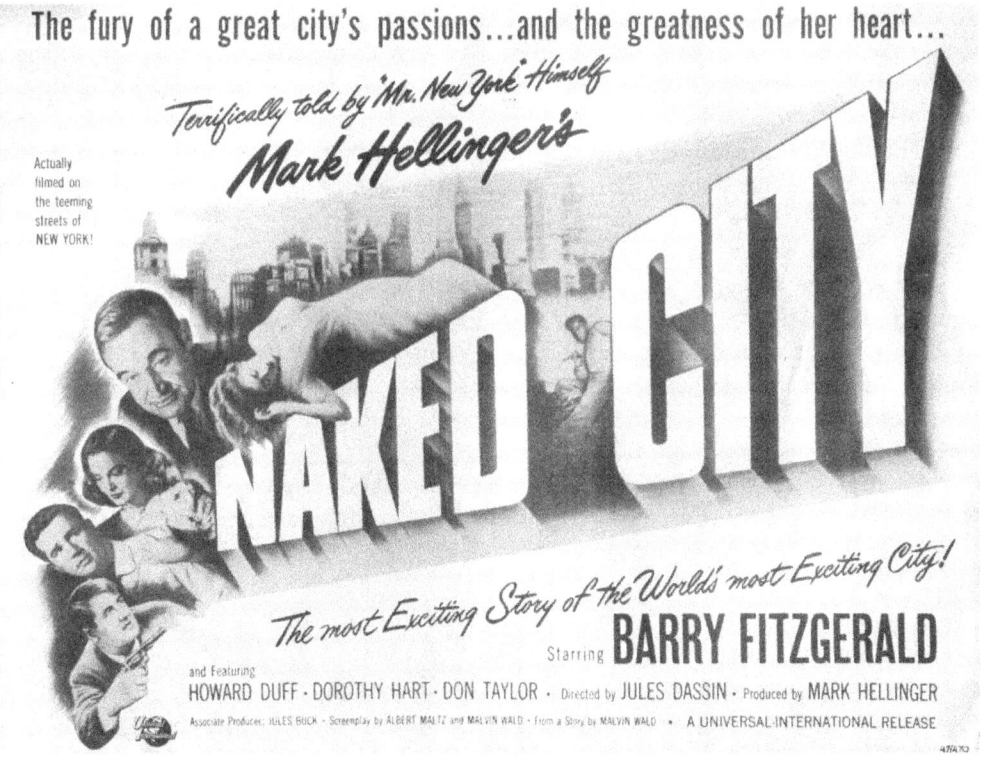

Poster for *The Naked City* (1948).

has deemed murder. The investigation questions Jean's physician, Lawrence Stoneman; model Ruth Morrison; and her ex-boyfriend Frank Niles, who is now engaged to Ruth. It is learned that Frank has pawned a gold cigarette case stolen from Dr. Stoneman and purchased a one-way ticket to Mexico. Ruth's engagement ring is also discovered to have been stolen, and they arrive at Frank's apartment to save him from being murdered by Willie.

Frank is arrested for robbery, and rookie detective Jimmy Halloran connects the body of Backalis to Jean's murder to a stolen jewelry operation being run by Jean, Stoneman and Frank, with Willie and Peter as the muscle. Lieutenant Muldoon learns about the scam from Stoneman, who was in love with Jean and helped her and Frank rob his society friends. Frank admits that Willie killed Jean and Backalis, but when Jimmy attempts to arrest him by himself, he is knocked unconscious. When he comes to, Jimmy calls in Muldoon, and they chase Willie through the streets. Just when it appears that he has gotten away, Willie draws attention to himself when he shoots a blind man's guide dog. Willie is shot by police and falls to his death from the top of the Williamsburg Bridge.

Notes

This crime drama, filmed on location, mixes documentary footage of daily life in New York City with an intermittent and contrived narration by producer Mark Hellinger (who, sadly, will be dead by the time the film is released). The police procedural narrative combines mystery and character revelation. While the murder investigation prefigures the documentary style common to television, Dassin provides some intensity in his character scenes and includes occasional humor. The music score continues the director's inexplicable fondness for unnecessary aural melodrama, but it does add tension to the climactic six-minute chase.

The film continues Dassin's favored theme of duplicity (this time backgrounded by murder), with the characters of Jean, Frank, and Willie offering plenty of moral ambiguity. Although we never see her conscious (so we cannot directly observe her behavior), we are told that Jean used men to elevate her social position, and she is described by the falsely confessing grocery boy as "immoral" and "beautiful, with no soul." She also recalls the femme fatales of the flashbacks in *Brute Force*—women who were responsible, either directly or indirectly, for men being put in prison. When we first see her as the victim of the murder, Jean inspires immediate audience empathy, which lessens as the narrative reveals her nature. Jean's notoriety as the bathtub murder victim in the tabloid headlines becomes a sad irony on her ambition.

Frank is a compulsive liar who betrays his fiancée and falsely wears a veteran's button, but he will save Dr. Stoneman from suicide. Willie murders Jean and Peter, and attempts to murder Frank, but he is strangely sympathetic when he becomes a hunted man at the film's climax.

The film begins with a daytime aerial traveling shot—a bird's eye view of the city's beautiful skyline. This establishes New York as the star of the picture, since the shot is not taken from any character's point of view. Hellinger's comment that the movie will be different from other films because it was photographed entirely on location (a claim reiterated by Dassin in his *Cine-Parade* interview on the DVD of *Night and the City*) comes into question because not only could some of the interiors have been recreated on a sound stage, the car-driving scenes and some other shots suggest that projected footage was used. Day turns to night (for the film to become film noir) as we hear the interior monologues of various people (the on-location shooting appears to have required some dubbing), although the majority of the treatment will occur in daytime.

Dassin's camera outside the apartment window of Jean shows us what appears to be a struggle inside, and when Dassin dollies in we see two male figures in shadowy profile with what appears to be Jean's corpse, since she is not struggling. We will only learn later that her inertia is due to her being chloroformed, so that she will not be dead until she drowns in the bathtub. Dassin cuts from the water pouring from Jean's bathtub tap to the water spraying from a street-cleaning truck the next morning.

The narrative is fragmented, so that the identity of a man being thrown into the East River is not disclosed to be Peter Backalis, and the murderer not shown to be Willie Garzah, until much later. We also don't know that these two men are the same two we saw in Jean's apartment. The fragmentation of the narrative will continue until the plot strands of the police investigating Jean's murder, the search for Philip Henderson (which will turn out to be an alias for Stoneman), and the later search for Willie all come together. The appearances of Willie are particularly intriguing, since we don't know why we are repeatedly being shown him observing the investigation. We see him outside the police station when Frank leaves after being questioned, buying a newspaper to read about the murder he has committed, walking by the East River where Peter's corpse emerges, and running from Frank's apartment building after the fire escape chase into the subway and escape on a train. Interestingly, Willie goes absent from the treatment once he becomes the pursued, since he knows how to hide in the city, and he only reemerges when found by Jimmy.

Willie throwing Peter into the river recalls Munsey being thrown from the tower in *Brute Force*. Willie then spitting into the river at Peter is a perverse touch for the character, and perhaps displays his contempt for Peter's drunkenness, since Willie, like Munsey, is positioned as another Nietchian superman figure. (Munsey's defeat also prefigures the defeat of Willie as a comment on the apparent fascism of the superman.)

An early injection of humor comes with our introduction to Jimmy. When seen by his son kissing his wife goodbye at his middle-class semi-detached house in Astoria, Jimmy responds to his own embarrassment by shaking her hand instead.

The casting of Barry Fitzgerald as Muldoon is a surprise, since his whimsical, eccentric, leprechaun-ish persona would seem to undermine the authority needed by a man in charge of an investigation. This apparent weakness also applies to Jimmy, who we will later see cannot defend himself against Willie's attack. Dassin inserts further humor via Jean's maid, Martha. At one point Muldoon compares hairs found on Jean's bedroom rug to the hair on Martha's head, with the maid's subsequent look of deluded coy romantic interest being funny. Muldoon's comment to Detective Constantino about Ruth gets another laugh: "Lovely young girl, isn't she? Lovely long legs. Keep looking at 'em."

Muldoon's speech in reaction to Frank's web of lies is noteworthy:

> I've been 38 years on the force. I've been a cop on the beat. I've been with the Safe and Loft Squad. I've been for 22 years with the Homicide Squad. But in a life of interrogation and investigation you are probably the biggest and most willing liar I ever met.

The appearance of the deluded Little Old Lady who wears a feather boa and thinks she is still a desirable girl adds more comic relief. Another laugh at the expense of a woman comes with the Stout Girl on Elevated Train, who asks a man near Jimmy if he read about the bathtub murder. The man replies, "I'll say—some figure that dame had." He then wolf whistles, looks at the Stout Girl disapprovingly, and looks away.

The issue of Jimmy being reluctant to beat his son Billy with a strap as punishment for wandering away from their home is interesting since it presents the police detective as weak, in spite of the modern thought that corporal punishment as education is poor parenting. (An argument is made by Dana Polan, film studies professor at New York University, in an interview on the DVD of the film that Jimmy's reluctance stems from his using force on criminals in his work.) Dassin highlights the comedic in the dilemma between Jimmy and his wife, despite the darker subtext of the issue, recalling the director's earlier MGM comedies. This scene and the later short one in which Jimmy is on the telephone at home represent the treatment's few wanderings from the murder investigation narrative.

The scene in which Jean's parents identify her body at the Bellevue Hospital Mortuary meets the expectation of a change in attitude in Jean's mother, Mrs. Batory, who goes from anger at Jean for the scandal her daughter has brought her family to sobbing grief upon seeing her daughter's corpse. However, the following scene, involving a conversation between the Batorys and Muldoon on a pier overlooking the river and the Manhattan Bridge, is upstaged by the sunset.

The crowds in front of Jean's Upper West Side apartment building, where some pose for photographs, are introduced by a shot of a man carrying balloons to highlight the circus mentality, the proletarian appetite for crass sensationalism, and the ghoulish appeal of the murder. Their callousness is reinforced by a joke made in reaction to a comment about Jean being "the bathtub girl": "Why didn't she take showers?"

The scene of Frank's rescue is well-staged by Dassin. In the exciting chase down the fire escape, the lights of the apartments turn on Willie and Jimmy descend, with the tenants appearing from their windows and inadvertently stopping Jimmy from pursuing Willie.

Muldoon saying to Frank, "While you're thinking about a nice story about what didn't happen, suppose you tell us what did," is amusing in light of Frank's earlier duplicity. Ruth's repeated slapping of Frank (almost perverse in its excess), with "You're lying, you're lying!" underlines his duplicity, as does our later view of him in a prison cell.

The Stoneman scene plays out with satisfying tension, and Muldoon counters Stoneman's melodramatic suicide attempt (trying to jump out of the Fifth Avenue Squid Building window) with, "I don't know much about medicine, doctor, [but] I'm pretty sure that's one prescription that never cured anything." This idea of jumping from a great height mirrors Peter being thrown into the river, and will also prefigure Willie's fall at the end.

The half-naked and sweaty Willie exercising and then showing off his body to Jimmy is charged with homoeroticism. This scene too has tension, since we wonder whether Jimmy will be strong enough to fend off Willie's expected attack. A view of the two men in a mirrored reflection presents their mutual duplicity (Jimmy here lies about Peter being alive), and this segues into Willie's attack, where he disarms the detective and uses the illegal "rabbit punch" that knocks Jimmy unconscious. Dassin uses a close-up to show Willie's perverse pleasure at his handiwork. Given that Willie has killed Jean and Peter, one expects that he will kill Jimmy also. Thankfully, he refrains (Willie, considering himself being a smart criminal, knows that killing a policeman will result in a much harsher punishment than killing ordinary citizens like Jean, Peter, and Frank). Jimmy being disarmed and defeated by Willie also undermines the rookie's initiative that he had shown in following the lead to find Willie.

French movie card for *The Naked City* (1948).

The cemetery behind Willie's Lower East Side tenement becomes visual foreshadowing of Willie's death, and Hellinger's advice to Willie as he runs makes the narrator the voice of the audience. Although Willie being stopped by the blind man's dog is a nice touch, the climactic chase is diluted by Muldoon's order not to pursue him up the bridge. This may be considered common sense, since we know Willie will have to come down eventually (because police are on either side of the bridge), but it leaves us with Willie continuing to climb as if still being pursued. Willie's decision to shoot at the police leads to them shooting back, and we presume from his scream when he falls that the shot he has received is not fatal. Of course, given that we have seen a man climb a bridge to its tower, the fall is expected anyway.

The narrative ends with shots detailing the fates of the main characters: Muldoon, Ruth, Frank in prison (recalling Howard Duff's prisoner of *Brute Force*), Jimmy and his wife, and the Batorys. We also see that Jean's murder has become yesterday's news when a street cleaner throws the newspapers that featured her headline story into a trash can. Hellinger's final lines would become the regular sign-off (and enter the language as an indelible catchphrase) for the television crime anthology series inspired by the film, *Naked City*, which was broadcast from 1958 to 1963: "There are 8 million stories in the naked city. This has been one of them."

In his *Cine-Parade* interview on the DVD of *Night and the City*, Dassin says that Hellinger promised him the film would not be re-cut after he had supervised the editing. However, when the director saw it at a gala New York screening, he described it as "hacked apart, mutilated, massacred." Supposedly, either Hellinger or Universal had removed anything that could have been interpreted as "red," meaning of communist sympathy (apparently the word "hunger" had such a connotation), and changed dialogue through over-dubbing. This "red" concern would seem to have come more from Universal than Hellinger. Perhaps because the film was released after the producer's death, Universal had more say in the matter than would otherwise have been expected. In his 2004 LACMA interview, Dassin would blame the studio for the cuts, stating they were made after Hellinger's death. In his article on Dassin in *Film Criticism*, Andrew Horton states he interviewed the director in August 1977, and describes two of the "offending" scenes cut from the film: At a real hotel in the Bowery called Hotel Progress, the camera pans down from the sign to a man stretched out in the gutter; and from jewelry store window filled with diamonds the camera pulls back to reveal two derelicts exchanging hats and shoes.

In an interview on the DVD, architect James Sanders adds some context to the making of the film. While some silent titles, like the D.W. Griffith crime short *The Musketeers of Pig Alley* (1912), had been filmed on the Lower East Side streets of New York City. The only sound features to have attempted this were the social drama *The Lost Weekend* (1945) and the spy drama *The House on 92nd Street* (1945), and they shot only *some* of their sequences on location. This made *The Naked City* a breakthrough feature in terms of on-location filmmaking. (In *The BFI Companion to Crime*, Phil Hardy calls *The Naked City* one of the most vivid pictures of tenement life that the early American cinema ever produced.) Story writer and co-screenplay author Marvin Wald had proposed the location-shoot idea to producer Hellinger, since Wald had come out of the Army Air Force Motion Picture Unit, where on-location film making had taken place. In his DVD commentary, Wald says he worked on 30 Air Force documentaries. (In their book *Tender Comrades*, Patrick McGilligan and Paul Buhle quote screenwriter Alfred Lewis Levitt as saying he was in the same army training film writing unit as Wald at Fort Roach.) Wald's interest in realistic locations reflected the current popularity of the Italian neo-realistic films, like Roberto Rossellini's war drama *Open City* (1945). (Sanders also mentions Vittorio De Sica's 1948 drama *The Bicycle Thief*, but that film was not released in America until 1949.)

Hellinger's friendship with the then New York Mayor, Bill O'Dwyer, helped secure cooperation from the Mayor's office. Even so, the production was not an easy one. Shooting at 107 locations over 84 days, the film went over-budget, and the police had difficulty controlling the crowds. Apparently there were on-site accidents, and one story goes that filming had to shut down when one of the lead actors got caught on a subway train and went the wrong way for a couple of stops. In his 2004 LACMA interview, Dassin claims that crowds followed the actors from their hotels, and the director had various means to avoid them so he could film. These included using a portable newsstand, a florist delivery truck with a see-through mirror, and a man on a ladder who waved an American flag and ranted against society, which would draw the crowd's attention.

Sanders claims that *The Naked City* is a social document of the last years of the old way of life on the streets of the city before the advent of television, which took people off the street and inside their homes. Additionally, he says the film presents a New York that is an ordered society, unlike the later presentations in films like *The French Connection* (1971) and *Fort Apache, the Bronx* (1981), in which the city was shown to be crime-ridden and unable to be properly policed.

In his DVD audio commentary, Malvin Ward claims that the treatment's view of the police as competent crimesolvers was a breakaway from the previous crime films that presented them as dumb and incompetent, so that it was up to individuals like Sherlock Holmes or private eyes to step in and do their jobs for them. However, this new look at police also deprived them of the so-called glamour that was attached to these individual crime-fighters, with the treatment demonstrating the drudgery and frustration of police footwork.

The brother of famed Warner Bros. producer Jerry Wald, Marvin had previously written original screenplays and stories for Columbia Pictures, 20th Century–Fox and independent producers. He researched the story of *The Naked City* by following real New York homicide detectives. Wald based his original screenplay (with dialogue added by Albert Matz) on the true-life story of Dorothy King, a model whose murder went unsolved, as well as additional details from other cases (and one Hollywood tale about a producer who would invite guests to his house so that theirs could be burglarized). Unlike in the film's screenplay, Wald says that the King case had been deliberately stopped by someone with influence after a tip had been received that she had been associated with a Philadelphia high society admirer. Hellinger may have responded to Wald's script because, according to Wald, he had been one of the newspapermen at the King crime scene. Hellinger also felt obligated to Wald since Hellinger had used some of Wald's (unpaid-for) material for a *New York Daily Mirror* column. (In his book *The Mark Hellinger Story*, Jim Bishop quotes Hellinger saying that Wald had contributed several times.)

Even so, Hellinger did not have much confidence in Wald's screenplay, according to the writer, because Hellinger had no experience producing a work with such strong documentary content (unlike Louis De Rochemont, who had produced *The House on 92nd Street*). It was Dassin who saved the project from being abandoned, since supposedly the director saw how pioneering it was. He brought on Maltz, since they were friends, and together they helped map out a new screenplay. Maltz was a playwright who joined Warner Bros. as a contract writer. He had written the screenplays for the Paramount film noir *This*

Gun for Hire (1942); the war documentary *Moscow Strikes Back* (1942), which won the 1943 Best Documentary Academy Award; the pro–Russian war drama *Seeds of Freedom* (1943); and the World War II sea drama *Destination Tokyo* (1943). He was nominated for the Best Writing Screenplay Academy Award for the World War II drama *Pride of the Marines* (1945); and the short subject documentary he had written and produced about racial tolerance, *The House I Live In* (1945), won an Honorary Academy Award. He would go on to write the screenplays for the spy drama *Cloak and Dagger* (1946) and United Artists' horror title *The Red House* (1947), though uncredited for the latter. A member of the Communist Party, Maltz was called before HUAC in 1947 and, as one of the "Hollywood Ten," was cited for contempt for being an "unfriendly witness." He was jailed and subsequently blacklisted in Hollywood, although he used the "fronts" of Michael Blankfort and John D. Sherry to continue to write screenplays. As Michael Blankfort he was nominated for the Best Writing Screenplay Academy Award for the western *Broken Arrow* (1950), a nomination that the Academy officially attributed to Maltz in 1991.

Wald advises that the film's title was appropriated from a 1945 book of crime scene photographs by a man named "Weegee" (real name Arthur Fellig). Weegee (a phonetic variation on "Ouija") was so nicknamed because he would always arrive at the crime scene before the police and other reporters (by listening to a short-wave radio in his car, which picked up police calls). In *The Mark Hellinger Story*, Jim Bishop said that Hellinger made Weegee the film's still photographer, which saved him from having to buy the book's name.

Wald makes the spurious claim that Dassin's casting of theater and radio actors unknown to filmgoers, like Tom Pedi and David Opatoshu, rather than recognizable Hollywood character actors, gives the film more realism because these unknown actors are not actors at all. Actually, although Pedi had acted on Broadway in the play *Beggars Are Coming to Town* in 1945 and *The Iceman Cometh* in 1946, he had been seen in a credited supporting role in the independent social drama *Native Land* (1942). Likewise, Opatoshu had previously acted on film, playing the lead in the independent Yiddish rural drama *The Light Ahead* (1939).

Wald states that Frank Skinner did the film's original score, but it was scrapped because Hellinger disliked it. Skinner had provided the score for Hellinger's earlier title *Swell Guy*.

Wald tells us that the producer had hoped to cast James Stewart in the part of the Lieutenant, but this hope was dashed after the character was written as an older man. Wald says that the 59-year-old Fitzgerald initially turned down the part because he thought it was better suited to someone like Humphrey Bogart, who could cope with the "running and shooting." However, Fitzgerald changed his mind when he saw that the police officers mostly sat and interrogated people, and the running and shooting scenes were left to the younger detective Jimmy. Fitzgerald had come to Hollywood from the Dublin Abbey Theatre in 1936 and signed with Paramount Pictures in 1944. He had won the Best Supporting Actor Academy Award for playing a priest in the religious comedy-drama *Going My Way* (1944), and was top-billed in the 20th Century–Fox mystery *And Then There Were None* (1945) and the gambling comedy drama *Easy Come, Easy Go* (1947). Fitzgerald had played an old man coupled with a young one (Bing Crosby) in the medical comedy drama *Welcome Stranger* (1947), a pairing repeated in the treatment of *The Naked City*. His prior title had been the Paramount Pictures musical comedy *Variety Girl* (1947), where he appeared as himself and sang in a chorus of stars. Apart from supporting roles, Fitzgerald would go on to play leads in the Italian comedy *Ha da venì ... don Calogero!* (1952) and his last title, the Irish independent comedy *Broth of a Boy* (1959).

Don Taylor had made his film debut in an uncredited bit part in the MGM homefront comedy drama *The Human Comedy* (1943). His first credited role came in 20th Century–Fox's World War II aviation drama *Winged Victory* (1944). Taylor's film immediately prior to *The Naked City* had been the MGM detective comedy drama *Song of the Thin Man* (1947). He would go on to play the groom of Elizabeth Taylor in the domestic comedy *Father of the Bride* (1950) and its sequel *Father's Little Dividend* (1951). Taylor would have a lead role in the postwar drama *Japanese War Bride* (1952), play Robin Hood in the British adventure *The Men of Sherwood Forest* (1954), and star in the Columbia "B" drama *Ride the High Iron* (1956). Taylor became a director for television and minor features in the 1960s and 1970s, and a producer of made-for-TV movies. One of the features he would direct is the comic western *The Great Scout and Cathouse Thursday* (1976), produced by *The Naked City* associate producer Jules Buck.

Dorothy Hart was a former model and Universal contract player who had made her film debut in the Columbia Pictures western *Gunfighters* (1947). Her title just prior to *The Naked City* had been the Douglas Fairbanks, Jr., independent romantic adventure *The Exile* (in an uncredited bit part). She would go on to play supporting roles in several Universal films, including the western *Calamity Jane and Sam Bass* (1949), again with Howard Duff. She received second billing (after Frank Lovejoy) in the Warner Bros. cold war drama *I Was a Communist for the F.B.I.* (1951), scored the role of Jane in the independent jungle adventure *Tarzan's Savage Fury* (1952), and co-starred with George Raft in the independent crime drama *Loan Shark* (1952), which was her last feature.

After his back to back supporting performances for Dassin, Howard Duff would go on to play more supporting roles at Universal, and earned leads in the crime dramas *Illegal Entry* (1949), *Johnny Stool Pigeon* (1949), the "B" spy drama *Spy Hunt* (1950), the newspaper drama *Shakedown* (1950), the western *The Lady from Texas* (1951), the independent "B" crime drama *Models, Inc.* (1952), the Monogram "B" car racing drama *Roar of the Crowd* (1953), the British science fiction *Spaceways* (1953), and the independent westerns *Blackjack Ketchum, Desperado* (1956), *The Broken Star* (1956), and *Sierra Stranger* (1957). He co-starred with his wife, Ida Lupino, in the television comedy series *Mr. Adams and Eve* from 1957 to 1958, then scored leads in the Italian adventure *War Gods of Babylon* (1962) and the independent melodrama *Panic in the City* (1968) before settling into television and supporting roles.

The Naked City would be the last film that Mark Hellinger produced; he died on December 21, 1947, from a heart attack at the age of 44. In *The Mark Hellinger Story*, Jim Bishop reported on a foreboding incident in July when Hellinger suffered a heart attack in the middle of the shooting of the climactic chase scene. In his 2004 LACMA interview, Dassin says that Hellinger had read a newspaper article reporting that Hellinger was second only to Winston Churchill as a great brandy drinker; and since the producer didn't want to be second, his subsequent increased drinking led to his early death. Wald tells us that Hellinger did see *The Naked City*—a week before he died—at a Los Angeles sneak preview, but that after his death Universal was reluctant to release the film, as they did not like it. (Bishop says the preview was on December 17 at the Loyola Theater.) Since Hellinger had self-produced the title, not Universal, his estate enforced the contract stipulation of a release.

Associate producer Jules Buck would go on to associate produce the independent Cuban drama *We Were Strangers* (1949), and produce the comedy *Love Nest* (1951), the war drama *Fixed Bayonets!* (1951) and the historical adventure *Treasure of the Golden Condor* (1953) at 20th Century–Fox. A later move to England would see him launch Keep Films, which allowed him to produce various independent titles, many which starred Peter O'Toole, though he didn't work with Dassin again. Buck is also credited as having been one of the founders of the Committee for the First Amendment, which attempted to protest the hunt for Communists in Hollywood by flying a group of celebrities to Washington in October 1947.

Release

March 4, 1948, with the taglines, "The Most Exciting Story of the World's Most Exciting City!" "The Soul of a City—HER GLORY STRIPPED! HER PASSIONS BARED!" and "RAW LIFE! REAL LIFE! RECKLESS LIFE!"

Reviews

"A boldly fashioned yarn.... Throughout, despite its omniscient, stark melodrama, there has been no sight lost of an element of humor."—*Variety*

"The drama is largely superficial, being no more than a routine and unrevealing episode in the everyday business of the cops. And the incidental details—the 'humorous' and 'poignant' vignettes—seem studiously over-written and even contrived.... Dassin has not preserved them from staginess which rends the 'actuality' disguise."—Bosley Crowther, *The New York Times*, March 5, 1948

"Fast-jabbing, empty Manhattan-set melodrama ... the film is visually impressive only."—Pauline Kael, *5001 Nights at the Movies*

"It would be hard to imagine a movie melodrama less cynical, less brutal and cheaply hard-boiled, more essentially kindly and sweet-tempered. And it would be hard to beat the setting and handling of the chase which climaxes the film by pulling the hair up on your head and keeping it there."—*Time* magazine, March 22, 1948

"The film lacks the distinctive edge of hysteria or paranoia that marks Dassin's other crime films, but the ending is justly celebrated."—Phil Hardy, *The BFI Companion to Crime*

Awards

1949 Best Cinematography, Black and White (William Daniel's award allowed the man who had filmed twenty-one of Greta Garbo's films at MGM, but whose career had suffered after he was fired for allegedly having one too many hangovers, to enjoy a career resurgence), and Best Film Editing Academy Awards. Nominated for Best Writing Motion Picture Story Academy Award.

···

Thieves' Highway (1949)

[aka *Collision*; *The Thieves Market*; *Hard Bargain*]
20th Century–Fox

Credits: Director: Jules Dassin; Producer: Robert Bassler; Uncredited Executive Producer: Darryl F. Zanuck; Screenplay: A.I. Bezzerides, based on his novel *Thieves' Market*;

Photography: Norbert Brodine; Music: Alfred Newman; Editor: Nick DeMaggio; Art Direction: Lyle Wheeler, Chester Corr; Set Decorations: Thomas Little; Costumes: Kay Nelson; Makeup: Ben Nye; Special Photographic Effects: Fred Sersen; Sound: Alfred Bruzian, Harry M. Leonard. B&W, 94 minutes. Filmed on location in San Francisco and Golden Delicious Apples Orchard, Sebastapol, California, from November to December 1948.

Songs: "The Pact" (Arthur Lange), played under the opening credits; "The Kleftman" (Traditional Greek folk song), sung by Morris Carnovsky; "I'll Never Be the Same" (Marty Malneck, Frank Signorelli), heard at the Oregon Restaurant; "Bye, Bye Blackbird" (Ray Henderson), "Honey" (Richard A. Whiting, Seymour Simms, Haven Gillespie), "Five Foot Two, Eyes of Blue (Has Anybody Seen My Gal?)" (Ray Henderson), "If I Could Be with You" (James B. Johnson), all heard in Hotel Colchester; "The Right Kind" (Charles Henderson, Lionel Newman), heard at Shorty's bar; "Snuggled on Your Shoulder" (Carmen Lombardo), heard when Rica tells the man his fortune.

Cast: Richard Conte (Nick Garcos); Valentina Cortesa (Rica); Lee J. Cobb (Mike Figlia); Barbara Lawrence (Polly Faber); Jack Oakie (Slob); Millard Mitchell (Ed Kinney); Joseph Pevney (Pete); Morris Carnovsky (Yanko Garcos); Tamara Shayne (Parthena Garcos); Kasia Orzazewski (Mrs. Polansky); Norbert Schiller (Mr. Polanksy); Hope Emerson (Midge). Uncredited: Walter Baldwin (Officer Riley); William Bendix (Italian Grocer); Robert Bice (Announcer); Howland Chamberlain (Mr. Faber); David Clarke (Mitch); Roy Damron (Motor Policeman); Al Eben (Newman); Robert Foulk (Taller Cop at Roadside Bar); Joe Haworth (Inspector); Percy Helton (Roadside Bar Manager); Ted Jordan, John Merton (State Highway Policemen); Frank Kreig (Clerk); Saul Martell (Stukas); Edwin Max (Dave); Ann Morrison (Mable); James Nolan (Small Cop at Roadside Bar); David Opatoshu (Frenchy); Frank Richards, Dick Wessel (Cab Drivers); Maurice Samuels (Mario); Mario Siletti (Pietro); Irene Tedrow (Mrs. Faber); George Tyne (Charles); Harry Wilson (Fifth, Ugly Man at City Bar).

VHS/DVD: DVD Criterion Collection released February 1, 2005.

Synopsis

Nick Garcos returns to his home in Fresno after being at sea but is shocked to learn that his father, Yanko, has lost his legs in an accident that occurred when he was transporting tomatoes for the San Francisco fruit and produce dealer Mike Figlia. Nick suggests to Ed Kinney (Nick's father has sold his truck to Kinney) that they go into business together to transport apples that Ed had arranged to transport with two other truckers, Slob and Pete. Ed agrees, though Nick is disturbed when Ed tries to cheat the orchard farmers. Ed drives Yanko's truck and Nick drives a surplus army truck to transport their loads. Ed is followed by the two disgruntled drivers, who are waiting for his damaged truck to break down so they can steal his apples. When Nick's truck blows a tire, he gets trapped under it when the jack fails, though Ed saves him. Although injured by the accident, Nick arrives first at Figlia's market, and his truck is sabotaged so that Figlia can legally take the load. Figlia has sent Rica to distract Nick, and they go to her hotel room.

When Nick learns that Figlia intends to pay him substantially less than what he has sold them for, he demands and receives cash and a check for the full amount. He then phones his girlfriend Polly Faber to come so they can be married. Nick celebrates his sale with Rica, but he is attacked by two of Figlia's thugs as they walk back to the market. Rica escapes with Nick's wallet, though the thugs chase her and take it. Meanwhile, Ed's truck falls apart on the Altamont hairpin curve and crashes down a hill, burning alive the trapped Ed. Figlia agrees to buy Ed's abandoned apples, and he and Pete go to collect them. Polly arrives and leaves when she learns Nick has lost all his money, as Rica predicted she would. When Slob tells Nick how Figlia is going after Ed's load, Nick goes after him and beats up Figlia in Bob's Roadside Café—payback for his father being robbed of his money and his legs. The police arrest Figlia but do not charge Nick for the assault, who goes back to Rica and proposes marriage.

Notes

A colorless trucking drama with a convoluted plot, this title has moments of resonant imagery and violence. The director's recurring theme of duplicity, deceit and betrayal permeates a treatment where opportunistic men (and women) value money over honesty. These latter concerns mark the picture as film noir, as does the theme of the peril of trusting others, although daylight scenes surround the extended night scene that is the film's sixty-seven-minute centerpiece. Continuing his favored use of long takes to emphasize performance, Dassin refrains from overusing the score by Alfred Newman, which is limited to credits and end titles. Regrettably, Dassin's attempts at humor fail in this effort. Fortunately, the broad presentation of ethnic stereotypes, recalling the broad comedy he created for MGM, also contains a mythic narrative association in terms of the protagonist's quest for revenge and retribution. The film also presents the director's interest in exploring female characters, an opportunity denied him with *Brute Force* and *The Naked City*, which only featured women in minor roles.

The rural location of Fresno, where the film opens, stands in contrast to New York of *The Naked City*; and the scene between Nick and his parents changes tone from comic celebration, where they applaud him kissing Polly, to intense drama in the discussion of his father's loss of legs. The kneeling Mrs. Garcos is shown with her face turned from the camera while she speaks of Yankos' accident and her deluded hope that he will grow new legs, with an expression of sadness over the tragedy mixed with the shame of the loss. Polly's disdain for the Japanese geisha doll Nick has brought her changes when he points out the ring the doll wears—a sign of the superficiality she will later demonstrate.

Nick uses occasional tough guy vernacular (which receives a visual parallel in the savagery of his beating of Figlia). He tells Ed, "You pull a trick like that on me, I'd climb all over your neck"; later he warns Figlia, "Touch my truck and I'll climb into your hair," and, "I've worked like a dog for that dough—gyp me and I'll cut your heart out." This way of talking may also suggest that Nick is a duplicitous character, though he actually isn't. Ed's betrayal of the deal he had with Pete and Slob somewhat justifies their later parasitic stalking of him, since their limited funds have left them unable to buy a full load from the farmers. However, at some point this following turns into opportunism, perhaps in light of their repeated torment and ridicule of his situation and our changed feeling towards Ed after he saves Nick's life. However, an argument could be made that Ed's attempt to chisel the farmers seals his fate for the truck crash later in the narrative.

Shots of apples rolling down a hill from the carts the sellers try to retrieve is a resonant

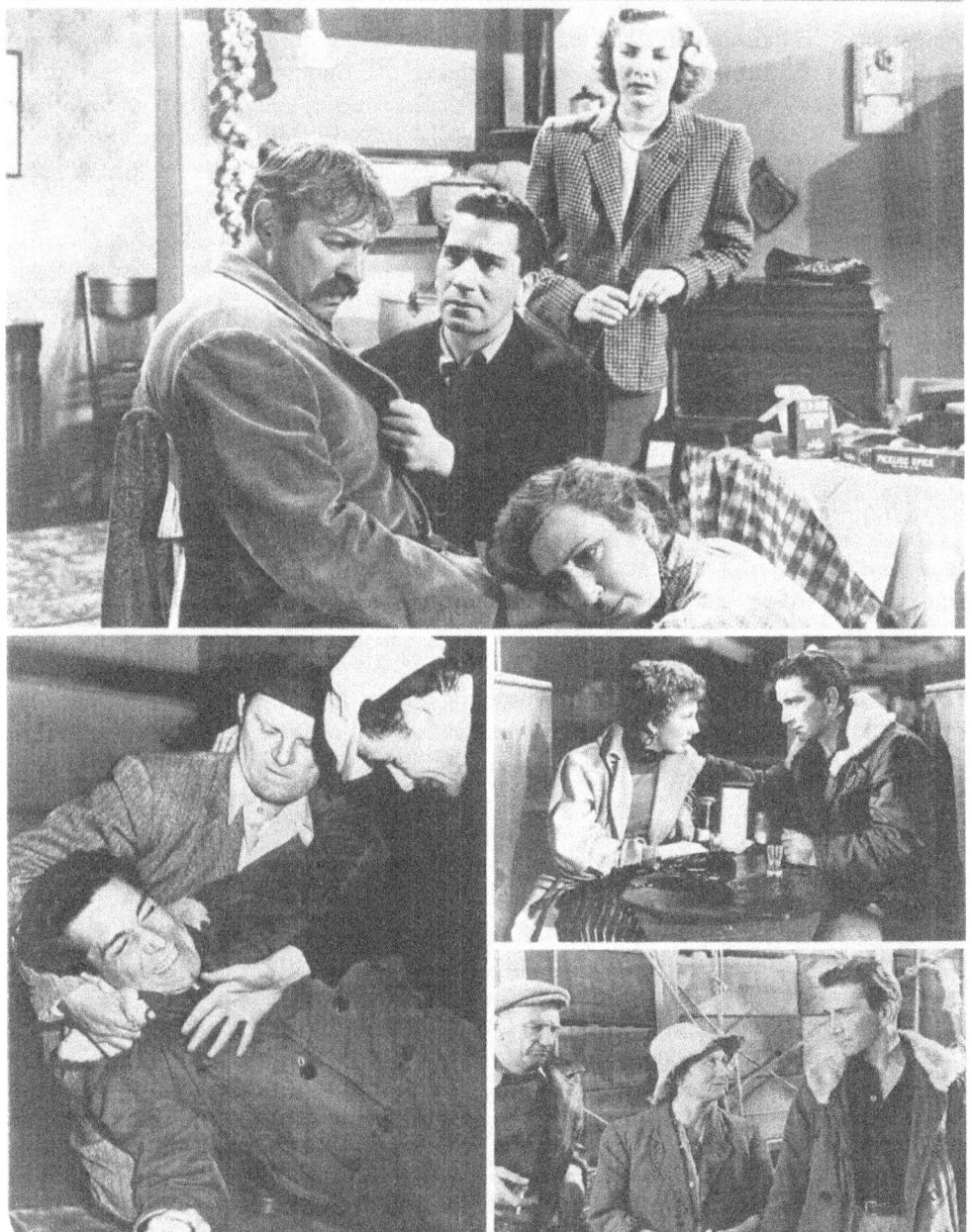

French movie card for *Thieves' Highway* (1949).

image, and one that prefigures Ed's fatal crash. An apple is also used by Pete when he puts one in Slob's mouth to stop him talking. This oral play will be repeated later by Figlia.

Dassin uses montage for the scenes of Nick driving, the first featuring the climbing needle of the speedometer, the speeding wheels of the truck, and Nick's POV of the road before he slows down and the tire blows. We get a long shot of the truck parking off the road, and we wonder where Ed's truck is, since Nick had insisted on traveling with him to the market. We also wonder whether Ed will stop and help Nick when he gets trapped under his truck, or whether he will leave him.

Nick being pinned recalls Yanko's similar predicament, and Ed saving of Nick comes as a surprise, with his attentiveness seeming almost paternal (appropriate, perhaps, since Ed drives Yanko's truck). Nick isn't able to thank Ed directly, and only comments on how silly they must look to the passing traffic. (The sexual component of the truck accident is highlighted by the erectile jack and the balloonish bubble of the tire inner tube that emerges next to Nick's head and bursts, causing the truck to fall on him.)

Dassin uses a second montage after Nick is back on the road, showing the truck wheels, his POV, and him nearly falling asleep (generating the worry that he might crash). Nick's sleepiness may well be the result of a concussion (suggested by blood on his bandage), although this plot point is dropped.

The nighttime market stands as counterpoint to the film's rural opening scenes, a noir underworld of violence, hostility and deceit. Its noisiness and anarchy presents the environment as an urban jungle.

The hatchet Dave uses to puncture Nick's truck's tire prefigures his hatchet seen in the climactic café confrontation. The first sight of it as it lies gleaming across a crate of grapefruit is almost sexual, a masculine image of penetration among feminine representations of productivity. The treatment's oral fixation continues when Figlia takes Charles' hand that is holding his pipe and puts the pipe in his mouth to stop him talking; and Charles does the same thing with Dave, who holds a cigarette.

Figlia is presented as a duplicitous character by his sabotaging Nick's truck, undercutting the price his providers seek, and ordering the theft of the money he had paid them (as with Nick and presumably Yanko). Figlia is a figure of connivance, deceit and betrayal, and Lee J. Cobb presents him as charmless and unlikable. Raucous, well-fed and repulsive, he is a cliché of avarice and swagger who chomps on a cigar and wears garish rings on his hands.

Rica's short, mannish hair and tight sweater worn under a trenchcoat makes her occupation seemingly apparent (aligning her with the playgirl Jean from *The Naked City* and the femme fatales of *Brute Force*). Her pursuit of Nick in the Oregon Restaurant gets a laugh when she asks Nick for a match for her cigarette, is immediately surrounded by three other men offering lit matches, and then uses Nick's cigarette to light her own. The idea that Rica is a known prostitute (if we are to believe that she is), fits with the milieu of transitory truckers. The honky tonk piano music heard in the Hotel Colchester Apartments, where Rica lives, conjures the ambience of a brothel.

The narrative here divides three ways—between Nick's relationship with Rica, Figlia selling Nick's load, and Ed in his truck on the road being pursued by Pete and Slob. Following the Nick-and-Rica thread, Dassin repeats the match business when Rica asks Nick again for a light to help her insert her key in the apartment door. He replies, "No match," as he had in the restaurant, but this time presents her with a flame. Nick's disparaging remark that Rica "looks like chipped glass" alludes to her worldliness, while Rica looking at the flying seagulls outside her window casts her in the same light as the opportunistic birds that feed off the market's produce. The power struggle between Rica and Nick over their attraction/repulsion reads as an odd presentation of the dilemma of a prostitute, with her moral ambiguity diluting the duplicity of her femme fatale role (she is the woman Figlia has paid to dupe Nick). This ambiguity prefigures her later being shown as the woman who truly loves Nick—and who he is willing to marry at the narrative's conclusion. Nick and Rica kissing is edited in jump cuts, perhaps to underscore the idea of their attraction/repulsion, with Rica more likely to rub her head on his chest than kiss him. While this coquettish action reveals her kittenish nature, it also creates suspicion and doubt about her honesty. Rica being Italian adds to her exoticism, but it also continues the ethnic flavor that Nick's Greek parents and the apple farmers (nationality unknown) had provided. (The Greek characters anticipate Dassin's later Greek connection in his relationship with Melina Mercouri, and the film *Never on Sunday*, made in Greece and the title for which he is probably best known.) Though the treatment doesn't explicitly indicate the couple has sex, Dassin shows Rica retrieving a robe from her closet to wear—presumably after the act—and returning to find Nick asleep (or unconscious from his injury).

Nick knocking the adding machine off Figlia's desk is enough to scare Figlia into giving Nick his full payment. This foreshadows Nick lashing out at market crates before he goes after Figlia, and Figlia's cowardice in the face of Nick's anger in the climactic cafe scene. Rica asks Nick to kiss her goodbye, his refusal to kiss her, her hands touching his face, and his suddenly kissing her reinforces their attraction/repulsion dichotomy. It is also telling that when Nick's wallet drops to the ground when he is attacked by Frenchy and Mitch, they don't notice but Rica does, and she runs away with it. Although later she tells Nick that she did this to protect his money, we have doubts about her intention. Nick's beating adds to his passion for revenge and also prefigures his own beating of Figlia. Dassin presents the thugs' later advance on Rica in another extreme long shot after a one-minute silent chase, adding tension to the threat. Later we will learn that the men do not harm her; rather, it is Nick who does, pulling her hair when he thinks she still has the money.

Peter and Slob's continued following of Ed creates the expectation that his truck will stop, so it is interesting that this expectation is not exactly met when the broken drive shaft causes the loss of brakes and Ed's crash. Dassin uses speeded-up footage of Ed's brake-less truck for horrific effect, with apples and crates dropping off to show their relative unimportance in the scene. We don't know why Ed is unable to get out of the burning truck, but the dropped crates on the hill resemble tombstones, prefiguring his death. Slob dropping an apple he has retrieved suggests his loss of interest in the load, and although we will see he and Pete bargaining with Figlia over the price of the apples they have brought to the market, Slob's unwillingness to retrieve the other apples reinforces his earlier abhorrence. The death of Ed reduces the narrative threads, with Nick/Rica/Polly and Figlia/Pete/Slob now being the remaining two scenarios; however, it also links Ed to Yanko's maiming as further loss for Nick and more motivation for his revenge.

The scene between Polly and Nick is enhanced by the sound of Rica's shower as a reminder of her presence. It is noteworthy that Polly's rejection of Nick because he has no money separates her from Rica, who remains with him. It doesn't take long for us to see Polly as a superficial and amoral woman, which should come as no surprise since Polly as a character was more or less abandoned by the narrative after the first scene, with Rica taking over as the female presence in Nick's life. However while Polly's quick rejection of

Nick allows for Rica to stay with him, it is a little disappointing dramatically since it might have been more interesting if Nick had two women to choose from.

Rica telling Nick about Figlia's use of Frenchy and Mitch leads him to deduce that it was they who got his father drunk and stole his money, and were indirectly responsible for the loss of his legs. But Rica divulging this information stands in contrast to the notion that Rica set Nick up to be beaten and robbed by the two thugs, again raising doubts about her duplicity and love for Nick. Rather than defend herself, Rica lets Nick believe that she is the femme fatale he thinks she is, which makes his return to her at the film's end slightly problematic.

As already mentioned, Nick's lashing out at the market crates before he heads after Figlia is testament to his explosive violence, prefiguring the beating Nick will deliver.

Nick's beating of the cringing Figlia, who pathetically throws money at him to try and stop his attacker is brutal, and the viewer begins to empathize with Figlia in spite of what he may have done or ordered done. This moral ambiguity adds further dimension to another duplicitous character, and Nick's repeated blows makes him less and less sympathetic, a point underscored by the attending policeman pointing out that the assault was legally unjustifiable. It is only the authorities' seemingly greater distaste for Figlia and his operation that allows Nick to go unpunished for the attack.

Nick's return for Rica sees her telling fortunes with cards, although she could be merely playing her customers. If she is, the behavior would present her as a duplicitous thief—something Nick is apparently prepared to overlook. We could read the fact that she had called the police to the café as an act protecting Figlia as much as Nick, although the cops appeared to arrive after he had stopped the attack. This then makes the union of Nick and Rica, given their attraction/repulsion dynamic, an odd and perhaps ill-fated one.

On the DVD interview with Dassin, he labels the film a "B" because of its "tight budget." (This claim is disputed by the author's criteria for a "B" title, and also by Alain Silver in his DVD commentary.) Dassin says it was shot in no more than 30 days, and that producer Darryl F. Zanuck made character and plot insertions that the director was not happy with. For instance, Zanuck insisted on creating the character of nice girl Polly—even though Dassin considered it "senseless and useless"—so that her bourgeois betrayal of Nick is a counterpoint to prostitute Rica's loyalty. (In his DVD audio commentary, Alain Silver maintains that the character of Polly is in the book the screenplay is based on and is therefore not an invention of Zanuck.) Zanuck also had the ending of the narrative changed while Dassin was in London (presumably preparing his next title, *Night and the City*, although the film would not go into production until July). Dassin says that the appearance of the police at the café to comment on Nick's beating of Figlia as an act above the law, and the happy ending with Rica, were Zanuck's creations. However, Silver claims that only the one shot of the policeman admonishing Nick for his vigilantism was inserted into the café scene as a concession to the production code requirements that one cannot take the law into one's own hands.

Silver also comments on the film's final scene, which he claims made further concessions to the production code. He states that the scene implies that Rica actually makes her living from telling fortunes and not selling her body, since the code would never allow a prostitute to be loved by any man. (The book apparently had Nick acknowledge that she is a whore and accept her as such.) We are supposed to believe that by helping to remove Figlia from the market, Nick has saved Rica from his clutches. Therefore, she is entitled to the treatment's happy ending, although we note that when she leaves she throws back her cards, as the symbol of her past life—but not the money she has taken.

Dassin reported that he only learned after weeks of filming that Jack Oakie was totally deaf and couldn't read lips, although Oakie never failed to pick up his line cues, even when an actor had his back to him. The director also reported that Valentica Cortesa had been brought to his attention by Gregory Ratoff, who had directed her in her prior title, the historical independent drama *Black Magic* (1949).

An actress in Italian films since 1941, Cortesa had played the double leading role in *Soltano un bacio* (1942), the lead in *Un americano in vacanza* (1946), another double role in *I miserabili* (1948), and had played a supporting role in the British/Italian co-production *The Glass Mountain* (1949) before coming to America for *Black Magic*. Cortesa would continue in Hollywood playing supporting roles, though she co-starred with her husband Richard Basehart in the Fox suspense melodrama *The House on Telegraph Hill* (1951), and essayed the lead in the British crime drama *The Secret People* (1952). She returned to Italy for the title role in the comedy *Lulu* (1953), the lead in the drama *Donne proibite* (*Angels of Darkness*, 1954), and the title role in the biographical drama *Adriana Lecouvreur* (1955). After that, Cortesa settled into supporting roles. She was nominated for the Best Supporting Actress Academy Award for François Truffaut's film about film-making, *La nuit americaine* (*Day for Night*, 1973), in which she played a fading alcoholic movie star.

The Turner Classic Movie website notes the claim that 20th Century–Fox contract players Dana Andrews and Victor Mature were considered for the part of Nick, and that the Zanuck-ordered retakes were done in March 1949. Richard Conte had actually worked as a truck driver before becoming a professional actor, which no doubt informed his performance as Nick. Conte was another Fox contract player who benefited from earning the roles that other leading men had abandoned in favor of performing military service during World War II. He had made his debut in a supporting role in the drama *Heaven with a Barbed Wire Fence* (1939), scored a lead in the "B" crime drama *The Spider* (1945), and co-starred in "A" titles with other Fox players. *Thieves' Highway* would prove to be his first and only "A" leading role at Fox; Conte would have better luck at Universal Pictures. He played leads in the medical drama *The Sleeping City* (1950), the prison drama *Under the Gun* (1951), the show business mystery *Hollywood Story* (1951), the independent historical boxing drama *The Fighter* (1952, with Lee J. Cobb), the western *The Raiders* (1952), Columbia Pictures' biblical adventure *Slaves of Babylon* (1953), the independent crime drama *Highway Dragnet* (1954), and the British car racing drama *Mask of Dust* (1954). In 1955, Conte played leading roles in the independent crime drama *The Big Tip Off*, the British "B" *Little Red Monkey*, the independent African crime drama *Bengazi*, and the Warner Bros. Korean war drama *Target Zero*. He starred in the independent gangster drama *The Brothers Rico* (1957), the independent mystery *The Eyes of Annie Jones* (1964), the Argentinean *Extrana invasion* (*Stay Tuned for Terror*, 1965), and the Italian *Sentenza di morte* (1968). He directed himself in his last leading role, in the Yugoslavian war title *Operation Cross Eagles* (1968). Conte apparently was considered for the title role of Don Corleone in the gangster drama *The Godfather* (1972), but he had to settle for a supporting role when Marlon Brando was cast instead.

In the interview with Dassin in their book *Tender Comrades*, Patrick McGilligan and Paul Buhle quote the director on the film: "[It] could have been good, but I think we shot it in something like twenty-four days" (as opposed to the thirty that Dassin remembers in the DVD interview). Dassin also comments on Lee J. Cobb and his later cooperating with HUAC:

> [He] was one of my closest friends. I loved him. I loved Kazan. I loved Odets. And this still hurts. I think they simply placed career before honor. It's that simple. The need to work is very strong. And particularly in the arts—it's your oxygen; it's your life. And their betrayal is a continuing pain because these are the guys I love. I saw him at a party with a group of old friends [in New York]. I got Lee aside and said, "Lee, there are rumors...?" He said, "I just want to know one thing. Do you believe them?" I said, "Of course I don't believe them." And the night before was when he had done it all! That, I think, was the one that broke me the most. That was the toughest one.... I turned my back on him.

Dassin's feeling about, and experience with, Cobb parallels the case of Elia Kazan, whom Dassin commented on his *Cine-Parade* interview on the DVD of *Night and the City*. Apparently Kazan told a group of his friends twenty-four hours before he was called to HUAC that he would never inform on them; not only did he inform, he also stated that he thought he had done the right thing. Dassin remembers Kazan describing the people he had named as "noxious for America." Dassin asks, "When did he discover this?" because he didn't feel that way twenty-four hours previously. The director would say of Kazan that he was a man who was lost without his work, and perhaps Dassin could have been more forgiving of him if he had admitted to that being his motive for doing what he did.

In the documentary *None Without Sin*, Kazan is said to have named 17 names (including himself) on April 11, 1952, after having refused to do so in his first testimony appearance. The case is made that the director's change of heart took place after the head of Fox, to whom Kazan was contracted, told him that if he didn't cooperate with the Committee then his Hollywood career was finished. The documentary notes that there was no blacklist on Broadway, so Kazan could have refused to cooperate and still have worked there. Ironically, naming names lost him friends both in Hollywood and on Broadway. Another factor for Kazan's change is said to be his loss of the Best Director Academy Award for *A Streetcar Named Desire* (1951)—thought to be the industry's punishment for his initial refusal to cooperate. Kazan would name Morris Carnovsky, Phoebe Brand, Lewis Leverett, Tony Kraber, Art Smith, J. Edward Bromberg, Clifford Odets, and Paula Strasberg as members of the Communist Party when he was a member, although reportedly he had asked for and received permission from Odets and Strasberg. All these people were fellow actors in The Group Theatre, though he also named party officials and others he knew to be communists. The documentary claims that all the people Kazan named had been named before, so he was giving HUAC nothing it didn't already know, but it is thought that his cooperation was seen as a validation of the Committee's actions, given Kazan's high profile.

Matters were not helped by the advertisement he placed in *The New York Times* two days after his testimony, in which he not only attempted to defend his actions but called for others to also name names. Labeled by some "the great apostate of Hollywood," Kazan's career following his testimony seemed bedeviled, given the box office failures of his two subsequent titles, the historical drama *Viva Zapata!* (1952) and the carnival drama *Man on a Tightrope* (1953). However, he made a comeback with *On the Waterfront* (1954), this time receiving the Best Director Academy Award. The film's treatment serves as an allegory for the director's own struggle—in that the character of the stevedore Terry Malloy informs on corrupt labor leaders, an action that is presented as heroic, and perhaps as a justification for Kazan's own Faustian bargain.

In his book *Naming Names*, Victor S. Navasky writes how the *On the Waterfront* screenplay is rife with talk of "rats," "stoolies," "cheesies," "canaries," and "squealers."

The protagonist, Terry Malloy, has to choose between the waterfront ethic (with the Waterfront Crime Commission able to be read as analog for HUAC), which holds ratting to be the greatest evil, and the Christian ethic, which suggests that one ought to speak truth to power. The former is represented by the vulgar, vicious, cigar-chomping corrupt labor boss, Johnny Friendly (Lee J. Cobb), and the latter by the clean-cut, gutsy, straight-talking priest, Father Barry (Karl Malden). Terry wins the girl (Eva Marie Saint) when he gains the courage to inform, achieves heroic stature by single-handedly taking on the mob at the risk of his life, and comes to true self knowledge. "I have been ratting on myself all these years," he tells Johnny Friendly, "and I didn't know it. I'm glad what I done."

After making his uncredited debut in the Universal Pictures serial *The Vanishing Shadow* (1934), and his credited debut in the independent Hopalong Cassidy "B" western *North of the Rio Grande* (1937), Lee J. Cobb played only supporting roles in films prior to *Thieves' Highway*. He would go on to play occasional leads in the independent police drama *The Man Who Cheated Himself* (1950), the independent biblical drama *Day of Triumph* (1954), the independent crime drama *Miami Expose* (1956), Columbia Pictures' fashion drama *The Garment Jungle* (1957), the melodrama *The Liberation of L.B. Jones* (1970), the Canadian *Ultimatum* (1973), and the Italian actioner *La legge violenta della squadra anticrimine* (1976). Cobb is perhaps better known as the stage actor who originated the part of Willy Loman in Arthur Miller's play *Death of a Salesman* in 1949 on Broadway, which was directed by Elia Kazan. Cobb appeared in the blacklist pamphlet *Red Channels* because of his earlier involvement with The Group Theatre and association with liberal causes, and initially refused to name names. (In *Bad Boys: The Actors of Film Noir*, Karen Burroughs Hannsberry states that Cobb had been named to HUAC by Larry Parks in 1951.) However, Cobb changed his mind and gave testimony on June 2, 1953, naming twenty people, including (according to Hannsberry) Lloyd Bridges, Jeff Corey, Marc Lawrence, Anne Revere (already named by Parks), Rose Hobart, and Gale Sondergaard. In Victor S. Navasky's book *Naming Names*, Cobb says that his blacklisting led to his wife being institutionalized and left him unable to provide for his children, so cooperating meant his career could be salvaged. (Cobb's claim of the blacklist affecting his employment prospects seems spurious given that in the approximate two-year period between his listing in *Red Channels* and his second HUAC testimony he worked on six features and three television anthology episodes.) Cobb would go on to be nominated for the Best Supporting Actor Academy Award for *On the Waterfront* (1954) and again for his work in the Dostoevsky drama *The Brother's Karamazov* (1959).

Barbara Lawrence was a Fox contract player who had made her uncredited debut in the Betty Grable musical *Diamond Horseshoe* (1945), and had appeared in numerous supporting roles. Her title prior to *Thieves' Highway* was the comedy *Mother Is a Freshman* (1949). The closest she would get to a leading role was in the independent science fiction title *Kronos* (1957), though she is probably best remembered for her cameo in the Bette Davis independent show business drama *The Star* (1952)—playing herself as a star that she actually never was.

Producer Robert Bassler was a former editor at Paramount who became a producer at Fox with the show business musical *My Gal Sal* (1942). Among his notable films are the horror title *The Lodger* (1944), the psychological mystery *Hangover Square* (1945), and the social drama *The Snake Pit* (1948). Bassler's prior title had been the western *Sand* (1949), and after *Thieves' Highway* he would go on to produce the television series *Naked City*, which had been inspired by Dassin's previous title.

In an interview on the DVD of *Rififi*, Dassin tells a story about baseball in relation to *Thieves' Highway*. After having been assigned the title, he was asked by Joe Mankiewicz if he could play baseball. Dassin replied that he could, and after he "auditioned" for Mankiewicz, the director was given the position of outfielder in a baseball game between Fox and MGM. Dassin turned out to be the "hero" of the game, and the next day his agent called him to ask if he had signed the contract for *Thieves' Highway*. When the director said that he had, his agent told him that after Dassin's heroic performance in the baseball game he could have gotten him more money.

Release

October 10, 1949 (on the DVD commentary, Alain Silver claims that the film had a September release; while TCM lists the Los Angeles opening as September 20), with the taglines "Rackets Ride the Roads!" and "You Need a Friend, Strong Man—And I'm Friendly!"

Reviews

"A flashy second-rate film ... [it] makes no pretensions to anything but entertainment; its only message, if any: think twice before going into the fruit-trucking trade. There have been better trucking movies (*They Drive by Night*), but none so fast or so violent.... Dassin's erratic direction of actors produces some mixed results."—*Time* magazine, October 10, 1949

"You will never be able to eat an apple again without calling up visions of trickery, mayhem, vandalism, and violent death ... a first-class melodrama which just misses—yes, just misses—being great."—Bosley Crowther, *The New York Times*, September 24, 1948

"Along with [a] highly visualized style, Dassin has effectively paced the movement of the plot to create a hard hitting drama."—Jay Robert Nash and Stanley Ralph Ross, *The Motion Picture Guide*

"Dassin keeps the story moving at a brisk pace, with good use of highways and the produce district of San Francisco."—Tony Thomas and Aubrey Solomon, *The Films of 20th Century–Fox*

"Intermingling menace and sex with social comment: superior of its kind."—Gordon Gow, *Films & Filming*

•••

Night and the City (1950)

20th Century–Fox Limited

Credits: Director: Jules Dassin; Producer: Samuel G. Engel; Screenplay: Jo Eisinger, based on the novel by Gerald Kersh; Photography: Max Greene; Editors: Nick De Maggio, Sidney Stone; Music: Franz Waxman; Art Director: C.P. Norman; Sound: Peter Handford, Roger Heman; Costumes for Miss Tierney: Oleg Cassini; Costumes for Miss Withers: Margaret Furse. Wrestling Technical Adviser: Mike Mazurki (uncredited). B&W, 95 minutes. Filmed at Shepperton Film Studios in Surrey, and at various locations around London, from July to October 1949.

Songs: "Don't Fence Me In (Cole Porter), heard in American Bar; "I'm Looking Over a Four-Leaf Clover (Harry M. Woods), heard in American Bar; "Here's to Champagne" (Noel Gay), dubbed vocal for Gene Tierney by Maudie Edwards, at the Silver Fox Club; "Again" (Lionel Newman), heard in Silver Fox Club; "The Right Kind" (Charles Henderson, Lionel Newman), heard in Silver Fox Club.

Cast: Richard Widmark (Harry Fabian); Gene Tierney (Mary Bristol); Googie Withers (Helen Nosseross); Hugh Marlowe (Adam Dunn); Francis L. Sullivan (Phillip Nosseross); Herbert Lom (Kristo); Stanislaus Zbyszko (Gregorius); Mike Mazurki (the Strangler); Charles Farrell (Mickey Beer); Ada Reeve (Molly the Flower Lady); Ken Richmond (Nikolas of Athens). Uncredited: Derek Blomfield (Young Policeman); Clifford Buckton, Clifford Cobbe (Policemen); Peter Butterworth, Arthur Lovegrove (Thugs); Edward Chapman (Hoskins—scene deleted in U.S. version); Patricia Davidson (Night Club Hostess); Maureen Delaney (Anna O'Leary); Aubrey Dexter (Fergus Chilk); Stanley Escane; Thomas Gallagher (Bagrag); Rex Garner (Waiter); James Hayter (Figler); George Hirste, John Mann, Leonard Sharp, Alan Tilvern (Beggars); Hamilton Keene (Charles); Kay Kendall (One of Helen's Girls); Hubert Leslie (Nightwatchman); Walter Magnee (A Second); Lew Marko (Referee); Gibb McLaughlin (Googin); MacDonald Parke, Eddy Reed (Americans from Chicago); Charles Paton (Watchman); Chunky Pattison (Dwarf); Frank Pettitt (Cabby); Philip Ray; John Rudling; Johnnie Schofield (Cashier); Betty Shale (Mrs. Pinkney); John Sharp; Tomy Simpson (Cozen); Ray St. Bernard (Strangler's Opponent); C. Denier Warren (Small American from Chicago); Freddie Watts; Brian Weske (Messenger Boy); Russell Westwood (Yosh).

VHS/DVD: Criterion Collection DVD released February 1, 2005.

Synopsis

Harry Fabian fails to get money from his girlfriend Mary Bristol, money which he says is for a proposed greyhound racing track but is actually to pay off a thug who has been chasing him. Harry works as a tout for The Silver Fox club, run by Phil and Helen Nosseross, where Mary works as a singer. When Harry takes potential suckers to a wrestling match, he sees Gregorius, a former champion wrestler who has come from Greece with his protégé, Nikolas, father of Kristo, a promoter and underworld racketeer. When Gregorius becomes disgusted by the phony show his son is staging with the Strangler, Harry sees an opportunity to move into another racket and promises Gregorius that he will promote classical

Harry Fabian (Richard Widmark) on the run in London in *Night and the City* (1950).

Greco-Roman wrestling in London. After Harry fails to get the needed initial investment from underworld lowlifes, Helen gives Harry the money on the condition that he will get her a liquor license for her own club; but Harry sells her a forged document. Phil decides to double-cross Harry by being his silent partner, promising Kristo that Gregorius will learn that Harry is not an honorable man.

Phil tells Harry that he is backing out of the deal unless he books the Strangler. Harry is forced to agree, and Harry goads the Strangler into challenging Nikolas. Gregorius agrees to let Nikolas wrestle the Strangler, and Phil withdraws his support. Harry takes Mary's savings, but at the gym the Strangler and Gregorius get into a fight, and Gregorius dies after defeating the younger man. Kristo puts out a hit on Harry, offering £1,000. Helen leaves Phil to start her own club, but a policeman identifies her license as a fake, and she returns to find that Phil is dead. On the run, Harry goes to Figler, king of the beggars, but suspects that he has tipped Kristo off and hides out on a barge owned by Anna O'Leary. Mary finds Harry at the barge, and Harry runs, falsely accusing her of turning him in for the reward. The Strangler catches Harry and kills him as Adam arrives with the police, who arrest the wrestler.

Notes

Perhaps Dassin's best film noir (with plenty of on-location shooting, á la *The Naked City*) this gangster melodrama is full of moral ambiguity and duplicitous characters. While the music score is again too effusive, and the female roles are minor, the director compensates with mood, visual invention and the great performance of Richard Widmark in the lead role. The film also features what may be Dassin's finest moment of pathos produced on film up to this time. It occurs after a rough four-minute wrestling duel (an extensive study of the director's seeming fascination with violence and sadism) that is nearly unwatchable in its tension.

The film opens with a narration ("Night and the city. The night is tomorrow night or any night. The city is London") that is soon dropped, and the picture proper begins with a chase. (It will also end with a chase.) Harry's pursuer stops when Harry enters Mary's apartment, indicated by the pursuer's shadow on the ground, though later we will see that the man waits outside for him.

Harry's loud checkered suit, carnation boutonnière, and white shoes mark him as flamboyant and common, with the fact of his being chased when we first see him an indication that he is not popular. However, Widmark makes Harry a likable character. At the same time, he shows us his weakness and vulnerability, making Harry perhaps the most interesting of Dassin's protagonists. He is also a classic film noir protagonist—dishonorable and doomed, a hollow man of ambition without values, described by the ceramic artist Adam as "an artist without an art." Harry is an infantile lost soul, his boastfulness masking inadequacy and insecurity, and his opportunism displayed by his attempt to rob Mary (only being stopped when he hears the sound of the door opening when she enters).

Unlike his previous pictures, *Night and the City* will provide few comic opportunities for Dassin. Even the introduction of the three (potentially comical) Americans at the American Bar, and Harry hustling for customers for The Silver Fox club, will fall by the wayside once Harry sees Gregorius at the fights.

Kristo's menace is demonstrated by the slap he gives a boxing attendant who tells his father to "take it easy" regarding Gregorius' dislike for the Strangler and the match. Gregorius' Greekness echoes the Greeks in *Thieves' Highway* and prefigures Dassin's later Greek work.

The idea of Mary working as a hostess at The Silver Fox aligns her with the alleged prostitute Rica of *Thieves' Highway*, Jean from *The Naked City*, and the femme fatales in the flashbacks of *Brute Force*. Mary's goodness is presented in the form of blind love in the face of what Harry does to her, and in her refusal to let him sacrifice himself for her profit. She is paralleled with the ambition and duplicity of the cold, calculating madam, Helen, who is the female counterpart to Harry. Gene Tierney being dubbed to sing at the club creates an expectation that Mary will be a more significant character than she actually is. Tierney was obviously cast merely for her box office draw (not that she isn't good in the film).

Francis Sullivan's corpulent Phil recalls Lee J. Cobb's well-fed Figlia. Here, as in *Thieves' Highway*, obesity symbolizes greed and self-indulgence.

Dassin uses a split-screen technique to show a conversation between Phil and Mary. He is seen in medium shot within the framed window of his office, with his back to the camera; and she is shown in long shot, in profile sitting on a chair. Both characters are compartmentalized as unhappy lovers.

A shadow on Phil's face when he decides to offer Harry 200 quid perhaps prefigures Phil's later betrayal; while Helen blowing smoking into Harry's face and suddenly kissing him in reaction to his tirade expresses her duplicity and manipulation in her offering him the money he needs—but only on *her* terms. Although she is attractive, she is not technically a femme fatale because she doesn't use erotic appeal to benefit herself.

The shadowed reflection of lines in his office presents Phil as a spider in his web, both entrapping Harry and being himself entrapped. Dassin places the camera outside an office window for the beginning of their negotiation, with Phil's change of heart explained by his silent discovery of Helen's missing fox piece (recalling the earlier scene where Helen's pleasure at the gift from her husband turns to disgust at his request for a thank you kiss). More shadows are used to show the danger inherent in Phil's deal, with his face in shadow when he gives Harry the money, and then Harry's face in shadow when Phil tells him that he wants to be a silent partner.

The narrative switch to daylight offers the only sustained happiness we will see Harry enjoy, as opposed to the unhappiness he suffers at night (although he will finally be killed during daytime). Widmark inserts a child-like joy into Harry's fleeting moments of happiness, even if they are based on duplicity. The actor also uses his balletic physicality to portray the character's euphoria. Widmark also employs a little of the giggle (labeled a "chortling laugh" by others) he had so memorably given the vicious hood Tommy Udo in his film debut, the crime drama *Kiss of Death* (1947), in a performance that had earned the actor a Best Supporting Actor Academy Award nomination.

The scene at the gym attached to Fabian Promotions recalls the homoerotic wrestlers from *The Naked City*, the bare-chested prisoners of *Brute Force*, and the bare-chested Nick from *Thieves' Highway*. Dassin again links eroticism with sadism in the wrestling training.

Dassin provides one of his rare close-ups when Harry awaits Gregorius' decision about whether Nikolas will fight the Strangler, since Harry is anxious to know whether the scheme he has instigated will pay off. Harry's pleasure at his success is expressed in Harry playing the drums in front of Phil back at the club. Phil's betrayal of Harry is expressed in his metaphorical line, "I am not giving you 200 quid; I am giving you the sharp edge of the knife," and he taps the cymbal on the bandstand as Harry leaves to parody Harry's previous drumming, after telling him, "You're a dead man." This last line, a classic film noir observation, will be repeated by Mary and Kristo, and prefigures the hit Kristo places on Harry.

A passing car nearly hits Harry when he leaves the club, and Dassin gives Widmark a long reaction shot. Our empathy with Harry's predicament is tested when he pushes Mary out of his way when stealing money from her apartment, his second attempt—this time successful.

The fight between the Strangler and Gregorius is Dassin's perfect set piece, generating audience empathy for both the drunken forty-year-old and the sixty-year-old champion of the old school. Both fighters have been manipulated by Harry to take advantage of their antagonism, but perhaps we empathize more with Gregorius because he is clearly not in the same physical shape as his opponent. This empathy will resonate in the old man's death afterwards. There is a moment of tension when the Strangler enters the room and we wonder whether Kristo will blame him for the death of his father. The Strangler's silent exit, unnoticed by Kristo, demonstrates his subtle determination to find Harry.

When Helen leaves Phil the following exchange occurs:

> PHIL: Helen, you don't know what you're walking into.
> HELEN: I know what I'm walking out of.

Phil's final comment—unheard by Helen—that she will come back to him and he will take her back are delivered with a sadness that prefigures Phil's death.

Harry as a man on the run can be equated to Dassin's flight from HUAC, although whether one considers the director to be as duplicitous as Harry probably depends on one's political point of view. Dassin ominously uses the subjective lights of the car that advances on Harry in front of the worksite of construction rubble over World War II bomb-damaged buildings, and the word "Danger" is written on the wall where Harry talks to the police constable, with the constable saving Harry from the occupants of the car. The director employs expressionist lighting and camera angles to show Harry's torment, with the ticking inside the shot tower adding aural tension. When Harry pushes away his pursuer in the shot tower, who brandishes a knife, we don't know if Harry has killed the man, who falls down the stairway. If the man *has* been killed, that colors our sympathy towards Harry, since we have seen him lie and manipulate but not kill before (even if the act can be interpreted as self-defense).

Helen's return to Phil creates the expectation that he will take her back as he had predicted. The sight of his back to her can initially be interpreted as his rejection of her, though it is soon revealed to be a sign of his death. There is ambiguity attached to the death, since we don't know whether he has committed suicide or whether he has been killed by the mad Molly, to whom Phil had bequeathed his money. Helen's horror at the realization of Phil being dead, and her loss of Phil's money as her last hope, is presented by her backing out of the frame into the darkness, as if she now ceases to exist.

The footsteps that Harry and Anna hear approaching his hiding place are revealed to be Mary's, one of the few people that mean him no harm. It's a relief of tension, but Harry looking away from her in shame rather than pleasure in seeing her is a sign of Harry's remorse over the way he has treated her. Mary rejecting his proposed idea that he sacrifice himself so that she can receive the reward as compensation again confirms her as a good person (ironically, he will go ahead with the plan anyway). Harry calling Mary a Judas paints him as a Christ-like martyr, and his running into the Strangler's hands when he runs away from her under the pretext of her supposed betrayal is a fateful move. Thankfully, Dassin spares us the sight of the Strangler killing Harry. Rather, his wretched demise has the Strangler throwing Harry's corpse into the river like garbage, recalling the disposal of bodies in *Brute Force* and *The Naked City*. Similarly, Kristo then throws his cigarette into the river, like Willy had contemptuously spit into the water after killing Peter in *The Naked City*. Kristo standing on the Hammersmith Bridge passively observing the murder of Harry is a sign that he has reasserted his control of the London underworld. The police arriving to arrest the Strangler seems to be a Production Code concession, because we don't know how they knew where to find Harry; while Adam, Mary's neighbor, arrives with the police to comfort Mary in another bit of narrative convenience.

In an interview on the DVD, Christopher Husted explains how the film had two released versions, one for the American market and one for the British (with a score by Benjamin Frankel). Apparently, Franz Waxman and Frankel worked simultaneously on their respective scores without the other knowing about it. Scenes from the film are shown on the DVD with Frankel's score for comparison, and, generally, his score is less melodramatic than Waxman's. Frankel uses a smaller orchestra and scores less of the film than Waxman. In particular, Frankel adds no music to Harry's chase at the worksite, and this reads as far more effective than Waxman's excessive attempt to evoke Harry's hysterical agitation. Husted advises that the British version of the film is longer and includes scenes, shots and characters not seen in the American print (presumably this additional footage was not filmed by Dassin). Husted also claims that the films are edited differently, and frequently use different portions of the scenes both versions have in common. Additionally, some scenes are missing entirely from one or other of the versions.

In the British version, Gene Tierney is first seen earlier than in the American, when Harry arrives at Mary's apartment and he asks her for money to finance a pill for fuel food. In the American Bar scene Frankel uses a wan drunken-ish score with banjo, as opposed to the slick Hollywood-style dance band arrangement that the Fox music department supplied in lieu of Waxman's lack of score. The British version has a scene where Mr. Hoskins tries to collect a hotel bill from Harry (the only indication of where Harry lives), and there is a shot of Helen kissing Harry from Phil's point of view before Harry asks Phil for the 200 quid. The British print also includes a scene between Adam and Mary where he cooks soup for her (continuing the gag of him being a bad cook), and they are visited by Fergus Chilk and Yosh, which allows them to learn about the reward for Harry and explains how Mary finds him at the end of the film (and how Adam finds her). Glenn Erickson in the DVD audio commentary describes two more scenes from the British version: one where Helen tries to steal a five pound note from Phil before he gives her the fox fur, and another where Adam meets Mary at the Silver Fox when Harry has stood her up. The ending of the two versions are also different, with the British print using a shot of the Strangler emerging from the riverbank after he has thrown Harry and before the police arrive, and the film ending with two shots of Adam and Mary walking up and across the bridge. This presents a more romantic notion of hope for them as a couple—a less cynical conclusion than in the American version.

In his interview with Gordon Gow in *Films & Filming*, Dassin called *Night and the City* "a film I've chosen to forget." However, in his interview with Patrick McGilligan and Paul Buhle for their book *Tender Comrades*, Dassin stated that the film "was certainly my

French movie card for *Night and the City* (1950).

best up to that time." The director also tells how a part was hurriedly written for Gene Tierney when he was very close to shooting in order to stop her from committing suicide after an unhappy love affair. This idea is supported by his interview on the DVD, where Dassin says that Tierney grew stronger from working. (The *Biography* episode on Tierney, "A Shattered Portrait," suggests the time period here is off. The actress had had an affair with John F. Kennedy while she was married to Oleg Cassini, but it ended in 1947 with Kennedy's refusal to marry Tierney if she divorced Cassini. Tierney's autobiography, *Self-Portrait*, makes no mention of a failed love affair at that time.)

The exotically beautiful Tierney was a successful Broadway actress who signed with Fox in 1940. After starting in supporting roles, she scored the leads in two independent productions: the World War II drama *Sundown* (1941) and the melodrama *The Shanghai Gesture* (1941). Tierney returned to Fox for supporting roles, then received top billing for the homefront aviation drama *Thunder Birds* (1942). She would continue as the lead in the oriental adventure *China Girl* (1942); the comedy *Heaven Can Wait* (1943); the murder mystery *Laura* (1944), the film Tierney is probably best remembered for; the World War II drama *A Bell for Adano* (1945); the film noir *Leave Her to Heaven* (1945), for which she was nominated for the Best Actress Academy Award; the historical drama *Dragonwyck* (1946); and the fantasy romance *The Ghost and Mrs. Muir* (1947). Tierney's title prior to *Night and the City* was the psychological drama *Whirlpool* (1949), which would also prove to be her last leading role at Fox. She would go on to be top-billed in Paramount's domestic comedy *The Mating Season* (1951) and the independent British crime drama *Personal Affair* (1953), but after more supporting roles, personal problems kept her off the screen for seven years. Tierney would return for three more supporting appearances and finish her career with three television roles.

Richard Widmark was a successful radio and Broadway actor who signed with Fox in 1947. After playing supporting parts in *Kiss of Death*, the crime drama *The Street with No Name* (1948), the melodrama *Road House* (1948), and the western *Yellow Sky* (1948), he secured the leading roles in the sea drama *Down to the Sea in Ships* (1949) and his prior title, the disaster drama *Slattery's Hurricane* (1949). After *Night and the City*, Widmark would play leading roles in films for the next twenty-seven years, as well as act as producer for his company Heath Productions, and uncredited director of the war adventure *The Secret Ways* (1961).

In the DVD interview, Dassin admits that he hadn't read the book the screenplay was based on before beginning shooting, since he didn't have time because the project came together so quickly. The director later learned that Gerald Kersh was angry that an entire subplot had not been included. Dassin's tenuous position as director was apparently solidified by his shooting the most expensive scenes first (although one might think that once those were done someone else could be brought in to complete the remaining scenes). In his DVD audio commentary, Glenn Erickson advises that this strategy was suggested by Zanuck, who thought if it was done this way Dassin might be allowed to finish the film. The director also says that Douglas Fairbanks, Jr., who was working at the British studio, had done most of the British casting. The climax was filmed over two days, at dawn each day, using six cameras and only requiring one take. The director attributes the success of the film's complex characterizations to his lonely state of mind when filming. After returning from London, Dassin found he was now banned from entering the 20th Century–Fox studio grounds because of his industry blacklisting; he cut the film by liaising with the editor by telephone.

Notes on the TCM webpage indicate that the Kersh novel was first sold to Chas. K.

Feldman Group Productions in 1946. Jacques Tourneur was engaged to direct, but the production was cancelled due to casting difficulties. Between 1946 and 1949 six writers, including Jo Eisenger, were assigned to the project. Then 20th Century–Fox bought the property from Feldman, and hired Eisenger to do further work on it. Part of the reasoning behind making the film in London was the "frozen" currency owed to Fox. TCM also says it is likely that sequences involving singer Adelaide Hall, a calypso band, and actors Eliot Makeham, Betty Shale and Betty Marsden are in the British version, but were dropped for the American release.

Producer Samuel G. Engel was a screenwriter who began producing "B" titles at Fox in 1936. He graduated to "A" productions with the western *My Darling Clementine* (1946), for which he also wrote the screenplay, and followed with the domestic comedy *Sitting Pretty* (1948) and its sequel *Mr. Beverdere Goes to College* (1949), *The Street with No Name*, the youth sea drama *Deep Waters* (1948), and the religious comic drama *Come to the Stable* (1949).

A 1992 remake of *Night and the City* was made by director Irwin Winkler, and was dedicated to Dassin. The treatment altered some aspects of the original's screenplay (e.g., the "Silver Fox Club" became the bar "Boxers," boxing replaced wrestling as the sport, the older fighter was the brother and not the father of the boxing promoter, and he fought with the venue's bouncer rather than another athlete, Harry is now an attorney dabbling in boxing, and Helen does not go back to Phil). The biggest change was in the relationship between Harry and Helen, with her part enlarged to accommodate the star casting of Jessica Lange, with Robert De Niro as Harry. This Helen had a romantic relationship with Harry, and she barely reacted to his selling her a forged liquor license (its exposure as a forgery comes about when Phil checks with the State Liquor Authority). Helen also flees with Harry during the climactic chase by the promoter's hoods.

The remake lacks the film noir fatalism of the original, with Winkler over-using the Platters song "The Great Pretender" for Harry's ambitions, which the treatment demonstrates by making him an effusive double-talker. It begins amusingly when muggers attempt to rob Harry at an ATM, only to learn that his balance is zero. The film is probably most memorable for the beating Harry receives from Phil, and the anger of Jessica Lange when Helen leaves her husband (although Phil throwing a woman who dresses as a nun out of his bar and onto the ground is a shocking image).

Jessica Lange and Robert De Niro in a publicity still for the remake of Jules Dassin's 1950 film that was also named *Night and the City* (1992).

Winkler had previously made the blacklist drama *Guilty by Suspicion* (1990), with De Niro playing David Merrill, a Hollywood film director that could be read as resembling Dassin. Despite the treatment's point in differentiating the director from Kazan, his anguish over whether or not to inform mirrors Kazan's plight. Merrill is said to have attended and been thrown out of Communist Party meetings, but unlike Dassin, he was never a member of the Party. Rather, named as a Communist sympathizer, he finally agrees to appear before HUAC after six months of unemployment and harassment by the F.B.I. Merrill is presented as heroic for refusing to name names, even though he is presumably found in contempt, facing a fine and perhaps jail time, and sacrifices a film deal with Darryl F. Zanuck. *Guilty by Suspicion* is also notable for its casting of Sam Wanamaker in an ironic supporting role—that of a lawyer urging Merrill to cooperate with the Committee—since the actor had been blacklisted in the 1950s.

Release

June 9, 1950. Glenn Erickson claims that in New York the film played at the Roxy Theatre with a live musical stage show starring Lucille Ball and Desi Arnaz.

Reviews

"A smash melodrama with a stirring climax. The action packs a wallop in every scene."—*Variety*

"[Dassin's] evident talent has been spent upon a pointless, trashy yarn, and the best that he has accomplished is a turgid pictorial grotesque.... It is all very bold and vertiginous, but what is delivered here is, in the end, just a lot of meandering in London's supposed lower depths."—Bosley Crowther, *The New York Times*, June 10, 1950

"A gaudy melodrama.... It gets some lurid effects out of a sordid story, murky backgrounds and a gallery of grotesque characters. Unfortunately, the excitement runs down well before the picture does.... Dassin's staging and Franz Waxman's overwrought musical score try to outdo each other in stridency."—*Time* magazine, July 3, 1950

"Should be a great help in sending American tourists to Paris."—*London Evening Standard*

"Several years before he made *Rififi*, Dassin directed this less flamboyant thriller, which is much less well known, but in some ways better. Dassin's shocking specialty—a kind of stifled violence that one fears will explode—finds the right milieu.... Widmark has what is possibly his best role."—Pauline Kael, *5001 Nights at the Movies*

···

Rififi (1955)

[aka *Du rififi chez les hommes*]
Pathé Consortium Cinema/Indusfilms/Primafilm/S.N.Pathé Cinema

Credits: Director: Jules Dassin; Producers: Henri Berard, Pierre Cabaud, Rene Bezard; Screenplay: Jules Dassin, Rene Wheeler, Auguste Le Breton, based on the novel by Auguste Lebreton; Photography: Philippe Agostini; Editor: Roger Dwyre; Music:

Georges Auric; Production Design: Trauner; Set Decoration: Auguste Capelier; Costumes: Rosine Delamere; Makeup: Anatole Paris; Sound: Charles Akerman, Jacques Lebreton. B&W, 117–122 minutes, French/Italian with English subtitles. Filmed at Photosonor studios, Courbevoie; Saint-Remy-les-Chevreuse, Yvelines; and in various locations around Paris, France, in 1954.

Song: "Le Rififi" (Jacques Larue, M. Philippe-Gerard), sung by Magali Noel.

Cast: Jean Servais (Tony le Stéphanois); Carl Mohner (Jo le Suedois); Robert Manuel (Mario Ferrati); Janine D'Arcey (Louise le Suedois); Pierre Grasset (Louis Grutter, aka Louis le Tatoué); Robert Houssein (Remi Grutter); Marcel Lupovici (Pierre Grutter); Dominique Maurin (Tonio le Suedois); Magali Noel (Viviane); Marie Sabouret (Mado les Grands Bras); Claude Sylvain (Ida Ferrati); Perlo Vita/Jules Dassin (Cesar le Milanais); Armandel (Second Gambler); Alain Bouvette (Footman L'Age d'Or); Alice Garan; Dalibert (Webb); Jacques David; Emile Genevois (Charlie); Marcelle Hainia (Fredo's Wife); Marcel Lesieur (Fredo); Daniel Mendaille (Lookout); Huguette Montreal; Lita Reccio; Fernand Sardou (First Gambler). Uncredited: Jacques Besnard (Third Gambler); Teddy Bilis (Teddy Laurentin); Jenny Doria; Rene Hell (Un Camelot); Gilbert Moreau; Maryse Paillet (Charlie's Mother); Marcel Rouze (First Gendarme); Roger Rudel (French voice of Jo le Suedois).

VHS/DVD: DVD Criterion Collection released April 24, 2001.

Synopsis

When Tony le Stéphanois gets out of prison after serving a five-year sentence, he is approached by his nephew, Jo le Suedois, and their friend Mario Ferrati to rob the Mappin & Webb jewelry store. After scarring his ex-girlfriend, Mado les Grands Bras, by beating her back with a belt because she had abandoned him, Tony agrees to the heist. Mario enlists the aid of Italian safecracker Cesar le Milanaise, and the four successfully pull off the robbery, scoring 240 million dollars in jewels.

Cesar gives a ring he has taken from the store to Vivianne, a singer at the L'Age d'Or nightclub owned by Pierre Grutter. Cesar informs on Grutter about Mario, who is killed by Grutter's henchmen. Tony finds Cesar tied up at the club and shoots him for his betrayal. Grutter connects Tony and Jo to Mario, and Jo's five-year-old son Tonio is kidnapped. Jo agrees to give Grutter his share of the money, which has been delivered by the heist's fence. Mado helps Tony discover where Tonio is being held, but is too late to stop Grutter from shooting Jo. Tony is wounded, though he shoots Grutter dead, and he drives Tonio back to his waiting mother before dying.

Notes

Dassin's return to filmmaking after five years of being blacklisted is an overlong heist movie peppered with film noir fatalism. It also features Dassin's first acting role in one of his own films. Although there is an extraordinary twenty-nine-minute dialogue-free set piece for the heist, the director again inexplicably over-uses a musical score, which culminates in a sequence of over-edited hysteria. While the narrative's interest dips after the heist and before the fatalism sets in, its exploration of duplicity is even more fascinating than in Dassin's earlier titles, given the resonance of his American blacklisting. The film also allows him to present multiple scene of perverse and sadistic violence. The treatment aligns the viewer's sympathy with criminals, enhanced by the comic sensibilities of Mario and Cesar, and by Jo having a family (which is exploited when fate turns against them after the heist).

The film begins with a faceless group of men playing poker. The camera moves up to reveal Tony's face, with Servais' tired appearance and lack of money symbolic of the anguish that Dassin must have felt during his period of banishment and unemployment. Tony's five years in prison parallels Dassin's five years of blacklisting, with Tony's noble action of taking the rap for Jo extending to the director taking the rap for others who named him as a Communist and named names to protect themselves. The final parallel can be made in light of Tony's release being on account of his good behavior, with perhaps Dassin's lack of considered subversive behavior allowing him to finally make another film. The idea that Tony was in prison for a jewelry heist, and his willingness to be involved in another so soon after his release, is a questionable plot point, since we would assume that the police would immediately think of him as a suspect. (The fact that he has no prospective alibi on the night in question, unlike the other three participants, doesn't help.)

Tony wearing a hand puppet as he pours coffee and talks to Jo, after playing with Tonio, adds a comic touch to the otherwise dour character, and Dassin manages to invest the treatment with other touches of humor. The search light in the interior of the L'Age d'Or nightclub (named after the 1930 Luis Buñuel film that the production designer, Trauner, also worked on) recalls the mirror-balled interior light of The Silver Fox Club in *Night and the City*, with the women employed here presumably also hostesses. Mado's character being a prostitute recalls the women of *Brute Force*, *The Naked City*, *Thieves' Highway*, and *Night and the City*, and her humiliation and beating by Tony adds moral ambiguity to both their characters. Tony loses more here, in terms of audience empathy, in spite of his perceived betrayal by Mado, since his action is in the present (even if not seen) and hers is merely hearsay from the past. Additionally, his action is a physical assault that results in a permanent marking, whereas hers, as a moral weakness, is judged less severely. Tony asking Mado to strip in his room creates the expectation that he will make love to her, although his asking her to remove her jewelry and fur coat as the emblems of her profit from other lovers reads as odd. Dassin protects the actresses' modesty when Tony pushes Mado behind a wall, which also spares us the sight of her being beaten, and the sadistic attack stands as counterpoint to the photograph of Tony and Mado that the camera looks at. Another duplicitous woman appears in the form of Mario's wife Ida, who betrays Tony to save her husband.

Dassin's appearance as the moustache-sporting Cesar comes as a surprise, and one wonders whether the director felt he still needed to hide his identity (in spite of his accredited direction of the film) by listing himself as Perlo Vita. It is also interesting that he only speaks Italian, like Mario. Although Cesar appears to understand French, he doesn't speak the language like Tony and Jo do, which allows him to utilize pantomime in his performance (highlighted in the montage when he is in the jewelry store on the pretext of being a customer). The treatment scores a laugh from Cesar being an effete womanizer, who wears ballet slippers for the robbery.

The performance of the title song in the film allows for a translation, with "rififi" said to mean "rough and tumble." The song has sadomasochistic overtones in Viviane's expression of her attraction to violent men, demonstrated by the use of shadowed dancers behind a screen as she sings. The male shadow dancer's use of a gun prefigures the fate of Cesar,

French movie card for *Rififi* (1955).

Jo, and Tony, who are all shot, and also Tonio's playing with a toy gun at the film's climax. The danger of violent men extends to Pierre's actions in pursuit of the heist jewels, although Tony is equally aggressive in his revenge upon Pierre.

The relationship between Pierre and his henchman Remi has homoerotic overtones, as well as perversity in the fact that Remi is a dope addict and carries a razor blade as a weapon. (Remi's dope addiction will eventually lead to his downfall at the climax, since his distracted minding of the kidnapped Tonio allows the boy to be rescued by Tony.) Pierre having drugs in his locked desk is a kind of tease for Remi, a means of control that Remi objects to by threatening Pierre with the blade. Pierre's repeated slapping of Remi, however, is evidence of his mastery over his subordinate.

Dassin creates two montages for the film. The first runs for five minute and covers the gang watching the neighborhood to note the delivery routines, taking an impression of a lock in order to make a key, and Cesar in the store identifying the safe and the model of the alarm system the gang needs to disarm.

Viviane's repeated singing of the "Rififi" song in rehearsal with the club's band plays over the scenes of Jo and Mario leaving their homes, Cesar leaving Viviane for the heist, and Tony shown having no one to leave.

The gang tying up the building concierge and his wife dents our sympathy for the criminals, but it resurges somewhat when they place a pillow behind the head of the struggling wife, which stops her struggle. This can be read as both a kindness and an act of practicality.

During the heist sequence Dassin uses no music, cleverly utilizing sound effects for realism (with a piano key accidently struck twice before the keyboard is covered). The director occasionally uses cut-aways to create tension. A cigarette pack left outside the building's door attracts the attention of a policeman, but the expectation of his investigating further is not met when he throws away the pack after seeing that it is empty (an action which also scores a laugh at the fact of his littering). As with the scene where the men try to figure out how to defeat the alarm system, the fun of the heist sequence, aligned with our wanting the gang to be successful, is seeing the ingenuity of their technique.

The dirt on their clothes from digging the hole in the floor above the jewelry store, and the sweat on Tony's face as he uses a fire extinguisher to disarm the alarm, only makes the gang seem more real and not superheroes. Jo and Mario seen drinking as Tony and Cesar work on the hole creates two expectations: that Jo and Mario's apparent carelessness will ruin the heist, and that Tony and Cesar will not like their behavior. But neither expectation is met.

Dassin moves outside to show a florist delivery and a street-cleaning truck, suggesting time passing and adding urgency, which is heightened by the staccato close-ups of the three other men watching Cesar using the contraption to create a hole in the back of the safe (which operates on the same principle as a can-opener). This staccato editing will be repeated at the film's climax, with Tony driving Tonio home.

Dassin then cuts to two policeman on bicycles who notice the gang's parked car in a side street, and our return to the gang sees that they are back on the upper floor. The parallel action creates more tension, since we don't want them to be caught when they are so close to succeeding. Tony spotting the police bicycle as he heads for the car and walking away creates an expectation that he will abandon the others, so that his opportunistic return to retrieve the car is a surprise.

The issue that the policemen have recorded the car's license plate is later resolved by

Tony dumping the car, and dialogue resumes with the gang sitting at a table as the jewels are shown. A newspaper seller gets a laugh from his line, "Biggest take since the Sabine women!" The police offering a ten million dollar reward seems excessive, although, as with the reward in *Night and the City*, it is a motivator for the gang to be apprehended. The irony of the heist, however, is that none of the participants profit from it.

The attack on Cesar uses a subjective camera for his point of view when Pierre's henchmen take him into the back of the club, and we only learn later that he has not been killed but only tied up. Mario tied up in a chair and threatened by Remi and his razor blade recalls the assault on Louie by Munsey in *Brute Force*, although here Mario is killed (off camera). Dassin places the lamp under which we know the jewels are hidden in the same frame when Mario is surrounded, and even though Ida tells Tony not to come after calling him, the fact that she has linked him to Mario and the heist is enough for Pierre's men. Her change of mind, which ensures she is killed with Mario, doesn't quite redeem her betrayal, even if it is done for the love of her husband.

Cesar seen tied up parallels the blacklisted director's restrictions, and Tony murders him for "ratting out" Mario. This may be Dassin's subtle judgment of what cooperative witnesses for HUAC deserve (like Kazan), since Cesar accepts his fate without protest, in spite of the language barrier. (This thinking is confirmed by Dassin, who, in his interview on the *Rififi* DVD, claims that the Cesar character is not killed in the novel.)

Tony has an interesting argument with Jo over giving the kidnappers money for Tonio, since Tony believes the boy will be killed anyway because he will be able to identify his kidnappers. Thus, Jo's share of the money would be given for nothing. Tony's cynical point of view is somewhat ameliorated by his intention to get Tonio back, although fate will stop Tony from being able to do so without Jo losing his life. Pierre's time deadline is little more than a motivator to get the money from Jo, but Jo's lack of faith in Tony prefigures his own death.

Dassin's second montage showing Tony visiting friends in an attempt to secure allies for the coming fight against Pierre recalls Harry Fabian visiting the lowlifes of London to borrow money in *Night and the City*, though Tony's intention is nobler. Mado betraying Pierre by helping Tony is a switch for her character after she had previously refused to help Tony, in light of his beating of her. Her change of heart is due to Pierre's kidnapping of Tonio, she claims; and Mado's duplicity—and the perversity of the drug dealer Charlie—is presented in the way he is revealed in the mirrored reflection of an open cupboard door. Tony's beating of Pierre's henchman, Louis, at the villa where Tonio is being held is again obscured by Dassin behind a pile of stones, with Tonio's toy gun mirroring Tony's real gun that he has used to shoot Remi. The death of Jo at the villa where he has come to give Pierre his money is presented as gunshots heard by Tony, and Tony stroking of the hair of his dead nephew is an act of homoerotic kindness as much as a suggestion that the wounded Tony is equally doomed.

Dassin returns to using music when Tony drives Tonio back to Louise, after a long absence of a musical score. This is the only scene in which music is used effectively. Unfortunately, as previously mentioned, the scene is over-edited into hysteria, with shots of Tony driving, Tony's point of view of the road, and Tonio laughing. Shots of Louise looking out her window are added until Tony's car crashes near her building, and her retrieval of Tonio without a care for Tony is rather shocking. Dassin retreats into a long shot showing the crowd gathered around Tony's car, with some ambiguity over whether Tony is dead or can be saved. A film noir reading of the narrative would indicate he is dead, so that the celebration of Tonio's rescue is soured by the death of the last of the four gang members, the narrative's protagonists.

In the article in *Picturegoer* by Henry Kahn, Dassin is quoted as saying that he felt he had to make the film when he read "how a simple umbrella is more useful to a skilled craftsman [breaking into a jeweler's shop] than anything else." (The umbrella is used to collect the tiles removed from the hole in the floor of the upper apartment.) He says he was given permission by executives of a British firm of jewelers to use their real store building in the Rue de la Paix of Paris. Dassin also says he asked police how to silence the shop's burglar alarm, but they would not tell him. When he lunched with officials of the alarm manufacturers, they couldn't suggest a way of silencing the machine either. The article claims that within 48 hours of the film being screened in Paris, an outcry arose from municipal councilors, jewelers, and righteous citizens. All Paris was saying that it had been given an elementary lesson in shop-breaking, and Dassin admitted, "I have been charged with teaching youngsters how to go about cracking open jewelers' shops." He continued: "I asked my seventeen-year-old son if he would 'have a go' after seeing the film. His answer was a prompt, 'No, thanks, I don't think I'll bother. It looks too much like hard work.'" However, on the *Rififi* DVD, Dassin advises that the film was withdrawn from screenings in Mexico after copycat robberies took place.

In his article in *Films & Filming*, Gordon Gow describes the picture as "a superior movie of the gangster genre and something to be noted with respect in the whole area of continental cinema of the time." In his interview with Gow, Dassin claims that making the film was very difficult because of the language problem. He was all right with the actors "because you don't need language to communicate." But talking with the technicians was not so easy. He sometimes asked himself whether so much of the film, apart from the robbery sequences, was silent because of his own lack of French, a language he was still learning. (In his interview on the *Rififi* DVD, Dassin says that silence was frequently used because professional thieves work in silence—since noise is their enemy—and he had the gang members wear noiseless shoes during the robbery.) Dassin believed that having Tony drive the car with Tonio in it at the film's climax, with the wounded Tony continually on the verge of blacking out, was the answer to the question of how to surpass the high level of suspense found in the robbery sequence.

In *Tender Comrades* Dassin claims that he was in Italy when he was called and offered the film by producer Henri Berard. Returning to France, he was told on a weekend (Dassin says in his *Rififi* DVD interview it was a Friday) that he had to answer yes or no by the following Monday. Unfortunately, the source book was in French, and, worse, in a local argot that even some native speakers can't read. Dassin got ahold of a friend (his agent, according to the director on the DVD of *Rififi*), "who sacrificed his love life" to read him the book. Even hearing it read aloud, however, didn't help, because the director felt he had no idea how to do it. Dassin went to answer no to the producer but heard himself say yes! He was told that he was the only person who could make the book into a film, because all the bad guys in the story were North African and at the time relations between France and Algeria were explosive. It was thought that Dassin could make the bad guys American, but the director stunned the producer by suggesting that they be made French. He was hired, with Dassin commenting in his 2004 LACMA interview that "I got the job for the same reason I was blacklisted"—presumably because he was perceived to be un–American. The director repeats this claim in his interview on the *Rififi* DVD.

On the DVD of *Night and the City*, Dassin says that he was told the film had copied the crime drama *The Asphalt Jungle* (1950), another fatalistic noir tale of an aging criminal involved in a jewelry heist. The director states that he failed to see the connection "except for the story element of a man undone by his attraction to a beautiful woman." While an argument could be made that Tony's beating of Mado eventually leads to his downfall, since it incurs the wrath of Pierre, the connection is only made in that the criminal in John Huston's title is caught because he delays his escape when spellbound by the sight of a jitterbugging female teenager. Both films feature an Italian safecracker and a gunshot-wounded man driving a car at the climax, and both engender audience empathy for the thieves, but *The Asphalt Jungle* differs greatly in its plot. In that film, the police are a presence in the narrative; it is the aging criminal who instigates the crime, the twelve-minute robbery sequence has dialogue, and the fence attempts to double cross the gang. Perhaps the greatest difference between the films is in Huston's superior control over the material (Dassin lets the last part of the film meander, weakening its interest), and in the treatment of the female characters. The women in *The Asphalt Jungle* are less marginal in the narrative than those in *Rififi*; Huston also manages to create far more sympathy for them than Dassin.

In the *Rififi* DVD interview Dassin says that when he met with Auguste Le Breton, the novelist told him, "I read your screenplay. I would like to know, where is my book?" Dassin tried to explain the difference between a novel and what is needed for a screenplay. The novelist, who dressed in a hat styled to make himself resemble George Raft, took out a gun and placed it on a table in front of them. Again he asked, "Where is my book?" Dassin says, "I looked at the gun and I looked at his hat and I began to laugh and because I laughed, because I showed no fear of his hat or his gun, he took me in his arms and we became very good friends."

Dassin also had trouble with Berard, a producer he acknowledges hired him to take advantage of the director's impoverished and desperate situation (and therefore could pay very little). The director refused to shoot in sunlight because he wanted a grey color palette, and he refused to include a fist fight in the treatment. Berard had wanted a fist fight to appear in the movie because at the time the biggest star in French films was Eddie Constantine, who had a fist fight in *every* picture. Dassin also advises that he played the part of Cesar because the actor who had been cast became unavailable.

The director admits that he had not liked the novel's cruel aspects (e.g., a necrophilia subplot was rejected for the screenplay). It was the passage about a robbery that takes place to finance a greater project that inspired him to build the screenplay around it.

Dassin also comments on the lack of music during the heist set piece. Both Berard and the composer, Georges Auric, had wanted to include music here, and music *was* written for it. Dassin asked Auric to view the edited film with and without the score, and the composer then agreed that music was unnecessary.

The director suggests in the interview that he is drawn to crime stories because he considers himself "a rebel" and likes to see authority conquered.

Dassin claims that the film's low budget (said to have been $200,000) affected casting, and that he was only able to get the 44-year-old Jean Servais for the lead because the actor had not worked for many years and was prepared to do so for little money. (It is rumored that the actor's lack of work was also due to him being an alcoholic.) Servais had been in movies since 1932 and had played Frederic Chopin in the German historical drama *La chanson de l'adieu* (1934). He also starred in the French war drama *Les réprouvés* (1936). However, he otherwise played supporting roles, with his prior title being the horror romance *Le chevalier de la nuit* (aka *Knight of the Night*, 1953). Servais would go on to play

Mexican lobby card for *Rififi* (1955). Jules Dassin is seen in the center picture, since he plays Cesar le Milanais in the film, although he is credited as "Perlo Vita."

more supporting roles and appear in Dassin's next title, *He Who Must Die* (aka *Celui qui doit mourir*, 1957).

Most of the crew and the editor of *Rififi* were not chosen by the director, but he was pleased with their work. Dassin also tells how he had Hollywood director Lewis Milestone, who happened to be in Paris, view the film and, that Milestone told him, "You go and make the same film all your life." This was a compliment from Milestone, who said that Hitchcock had great success making the same film over and over again, and that Dassin could have success doing the same.

Producer Berard had previously made the Fernandel comedy *Adhemar ou le jouet de la fatalité* (1951), and the French titles *Le plus heureux des hommes* (aka *The Happiest of Men*, 1952), and *Le guérisseur* (1953). He would go on to work with Dassin on *He Who Must Die* (aka *Celui qui doit mourir*, 1957).

Rififi was the first producing title for co-producer Rene Bezard, who had previously executive produced the French adventure comedy *Cadet Rousselle* (1954) with fellow co-producer Pierre Cabaud.

Release

France—April 13, 1955; Italy—February 7, 1956; USA—June 5, 1956; with the tagline "Rififi ... means Trouble!" At the 1955 Cannes Film Festival, where the film represented

France, it was nominated for the Golden Palm, and Dassin shared the Best Director award with Sergei Vasilyev (for his Bulgarian historical drama *Geroite na Shipka*; aka *Heroes of Shipka*). The film would also win the Critics Award from the 1956 French Syndicate of Cinema Critics.

Reviews

"Perhaps the keenest crime film that ever came out of France ... beautifully fashioned."—Bosley Crowther, *The New York Times*, June 6, 1956

"A 30-minute stretch of wordless moviemaking is one of the most engrossing sequences since the invention of talking pictures.... But once the burglary is over, Dassin's imagination fails him. The remainder of the film seems to have been made by a sadly inferior second team."—*Time* magazine, July 16, 1956

"The granddaddy of a batch of suspense films featuring how to knock over safes or break into banks and museums, but its own chief distinction is its nasty tone."—Pauline Kael, *5001 Nights at the Movies*

"The best crime film I have ever seen.... The direction is a marvel of skill and inventiveness ... [and through it] we divine the filmmaker, a tender, indulgent man, gentle and trusting."—François Truffaut, *The Films in My Life*

"Perhaps the greatest of all 'heist' movies.... The long scene of the actual theft, completely in silence, will have your heart in your throat."—Jim Craddock, *VideoHounds's Golden Movie Retriever*

....

He Who Must Die (1957)

[aka *Celui qui doit mourir*]
Indus Films/Prima Film/Cinetel/Filmsonor/Da Ma Produzione

Credits: Director: Jules Dassin; Producer: Henri Berard; Screenplay: Ben Barzman, Jules Dassin, Andre Obey, based on the novel *Le Christ Recrucifié* (aka *The Greek Passion*) by Nikos Kazantzakis; Photography: Jacques Natteau; Editors: Roger Dwyre, Pierre Gillette; Music: Georges Auric; Production Design: Max Douy; Sound: P. L. Calvet; Costumes: Christiane Coste. B&W, 122 minutes. French language with English subtitles. Filmed in Crete, Greece, in 1957.

Cast: Jean Servais (Father Photis); Carl Mohner (Agha); Gregoire Aslan (Lukas); Gert Froebe (Patriarcheos); Teddy Bilis (Hadji Nikolis); Rene Lefevre (Yannakos/Peter); Lucien Raimbourg (Kostandis/James); Melina Mercouri (Katerina/Mary Magdalene); Roger Hanin (Panayotaro/Judas); Pierre Vaneck (Manolios/Jesus Christ); Dimos Starenios (Ladas); Nicole Berger (Mariori); Maurice Ronet (Michelis/John); Fernand Ledoux (Father Grigoris); Anna Armaou; Nitza Avantagelou; Joseph Dassin; Pannayotaros Karavoussanos; Thanassis Kedrakas; Yanni Migadis; Rita Moussouri; Panagiotis Neranzoulis; Nikos Papadakis; Dimitri Papadimos; Olympia Papadouka; Rena Peza; Stephanos Skopelitis; George Stupakis; and the population of Kritsa, an isle of Crete.

VHS/DVD: Not available in either format.

Synopsis

In 1951 a Greek village is ransacked by invading Turks, and the survivors walk for three months to find a new home. They arrive at another town of Greeks who live peacefully with Turkish forces, headed by Agha, and who are planning to celebrate the St. Elijan holiday by reenacting a passion play. The refugees are shunned by order of the town's priest, Father Grigoris, who convinces the townspeople that they have cholera. So the refugees set up camp in the Sarakina, the hills near the town. Blessed by the generosity of some of the townspeople who fear the refugees will starve to death, their plight is expressed by Manolis, who has been cast as Jesus in the play. Manolis is ex-communicated by the town when it is learned that his cohorts have stolen food for the refugees, and his friend, Michelis, joins him in sympathy. When Michelis' father Patriarcheos, the town's council leader dies, Michelis inherits land. He desires to sign it over to the refugees, but this plan is rejected by Father Grigoris. The refugees, under the leadership of Father Photis, decide to attack the town and demand their rights. A battle ensues. Agha negotiates a peace with Manolis, but when Manolis tries to take the Turk's machine gun, he is taken captive and killed in the town's church. The refugees permit revenge killings and await the reinforcements ordered by the Turks.

Notes

Although competently staged, this earnest Christ allegory is only occasionally arresting, with a ten-minute set piece and an intimate two-hander scene that both feature satisfying narrative transitions, and one innovative use of the subjective camera. Otherwise, Dassin indulges in extended scenes that read as overlong, although once again the treatment allows him to explore the theme of duplicity (here in a particularly shocking manner, since the duplicitous character is a priest). The film is notable as the first of eight that the director would make with actress Melina Mercouri, even if her role (as yet another of his cinema prostitutes) is marginal to the male dramatic dynamics. Thankfully, Dassin uses source music and singing on the soundtrack, rather than his standard overdone score, and limits himself to building drumbeats for the film's climax.

Under the opening credits are images of the Turk attack: buildings on fire, horses running, a burning crucifix, and women crying. A bouzouki-playing-and-singing boy, Youssoufaki (perhaps the son of Agha), whips a guard in an act of perversity and class privilege. Katerina is judged in the same manner, since, as a whore, she is considered inferior to other women (which is ironic given that she probably does for men what other women won't) and objectified by the men in the street. The antagonism of the women towards her is exemplified by Panayotaro's wife fighting with her when Katerina tries to enter the church. At least, this is ostensibly the reason, although Panayotaro's later meetings with Katerina (hardly surprising given the older age of his wife) would suggest that his wife has another agenda. The casting of the passion play is done by Father Grigoris to demonstrate his power in the council, with Panayotaro's objection to being cast as Judas momentarily amusing, though later it will be Panayotaro who executes the Christ-figure Manolis.

The new people are initially considered beggars by Grigoris, and later called refugees by Katerina. The priest's lack of compassion for the people is demonstrated by his refusal

Poster for *He Who Must Die* (1957).

to let them even have uncultivated (i.e., useless) land, and it is Grigoris who reads the death of a woman as a sign of cholera rather than death from hunger (as Father Photis deduces). Fear of the refugees is fear of outsiders, and one can imagine Dassin could relate to them since he himself was the victim of fear-mongering; the fear of infection from the supposed disease can be equated to the fear of association with Communists and other subversive undesirables. The refugees setting up camp relatively close to the town would seem to be an act of provocation. It certainly makes it easy for their encampment to be visited by townspeople.

A flute is heard coming from the refugee's camp during a long scene of Yannakos getting drunk, as a reminder of the presence of the aliens (a device later repeated with singing). The sequence ties in narratively to the later scene when the equally drunk Manolis goes to Katerina. Their scene together is (along with his later sermon to the townspeople) one of the best in the film, even if its transitions are predictable. It is also perhaps Mercouri's best scene, since she gets to change from being sexually aggressive to angry in her rejection of Manolis, who only gets brave enough to have sex with her out of the shame of being silenced by Patriarcheos.

The fight between Manolis and Panayotaro is framed with the battling men on the left of the frame in semi-darkness, and a fountain on the right. The aggression, instigated by Panayotaro's jealousy over seeing Manolis leaving Katerina's house (in spite of the fact that we know he didn't have sex with her), is more of Dassin's taste for violence, but is also restrained in its abbreviation. However, the antagonism will be used to flavor Panayotaro's eventual Judas-like murder of Manolis. Panayotaro's frustration in not finishing the fight is carried over into the extended scene where he drunkenly plays with a whip. The narrative uses Panayotaro's anger at Katerina to create the expectation that he will kill her, something he threatens to do because she has refused to see him again, but this is an expectation that remains unfulfilled.

The scene of Manolis arriving to speak to the townspeople on the day of the St. Elijah celebration times out at ten minutes. The laughing of the mocking crowd creates the question of whether or not Manolis will be able to overcome his stammering, and whether his address will result in humiliation or triumph. If Manolis' sudden "God untied my tongue" is a tad convenient, his resultant speech to the crowd is satisfyingly ineloquent, with Dassin using an unexpected long shot to distance the impact of what Manolis says. Manolis convinces the crowd that the refugees do not have cholera, and people offer up gifts. But Patriarcheos' appearance to inform the people about Yannakos' theft and Father Grigoris' ex-communication of Manolis sways the crowd back to their earlier indifference. Interestingly, when Michelis joins Manolis in banishment, Michelis' betrothed, Mariori (who we have seen speak of her love for Michelis in earlier romantic scenes), does not volunteer to join him now. Michelis exits after delivering two good lines to Father Grigoris, dialogue that prefigures the death of Manolis: "If Jesus came back to Earth, He would be crucified again. And you'd be the one driving the nails in!"

The film appears to have suffered some cuts, since Patriarcheos is seen dying with cuts on his face that we have not seen applied, and later Father Photis will be seen with an unexplained bandaged broken arm.

After the refugees attack the town, the Agha eating on the right of the frame as the townspeople lay out their dead on the left is more of Dassin's expressionist framing, with his use of a subjective camera point of view for a gun assault on Manolis an example of the director's rare visual invention in the film. The attack on Manolis creates the false expectation of his immediate death, and even the cause of his eventual death is ambiguous since we don't see Panayotaro's switchblade being applied. Manolis cast as a Christ figure is heightened by his being brought to be tortured in a church, surrounded by a circle of enemies in the manner of a Greek tragedy, though it is odd that he is considered the most prized ally of the refugees when the business of Michelis' gift had seemed to make him a greater one. Dassin's restraint in not showing Manolis' attack from Panayotaro is, for once, frustrating, and also colors our feeling of later seeing Panayotaro lying dead on the ground, since we don't know who has killed him. We also are frustrated by not seeing Father Grigoris dead, since it was he who had given the order to "get Manolis."

Father Photis' story of the devil that attacked an angel who kept multiplying in response is cloying, as told to a child, and the sight of the refugees behind the town's gate as they await the return of the Turkish soldiers prefigures the students behind the gate of the captured school in Dassin's later title *The Rehearsal* (1974). The increasing drumbeat on the soundtrack at the film's end implies that the refugees, now allied to the townspeople, are ready to fight and die against more invading Turks, recycling the narrative from the film's beginning but reinventing it as polemic activism.

In his interview in *Continental Review* about the film, Dassin said, "All that is violence interests me." He continued:

> I was captivated by the under-currents of violence vibrating inside the characters, and the unexpected outburst of this violence in each one. Katerina, a loose woman, fights a violent battle to defend her innate virtue. Manolis, the very image of kindness, becomes an eager fighter. A Greek priest—the very essence of patience—breaks away to lead a bloody battle. And Judas kills, for love.... Dependent on its driving force, violence can be either destructive or constructive—these are the factors which enthused me and drove me to make [the film]. Violence is intensified strength—and I never cease to marvel at this power inherent in man.

In his article for *Films and Filming*, Gordon Gow calls the movie "somewhat overemphatic, perhaps, it can be seen as related to a predilection which is evident again in later Dassin films: a taste for allusions and parallels."

In Melina Mercouri's autobiography, *I Was Born Greek*, she tells of observing Dassin working in between her scenes. She also tells of two events that slowed the shooting. The first involved filming the largest crowd scene, where there was talk of a strike because of an unnamed seventeen-year-old girl. She had whipped up the crowd by saying that they should be paid more, in spite of the fact that in working for only a few weeks they had earned more than they normally made in a year. The producer threatened to cancel the production, and the girl was shouted down. However, Dassin let the girl speak, and he agreed with her, so that the producer paid the extras more money. The second problem was the behavior of one of the actors (who Mercouri does not name), who, she says, was not very bright but was conceited enough to picture himself as a martyr to his art. Apparently, the actor had written an article about the unsatisfactory shooting conditions which mentioned how the food was inedible, how there was a shortage of water, and that the people were illiterate and savages. When the article was published in a foreign newspaper, the story found its way back to Kritsa; the men formed a vigilante posse and wanted to kill the actor. They went to Dassin, who agreed with their outrage and promised to turn him over to them when the film was finished. However, the director didn't do this; rather, the actor was smuggled out of the country, and Dassin was forgiven because he was loved by the villagers.

Mercouri also writes about the change in the character of Manolis from the novel,

He Who Must Die (1957)

Manolis (Pierre Vaneck) with Katerina (Melina Mercouri) in *He Who Must Die* (1957).

where his face and body were covered in sores, which, in a miracle, disappear. Working with a low budget, and disinclined to use photographic trickery, Dassin suggested the character have a stammer instead and use its cure to dramatize the miracle. The director drew inspiration from when he was working in summer camps where workers came for their vacation, and he had asked a young waiter to play a part since Dassin would cast plays with people who worked in the camp, being unable to pay professional actors. This waiter did not want to do it because he spoke with a painful stutter. But unable to secure anyone else for the part, Dassin told him, "You will play the part and you will not stutter." Unknown to the waiter, the director rehearsed with the others, preparing to cover for him if the stutter kept the young man from going on or slowed him too much. However, on the evening of the performance, after Dassin had again said to the young man, "You will not stutter," he played the part well, and not once did he stutter. Kazantzakis agreed to let Dassin use the stutter in the film.

Mercouri also tells of another "miracle" that occurred during shooting, in the scene where women were lamenting the death of their men killed by the Turks. Apparently Dassin noticed a woman standing apart from the female villagers in black, and just before the cameraman was to start shooting the director led her into the scene, wanting to include her noble, tragic mask of a face. The women objected, telling him that the woman had been struck dumb by the death of her son thirty years previously. Dassin insisted on keeping her in, even if she was silent. However, when the cameraman began shooting, the woman suddenly began to scream. She had regained her speech, and shouted lamentations for her son, dead thirty years. Although some of the other women rushed away from the camera in fright, presumably the screaming woman was kept in the film, because Mercouri doesn't say otherwise. Her scream may be the crying heard in the movie under the opening credits. Mercouri also notes that after the film was finished, the standing village became a shrine to Kazantakis for years, but finally was worn away by the wind and rain so that it no longer existed in 1971 (the year her book was published).

In Tony Crawley's interview with Dassin in *Films Illustrated*, Dassin is quoted as saying, "Something very close to me, that film. The whole making of it, in that far-flung village in Crete, and everyone in the village acting in the film. *That* was a labor of love." The film would be the last ever made by producer Henri Berard, although in *Tender Comrades*, Norman Barzman tells of a possible follow-up production that Berard wanted to do with Ben Barzman directing, but that it never materialized. Apparently Berard had told Ben, "I think you could direct a picture, I think you should direct a picture, and I will let you do it. If, that is, Dassin agrees to back you up." Supposedly, Ben went to Dassin and asked him to provide whatever assistance he might need. Dassin is said to have turned purple, and the following exchange reportedly occurred before Ben picked up a chair with which to hit Dassin:

> DASSIN: What makes you think you can direct?
> BARZMAN: You mean, you won't help me?
> DASSIN: Of course not. That is what I do, direct. That's me.

In his article on Dassin in *Film Criticism*, Andrew Horton describes the film as

> uneven at best. But as a project shot with a French/Greek cast shot in French, it was Dassin's baptism of fire with filmmaking in Greece. Clearly it was too much to expect the director from a Harlem ghetto who had made *Rififi* and *Brute Force* to immerse himself in a new culture and successfully interpret a powerful Greek novel that depends in large extent on its understanding of the Greek peasant character for its effect.... It is, in fact, the stark photography by Jacques Natteau [who was to also shoot *Never on Sunday* and *Phaedra*] of the rugged beauty of Crete that one remembers most about the film.... While the film is flawed by Dassin's overly ambitious scheme, it nevertheless served as a transitional film, one in which American codes are beginning to dissolve towards a more open and thus multinational approach.

It is worth noting that a number of sources give the time period for *He Who Must Die* as 1921. However, it appears to be 1951, since one character states that the passion play has not been performed for seven years, since the end of the war in 1944.

Release

France—May 4, 1957; Cannes—May 7, 1957; U.S.A.—December 28, 1958. At Cannes the film was nominated for the Golden Palm, and won the OCIC Award for Special Mention for Dassin.

Reviews

"Powerful and frightening.... Dassin has constructed a film that is as brutally realistic as the bare town and the stony hills in which it was photographed. It abounds in a daring sort of candor and relentless driving toward its points of allegorical contact in a succession of searching and searing episodes."—Bosley Crowther, *The New York Times*, December 29, 1958

"One of the most powerful religious statements the screen has made in many a year.... Dassin may in fact be a broadly and intensely gifted artist, one of the best in the film business.... The film is fidgety with small faults. Yet all the faults are defects of execution, not of conception."—*Time* magazine, December 29, 1958

"Big [and] emotionally overwrought.... It's about oppressors and oppressed, those who believe in the forms of Christianity and those who believe in the spirit.... You may be left with the uncomfortable feeling that Christ is being claimed for the underdogs in much the same terms that Abe Lincoln and Tom Paine were in the 1940s."—Pauline Kael, *5001 Nights at the Movies*

"There is nothing but nobility, nobility, and more nobility—too much nobility for a film that displays an intellectual confusion seldom equaled in the history of cinema."—François Truffaut, *The Films in My Life*

"Occasionally striking, but mainly arty and pretentious parable; however well meant, a bore to watch."—John Walker, *Halliwell's Film & Video Guide 2000*

Where the Hot Wind Blows (1959)

[aka *The Law/La Legge/La Loi*]
Le Groupe des Quatre/GE.SI. Cinematografica Titanus S.P.A./MGM

Credits: Director/Screenplay: Jules Dassin; Producers: Jacques Bar, Maleno Malenotti (uncredited); Screenplay: Françoise Giroud, based on the novel by Roger Vailland; Photography: Otello Martelli; Editor: Roger Dwyre; Music: Roman Vlad; Production Design: Mario Chiari; Art Direction: Robert Giordani; Set Decoration: J. d'Ovidio, P. Romaino; Sound: William R. Sivel. Filmed June 3 to September 20, 1958, in Paris Studios Cinema, Billancour, Hauts-de-Seine, France; and exteriors in Carpino, Foggia, Apulia, Italy. B&W, 113–126 minutes. French language with English subtitles.

Cast: Gina Lollobrigida (Marietta); Pierre Brasseur (Don Cesare); Marcello Mastroianni (Enrico Tosso); Melina Mercouri (Donna Lucrezia); Yves Montand (Matteo Brigante); Raf Mattiolo (Francesco Brigante); Vittorio Caprioli (Attilio); Lydia Alfonsi (Giuseppina) ; Gianrico Tedeschi (First Loafer); Nino Vingelli (Pizzaccio); Bruno Carotenuto (Balbo); Luisa Rivelli (Elvira); Annamaria Bottini (Maria); Edda Soligo (Giulia); Anna Arena (Anna); Herbert Knippenberg (Swiss Tourist); Franco Pesce; Joe Dassin (Second Loafer); Sonia Barbieri (Tourist's Wife); Marcello Giorda (Priest); Teddy Bilis (Judge Alessandro); Paolo Stoppa (Tonio).

VHS/DVD: DVD released under the title *The Law* by Image Entertainment on April 11, 2000.

Synopsis

Engineer Enrico wants to hire Marietta as his servant. But Marietta is already the housemaid of Don Cesare, the landowner of Porto Manacore, a small Sicilian fishing village. Marietta refuses Enrico's offer, predicting she will become his wife instead. Marietta is also desired by the policeman Brigante, though only as a lover and not a wife. Marietta spots the bulging wallet carried by a Swiss Tourist and steals it from his car, while Brigante sadistically orders Marietta's brother-in-law Tonio to drink copiously. When Marietta returns to Cesare's house, her mother and sisters tie her down and whip her for being a "slut." Tonio returns home to stop the fight, and after he releases Marietta, she leaves the house to live in an orange grove storehouse.

When Brigante visits Marietta, he finds the Tourist's money. When he attempts to rape her she slashes his face with his own knife. As Brigante washes the blood from his cut, Marietta plants the Tourist's wallet—without the money—in the policeman's jacket. When Brigante pulls out money to pay for a drink at the bar, Tonio notices the tourist's wallet in his pocket.

In her storehouse, Marietta is visited by Enrico, who tells her he cannot afford to marry her. She shows him the money she has stolen, but Enrico demands that she give it back. Marietta returns to Don Cesare when she gets word that he is ill, and gives him the stolen money. He calls the Judge to his apartment, who brings Brigante, who has been accused of stealing the money. Don Cesare shows that he has the money, but falls ill. Marietta comforts the man when he dies and inherits his wealth. Marietta bans the use of whips in her new house, and she and Enrico plan their marriage.

Notes

This comic drama is another of Dassin's European films with a bloated treatment that only occasionally comes alive. Although his framing and blocking of actors is admirable, and the village milieu creditably portrayed, performances here verge on the hysterical, although the use of a music score is pleasingly minimalistic, and aided by source music and singing. While Gina Lollobrigida receives top billing, her character cannot be considered the main protagonist because she is but one of an ensemble in the dense narrative. Again the treatment explores duplicity, with many women considered as prostitutes, and again Dassin's taste for perversity and violence is on display. The whipping scene, often considered the film's highlight, is actually outdone by two other scenes that coincidently feature Melina Mercouri and not Lollobrigida. The director also gets to insert more humor and visual invention than in his prior title.

After the opening credits, Dassin begins with the humor of Luigi, a sleeping man awakened by the cooing of a white pigeon, with the pigeon also used for the film's end. Luigi, who sits with other men in the village's courtyard, represents a relaxed lifestyle in opposition to the high drama that the main characters will endure. The men, in unison, watch the pigeon fly, and it joins other pigeons on a rooftop. Dassin pans down the building and stops at the first window, which is closed, although we can see partially Melina Mercouri with a man. She walks to the window and opens one side to tell a young man who sits outside "I love him" to his "I love her." This behavior establishes Lucrezia as a duplicitous woman who loves Francesco, though she is married to the Judge. The camera pans down a second time and we see an open window where two women are framed, sitting in front of two girls. On the left, Giuseppina sews, and on the right, Anna knits. The camera pans down a third time to another open window which appears to be the police office, with a man typing in the background, then pans across to what appears to be a prison, stopping to the side of a barred prison window. We do not see inside it, but the typing man reacts to the singing we have been hearing, which is later revealed to come from Marietta.

Marietta cleaning a long boot and holding some lace across her face suggests a kinkiness in her nature. Although this expectation is not met, the narrative will have her suffer a kinky whipping and an attempted seduction by Brigante, to which she responds violently. Marietta's sister, Marta, responds angrily to the attention her husband Tonio gives Marietta, resulting in the following exchange:

> MARTA: Look at that neckline.
> MARIETTA: If you could show your husband one like that he wouldn't chase other girls.

This exchange establishes the contempt her family has for Marietta, considering her sexually promiscuous and provoking the attentions of men. This contempt will lead to the whipping the women will give her.

The Greek statues at Don Cesares' apartment, and his telling Enrico that the village was once a Greek colony, continues the Greek connection Dassin had presented in *He Who Must Die*, as well as the Greek characters in *The Naked City*, *Thieves' Highway* and *Night and the City*.

Dassin offers more humor via the band of boys who dismantle a police motorbike, when they suddenly switch to playing cards when warned by Marietta that someone is coming. Leaving the bike's number plate as the only remnant of the vehicle is a nice touch. Acting as the boys' lookout presents Marietta as complicit in criminal behavior, a character trait that is reinforced by her later theft of the Tourist's wallet. These actions challenge audience sympathy for her, as Lucrezia's affair with Francesco does the same for her, though to a lesser degree.

Brigante touching Marietta with his knife when he talks to her is another sign of perversity, and it receives a narrative payoff later when the knife is used against him during his attempted rape of her.

Dassin devotes thirty minutes to the nighttime dance, intercutting between the Law Game, Marietta pursuing the Tourist for his money, and the concealed affair of Lucrezia and Francesco, who plays in the orchestra. The Law Game seems to have an arbitrary way of deciding who is the "Boss," but it provides more narrative perversity in the way it humiliates Tonio by first denying him, then over-supplying him with wine. Thankfully, the narrative pays off the Game later when Brigante is humiliated by Marietta in an abridged version of the game played for Don Cesare. The lights-out moment at the dance recalls the same effect in Dassin's earlier *Two Smart People*, as Marietta's use of her belt recalls the robbery technique of *Rififi*, even when we wonder why the Tourist has left his wallet in his car. Marietta's theft makes the subsequent punishment by the women justifiable although their reasoning is her perceived promiscuity and her refusal to accept the servant job offered by Enrico.

The whipping scene offers the same combination of brutality and eroticism inherent in other similar acts in Dassin's filmography, and it's interesting that the brief attack does not leave marks on the victim. Tonio's delayed rescue of Marietta creates the expectation of an opportunistic molestation, an expectation that is not met after he climbs on top of her but then apologizes for his attentions. Her sympathy towards him, when she tells him he is a good man, is also a surprise.

Music becomes noticeable in the scene of Brigante's attempted rape of Marietta, although the line between rape and seduction is blurred, given her apparent willingness; and the mixture of desire and disgust she has for Brigante will be described to Enrico later. The scene begins with an expectation of violence after Marietta spits at Brigante and he slaps her (Brigante is a character who enjoys repeatedly slapping people, since he also does

Mexican lobby card for *Where the Hot Wind Blows* (1958), featuring Marcello Mastroianni (Enrico Tosso) and Gina Lollobrigida (Marietta). At left Gina Lollobrigida appears with Yves Montand (Matteo Brigante) at her chest.

it to Giuseppina, Fassitio, and Francesco). The film offers the same ambiguity with Brigante's later attempted seduction of Lucrezia, although that too will have a surprising result.

Anna seen on the beach creates another expectation that is not met: that she will be laughed at because of how the bathing suit she wears cannot conceal her fatness. Rather, she is noticed by men but not judged negatively—either a recognition of the aesthetic taste of the village's men or an example of their sensitivity.

Brigante choking Giuseppina with the neck string of her sun hat is another manifestation of his sadism, like the slapping, and the cut on his face is an appropriate marking for his cruel perversity. Dassin uses a subjective camera for Brigante's point of view as he approaches the row of men sitting around the courtyard, and he will later use another subjective point of view shot for Lucrezia's suicidal fall from the window.

The scene inside the bus, where Brigante confronts his son, Francesco, about the plan to leave with Lucrezia is perhaps the best in the film. Before it, the kind of kiss the Judge gives Lucrezia—and her reaction to it—tells us what kind of marriage they have, which lessens our antipathy towards her as a cheating wife. In the bus Dassin uses a dramatic score and edits to show first Francesco's humiliation by his father (as witnessed by Lucrezia and the other passengers), and then Lucrezia's shame at being abandoned by Francesco and left to be gawked at.

Brigante takes Lucrezia to a private room in what is perhaps the film's second best scene. When she turns up the volume on the radio, it raises the expectation that they will have sex. However, our knowledge of her feeling for Francesco and her particular reactions to Brigante warn us that something is not quite right about the idea of their sex being consensual. We even expect her to attack him, the way Marietta had earlier. Though Lucrezia doesn't, the scene concludes even more disturbingly when she jumps out the window. Dassin cuts from Lucrezia's point of view during the fall to a shot of the dead Don Cesare, sparing us the sight of a mangled Melina Mercouri (and also presenting the double deaths).

Marta tied to the same table that Marietta had been tied to creates the expectation of a revenge whipping, since Marta had instigated Marietta's beating. So it is a surprise when Marietta whips her mother and her sister, Elvira, only to tell them that whips will no longer be used in what is now Marietta's inherited house.

Dassin finishes the film by dollying forward towards the empty courtyard bench that the men have now vacated to go drinking, and has the white pigeon from the film's beginning land on the bench as a cyclical closer.

In his interview with Gordon Gow in *Films & Filming*, Dassin would say, "I had such an unpleasant experience in Italy; that whole film was a mess.... I still consider, looking back on any writing I ever did, that it was the best screenplay I'd ever written." In the interview the director says he rewrote the script for Lollobrigida in three days (not the four days Melina Mercouri claims in *I Was Born Greek*). He also says the he invented the character of Enrico to create a part for Marcello Mastroianni. "It was all a nightmare, just sheer nightmare. And it was, I really believe, a marvelous script—but it just ... went. It was just condemned before it began. And we knew it, we knew it."

In her book, Mercouri says that she and Lollobrigida disliked each other intensely, so perhaps it's just as well Marietta and Lucrezia have no scenes together. Perhaps Dassin planned it that way because of the actresses' animosity. Mercouri says that when she saw a rough cut of the finished film in the projection room, Lollobrigida's performance was better than she thought it would be, which bothered Mercouri. But she also says that upon seeing the film, what immediately became clear was that it was not the picture Dassin had set out to make. She says the director thought perhaps that this other film could work, but Mercouri believes it didn't.

In his article on Dassin in *Films Illustrated*, Tony Crawley describes the movie as "overly hyped during shooting and badly dubbed and drummed up by MGM for world release, as little short of a disaster." Crawley claims that it was the film's producer who wrecked the project from the start by insisting on casting Lollobrigida.

Gina Lollobrigida, the earthy, voluptuous Italian beauty whose signature hairstyle was dubbed "the tossed salad," started making films in Italy in 1946. She toiled in uncredited roles and supporting parts, and scored her first lead in the drama *Campene a martello* (1949). She followed this with *Miss Italia* (aka *My Beautiful Daughter*, 1950), a film that reflected the actress' own experience with beauty competitions; the title role of *Alina* (1950); *The White Line* (1950); the crime drama *Four Ways Out* (1951); the war drama *Attention! Bandits!* (1951); and the comic dramas *The Unfaithfuls* (1953) and *The Wayward Wife* (1953). She played a supporting role in the John Huston crime comedy *Beat the Devil* (1953), which was partly filmed in Italy; played a dual leading role in *Flesh and the Woman* (1954); starred with Errol Flynn in his production company's adventure *Crossed Swords* (1954), filmed in Rome; and was the *Woman of Rome* (1954). After playing the lead in the romantic comedy *Beautiful but Dangerous* (1955), she supported Burt Lancaster and Tony Curtis in the circus love triangle movie *Trapeze* (1956), filmed by director Carol Reed in Paris;

received top billing over Anthony Quinn's Quasimodo in the historical horror remake of *The Hunchback of Notre-Dame* (1956); and played the lead in the comedy *Fast and Sexy* (aka *Anna of Brooklyn*, 1958).

Lollobrigida would continue to play leading roles in films like the romance *Go Naked in the World* (1961), *La bellezza di Ippolita* (1962), the comedy *Mare matto* (aka *Mad Sea*, 1963), the mystery *Woman of Straw* (1964), the comedies *Me, Me, Me ... and the Others* (1966) and *Hotel Paradiso* (1966), the crime thriller *Death Laid an Egg* (1968), the comedy *Buona Sera, Mrs. Campbell* (1968), and the Italian made *Un bellissimo novembre* (1969). Lollobrigida's last lead was in the comedy *King, Queen, Knave* (1972), and she would go on to write, produce and direct a short interview she did with Fidel Castro, *Ritratto di Fidel* (1975).

Pierre Brasseur started in French silent films, and had played the lead in the war title *Feu!* (1927). After playing supporting roles, he scored leads in the title role of *Jonny, haute-couture* (1935), *Une femme qui se partage* (1936), the comedy *Le mari rêvé* (1936), *Claudine a l'école* (1937), *Visages de femmes* (1938), and *Grisou* (1938). He continued to play occasional leads, in *Two Shy Ones* (1943), the fantasy *Gates of the Night* (1946), the comedy *Noah's Ark* (1947), the title role of *Rocambole* (1948) and its follow-up *La revanche de Baccarat* (1948), and *La nuit blanche* (1948). In the 1950s he was the lead in *Skipper Next to God* (1951), *Dirty Hands* (1951), *The Drunkard* (1953), the Italian comedy *Vestire gli ignundi* (1954), the title role of *Raspoutine* (1954), the crime drama *The Gates of Paris* (1957), and the comedy *La vie à deux* (1958). After his supporting role in *Where the Hot Wind Blows*, Brasseur continued to play leads in *Head Against the Wall* (1959), the horror classic *Eyes Without a Face* (1960), the adventure *Carthage in Flames* (1960), *Spotlight on a Murderer* (1961), *Pas de caviar*

Marietta (Gina Lollobrigida) and Don Cesare (Pierre Brasseur) in *Where the Hot Wind Blows* (1958).

pour tante Olga (1965), the crime drama *Two Hours to Kill* (1966), the adventure film *Pas de panique* (1966), the war comedy *King of Hearts* (1966), and *Goto, Island of Love* (1968).

Described as "the Italian Gregory Peck," it has been argued that Marcello Mastroianni was one of the few Italian male actors to achieve the equivalent stardom of his female contemporaries Sophia Loren and Lollobrigida. The actor's international success is indicated by the three Best Actor Academy Award nominations he received over a period of three decades. They were for the comedy *Divorce—Italian Style* (1961), the war romance *A Special Day* (1977) (both co-starring Loren), and the romance *Dark Eyes* (1987). Mastroianni made his cinematic debut in Italian films in 1939, acting in uncredited and supporting roles. He played the lead in the crime drama *Against the Law* (1950), and he and Gina Lollobrigida had supporting roles in the comedy *Vita da cani* (1950). Mastroianni was the lead in *The Eternal Chain* (1952), *Black Feathers* (1952), and the comedy *Days of Love* (1954). The late 1950s saw him in more leading roles: *The Bigamist* (1956), the German thriller *Sand, Love and Salt* (1957), *Il momento più bello* (1957), and the comedies *Love and Troubles* (1958) and *Il nemico di mia moglie* (1959). After playing support to Lollobrigida in *Where the Hot Wind Blows*, Mastroianni's next leading role was perhaps his most famous—as the decadent gossip columnist in Federico Fellini's comedy *La dolce vita* (1960). He followed this with leads for the next eight years. In the 1970s and 1980s the actor continued to be cast in leading roles, though he did not work quite as regularly as he had in the 1960s. Mastroianni's output lessened in the 1990s, but he remained a leading man to his last role—in the biographical drama *Voyage to the Beginning of the World* (1997), which was released after his 1996 death.

Debonair Yves Montand was also born in Italy and was discovered as a singer by French chanteuse Edith Piaf in 1944, which no doubt enabled him to begin his film career in a supporting role in her vehicle *Star Without Light* (1946). He played the lead in *L'Idole* (aka *The Idol*, 1948), the thriller *The Wages of Fear* (1953), the adventure *Heroes and Sinners* (1955), the romance *La grande strada azzurra* (aka *Wide Blue Road*, 1957), and the comedy *Premier mai* (1958). After *Where the Hot Wind Blows*, Montand next appeared opposite Marilyn Monroe in the Hollywood musical *Let's Make Love* (1960), his casting presumably aided by the winning of the Best Actress Academy Award by his wife, Simone Signoret, for her performance in the romance *Room at the Top* (1959). Considered the most successful continental star since Charles Boyer, Montand would always be billed under his leading leadies in his subsequent Hollywood films but sustained leading man status in Europe. He had leading roles in the war drama *The War Is Over* (1966), *Live for Life* (1967), the fantasy *Un soir, un train* (1968), the crime drama *Z* (1969), and the comedy *The Devil by the Tail* (1969). In the 1970s Montand continued as the lead in European titles, including being billed above Jane Fonda in the French *Tout va bien* (1972). Though his output slowed down considerably in the 1980s, he managed to end his career in the leading role in *IP5:L'île aux pachydermes* (1992), which was released after his death in 1991.

French producer Jacques Bar had founded his company Cite Films in 1949, and had been a prolific filmmaker in the years prior to *Where the Hot Wind Blows*. He had experience with multi-language co-productions, and had worked repeatedly with the French comic Fernandel in his later films. Maleno Malenotti was a screenwriter and producer of Italian films who had worked with Lollobrigida in the musical comedy *Mad About Opera* (1949), the musical biography *The Young Caruso* (1951), and *Beautiful but Dangerous*. Malenotti worked with Yves Montand in the romance *La grande strada azzurra*, which he co-directed with Gillo Pontecorvo. Neither producer would work with Dassin again.

Release

France—January 25, 1959; Italy—March 26, 1959; U.S.A.—November 1960, with the taglines "Get set for the kind of male-female explosion of excitement you haven't seen in years," "One stunning scene after another explodes the most dangerous game its sensualists ever played with life!" "Lollobrigida is the Flame ... Montand is the Fuse That Sets Them on Fire!" "Desire Catches Fire With Lollobrigida and Montand," and "GINA AND MONTAND TURN DESIRE INTO FIRE WHERE THE HOT WIND BLOWS!" The film would be re-released in the United States in 1962 to art house theaters under the title *The Law*, capitalizing on the popularity of Mastroianni and the success of Dassin's next title, the comic drama *Never on Sunday* (1960).

Reviews

"A vibrant visual flow of reality that is consistently arresting. The acting is almost flawless. Lollobrigida gives her best performance in years."—Howard Thompson, *The New York Times*, November 12, 1960

"A complicated game of sex and power ... a heavy-breathing drama set in an Italian village."—John Douglas Eames, *The MGM Story*

"Sure-fire cast is wasted in a pedestrian drama."—Leonard Maltin, *Movie & Video Guide*

"Dassin's B-movie [is] a scattershot melodrama set in an Italian coastal village.... Elegant and sultry, Melina Mercouri transcends the slightly sordid material."—Kent Turner, *Film-Forward.com*

"Dassin still in sharp form, even if his material doesn't quite live up to his direction's high standards.... Film overflows with conflicts of a political and amorous kind, and there's a definite soap-operatic quality to the myriad roundelays crowding the screen, never more so than in a free-flowing nighttime festival sequence."—Nick Schager, *Slant Magazine*

···

Never on Sunday (1960)

[aka *Pote tin Kyriaki*]
Melina Film Production

Credits: Director/Screenplay: Jules Dassin; Associate Producer: Vassily Lambiris; Photography: Jacques Natteau; Editor: Roger Dwyre; Music: Manos Hadjidakis; Costumes: Deni Vachliotou; Art Director: Alekos Tzonis; Sound: Antonis Bairaktaris; Makeup: Malvina Tsougiopoulou, Anna Armau; Choreography: Giorgos Provias (uncredited). B&W, 91–97 minutes. English and Greek language with English subtitles. Filmed in Piraeus, Greece, from March to April 1960.

Songs: "The Joys of Illya," aka "The charms of Illya" (Manos Hadjidakis), sung by Titos Vandis; "The Piraeus Lads" (Manos Hadjidakis), sung by Melina Mercouri; "Ein Schiff Wird Kommen" (Manos Hadjidakis, Fini Busch), sung by Melina Mercouri; "Ta Paidia tou Peiraia," aka "Never on Sunday" (Manos Hadjidakis), sung by Melina Mercouri.

Cast: Melina Mercouri (Illya); Jules Dassin (Homer Thrace); Georges Foundas (Tonio);

Titos Vandis (Jorgo); Mitsos Lygizos (Armathis, aka the Captain); Despo Diamantidou (Despo); Dimos Starenios (Poubelle); Dimitri Papamichael (Sailor); Alexis Solomos (Noface); Aleka Katselli; Nikos Fermas (Waiter); Thanassis Veggos; Giannis Fermis; George Foras; Panos Karavoussanos; Stefanos Skopelitis; Artemis Matsas; Koula Agagiotou; Popi Gika; Faidon Georgitsis (Sailor); Kostas Nikoloudis; Kostas Doukas; Christos Zikas; Tasia Kyriakidou. Uncredited: Nikos Tsachiridis.

VHS/DVD: DVD released by MGM Video & DVD July 1, 2003.

Synopsis

Homer Thrace, an aging American intellectual and self-confessed amateur philosopher, comes to the Athenian port city of Piraeus to find the truth about the fall of ancient Greece. He meets Illya, a headstrong life-loving prostitute, and decides her amorality is what personifies the fall. Horrified at her ignorance of the theater of Greek tragedy, he accepts an offer from Noface, the landlord of the apartment building where the prostitutes work, to pay her to stop working and educate her in two weeks. The plan appears to work until another prostitute, Despo, learns of Homer's deal with Noface and tells Illya. Illya revolts and leads all the prostitutes in a strike because of Noface's high rent prices — just when a navy fleet pulls into port. Noface's lawyer pays the women's fine and negotiates a new lower rent, and they are released. The men at the local café are antagonistic towards Homer, particularly after he has convinced their bouzouki player, Taki, that he is not a real musician because he cannot read music. After Illya convinces Taki to play again, Homer is initially taunted, then joins the drinking and dancing Greeks. As he sails away, Homer throws his notebook into the sea.

Notes

This Greek comic drama is an improvement over the director's prior titles with extended narratives; however, there are still longueurs in the treatment. What redeems the film is the performance of Melina Mercouri in her third title for Dassin (and her first starring role for him). Her charisma and likability elevates her beyond the archetypal figure of the whore with a heart of gold, even when her character has to endure a Pygmalian attempt at re-birth by an asexual intellectual. Apart from one montage, the film seems devoid of Dassin's usual visual invention, though it makes up for it in its celebration of the Greek spirit, with the director using singing and dance sequences to make the title qualify as a musical. The treatment also features duplicity in the deal the intellectual makes to educate the whore, although the imbalance in the character's intention makes the endeavor a predictable failure.

Before the delayed opening credits, the film begins with the image of a bouzouki being played, superimposed over views of the port of Pitraeus, with the shipping industry recalling the fishing island in *Where the Hot Wind Blows*. The opening scene of Illya jumping into the bay is different from that described by Dassin in his attempts to obtain funding for the production, since here she is not naked but rather wears a two-piece bathing suit. The director protects Mercouri from exposure by showing the clothes she discards as a trail behind her before we see the actress from behind before she jumps. The bathing suit and Illya's jumping into the bay will later be juxtaposed to the parallel scene of her swimming after her "education."

The Captain tells Tonio that Illya is a whore who makes no prices, meaning she considers what is offered, and only goes with someone she likes. This philosophy is meant to separate her from the other town's whores, who Dassin will objectify in a repeated and resonant image of four women's legs walking in unison, with the women presumably arm in arm (interestingly, it's an image first seen under the director's name in the opening credits). Illya is different from the others because she is an independent, not living in the apartment where the others do; and it will be this independence that will enable her to help the others at the film's climax. However, because she isn't like the others, that makes her the receiver of the advances of Noface, via his errand boy Filippe, whom she calls "Garbage." Illya's policies are demonstrated in a later scene where two sailors come to her and she rejects the vocal one in favor of the silent one. Her policies will also impact on her relationship with Homer, since she likes him and makes an advance—which he does not take advantage of, although at the climax he will confess, "I've been dying to sleep with her from the first minute."

This image of Illya (Melina Mercouri) from *Never on Sunday* (1960) became iconic when it was used on the poster for the stage musical adaptation, *Illya Darling*.

Homer is described as an intellectual by someone onboard the ship he arrives on before he is seen, and Dassin presents our first view of him in an unusual manner. The camera is at ground level as Homer enters the frame—but it is his feet, rather than his face, that come into close-up. Homer as an intellectual is represented by his camera and his notepad, and Dassin's graying hair adds to the idea that he is an aging bachelor, missing romance in his life because of his intellectual preoccupations. (Dassin's grey hair, at his real age of 48, may be due to the stress his personal life had endured.) The screenplay will score points off Dassin's lack of height—and his nose—which Illya will repeatedly comment on as being big. Dassin gets to engage in some comic physicality and slapstick for the bar scene, an ability he had also employed in his previous film appearance in *Rififi*. Homer's admission that he is from Middletown, Connecticut, is a direct take from Dassin's own life, since that is where the director was born.

Later Homer will call the Greeks "barbarians," though, ironically, he himself is quick to become violent. The bar is a male bastion, since we see no women in it, and is perhaps a symbol of Greek society, since the only women we see in the narrative are whores, the actresses in Medea, and patrons of the amphitheater. The business of Homer not being able to drink the coffee he is served remains ambiguous, since we do not know whether he rejects it because it is Greek and too strong or because it is hot. His frightened reaction to Jorgo throwing a glass onto the floor is an ignorance of Greek tradition, something Homer will ultimately embrace and imitate at the climax, and Jorgo's repeated drinking then smashing of the glasses heightens Homer's fear. The ringing of the cash register each time a glass is smashed on the floor adds to the comedy, a device that will be repeated, and Jorgo lifting a bottle of ouzo from the floor with his mouth is seen from Homer's point of view as public entertainment. Subsequently, Homer's loud applauding of Jorgo is later explained by Illya to be inappropriate, and this explains Jorgo's anger at him, represented by his dropping the bottle which smashes. The fight that ensues, punctuated by the ringing cash register, is more comic than real, using Dassin's buoyancy as humor. The intention is underlined by Homer's initial reluctance, when he states, "I don't want to fight with you; I came here to love," though later we will see how Homer enjoys fighting, with a bruise over his right eye that he sports for the remainder of the film evidence of that enjoyment.

Homer is seen from Illya's point of view when she looks through his camera, and his face in close-up is covered by a checkerboard pattern. (The camera will inexplicably disappear from the narrative, and Homer's notebook only reappears for the film's end.) Her comment, "In the camera you look more beautiful," can be read as one made by someone who enjoys fantasy but can also understand the difference between it and reality.

The scene where the second sailor apologizes to Illya for presumably not being able to get an erection (this problem is not specifically stated) is a surprise for its time, though the fact that he is English and not Greek makes it a little more acceptable. His change of condition in response to Illya playing bouzouki music is a comic payoff for his earlier embarrassment, and Dassin gets a laugh in the way the couple fall back out of frame in an embrace.

The scene in which a man carrying an armful of parcels runs for a streetcar that fails to stop for him is a little comic gem. The humor comes from the man's exasperated anger, as he yells to the car driver, "You're a heathen. Your grandfather. Your father. You and the children to come." The car subsequently stopping to allow Illya to get on but not the man results in his "Do I have to wear a skirt for you to stop? Even then you wouldn't because you're a mule."

Homer and Illya have a funny exchange on the streetcar, even if the payoff is expected:

> HOMER: French, English, Greek.
> ILLYA: Italian, a little Spanish.
> HOMER: That's extraordinary. Where did you learn all those languages?
> ILLYA: In bed.

Illya's birthday party creates the initial expectation of her rape by Tonio, after he tells her he has sent away her guests and attempts to seduce her; but the expectation goes unfulfilled when we see that Tonio has lied about sending the guests away. The small frail man from the opening scene reappears for the party, laying over the shoulders of three men when they enter, and the party being attended solely by men suggests that the guests have all been Illya's customers. As in the later bar scenes, the extended singing here echoes the chorus that Dassin used in *He Who Must Die*, though the addition of a wind-up organ adds character. The attempt of Filippe to offer Illya a present gets the expected rejection by her, but Filippe being thrown down a flight of stairs is a rather disturbing surprise, unredeemed by the business of Illya throwing the present out of her window and it landing on his head as he walks down the street.

Dassin shoots Illya's telling of the story of Medea to her guests in an interesting way. She is in the center of the frame but in the background, with Homer and the Captain on either side of the frame in the foreground. Homer provides asides to the Captain, telling him how Illya gets the story wrong. Her telling of the story is also aided by the sound of the organ, and the telling creates a context for the forthcoming scene where Illya and Homer go to see the production at the amphitheater. Illya's take on Medea, in her denial of Medea's nature of being a poisoner and a murderer of her own children, convinces Homer that she needs to change so that reason will replace fantasy and morality will take the place of immorality. However, Homer will not directly try to educate her until after they go to the amphitheater, when he receives the offer from Noface to close her business.

The sign on her door, "Closed on account of Greek tragedy," is the indication that they have gone to see the play, and the sign is a device that the narrative will repeat for comic effect. Dassin uses a thrice repeated right pan over the same patrons at the theater for us to see Illya's inappropriate reactions of crying and laughing at what is occurring in the play, and Homer's disbelief and exasperation. He adds an echo to their voices as they argue in the empty amphitheater after the play is over; while Homer's attempt to correct Illya's interpretation of Medea, and her resultant unhappiness, presents Homer as an unlikeable spoilsport. The fact that he has made enough of an impact on her to put Illya off wanting to go to the theater again shows she has sensitivity, and helps to make the later fact of her change through his education more believable. However, there still exists an imbalance in the audience's empathy with their characters, so that Illya's eventual rejection of Homer's education, and his change of viewpoint, will make a satisfying conclusion. Even if we may agree that Homer is right in pointing out Illya's ignorance of certain matters, we still don't want to see them end up as a couple.

The bar scene where Jorgo sings to Illya to try to shuck off her blues reads as indulgent because, in spite of Jorgo being successful in his attempt, the song is unremarkable and his performance of it bad. However, Homer's observation that the song's idea that all women are whores reveals to him that Jorgo hates women because he hates his mother is treated with pleasing suspense. After Homer tells Illya his theory, she suggests he tell Jorgo, knowing that it will infuriate the Greek. The expectation that Homer's observation will earn him another fight comes to full fruition, but the surprise is how more aggressive Homer is in response to Jorgo's attack, with the ringing cash register device again used.

Noface's proposition to Homer uses an interesting turn of phrase, since he says Illya's education is "to prove that the American way of life is better than hers." Although Noface's agenda is to shut down Illya's business, the idea that she is not happy is one that Homer agrees with and which makes him accept the offer. Happiness will be defined by Homer as "coming from the pleasure of the mind" and not from sensuality, which Illya represents. Again, we can see that Illya *is* happy, so we know that any education is doomed to fail, but particularly when it is being administered by someone like Homer, who we sense is actually unhappy himself (despite his claims of satisfaction with his life of the mind).

The idea of allotting two weeks for the education is in itself a preposterous one, but is an acceptable dramatic challenge. Amusingly, the second sign on Illya's door reads "Closed on account of studies." Dassin creates a no-dialogue montage for Illya's studies, with mournful classical music as background, as opposed to the bouzouki music we have previously heard. In the montage we see a piano being delivered, a Picasso print replacing a framed photograph of a soccer team on the wall, and Illya drawing a cube. The joyous opening jump into the water is now contrasted with the way she uses a changing room on the bay, her appearance in a demure one-piece bathing suit, and how she tentatively walks into the water. Her change is underscored by the reaction of the working men who initially whistle at her, then stop when they observe her new behavior. The Captain sums up Illya's transformation with: "And Illya ate of the apple of wisdom and she knew shame." The montage ends with the sign on her apartment door now reading simply "Closed."

Homer's rejection of Illya's physical advance leads to her rebellion, where she plays bouzouki music and sings as she looks at the photograph of the soccer team. While Mercouri is an unremarkable vocal performer (like Titos Vandis' Jorgo), we endure the long musical sequence because it is the film's theme song (which would become famous). The blare of the fleet arriving in port breaks the mood (Illya's binocular view of the ship appears to be stock footage). But as she opens the door to her apartment we hear the same mournful classical music, and, whether real or imagined, it stops her and she closes her door again.

Illya playing a few notes on the piano when Despo arrives is both a surprise and a realistic accomplishment for the two-week period, and Despo makes an amusing retort in response to Illya's comment about her as an aging whore: "The older the chicken, the better the juice." Despo's specific observation of Homer with Noface in regards to the envelope of money Homer has in his pocket leads to Homer's duplicity being exposed, with his initial denial bringing further shame on his character. Dassin has Despo play the wind-up organ when Illya rages in anger after Homer admits the truth, but the scene confounds expectations about her trashing the room. Rather, it is perhaps Mercouri's best scene in the film, since Illya makes fun of Homer while she makes only a mild mess, mocking the lines he has attempted to teach her by rote. Her putting on the soccer jersey we have seen the players wear in her photograph signals her return to her origins and her intention to greet the fleet's sailors. Dassin cuts from her line "The sailor boys will make like wolves" to the sailors howling outside the apartment building of the whores. Illya's return to a life of immoral sensuality is her rejection of Homer the intellectual, and her intention of sleeping with other men is her personal rejection of him as a man.

Although Illya seen in the whores' apartment building creates the expectation that she will work there, this expectation is not met, since she plans to punish Noface the landlord as much as Homer. The lock seen on the front door suggests that something is amiss, and the women throwing their beds out the windows is the sign of their strike, with the ruckus of the sailors outside remaining ambiguous as to whether they are vocalizing their frustrations or their support for the women's activism. The sound of a police siren makes the sailors run away, and the mattress and pillow stuffing on the street is an ironic comment on the debris of a whore's work.

The women singing in jail continues the treatment's expression of the supposed Greek tendency to sing, with the whores standing behind the jail bars recalling people behind bars in *Brute Force* and *He Who Must Die*, and prefiguring *The Rehearsal*. That Illya is the instigator of the strike and the successful negotiator for reduced rents, over a matter that doesn't immediately affect her, indicates her generosity and also the weakness of the other whores who haven't resisted Noface's opportunistic use of them. It's a pity that the narrative only provides Noface's lawyer as his representative, rather than let Illya directly confront Noface himself, something that she never does in the entire film.

The film's climax is a return to the bar, where the men silently glare at Homer. Although we don't know if they are aware of what he has done to Illya, we will learn of his new humiliation of Taki, which justifies the men's animosity. Dassin employs a brief montage of glasses being smashed, swept up, and the cash register ringing as Taki returns and the bouzouki music and dancing begin. However, this time the expected third fight between Homer and Jorgo, as Jorgo taunts Homer with his dancing, fails to materialize. The real surprise is Homer's reaction, which is not defensively violent but rather an acquiescence to the Greek way of life. Homer's "education" begins with his own changed behavior, when he drinks and smashes glasses, as he has seen the Greek men do. Dassin exploits his gift for physical comedy in the way Homer behaves, culminating in Homer balancing a tray of glasses on his head, which he lets fall to smash onto the floor, and in his silly dancing style in an attempt to emulate the Greeks. Another expectation is created when Homer says that he has been dying to sleep with Illya—of them becoming a romantic couple. But this comes to naught when she is taken away by Tonio.

The film ends with Homer sailing away, presumably back to America (which is a kind of wishful thinking on the part of the still-blacklisted director), leaving Illya and Greece behind, whose sensuality and amoral happy ignorance is demonstrated by Illya and the men in the small boat tailing Homer's ship jumping into the sea after they wave to him. After Homer wordlessly throws his notebook into the water, Dassin ends with the image of the legs of the four whores walking, which dissolves to a rather sad long shot of the ship in the distance at dusk.

In his interview with Gordon Gow in *Films & Filming*, Dassin said:

> I must have failed. It was a very successful film in terms of audience, yet I thought I was making a point there which people didn't get. Strangely enough, it was most understood by the Americans whom I was criticizing. I was trying to criticize in comedy this awful tendency that Americans have to try to remake the world in their image, in their thinking, in their imposition of what we call the American way of life. Often half-baked, often without any real understanding of what different countries are about. And I'm always distressed about America backing the wrong guys: we're always with the Francos and so on. And I took this rather idiotic boy-scout character and, because of the very falseness of his position, he's tied up automatically with the character called Noface, who is the guy who exploits people.... I thought I was making the whole point very clear, but I guess it didn't come out. Not here. The Americans were much more sensitive to it.

In *I Was Born Greek*, Melina Mercouri writes that the small frail man for whom Dassin invented the business with his glasses was impeccable when he came to shoot the scene. "He calmly took off his glasses, jumped, with easy timing put the glasses on again, swam a single stroke out of the shot then proceeded to sink like a stone. He couldn't swim!" (This was in spite of the man telling Dassin at the call for swimmers, "I'm great. Esther Williams. I grew up in the islands. I swim with the dolphins.") Apparently the small frail and bespectacled man was not the only one who needed saving, since a lot of the men who had answered the casting call for swimmers risked drowning in the Bay of Pireaus because they needed work so badly. Mercouri also writes about her reaction to the bay. "The water was cold that day. When I hit the water, I wanted to cry out with the shock. But I had to be laughing and provocative. And laugh gaily I did, through chattering teeth."

Mercouri says she researched the part of Illya in Notaras Street, the red-light district of Piraeus:

> The girls received us graciously and in the most bourgeois manner. There was tea, little cakes, and polite conversation. They liked me. [In the film] I became the mascot of the whores of the world. I received letters from everywhere thanking me for portraying their profession with dignity.

She also writes about how shooting came to a stop after five days when Dassin dislocated his back after playing a scene where he climbed a ladder to reach a dock. He was bedridden for three weeks; the crew agreed to stay together and wait for him to recover—without being paid. However, Dassin would not accept this, and they were paid while they waited. Unbeknownst to United Artists, the film was made without any insurance policy, contrary to all business custom. Dassin's doctor allowed him to resume work on the condition that he wear a neck brace, a look that made the crew refer to him as "Mr. Von Stroheim."

The neck brace didn't stop Dassin from giving Mercouri the hardest slap she ever received in her life. He had rescheduled the order of shooting so that his scenes could wait for the brace to be removed. When they were shooting the scene where Mercouri sang the title song, the actress had to lip-sync to a pre-recorded playback. She had never done something like this before, and Dassin had to keep shooting take after take because Mercouri was out of sync. Fed up with the re-takes, she stormed off the set; but after seeing Mercouri slap an assistant who had pushed her back, Dassin slapped *her*. After screaming and yelling at each other, they began to laugh, and continued laughing for ten minutes. Then when the director led her back into the scene, Mercouri synced with the playback perfectly.

She also writes that when they saw the first rough cut of the film, Dassin loved her in it but hated himself. Mercouri says that she thought she was good but that he was better, and that the film had charm. In his *Films Illustrated* article, Tony Crawley writes that Dassin's sole regret about the film was that he could not afford a better actor than himself to play Homer. "[But] for all its rough-hewn faults, cinematic and artistic, it remains one of the most zestful of movies."

In his article on Dassin in *Film Criticism*, Andrew Horton writes that this movie and his next, *Phaedra*, show Dassin at his best, "as the American director gained a surer knowledge of Greek culture and found material more in tune with his capabilities." Horton continues:

> The strength of the film derives from Dassin's growing ability to blend his talent for American-styled comedy with a clearly Greek comic tradition of film and stage which stretches all the way back to Aristophanes' social comedies.... Aristophanic comedy is characterized by its use of a wide combination of elements, including dance, farce, song, and lyrical moments, in addition to witty dialogue. Dassin captures a hauntingly muted moment as Illya sings the theme song of the film [which] may well be [his] finest moment to date. Here in a simple scene, neither overstated nor overacted, comedy, pathos, music and emotion come together effortlessly.

Giorgos Foundas had started acting in Greek films in 1944 and played uncredited and small parts until his lead in *Mavri gi* (1952). He also played the leading role in *Magiki polis* (1954), *Women Without Men* (1954), the romance *The Sheperdess' Lover* (1955), played opposite Melina Mercouri in *Stella* (1955), the adventure *Gerakina* (1958), the romance

Prostitute Illya (Melina Mercouri) is amused by the efforts of Homer Thrace (Jules Dassin) to educate her with a globe in *Never on Sunday* (1960).

Mono gia mia nyhta (1958), the romance *Antio zoi* (1960), and played a supporting role in his prior title, *Take Me Away, My Love* (1960). After *Never on Sunday*, Foundas continued playing leading roles in Greece, and during this time took an uncredited supporting role in Elia Kazan's Greek drama *America, America* (1963), and a supporting part in the adventure *Zorba the Greek* (1964). His last leading role in successive years was *O megalos enohos* (1970); after that he slipped into television work and supporting roles.

Release

Released for Cannes screening May 1960, where Dassin was nominated for the Golden Palm, and Melina Mercouri won the Best Actress award in a tie with Jeanne Moreau for *Moderato cantabile* (1960). Released in U.S.A. October 1, 1960. Nominated for Academy Awards for Best Director, Best Writing Screenplay, Best Actress, and Best Costume Design, and won for Best Song.

Reviews

"A catchy comedy ... serves to establish Mercouri [in a] brilliant execution of a larger-than-life character which is the anchor and very reason for the pic.... Dassin is better with his behind-the-camera work because he does not quite instill the right note of naivete into his role."—*Variety*

"A gay Greek-American comedy neatly and nimbly handled by Dassin. He and Mercouri are both superb.... Dassin is perhaps the most amiable serpent ever to glide onto the screen and attempt to entice an innocent woman away from a life of heroic sin."—Bosley Crowther, *The New York Times*, October 19, 1960

"A rambunctious little politico-philosophical fable.... Dassin's satire is obviously directed at the U.S., but his touch is light and his affection for the object of his satire unmistakable.... The idea is scarcely original, but Dassin expresses it in a wonderful rush of animal spirits and earthy humor."—*Time* magazine, October 31, 1960

"Jules Dassin's clumsy fable about the joys of amorality and the stupidity of virtue.... Pinhead Shavian ironies and an exhaustingly robust heroine, but a great success."—Pauline Kael, *5001 Nights at the Movies*

"Extremely naïve and contrived. But it was one of the rare portrayals in the cinema of an unrepentant happy hooker.... Dassin plays a pedantic writer ineffectually."—Ronald Bergan, *The United Artists Story*

Phaedra (1962)

Lopert Pictures Corporation

Credits: Producer/Director: Jules Dassin; Associate Producer: Noel Howard; Screenplay: Jules Dassin, Margarita Liberaki; Photography: Jacques Natteau; Editor: Roger Dwyre; Music: Mikis Theodorakis; Art Director: Max Douy; Set Dresser: Maurice Barnathan; Costumes: Denny Vachlioti (aka Theoni V. Aldredge); Sound: Jacques Carriere, Athanassis Giorgiades, Jacques Lebreton; Makeup: Jill Carpenter, Anna Armaou; Opticals and Main Title Design: Jean Fouchet. B&W, 115 minutes. Filmed at Studios De Bouloche in Paris, and Studios Alfa in Athens; on location in Paris and London; and on the islands of Hydra and Piraeus in Greece; from July to October 1961.

Cast: Melina Mercouri (Phaedra); Anthony Perkins (Alexis); Raf Vallone (Thanos); Elisabeth Ercy (Ercy); T. Karoussos; George Sarris (Ariadne); Andrea Philipides (Andreas); Olympia Papadouka (Anna); Stelios Vocovitch (Stravos); Nikos Tzoyas (Felere); Depy Martini (Heleni); Alexis Pezas (Dimitri); Tasso Kavadia; Dimos Baladimas (Dimo); Phaedon Giorgitsos; Yannis Bertos; Phaedon Papamichael; George Txanis; George Pantzas; E. Zachiades. Uncredited: Elisabeth Mottet; Marc Bohan; Jules Dassin (Christo); Giorgos Karoussos (the Old Man); Lillia Ralli.

VHS/DVD: Not available in either format.

Synopsis

In Athens, Thanos Kyrilis is a Greek shipping magnate who launches his new ship, the *Phaedra*, named after his second wife. She is bored by a life in which her husband's work is his priority, and agrees to go to London to meet Alexis, Thanos' 24-year-old son by a previous marriage, though she doubts she can convince him to come to Greece. Phaedra and Alexis are attracted to each other and become lovers in Paris, where she has gone to shop for clothes. However, wracked by guilt because of the seeming inappropriateness of the relationship, Phaedra leaves Alexis and returns to Thanos' home on the Aegean island of Hydra. Still in love with Alexis, and unable to make love to Thanos, her sadness lifts when she learns Alexis will come to the island to visit his father. However, upon arrival Alexis declares his hatred for Phaedra, who he feels has rejected him.

He entertains the idea of seducing Ercy, the daughter of Phaedra's sister Ariadne, as revenge on Phaedra. Thanos wants Alexis and Ercy to marry so he can merge his business with that of Andreas, who is another shipbuilding tycoon and Ariadne's husband. However, Phaedra is determined to stop the marriage. She tells Thanos about the affair—just when the news of the sinking of Phaedra's namesake ship is announced. In a rage, Thanos beats his son then banishes him from the business and his father's life. Rejecting Phaedra's advance, Alexis is killed when his car drives off a seacliff road. Phaedra takes a lethal dose of sleeping pills.

Notes

A family drama of duplicity, and toying with the theme of incest, this is another extended treatment by Dassin, though one that features some arresting visuals and an interesting attention to aural detail. A blood-drawing slapping attack serves as an example of the director's fondness for violence, while another of his unfortunate penchants—the overused score—draws attention to itself. In her fourth performance for Dassin, Melina Mercouri is appropriately intense and brooding; and as her surprising love interest, Anthony Perkins makes up for his lack of emotional conviction with physical playfulness. Dassin's world of Greek wealth and shipping magnates also parallels that of the topical romance between Aristotle Onassis and opera star Maria Callas.

Behind the opening credits are images of Greek sculptures that prefigure those later seen in the British Museum sequence, suggesting the tragic resonance of the narrative to come. There is a funny exchange at the launch of the ship *Phaedra* in the first scene between Thanos and Dimo, which also attests to Thanos' materialist nature:

> DIMO: At every baptism of a ship I have designed he gives me the same present, the gold cigarette case.
> THANOS: That's not to break my luck. Don't you like them?
> DIMO: I love them. But I keep telling you I don't smoke.

The exchange also prefigures the back luck naming the ship after his wife will bring to Thanos—and to Phaedra.

Dassin zooms in on Mercouri for our first sight of Phaedra, and then cuts to a shot of Ariadne and Andreas watching her disapprovingly, their looks changing to smiles when Dimi touches Andreas' shoulder. They see Phaedra put on a ring to bring Thanos luck—another harbinger of fate, as she will later sacrifice the ring to prove her love for Alexis. Ariadne's contempt for her sister is based on our being told how Phaedra had stolen Thanos from her, which marks Phaedra as a duplicitous character, a trait that will resurface in her affair with Alexis and her deception of Thanos.

The fireworks at the launch party recall the fireworks of Dassin's title *Two Smart People*, and the observing village women dressed in black will behave like a Greek chorus, becoming a recurring visual motif. Here one comments on the Kyrillis: "They are powerful. They speak many languages. And they celebrate with fire in the sky." The fireworks that spell out Phaedra's name, which initially dazzles then dies, is also symbolic of her fate.

The fireworks scene offers a telling exchange between Ariadne and Andreas about Phaedra:

> ARIADNE: She has everything she could want.
> ANDREAS: But so do you.
> ARIADNE: Of course. [Her look of misery expresses her true emotional condition.]

The idea that Alexis does not accept Phaedra as Thanos' second wife, in spite of his own mother having remarried, recalls the real-life disapproval of Mercouri by Dassin's children (especially since their union had begun while they were both still married to others). Thanos' first wife will be referred to as "the foreigner," which also applies to the Greek Mercouri in regards to Dassin's American family, though his first wife, being Hungarian, was equally a "foreigner."

Phaedra's servant, Anna, is said to be a witch who has premonitions. (Her being a witch allows us to accept her seemingly questionable pseudo-lesbian relationship with her mistress.) While Anna's dream of Alexis fighting another man with spears—how's that for phallic symbolism!—doesn't eventuate in a literal sense, her premonition of the danger of Phaedra meeting Alexis is justified. The antagonism between two males can also be applied to the rivalry between Alexis and Phaedra's son, Dimitri, as the heir to Thanos' empire. Phaedra's rather dismissive treatment of Dimitri is demonstrated by the expressionist venetian blind lighting that Dassin gives the room where the child sleeps in bed, unseen by the camera, as Anna voices her warning.

Dassin dissolves from Anna to use the first of three repeated aural effects of the roar of a flying airplane for scene transition, here providing an aerial view of London. He also superimposes a pan of the barred fence of the British Museum over Phaedra's subjective camera walk through the interior, the bars suggesting that she is entering a trap. Her dropping her handbag as she finds Alexis is perhaps too coy, and he is photographed from her point of view, framed in the foreground and to the right of a male Greek statue in the background. While Anthony Perkins is attractive, the idea of comparing him to a perfect Greek god is a bit much, though later in the scene Alexis will parallel Phaedra with the statue of Aphrodite. He begins telling her how she is not pretty but has a unique face, which is both the expression of his aesthetics as a painter and an acknowledgment of Mercouri's androgyny. Alexis' comment about her not being pretty will devolve later into him telling her, in anger, how she is "ugly."

Alexis' initial form of duplicity is in being a painter (although we never see his work) while allowing his father to pay for him to attend the London School of Economics, where he never goes. This disparity between the artistic and the materialistic world is what defines Alexis as being unsuitable to inherit Thanos' business, but also rationalizes his willingness to have an affair with his stepmother and disregard the norms of society. Phaedra's complicity in the affair also aligns her psyche with the artist, although we do not see any other expression by her of an artistic sensibility.

Dassin uses a camera at feet level for an amusing moment after Phaedra buys new shoes, when she and Alexis exit the store and are approached by the shoes of another man. At this, Alexis says, "Sir, don't stare at my mother." His comment makes the third pair of shoes exit the frame, with the idea of Phaedra being his mother much discussed in the following scenes, even though technically she is not. Alexis repeating his own mother's opinion that Greeks are "savages" is echoed in the animal print scarf Phaedra wears, and Alexis' own perversity is demonstrated in his romantic attachment to a car (which he considers female).

Phaedra throwing her ring into the Thames is said to be a sacrifice intended to make her wish that Alexis come to Paris with her come true. The sacrifice shows Phaedra's bravery in love, and Alexis' attempt to retrieve the ring—before being stopped by her—displays his matching bravery (in his willingness to sacrifice his own comfort for her).

The second airplane roar is used for the scene transition to Paris, with an aerial view and a subjective camera moving down the Champs Elysees eventually superimposed over a shot of Phaedra and Thanos kissing. Despite Thanos' sexual attractiveness—a confirmation of his Greek "savagery," if you will—it is his neglect of Phaedra that leads to her affair, although a lingering touch of Alexis' face by Thanos seems more than paternal (perhaps a reminder of the homoeroticism Raf Vallone brought to *Vu du pont* [aka *A View from the Bridge*, 1962] when he kisses the boyfriend of his niece on the lips to prove that the boyfriend is allegedly gay).

The love scene begins with perverse blocking in the way Alexis kneels with his back to Phaedra and their hands twist when their fingers intermingle. They move so that they are seen face to face in front of a raging fire, and the pauses before they slowly come together creates an expectation of rejection that is not met. Phaedra's tears and apparent shame may be ambiguous; who knows when she last made love to Thanos? Dassin transforms the shot into an out-of-focus tableau for the extended love scene. This is another of the director's fast-edit set pieces, with cut-aways to the fireplace and record player, a dolly into a window, shots of rain on the window, and the actors kissing. The couple is

Phaedra (Melina Mercouri) is willing to sacrifice a ring to prove her love for her stepson, Alexis (Anthony Perkins), in *Phaedra* (1962).

photographed to show only abstract body parts during their coupling, with the flames from the fire almost engulfing their supposed passion.

While the musical score is over the top, it complements the style the director uses for the love scene, something that almost always becomes comic in its expression. Dassin comes up against the classic problem of cinematic love stories, where the period of being in love slows down the narrative, and he fails to overcome it through the extended use of a Greek song Phaedra sings (with translated lyrics like "I gave you milk and honey/In return you gave me poison"). Things pick up when Thanos telephones, with the melodramatic score becoming acceptable, and Phaedra lies about Alexis being with her. Thankfully, this leads to Phaedra wanting to leave and telling Alexis not to come. Perkins supplies some convincing anger at Alexis' perceived rejection, his hooded eyes working against the notion of him as an innocent (this is in spite of his post–*Psycho* career carrying the baggage of the mother-fixated Norman Bates). Alexis' anger leads him to rip off Phaedra's dress (shot by Dassin in a way to protect Mercouri's modesty), and we transition back to Greece with the third airplane roar and aerial view.

Phaedra at the airport photographed by paparazzi presents her as a celebrity by association, the wife of a magnate. Her rejection of Thanos' romantic advance tells us she is still in love with Alexis, or at least still feeling guilty, with her sadness underlined by the music. While Anna's stroking of the negligee-wearing Phaedra's skin can be interpreted as either maternal or romantic, Phaedra slapping and choking Anna when she badmouths Alexis suggests Phaedra's passion. It also shows her sense of entitled sadism, although it is the only act of physical violence we will see her perform. Phaedra's admission to Anna that she loves Alexis works because of the pain and fear Mercouri gives to the confession, aided by her wild hair and insomniac-ravaged beauty.

The treatment now becomes fun in the exquisite observation of Phaedra's tortured love and our waiting for the secret to be discovered (and the lovers punished). Thanos buying the car Alexis was seen earlier "romancing" prepares us for his arrival, and Phaedra laughing hysterically when told the news only fools those that can be deceived that she is happy about seeing her lover again. Dassin makes a cameo appearance wearing a big Greek moustache and tan as an old man that comments prophetically on the sports car Thanos has bought and shipped over for Alexis: "To me it looks like big coffin." The director films Alexis' return as if it is Phaedra's mirage, and she states, "I love you." Backlit by the sun, Alexis asks her, "Why did you make me come here? How do you plan it? How much time in my father's bed? How much time in mine? You're ugly. You're ugly." Phaedra's momentary joy changes to her covering her face in pain. Naturally, Alexis has to be horrible to Phaedra for her to feel the way we want her to feel ... after all, who wants any more sappy love scenes?

Dassin employs another aural device—the sound of Alexis' car before we see it—to create the expectation that he will be killed in the car. While this expectation is fulfilled only later in the narrative, this adds suspense whenever we see Alexis in the car, which is enhanced by the woman in black also seeing him (although the obvious studio-bound shot of Perkins in the car with rear projected imagery is disappointing—but the only apparent process work in the film).

The montage of Alexis wandering the island in different outfits seems like filler, although the accompanying music redeems it, with the following party scene heightening dramatic tensions. The expectation of an affair between Ercy and Alexis, and Phaedra's subsequent jealousy, is met. The dance source music drowns out the dialogue in the scene around a table so that our focus is on Mercouri's point of view and her reactions, including cuts to the legs of the dancing people, recalling the earlier shot of shoes, and the body parts in the love scene. Phaedra is funny in her unhappiness as she dances with Andreas while Alexis dances with Ercy; and when Alexis slow dances with Phaedra his anger is expressed by his refusal to make eye contact. His "Please help me—let me go" is an acknowledgment of his feelings for her and an awareness of its inappropriateness. However, we know that Alexis' arrival on the island has stiffened Phaedra's resolve; she will not let him go and will resist his proposed marriage to Ercy. She only lets him go when he drives away to his death.

The scene where Thanos and Alexis ride in an open elevator allows us an aerial view of the shipyard, and lets us view the possibility that Alexis can repair his relationship with his father without having to admit to the affair. However, the later scene in which Alexis provokes Phaedra into confessing her love for him makes clear Alexis' desire to be exposed. Dassin creates tension from the expectation that Phaedra will be overheard, though the cacophony from the adjoining apartments ensures that she is not. The scene plays out with Phaedra aware of the possibility of her being exposed, and challenging Alexis by kissing him, an act that is only seen by Anna. Dimitri's playing of the traditional song/nursery rhyme "London Bridge Is Falling Down" represents the threat of Alexis "falling down." Alexis' admission that his provocation has failed is made clear by his comment to Phaedra, "Let me alone or I'll kill you."

At the change-partners dance, Alexis flirts with many women, seemingly to support the charge he denies—that he is not a "woman-eater." This scene, with his supposed interest and then sex with Heleni (implied by the closing of doors on a boat), and the extended game of throwing plates into the sea, reads as extended filler.

Ercy is seen to enter Phaedra's room by a mirrored reflection, and her asking the older woman what she can do to make herself attractive to Alexis as she undresses to her underwear shows Phaedra's reaction in the same mirrored reflection. Phaedra going to see her father in Athens, to ask him to finance Thanos' new ship (so as to stop Andreas' merger), is undercut by a telephone call her father receives announcing the news of the marriage of Alexis and Ercy. Dassin has Phaedra wearing sunglasses when she is told the news so that her reaction is hidden, although we know she won't be pleased (and isn't when she predicts "Everything will fall"). The shot of her leaving is superimposed over the zoom-in on a man in Thanos' office receiving the news of the *SS Phaedra*'s loss in a storm and the death of its crew.

The village women in black run as a group down to the pier, and appear as a roiling sea of black in the office. Phaedra, dressed in white and sporting sunglasses as she struggles to get through the crowd, stands in stark contrast to the women in black (although when told she can enter through a private entrance we wonder why the other women don't follow her). Dassin adds more aural touches via the wailing of the mourning women and their knocking on the door.

The appearance of the women in reaction to the loss of the ship prefigure Phaedra's admission to Thanos about her affair, told to him to stop the marriage rather than as any personal vindication. Dassin has Raf Vallone's Thanos react slowly to the news, and his sorrow, shown in close-up, is a surprise. Thanos does not punish Phaedra, saving his violence for Alexis, and Thanos slapping Alexis' face with a ringed hand that draws blood joins Dassin's canon of brutal set pieces. Alexis makes the valid point that he blames his father for sending for him from London, although the offer didn't also include sleeping with Phaedra. Alexis' bloody face adds a bit of gore to the treatment, and (apart from the metaphorical blood of Alexis on Phaedra's hands) it is the only gore we will see in the film. Phaedra tenderly washing Alexis' face, which leads to a kiss is not a surprise, although the scars from the ring on his face are. Phaedra tells Alexis: "There is only one more terrible thing than what we have done and that is to leave each other." However, this is not enough to stop Alexis leaving her again. Dassin will intercut between Alexis driving and Phaedra in her room, to suspend the expectation that he will drive to his death.

The washing of her hands, the undressing to her slip and asking Anna for her nightgown, her closing the window shutters and the doors of a wall icon all read as preparation for something from Phaedra, although at this stage we do not know it to be suicide. As with the love scene and the climactic drive in *Rififi*, Dassin employs quick edits for Alexis' final car ride, alternating aerial views, shots of Alexis in the car, and finally his point of view as he approaches the truck driving down the middle of the road. Alexis sings along hysterically with Bach's Toccata and Fugue in F Major, and yells Phaedra's name twice before he swerves to miss the truck and heads over the hill to crash, with the rocks obscuring whether or not he falls into the sea. Dassin dissolves to a shot of Phaedra lying on her bed, and though we don't see her take the sleeping pills, a pan from Anna, who retrieves Phaedra's sleeping mask, to the pill bottle on the table suggests she has taken some.

Phaedra kisses Anna on the mouth, Anna pulls the sleeping mask over Phaedra's eyes, and Dassin cuts to the mourning women in black at Thanos' office. While Thanos reads out names of the dead, we cut to a shot of Anna, then a wrapped body (presumably Alexis) being carried into the apartment grounds, and then to the sleeping/dead Phaedra, and fade out on Mercouri's face. In spite of the satisfaction one should feel about both Alexis and Phaedra being punished, the film's outcome does not satisfy, perhaps because Phaedra's death is too easy. Although it may seem a more Hollywood choice, perhaps a better one may have been for the couple to have been together in the car when it drives off the cliff, killing them both together.

In his *Films & Filming* article, Gordon Gow claims that the picture gave Mer-

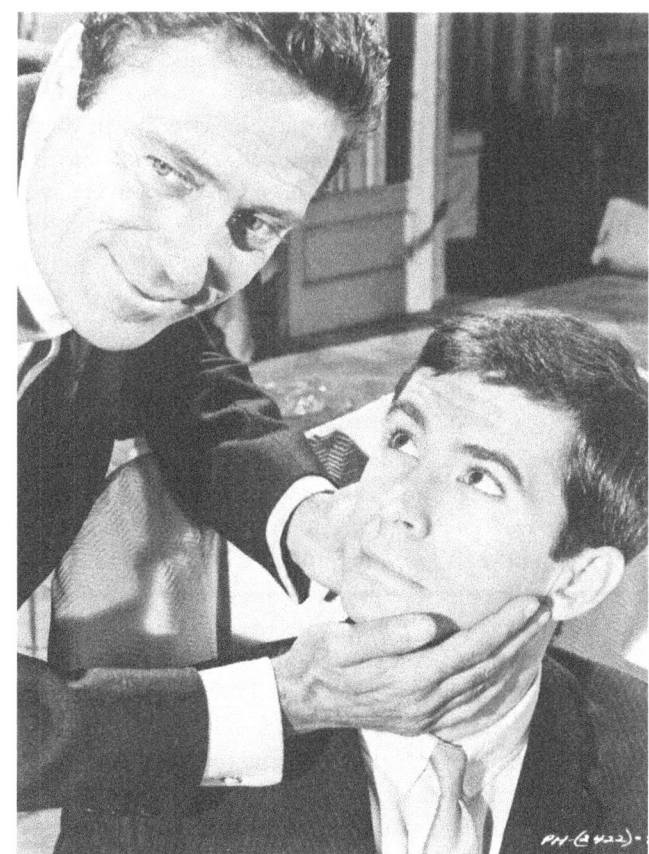

Thanos (Raf Vallone) with his son Alexis (Anthony Perkins) in *Phaedra* (1962).

couri her best chances since *Stella*, and that the love triangle was pitched at just the right key, with atmospheric use of authentic locations. Gow also quotes Dassin on the use of the black-clad women:

> We had a marvelous boy who was our assistant and I had scouted locations where we could use the black-clad women appearing from all parts of Piraeus to find out what happened in the shipwreck towards the climax. We scouted the places about two months before I began to shoot, and the boy had written down all the streets and positions at the port and so on, but when we came to shoot he'd lost them. And there were all our black-clad women and all our crew ready, and he couldn't find the bloody streets. Also, at that time, we were running out of money fast. But it was a marvelous day. So I said, "Come on, everybody, follow me." And we just walked, and every time we saw a possible position, bang, we just placed the women there and shot it; that was complete improvisation out of desperation. Of course, the whole port area lends itself to compositions, so it wasn't too hard.

Dassin also spoke about the love scene of the film, which Gow describes as heightened romanticism, misted, and intensely physical. "I knew that I wanted something basically unreal, basically impossible, and there was a need for this moment to have a formally beautiful quality."

In *I Was Born Greek*, Mercouri writes how the film was shot in an old house in Hydra, built by the famous Hydra Kapetanios. Everything was white: the ceilings, the walls, the floors. Mercouri reports how the company had arranged to shoot the opening ship-launching scene in a giant shipyard in Scaramanga in Athens, owned by Stavros Niarchos, where there happened to be a boat that was in repair at a floating dock. Holes in the sides were covered with colored streamers and ribbons. After shooting brass bands and marches, and the Thanos character going through a crowd of handsomely dressed guests distributing gifts, the company stopped for lunch. After lunch they were told that no more shooting would be allowed, on the orders of Mr. Niarchos. Since Niarchos could not be reached by telephone, Dassin decided to shoot anyway. He was warned that the boat would put to sea, but they knew that was a bluff because of its condition, as it would have sunk. When the company reached the boat, a voice came from a loud speaker telling them to remove the cameras or they would be sunk with the dock. The actors and crew shouted in protest, and Dassin went to the dock and ordered "Go ahead" to the cameras.

Niarchos' employees began to flood the dock, so that Dassin stood in ankle-deep water. Apparently the shipyard workers had mistakenly heard that the film was a vicious attack on the Greek royal family, which motivated their aggression. The actors and crew and extras all stood with the director, and the dock kept sinking. The water was now knee-deep, and the men lifted the cameras to their shoulders. Then Mercouri, wearing a chiffon dress, and the other women joined the men, lifting their skirts high above their waists. Anthony Perkins and the stills photographer, Corbeau, took photos to prove that the boat had holes in it and was not seaworthy. After the women had entered the scene, Niarchos' men stopped submerging the dock, and it rose again. Naturally, Niarchos wanted the photographs, but Mercouri had hidden them. The police arrived and demanded the photos, but, refusing to hand them over, the company stayed. That night Mercouri called a lawyer and, after negotiations, the company were allowed to leave with the photos. The next morning reporters and photographers from the local and foreign press came to see them, and Dassin and Mercouri were summoned by the Minister of Commerce, with whom they had made arrangements to shoot in Greece. The Minister sided with the company and gave permission for them to go back to the shipyard and finish shooting on the condition that the photos would not be published. Two days later shooting was completed in the shipyard.

In his *Films Illustrated* article on Dassin, Tony Crawley describes the movie as "patently silly." In his Los Angeles County Museum of Art interview, Dassin advised that he had wanted to film a scene in the British Bridges Museum with the Parthenon marbles in the background and a sculpture of a horse, since in the original tale the Hippolyte character was killed by charging horses. However, the company found it hard to obtain permission, and kept being put off. Mercouri apparently confronted the Museum authorities, stating, "They are our statues." The marbles were originally part of the Parthenon and other buildings on the Acropolis of Athens, and had been transported to England between 1799 to 1812 by the agents of Thomas Bruce, the 7th Earl of Elgin, then purchased by the British Government in 1816. However, Mercouri's stance still did not sway the museum authorities. Later, when Mercouri was appointed Greek Minister of Culture, a British reporter apparently asked her what her first act would be, and Mercouri replied, "I would ask for the return of the Elgin Parthenon marbles." In 2007 the Greeks were building a museum, to be called Melina's Museum (Mercouri died in 1994), to receive and house the marbles. To date, however, they remain in England.

In his article on Dassin in *Film Criticism*, Andrew Horton had written that *Never on Sunday* and this film show the director's work at his best. Horton writes that "at first glance the classical genre of Greek tragedy would not have seem suited to the basic American realism of Dassin's approach. But here again [he] found his own way of interpretation so that the result would be a multinationally spirited work in tune with his own interests." Horton defends the "seemingly incongruous" casting of Mercouri and Perkins, which was much criticized, by stating:

> The seeming mis-match between lovers can be seen as a serious rendering of the Homer/Illya relationship in *Never on Sunday*. But while passion leads to reconciliation and liberation in a world of comedy, the opposite is true for Greek tragedy. Dassin's script follows the destructive path of passion as it unfolds in a modern setting which echoes timeless mythic-tragic patterns. His decision to do a loose adaptation of the original tragedy allowed him the freedom he needed to re-shape the myth as he wished. Thus Dassin uses the ancient text as a starting point rather then as an end. [The film] pulls us into a timeless tale through a realistic contemporary setting. After an "American" documentary[-style] opening, Dassin proves he has become more truly "multinational" by working out his own form of stylized drama to approximate in cinematic terms the power of Greek drama. [His] film both reinforces and contrasts with the classical version, and by using human nature and the Greek landscape, has neither imprisoned himself in the dramatic form of tragedy nor become a slave to the written or spoken text.

Horton says that Dassin was condemned for his mixture of documentary-like background and staged tragic excess in the foreground by those who judge films on the basis of realism; but Horton claims these elements have always been present in Dassin's work, to greater or lesser degrees, and that what he understood was that

> the emotional truth is often more successfully captured through such stylized exaggeration rather than through realism. The initial realism of the film enables Dassin to intensify our involvement with the characters who then appear in more stylized settings. There is, for instance, the simplicity of Phaedra's flowing gowns, the framing of the characters in the island villa in such a way as to make them appear as if they were on a stage, and the use of the black-clad widows and mothers who act as a chorus in the closing scene. These elements could easily be over-done. But Dassin uses no chorus chanting in unison and no stilted formal speech. The effect of *Phaedra*, as in his earlier American films, remains dependent on the blend of these theatrical and realistic elements.

In his book on Anthony Perkins, *A Haunted Life*, Ronald Bergan says that United Artists had not wanted Dassin to cast the actor, thinking him not "masculine enough," but Dassin had insisted. Perkins describes the role as "awkward and difficult." The actor continues:

The servant Anna (Olympia Papadouka) witnesses the suffering of her mistress (Melina Mercouri), the title character in *Phaedra* (1962).

> I think the picture had great originality. We shot it under the adverse conditions that Dassin particularly seems to enjoy. He is a singular director in that the thing that makes him work most heatedly is to have technical and, well, any kinds of problems that seem insurmountable, and in the conquering of these problems he finds his inspiration to film. The most difficult part was literally lugging equipment ourselves up the rocks and over the mountains, that's the kind of thing he likes.

Dassin would say that Perkins protected Mercouri for their big love scene: "He would nudge her into a better light so she would look better." Perkins says that the climactic car scene was filmed

> in the most dangerous, foolhardy way. We were in a car with the camera mounted on the hood which made it absolutely impossible to see. I was driving at breakneck speed around the mountain turns, yelling and crying the dialogue. It could have been done in any number of different ways just as well, but this was the hardest way and this was damn well the way he wanted to make it, and I think it was good for the picture.

Dassin would say, "Tony was the worst driver ever. An Aston Martin can run away with one. I sat beside him with the mike. The emotion of the scene made him close his eyes, and I'd have to kick him to watch the road." Perkins would say of the director and Mercouri (who would marry five years later), "[It] was an emotional circus—to cohabit with their vitality is unforgettable. They were at the pinpoint in time when they were riding high after their success in *Never on Sunday*, and during our last day of shooting the three of us cried so much that we had to reshoot the next day—our eyes were so puffy."

Bergan quotes Dassin on his second thoughts about the film. "I would have liked to have made it in Greek and closer to the Euripides tragedy, but as it was it became merely a melodrama. My idea was to replace the kings with the shipping magnates. Onassis liked it, but he thought he was better looking than Raf Vallone." Dassin also said of working with Perkins that "there was not a single moment that wasn't enjoyable. Everybody liked him. On Hydra, where we filmed, the islanders would bring him nuts and honey." In his book on Perkins, *Split Image*, Charles Winecoff quotes Mercouri on the actor:

> We were great friends. He was the most intelligent and the most beautiful actor that I played with. He was extremely generous, a gentleman. [The film] was one of the most happy films that I made in my life because of Tony. I knew him not many years from *Phaedra*, and it was a big love, a big big love. But really love. He helped me a lot. I had only made three or four films before [it] and Tony had experience. I learned many technical things from him, about lighting, and how to be on screen for close-ups. And about life, about love. I have his photo near my bed, and every night I look at him.

About the climactic car scene, Winecoff adds that Dassin was crouched in one corner watching Perkins through a mirror so he could see what the actor was doing, with three old ladies stopping traffic ten miles down the road as Perkins drove at full tilt around hairpin curves. Winecoff also says the film's love scene took two days to shoot, and that Dassin got the idea to intercut the shots of torrential rain running down the window panes from seeing rain splashing on the windows of cars on the way to the studio that morning. The scene was difficult to shoot because, supposedly, Perkins couldn't act it. Mercouri is said to have commented on the actor's frigidity to Dassin: "I cannot do this with him. There's nothing there. I can't feel anything. He's like ice." This inability of Perkins may explain the director's piecemeal approach to the scene.

Winecoff quotes Perkins saying after the film wrapped, "This is one film people won't come out of with a shrug. They may come out furious, but they won't be indifferent. There are scenes and dialogue that are absolutely daring in a cinematic sense." Winecoff blames the failure of the film on Perkins' miscasting. His use of "miscalculated, downright campy eye movements—meant to denote smoldering passion—heightened the impression of his American masculinity level hitting an all-time low." Winecoff adds, "Ironically, his scenes with Raf Vallone carry more of a sexual charge." Despite the supposed effeminacy which made Perkins a "laughingstock" in the United States, *Newsweek* magazine reported in late 1962 that the actor's popularity in France was rivaled only by that of Jean-Paul Belmondo. Mercouri told *Newsweek*: "Ah, Tony. He is attractive to women. He is dangerous to women. When you touch him, he goes away a little." Apparently what the Americans considered effeminate was considered almost a virtue by European audiences, who appreciated his "sensitivity."

The tale of Phaedra would be retold in a West German television version entitled *Phädra* (1967), based on the Jean Racine play version.

The Dassin film was the second and last to be associate produced by Noel Howard, his prior title being the Gene Kelly directed French-American co-production of the comedy *The Happy Road* (1957). Howard had been a Hollywood second unit director and uncredited production designer, and would go on to write the screenplay and direct the French Johnny Hallyday musical *Where Are You From, Johnny* (1964), and co-direct the multi-national biographical adventure *Marco the Magnificent* (1965).

Since *Never on Sunday*, Mercouri had played supporting roles in the comedies *Vive Henri IV ... vive l'amour!* (1961) and *The Last Judgment* (1961). She would go on to work with Dassin on his next title, the comic crime drama *Topkapi* (1964).

Anthony Perkins was age 29 at the time of filming, playing a 24-year-old; while the

41-year-old Mercouri played a 34-year-old (in the screenplay Phaedra says that she is ten years older than Alexis). Coming from Broadway, Perkins had made his film debut in a supporting role in the domestic comedy *The Actress* (1953), and scored the lead in the psychological baseball drama *Fear Strikes Out* (1957), playing the baseball player Jim Piersall who suffered from mental illness. He continued in supporting roles until the college comedy *Tall Story* (1960) and *Psycho*. After *Phaedra*, the actor continued to alternate between leading and supporting roles, and had leads in the Orson Welles–directed version of the Kafka novel *The Trial* (1962), the crime drama *Le glaive et la balance* (1963), the melodrama *The Fool Killer* (1965), and the crime dramas *The Champagne Murders* (1967) and *Pretty Poison* (1968).

By the 1970s Perkins' output had diminished, but he still played leadings roles in *Ten Days Wonder* (1971) and the romance *Lovin' Molly* (1974). He returned to playing Norman Bates in *Psycho II* (1983); *Psycho III* (1986), which he also directed; and *Psycho IV: The Beginning* (1990), a made-for-television movie. Perkins continued in horror titles by playing Dr. Jekyll and Mr. Hyde in *Edge of Sanity* (1989), directing but not appearing in the comic horror *Lucky Stiff* (1990), and playing his last leading role in *A Demon in my View* (1991). The actor was also the screenwriter of the mystery *The Last of Sheila* (1973), though he did not appear in the film.

The Italian born Raf Vallone was a soccer player and journalist who began making films in Italy in 1942. After playing supporting parts, he scored the lead in the crime drama *Il bivio* (1950), and continued as the lead in multiple titles for the next three years: *Under the Olive Tree* (1950), *Path of Hope* (1950), the war drama *Strange Deception* (1951), *Carne*

Ercy (Elisabeth Ercy) exposes her youthful body to her romantic rival, Phaedra (Melina Mercouri), in *Phaedra* (1962).

inquieta (1952), the adventure *Don Juan's Night of Love* (1952), *Los ojos dejan huellas* (1952), *Sunday Heroes* (1953), and *Perdonami!* (1953). After the comedy *Storm* (1954), Vallone then played a series of supporting roles until *No Escape* (1958), *La garçonniere* (1960), *Recourse in Grace* (1960), and *Vu du pont*. The actor's international successes had him in supporting roles: *Bitter Rice* (1949), the war drama *Two Women* (1960), and the biographical actioner *El Cid* (1961). After *Phaedra*, he continued in supporting roles in international productions like the historical drama *The Cardinal* (1963), the war actioner *The Secret Invasion* (1964), the biography *Harlow* (1965), the western *Nevada Smith* (1966), and the crime comedy *The Italian Job* (1969), although he did have the lead in *Una voglia da morire* (1965). In the 1970s Vallone played the lead in *La morte risale a ieri sera* (1970), but otherwise was reduced to supporting roles, one of which was another Onassis-inspired tale of a Greek magnate, *The Greek Tycoon* (1978). He bounced back for the lead in *Return to Marseilles* (1980), but it was to be his last, as he followed it with more supporting roles and work in television.

Release

October 18, 1962, with the taglines "A violent drama of profane love" and "The passion of Phaedra ... who at the same moment embraced her love and her destruction." Nominated for the Academy Award for Best Costume Design, Black and White.

Reviews

"Explosive drama that simply evolves as tour de force for its expert director and principals.... Dassin's directorial touches are neat, colorful, and effective."—A. H. Weiler, *The New York Times*, October 19, 1962

"Dassin's glossy novelistic version of the classic story is undermined by a lunatic piece of miscasting [Anthony Perkins].... With its snazzy cars and fabulous jewels that can be thrown away into the sea this is like a Joan Crawford picture, only more so."—Pauline Kael, *5001 Nights at the Movies*

"Dassin's direction, is lean and fluid.... [He] succeeded in bringing to the screen that most treacherous of all dramatic forms: high tragedy.... Melina Mercouri is as achingly believable as a tragedienne as she was believably zany as a comedienne (in *Never on Sunday*). Only Perkins seems too Ivy to wear Greek laurels."—*Time* magazine, October 26, 1962

"One of the most maddening films in [Dassin's] oeuvre ... manages to justify [his] most ardent champions and his most vehement detractors, often within the same scene."—Frank Miller, *TCM* article

"Ludicrous, awesomely folly-filled attempt to modernize and sex up Greek tragedy."—John Walker, *Halliwell's Film & Video Guide 2000*

•••

Topkapi (1964)

Filmways/United Artists

Credits: Producer/Director: Jules Dassin; Associate Producers: Roger Dwyre, Lee Katz (uncredited); Screenplay: Monja Danischewsky, based on the novel *The Light of Day*

by Eric Ambler; Photography: Henri Alekan; Music: Manos Hadjidakis; Sets: Max Douy; Costumes: Denny Vachlioti; Editor: Roger Dwyre; Sound: William Sivel; Makeup: Amato Garbini; Main Title Optical Effects: Jean Fouchet. Color, 116–120 minutes, in English, French, Greek, German and Turkish. Filmed on location in Istanbul, Turkey; Kavala, Greece; Paris, France; and at the Studios de Boulogne-Billancourt/SFP, Hauts-de-Seine, France.

Cast: Melina Mercouri (Elizabeth Lipp, aka Elizavetta Lippmanova); Peter Ustinov (Arthur Simon Simpson); Maximilian Schell (Walter Harper, aka Walter Haberlee); Robert Morley (Cedric Page); Jess Hahn (Hans Fisher); Gilles Segal (Giulio); Akim Tamiroff (Gerven); Titos Wandis (Harback); Ege Ernart (Major Ali Tufan); Senih Orkan (First Shadow); Ahmet Danyal Topatan (Second Shadow); Joseph Dassin (Josef); Despo Diamantidou (Voula). Uncredited: Bedri Cavusoglu (Police Officer); Amy Dalby (Nanny); Jules Dassin (Turkish Cop).

VHS/DVD: DVD released by MGM (Video & DVD) December 11, 2001.

Synopsis

The thieves known as Elizabeth Lipp and Walter Harper plan to steal an emerald dagger from Istanbul's Topkapi Museum. To this end they recruit a team of amateurs. These are Cedric Page, an eccentric British inventor; Giulio, a mute athlete; and Fischer, a strongman. In Greece, con man Arthur Simpson is hired to drive a car over the border and meet them in Istanbul, but he is stopped by the Turkish border security who discover a rifle and six grenades hidden in one of the car doors. Major Ali Tufan allows Simpson to enter Turkey on the condition that he spies on the gang, which he agrees to do.

At their villa headquarters, the gang plans the robbery as Simpson leaves messages for the Turks about what he learns. When Geven, the drunken cook, accidentally smashes Fischer's hands in a door, Simpson is enlisted to take Fischer's place—after he reveals his spying. Walter thinks of a way to perform the robbery without using the arms that are in the car. Distracting the Turks who shadow the group, the robbery is a success, and the dagger is given to Josef, who will smuggle it out of the country by hiding it in his traveling carnival. The gang go to Tufan to explain about the arms in the car, but they are trapped when Josef is arrested with the dagger. Imprisoned, the gang listens to Elizabeth's plans for their next job—the theft of the Romanoff jewels from the Kremlin.

Notes

Dassin's first color feature is a bloated crime drama that's an uneasy repeat of the jewelry robbery seen in *Rififi*, though lessened by an unfocused narrative. While this title lacks the former's film noir fatalism, the attempt to replace it here with comic charm proves unsuccessful. The protagonists, which include Melina Mercouri in her fifth film for Dassin, fail to raise audience sympathy (like the characters did in *Rififi*), although we still wish for them to be successful in the heist. The treatment includes studies of the duplicity of criminals in general, and also specifically in terms of the character of Arthur Simpson (since he spies on the team for Turkish authorities). While the heist set piece isn't as spectacular as that in *Rififi*, the director still impresses with some visuals, including primary

Spanish poster for *Topkapi* (1964).

wardrobe colors and candy-color set design, and the comic performance of Peter Ustinov (which won him the Best Supporting Actor Academy Award).

A pre-credit sequence begins with a bejeweled optical effect as Melina Mercouri sings a song about the Istanbul emerald, accompanied by bouzouki. We then go to attractions at the fair locale that will be featured in the narrative, with Dassin using a numbered spinning wheel, a ring-the-bell test of strength game, lights, and a curtain pulled back with a scream to reveal a blindfolded female mannequin. Bursts of fire are followed by the sound of Mercouri laughing—a sound that will later be used as a decoy during the heist—and small circle images of the actress shown around the spinning wheel. She appears as the camera zooms in on her; and after talking directly to the camera, Mercouri moves her focus back into the film and speaks to Josef, who works at the fair. An aerial view of the fairground spins and dissolves to Mercouri superimposed over the blue and red jeweled lighting effect, as she again speaks to the camera. Her character's admission that she doesn't tell us her real name suggests her duplicity, although this will turn out to be misleading (apart from the general duplicity of her being a criminal in attempting to steal the Istanbul dagger). The camera follows her as she enters the Hazine Treasury of the Topkapi Museum, and the jeweled effect is used again under the film's opening credits.

Walter tells Elizabeth his three cardinal rules of theft: "Plan meticulously, execute plainly, and don't get caught before, during or after." However, his new idea to use amateurs and not professionals, who the police would immediately suspect, is what condemns the robbery to failure. Walter and Elizabeth tossing their drinking glasses away to indicate they agree to work together on the heist recalls the Greek behavior of throwing glasses in *Never on Sunday*.

The narrative location moves from Istanbul to Kavala, Greece, where Elizabeth and Walter come to see Arthur Simpson. The fact that they think him a "schmo" (i.e., a failed hustler acting as a historian and guide) weakens their decision to entrust him with transporting the car that holds the rifle and grenades they need for the robbery. The expectation is created that Arthur will be caught at the Istanbul border, an expectation that is borne out. This makes rather inexplicable the surprise of Walter and the gang of thieves when they learn of Walter having been caught. This misguided faith in Arthur, an acknowledged amateur, seems to violate Walter's rules of theft, so that the plan is doomed from the outset. However, this also serves to create the expectation that Arthur will also be a failure as a spy. His arrest at the border is compounded by Arthur lacking a current passport (recalling Dassin's own personal passport problems), and the director uses silent reactions for the Turks' discovery of the arms and explosives in the car door.

Arthur's interrogation about the "Sigma group" recalls HUAC and the questioning Dassin never received, with the room dark and Arthur seated under a spotlight. Arthur being called a "terrorist" also recalls the term the director was labeled with, although Dassin didn't harbor weapons. Although the Turks falsely believe that the arsenal is to be used to disrupt the Army Day parade, the blackmailed agreement they make with Arthur is another form of "purging." While he doesn't name names (since at this point he is not aware of the robbery, and only knows Elizabeth and Walter), he is still prepared to spy on them and act duplicitously. Though Arthur will eventually abandon this betrayal—when the betrayal is exposed by his slip of the tongue—his willingness to do so sets up his mistakes during the robbery, and the gang's eventual arrest and imprisonment. Both Arthur's entrapment and duplicity is expressed in his face being seen in the car's side view mirror as Harback speaks to him; and his exit line "You can rely on me" gets a comic if obvious button when he backs up the car and nearly crashes into one of the tailing Turks.

Dassin creates a montage of Turkish people and locales, shot from the backseat of Arthur's car, recalling the same device used in *Night and the City*. The montage quickens in edits, which recalls Dassin's fast-edited sequences in *Rififi* and *Phaedra*.

The director casts himself in a cameo role as a mustachioed Turkish parking officer, seen only once, who stops Cedric from driving the car. This plot point allows Arthur to continue to be involved with the gang, as will his later replacement of Hans, with the scene given an odd touch when Arthur tries to walk away reading a Mr. Universe magazine. This body builder motif will be repeated in the athleticism of Giulo and the later wrestlers in the stadium.

Dassin intercuts between the gang and Arthur reporting to his "Shadows," and an exchange between he and Tufan shows the idiocy of the relationship:

> TUFAN: What made you suspect they are Russian spies?
> ARTHUR: I deduced it.
> TUFAN: From what?
> ARTHUR: From the cook.
> TUFAN: What did the cook say?
> ARTHUR: That they were Russian spies.
> TUFAN: Clever deduction.

Our initial surprise at Walter slapping Guilo for looking at a magazine advertisement for a sportscar is later explained by him saying, "The sudden heavy spender, the overnight

The heist gang from *Topkapi* (1964). From left: Walter Haberlee (Maximilian Schell), Elizavetta Lippmanova (Melina Mercouri), Giulio (Gilles Segal), Arthur Simon Simpson (Peter Ustinov), Hans Fisher (Jess Hahn), and Cedric Page (Robert Morley).

millionaire will be caught in a spotlight from East Istanbul to Peru." Walter's use of the word spotlight prefigures the spotlight that Guilo will need to avoid during the robbery. Just as Walter slaps Guilo Elizabeth later slaps Hans. These violent urges expressed by Walter and Elizabeth reveals their volatile natures (and the tension created by the stress of criminal activity). However, there is the suggestion of perversity between Walter and Elizabeth, who declares herself a nymphomaniac (in line with Dassin's prior filmic presentations of women as prostitutes), in the way he whips her with a piece of rope he toys with, and roughly removes a ribbon she wears around her neck, before they have off-screen sex. The idea of Elizabeth as a nymphomaniac is repeated in her kissing all the men on the mouth after Walter announces about the robbery, "We go tonight."

When Walter has to come up with a new way to cope with the searchlight and the guards during the robbery, Dassin provides him with an unusual full minute of time in which he thinks, while the other gang members wait and watch him. It's a daring cinematic device that both enhances Walter's character and builds tension.

Like the studio set of the street in the first post-credit scene and the end credits' faux curtain call (where the actors walk together on another studio set), Dassin draws attention to his use of artifice when he cuts from an on-location long shot of the gang driving to a medium shot which employs rear-screen projection. While the stadium parade and wrestling exhibition is used as a decoy for the Shadows surveillance of the gang, the footage still reads as filler, particularly when individual members leave their seats to wander seemingly pointlessly around the fair so that they can be followed, and then return. These eight-minutes of footage offers little or no dialogue, which creates the expectation that Dassin will repeat or even try to improve upon the extended robbery scene from *Rififi*, which had no dialogue.

An expectation is also created that the robbery will take place in broad daylight, which would up the ante on the *Rififi* scene (which occurred at night). This latter expectation is only half met in the face of Arthur's initial refusal to climb over the roof of the Museum. (In the book *Larger Than Life*, Margaret Morley tells how Robert Morley's Cedric *was* supposed to be on the roof, but the actor, afraid of heights, talked himself out of doing it and spent four days watching the others.) Consequently, he, Guilo and Walter must sit and wait until night before they continue their action. However, when Arthur is finally persuaded to try, Dassin uses a subjective camera for his point of view, with the image distorted and multiplied as if colored by Arthur's fear of heights.

At the nighttime resumption of the break-in, Dassin disappointingly keeps using dialogue (though, thankfully, no music), but still manages to sustain tension over the eighteen-minute sequence. He initially succeeds by inter-cutting between Guilo hanging suspended by Arthur and Walter, and Elizabeth and Cedric distracting the spotlight manager (she playing Turkish backgammon with him as Cedric surreptitiously slows down the spotlight's movement to allow Guilo to enter the barred window). When Guilo is inside and Walter tells Arthur, "Guilo's on the [window] sill. I'll help you lower him down," Arthur answers, "Can't he do anything by himself?" While this response reads as funny, it also creates the expectation that Arthur is going to weaken and perhaps unintentionally sabotage the operation. We have seen how after he had blown his cover to the gang, he had discarded the cigarette pack containing his last message for the Turks, although this message will find its way to Tufan and help get the gang caught. But in spite of his avowed refusal to continue to spy, Arthur's lesser abilities as Hans' replacement is troublesome.

This fear manifests itself in our feeling that Arthur will not be able to hold Guilo's weight on the rope by himself (Walter must leave him to handle it alone since Walter must work the second rope, used to lift the glass case). The expectation that Arthur will fail had nearly come to pass when Arthur's weakness had let Guilo fall past the window outside the tower, and Arthur had slid down, needing to be rescued by Walter. But the real shock comes when Guilo suffers a momentary loss of balance and nearly drops a dagger and bumps the sultan mannequin (holding the real dagger) so that it teters, threatening to fall over. Dassin heightens the suspense by employing quick edits for the replacement of the removed glass case, inter-cutting between the faces of Walter and Arthur, the upside-down Guilo, the case, and the cord holding it (which is moving towards the mark Walter has made previously to measure the correct length needed to replace the cover).

Dassin cuts from Walter's "It's done" (when Guilo has motioned with his hanging rope that he has the emerald dagger) to the roar of the crowd at the stadium in response to the wrestlers. The little bird that flies through the window, unseen by Guilo, will be paid off when it sets off the alarm after the three have left, as Cedric's earlier recording of Elizabeth laughing will be paid off when we see how it is used to distract the museum guard.

We question why the gang feels the need to go see Tufan, rather than just flee Istanbul, since it seems to exist as a plot point solely to make it easier for them to be caught. Dassin also fumbles in timing the connection between Tufan with the gang at the police station, Josef at the fair, and the bird setting off the alarm at the Treasury. However, he redeems himself somewhat with the montage of telephones ringing and being answered following the alarm being tripped by the bird.

Giulio (Gilles Segal) and Walter Haberlee (Maximilian Schell) try to comfort Arthur Simon Simpson (Peter Ustinov), who is not used to roof-climbing, in *Topkapi* (1964).

Elizabeth in close-up for her mug shot (with her hair cropped) signals the arrest, with the prison locale recalling similar circumstances in *Brute Force* and *Never on Sunday*. The fact that the heist is unsuccessful and the thieves are imprisoned is narratively satisfying, making the happy-ending fantasy scene unnecessary and only acceptable as a curtain call.

In his *Films & Filming* article, Gordon Gow would describe the film as "Fitful ... notable chiefly for the acrobatics of Giles Segal and the concomitant Dassin tension-notes in the beautifully sustained passage where a dagger encrusted with precious stones is filched from its security-case in the Istanbul museum."

In *I Was Born Greek*, Melina Mercouri reports that this was the first time she did not enjoy making a film. She writes that, after enduring a period of illness, she was "nervous and not too enamored of the role I was playing. It got me the Donatello prize [the Italian equivalent of an Academy Award] in Italy later. I've always wondered why." (Mercouri's claim of winning a Donatello for the film cannot be substantiated.) Since *Phaedra*, she had played a supporting role in the war drama *The Victors* (1963), which was a Hollywood film shot in Europe; and Mercouri would next work with Dassin on his melodrama *10:30 P.M. Summer* (1966). In his book *Dear Me*, Peter Ustinov would write of Dassin and Mercouri:

> [He was] a fine, meticulous director with a great sense of humor, who dedicated his career to his wife, Melina Mercouri. It is no reflection on her to suggest that perhaps he could have had a rather more remarkable career if he had not dedicated himself so devotedly to her service. It is, I believe, ever so with husband and wife teams, with the undoubted exception of the Lunts, who possessed an uncannily integrated style in which neither seemed to be making concessions to the other.

In the book *Ustinov in Focus*, by Tony Thomas, the actor said:

> I have a special affection for *Topkapi*. The character is so absurd. I love the idea of a man who aims low and misses. Simpson is the kind of man who wears blazers a little too consistently, the kind with military presumptions, who has to belong to a cricket club. He's a man who hovers between the more reprehensible columns of *The News of the World* and oblivion.

The burly, multi-talented, British-born Ustinov had made his film debut in a supporting role in the British war drama *One of Our Aircraft Is Missing* (1942), and continued playing supporting and uncredited roles. After army service in World War II, he played the title character in (though not top-billed), and co-directed, the war comedy *Private Angelo* (1949), and continued in supporting parts. He made his first Hollywood film as Emperor Nero in the historical adventure *Quo Vadis* (1951), which was filmed in Rome, and for which Ustinov was nominated for the Best Supporting Actor Academy Award. He then went to Hollywood for the epic *The Egyptian* (1954), and the crime comedy *We're No Angels* (1955), and scored the leads in the Italian *I girovaghi* (1956) and the comic fantasy *The Man Who Wagged His Tail* (1957). Ustinov's role as a clown in *Spartacus* (1960) would win him his first Best Supporting Actor Academy Award (*Topkapi* being his second); and he would direct and star in his own adaptation of the Shakespeare play for the comedy *Romanoff and Juliet* (1961). He followed this with directing the sea drama *Billy Budd* (1962), in which he played a supporting role and which was his prior title before *Topkapi*.

After *Topkapi*, Ustinov played more supporting roles and the occasional lead, such as in the comic fantasy *Blackbeard's Ghost* (1968), the crime comedy *Hot Millions* (1968), for which his screenplay was nominated for the Best Writing Academy Award, and the comedy *Viva Max* (1969). In the 1970s the actor returned to a leading role as Hercule Poirot in the mystery *Death on the Nile* (1978), a character he would revive in *Evil Under the Sun* (1982) and *Appointment with Death* (1988). He also starred in various made-for-television movies and the French comedy *We'll Grow Thin Together* (1979). He essayed another mythic detective in *Charlie Chan and the Curse of the Dragon Queen* (1981), directed and starred in *Memed My Hawk* (1984), and played the leads in the comedies *There Was a Castle with Forty Dogs* (1990) and *Stiff Upper Lips* (1998). Ustinov had also directed Elizabeth Taylor and Richard Burton (and played a supporting role) in the comedy *Hammersmith Is Out* (1972). He was a film producer, and a writer and director of stage plays, and was knighted in 1990.

Austrian born Maximilian Schell entered films in Germany in 1955 in supporting roles, including the Hollywood war drama *The Young Lions* (1958), which was filmed in Germany. After playing the German defendant Hans Rolfe in the *Playhouse 90* television production of the historical drama "Judgment at Nuremburg" (1959), he repeated the role for the 1961 film version and won the Best Actor Academy Award (although he was not top-billed in the movie). Schell scored a lead in the comedy *The Reluctant Saint* (1962), his prior feature before his supporting turn in *Topkapi*. After that film, the actor was top-billed in the British thriller *Return from the Ashes* (1965), the German mystery *The Castle* (1968), the adventures *Beyond the Mountains* (1968) and *Krakatoa: East of Java* (1969), and the biographical drama *Simon Bolivar* (1969).

In the 1970s Schell's interest seemed to stretch beyond being a leading man. He co-wrote, directed and also played a supporting role in the romance *First Love* (1970), and performed the same duties for the drama *The Pedestrian* (1973); both were nominated for the Best Foreign Language Film Academy Award. After a cameo in Dassin's *The Rehearsal*, he resumed playing supporting parts, though returning to leads in the theatrical drama *The Man in the Glass Booth* (1975), which earned him a Best Actor Academy Award nomination, and the science fiction adventure *The Black Hole* (1979). Schell was also nominated for the Best Supporting Actor Academy Award for his performance in *Julia* (1977). The 1980s saw the actor essay the lead in *The Chosen* (1981), the fantasy *The Islands* (1983), and the German thriller *Morgen in Alabama* (1984). In the 1990s he returned as the lead in *Justiz* (1993) and the German romance *On the Wings of Love* (1999), which has been his last leading role to date. However, Schell continued as a screenwriter and director, making the noteworthy documentaries *Marlene* (1984), with the heard-but-not-seen Marlene Dietrich, which was nominated for the Best Documentary Feature Academy Award, and *My Sister Maria* (2002), about the alleged mental deterioration of his actress sister.

The jovial and portly British actor Robert Morley had appeared on the London stage as Oscar Wilde in 1936, and the hit was transferred to Broadway in 1938. This led to his film debut in the Hollywood historical romance *Marie Antoinette* (1938), for which he was nominated for the Best Supporting Actor Academy Award. Back in England, Morley would carve out a career as an erudite character actor, with the occasional leading film role. He starred in a dual role in the British musical *You Will Remember* (1941), and scored leads in the comic fantasy *The Ghosts of Berkeley Square* (1947), the comedy *Curtain Up* (1952), the 1953 biographical musical *Gilbert and Sullivan* (as William S. Gilbert), and *The Rainbow Jacket* (1954). He joined Peter Ustinov in a supporting role in the biography *Beau Brummell* (1954), and, after more supporting parts, got to film his stage success, *Oscar Wilde* (1960), which was to be his last leading role on film. After *Topkapi*, he continued with supporting roles, again with Ustinov in *Hot Millions*, and though his output slowed down in the 1970s, the actor would work into the late 1980s before his death in 1992.

Morley was also a screenwriter, and he adapted the play he had co-written, *Edward, My Son*, for the 1949 Hollywood film version, with Spencer Tracy playing the role Morley had originated on stage.

The short and flamboyant Russian born Akim Tamiroff, with the guttural baritone voice and thick accent that lent itself to a variety of nationalities, started in movies in 1932, playing uncredited or minor roles. He graduated to supporting roles and was nominated for the Best Supporting Actor Academy Award for playing the title character in the adventure *The General Died at Dawn* (1936). Tamiroff scored the title role in the "B" mystery *The Great Gambini* (1937) and the lead in the "B" western *Ride a Crooked Mile* (1938). The actor played the lead (a dual role) in the "A"-level *The Magnificent Fraud* (1939), and played the lead in the crime drama *The Way of All Flesh* (1940). Although Tamiroff's output slowed in the 1940s, he was again nominated for the Best Supporting Actor Academy Award for the adventure *For Whom the Bell Tolls* (1943). After more than a decade of playing supporting roles, he returned for a lead in the British comedy *You Know What Sailors Are* (1954). The actor had made repeated appearances for filmmakers like Cecil B. DeMille, Preston Sturges and Orson Welles, and had previously appeared with Peter Ustinov in *Romanoff and Juliet*, and Maximilian Schell in the comedy *The Reluctant Saint* (1962). After his relatively minor role in *Topkapi*, Tamiroff continued in supporting roles, appearing with Robert Morley in *Hotel Paradiso*. He would score leads in the spaghetti western *A Man Called Amen* (1968) and *Moto Shel Yehudi* (1970), and receive a posthumous credit for his performance as Sancho Panza in Welles' unfinished *Don Quixote* when a version of it was released in 1992.

Topkapi was the only title produced by associate producer Roger Dwyre, who had been Dassin's editor on *Rififi*, *He Who Must Die*, *Where the Hot Wind Blows*, *Never on Sunday*, and *Phaedra*. Dwyre would go on to work with Dassin again on *10:30 P.M. Summer*. Uncredited producer Lee Katz had been a screenwriter and assistant director for films made in the 1930s and 1940s, and had become a production manager in the 1950s. As an (often uncredited) associate producer, his prior titles had been the adventure *Moby Dick* (1956), the comic romance *Love in the Afternoon* (1957), the adventure *The Vikings* (1958), the romance *The Journey* (1959), *Scent of Mystery* (1960), and the musical *Paris Blues* (1961). *Topkapi* would be his last producing credit. Filmways Pictures' only previous feature had been the comedy *The Wheeler Dealers* (1963), and they would not produce any future Dassin titles.

Release

France—September 2, 1964; USA—September 17, 1964, with the taglines "(where the jewels were!)," "(where the jewels are!)," "Join us—we'll cut you in on the theft of the century!" "Let us introduce ourselves ... we're crooks (honest)!" and "Come on—you're cut in on the theft of the century!"

Reviews

"Delightful and suspenseful comedy spoof of [Dassin's] own *Rififi*.... Mercouri has a holiday in a role that asks her to be equally enamored of gems and males.... Ustinov has probably the meatiest part in the film and one that allows him to use many of the unsubtleties in dominating scenes he has at his command."—*Variety*

"Another adroitly plotted crime film, played this time for guffaws.... Being something of a musical-comedy pastiche, this is not one of Mr. Dassin's finer films. But it is a diverting entertainment.... Ustinov is the salvation of the film."—Bosley Crowther, *The New York Times*, September 18, 1964

"[Dassin] has pulled off the niftiest caper seen on screen since the jewel job he engineered in *Rififi*. As in *Rififi*, unfortunately, the rest of the film seems a bit Dassingenuous. The director's jokes are often too laboriously explained, and the camera's adoration of Melina Mercouri is sometimes boring and always embarrassing."—*Time* magazine, September 18, 1964

"It's a swell exercise in suspense, and one of Dassin's finest illustrations of men at work, but it doesn't come till 85 mins. into the movie. Most of the rest is airy banter, suggesting that Dassin & Co. had a better time making *Topkapi* than most people do watching it."—Richard Corliss, *Time* magazine April 6, 2008

"Comic grand larceny ... [the actors] all work too hard at being merry, lovable scoundrels."—Pauline Kael, *5001 Nights at the Movies*

10:30 P.M. Summer (1966)

Jorille and Argos Productions/United Artists

Credits: Director: Jules Dassin; Uncredited Producer: Anatole Litvak; Associate Producer/Editor: Roger Dwyre; Screenplay: Jules Dassin, Marguerite Duras, based on the novel *10:30 on a Summer Night* by Marguerite Duras; Photography: Gabor Pogany; Music: Cristobal Halffter; Additional Music: Dimitri Shostakovich, Salvador Bacarisse; Art Director: Enrique Alarcon; Costumes: Dimitri Kritzas; Sound: Johnny Dwyre; Makeup: Julian Rutz. Color, 85 minutes, in English, Spanish and French. Filmed in Provincia De Segovia, Castile, and Estudios Roma, Madrid, in the Winter of 1965.

Cast: Melina Mercouri (Maria); Romy Schneider (Claire); Peter Finch (Paul); Julian Mateos (Rodrigo Palestra); Isabel Maria Perez (Judith); Juan Estelrich; Beatriz Savon (Rodrigo's Wife); Tupe; Cuatro; Tota Alba; Rafael; Luis Rivera; Tereza.

VHS/DVD: DVD released by MGM (Video & DVD) on July 24, 2007.

Synopsis

Travelling in Spain are the Englishman Paul (surname unknown), his wife Maria, their daughter Judith, and their companion, Claire. During a thunderstorm, they stop over at a hotel, but because of overcrowding they are forced to take accommodation in the hotel corridors. The police storm the hotel in search of Rodrigo Palestra, a young peasant who has shot and killed his nineteen-year-old wife and her lover, Amado. Maria drinks heavily, presumably depressed by the affair that she assumes Paul is having with Claire. While the others sleep, Maria sees someone she assumes to be Rodrigo hiding on the roof of a building near the hotel, and she offers to rescue the wet fugitive.

After avoiding police patrol trucks and a spotlight, Maria drives the black-clad person ten kilometers outside of town to a field that is marked by signs that say "Pegaso." When they stop in a deserted area, the mute person reveals himself to be Rodrigo, and Maria comforts him. She tells him she must go back to her companions but will return to take him across the border. Maria tells Paul what she has done, and the four drive back to find the peasant. However, they discover that he has shot himself with the gun he used to murder his victims. The four go to another hotel, where the alcoholic Maria dreams that Paul and Claire make love. After a drive to Madrid, the three adults drink at a bar, seemingly reveling in the Spanish music and dancing. However, after Maria leaves suddenly, Paul and Claire are unable to find her.

Notes

Although this melodrama begins promisingly, and the treatment features a twenty-minute non-dialogue set piece, ultimately the film disappoints in the languor of its pacing, a general lack of humor, and the frustrating ambiguity of the narrative. Roger Dwyre's editing is a highlight of the film's centerpiece, and Dassin repeats the quick-edit technique he had used in *Rififi* and *Phaedra*. While the director utilizes his gift for visual invention, he also, regrettably, overindulges in his use of the musical score. Whether the subject of duplicity is explored (a recurring motif of the director) remains uncertain, given the unexplained nature of the love triangle presented.

Under the opening credits multiple clapping hands are shown, objectified via black lighting, and their increasing fervor associates them with Spanish music and dance, prefiguring the passion that leads Rodrigo's wife to became an adulteress, her lover to cuckold another man, Rodrigo to kill both of them, and the assumed passion felt by the three protagonists in their love triangle. The building rhythm of the clapping leads to anarchy, symbolizing Rodrigo's actions, and also perhaps Maria's passion in wanting to help Rodrigo elude the police (since she empathizes with him as another tortured creature). While this passion can be applied to the participants of the love triangle, their unhappiness is shown to be the negative result of their dangerous behavior. Dassin will use the image of hands repeatedly in the treatment; and the clapping also presents the scene as a musical number, prefiguring other sequences in the film that have the tone of a musical (e.g., Maria's singing of songs, and the dancers in the climactic bar scene).

The storm cloud that appears after the credits, and the thunder and rain, allude to both passion and the convention of a horror film (which the following three-minute sequence suggests). An advancing camera sees a light bulb blown out, and a person dressed in black holds a gun. Dassin uses rapid edits for shock effect, and he conceals the identity (and the gender) of the person with the gun so that they are presented as a horror movie monster, with the gun they hold representing their threat. A boy with a whistle stops whistling and runs away when he sees the person, after we have seen a dog run away when the light bulb had been broken. The black-clad figure's feet are shown, and a pan moves up and stops at the person's lower body. A woman is heard singing, and the person opens a door to reveal the singer with her back to him, half-naked as she bathes while standing. A man is seen in the room smoking but does not react to the sight of the intruder. Has he been expecting him? Or is he just not afraid?

The gun is raised, and the man gestures the sign of the cross over his face before he falls when shot. The woman slowly turns around, and the mystery person is revealed to be Rodrigo, in close-up, shrouded in smoke. Is the smoke steam from her bath or smoke from the discharged gun? She retrieves a blouse to cover her nudity, and Dassin cuts to the exterior thunder as the woman approaches him, unafraid. Dassin again cuts to an exterior shot, and we hear the sound of another gunshot. The scene then cuts to a car driving. A man's hand on the gear shift is touched by a woman's hand, and a pan upwards shows Paul to be the driver, with Claire next to him and Maria in the backseat. A shot of an empty alcohol bottle is enough shorthand to show Maria has a drinking problem, though this doesn't stop her attentiveness to Judith. This is the first time Dassin has presented Mercouri as a mother, and her later behavior towards Rodrigo can be interpreted as more maternal than sexual, although we remember the presentation of Mercouri as the older lover of a younger man in *Phaedra*.

Maria wandering the streets at night looking for a drink recalls Harry Fabian in *Night and the City* on the streets of London, and her entering an all-male bar recalls the all-male bar of *Never on Sunday*. The men we have heard loudly talking, and who sit at tables, go silent when she enters, and stare at her as she sits at the bar to drink. Rather fortuitously, an English speaking man, Emilio, is called to communicate with her (in spite of Maria being Greek), and it is he who explains the feeling that Rodrigo's wife was a whore: "After six months married she wants every man in town." He also rationalizes Amado's affair with a married woman as being the woman's fault: "A woman wants you; you do not refuse her." Although we do not know how Claire has been introduced into the marriage of Maria and Paul—in fact, this is never explained—we naturally make the parallel between Claire and Rodrigo's wife as a whore, with Maria (like Rodrigo) as the cuckolded party. Perhaps this is the reason for her alcoholism.

The fugitive Rodrigo Palestra (Julian Mateos) is told the time by Maria (Melina Mercouri) in *10:30 P.M. Summer* (1966).

Dassin frames four men around Maria and Emilio in an expressionist pose as she leaves the bar, and then presents quick edits for looks between Paul and Claire, culminating, when Maria approaches, with Claire's amusing line, "If she wants so much to find me in your arms, it won't be in a doorway." This comment remains ambiguous—it can be read as presenting Claire (and Paul) as duplicitous characters, but it also supports the later idea that it is Maria who has brought Claire into the marriage for Paul as part of a "game," thereby making Claire less duplicitous (though hardly innocent).

Dassin's use of candlelight in the hotel's restaurant recalls the candlelit restaurant of *Phaedra*, and the blackout recalls the blackout of *Two Smart People*. However, the thunder and lightning emphasized by the glass ceiling of the restaurant returns to the horror movie tone, particularly in regards to the fearful reactions of the patrons. The love seat that Maria and Claire sit in is an obvious metaphor for them as alternate lovers for Paul, but it also suggests the women as potential lovers for each other, an idea that is furthered by Maria's unthreatened attitude toward Claire and their later shared shower.

Paul dressed in all white can be read as an ironic representation of his supposed innocence while committing adultery, reinforced by the primary colors of Claire's dresses, though later he will change into a green sweater to divide the metaphoric presentation. He scores a laugh when translating the Spanish policeman on the telephone for Claire and Maria by saying "Ha ha ha" for the policeman's cackle. Dassin employs a semi-circular movement of the camera to show Maria standing on a balcony watching Paul and Claire kissing on a higher balcony, with Maria's tears matched by the falling rain. Dassin presents the couple's passion via tilted angles and the idea that they don't care that they are being rained on as they embrace. Dassin goes a little overboard in Mercouri's numerous reaction shots, but given the later idea that Maria *wants* Paul to have Claire, we might wonder whether they are kissing on the balcony so that they can be seen by Maria. However, Paul and Claire never look down to Maria's balcony to show that they are aware of being seen by her.

The narrative partially redeems its previous lugubriousness by the inclusion of the pursued Rodrigo (although, as in the opening sequence, Dassin withholds showing us his face so that we can identify him). He is seen by Maria, appearing on a rooftop like a horror movie monster, and the way he scrambles down the roof in a black covering to hide suggests a cockroach. Rodrigo's vulnerability as a hunted figure, in spite of our knowledge of him as a murderer, is enhanced by his being caught in the storm—wet and alone and presumably frightened. Dassin uses this divided interest of Maria's to show Mercouri's alternate reactions to both spotting Rodrigo and her torture at seeing Paul and Claire kiss. Paul and Claire are seen as profiled shadows on the wall when they come to Maria, who has returned to her corridor mattress. (Curiously, the hair of all three is now miraculously dry.)

When Paul leaves Claire alone with Maria, the expectation in created that Maria will attack Claire. Mercouri then stretches out her palm in an odd fashion, seemingly in preparation for the expected strike. However this expectation is not met, and Maria's palm covering her view of Claire removing her dress can be read as both a continuation of Maria's odd hand play (as another example of the use of hands, like the clapping) and a way for Dassin to conceal Claire's stripping. The gesture can also be read as a way for Maria to make Claire disappear, since her hand covers her view of the other woman.

Paul stroking Maria's shoulder and telling her how he loves her creates an expectation that they will have sex, although since they are in a populated corridor, this seems unlikely. While Paul's declaration may be read as that of a guilty man, it may also be sincere, and

Dassin continues the hand motif by showing the shadow of Paul's hand on the wall, from Maria's point of view.

The whistles of the police in their search for Rodrigo recalls the boy whistling before the murder, and the stillness of Rodrigo on the roof as his covering is blown by the wind suggests that perhaps he has died. This suggestion is proven wrong when he moves, with Dassin focusing on his hand moving like a horror movie creature. We then wonder if he still has the gun he used before and, if he does, whether that makes him a continuing violent threat. A subjective camera is used for Maria's point of view as she moves down the corridor of sleepers, down a stairway, through the restaurant (which his now closed, with chairs placed on tables), and into the foyer. Dassin errs in using an unnecessary heartbeat sound effect, but returns to his quick editing when Maria gets to the garage, and we see her point of view of the streets she drives through. The police spotlight playing over the rooftops recalls the spotlight that had to be avoided in *Topkapi*, and Rodrigo's hands clinging to the rooftop tiles is another image casting him in the role of horror movie monster (and further hand imagery for the recurring motif). Dassin continues Maria's point of view when she drives Rodrigo out of town, alternating with shots of her and Rodrigo, although he adds a melodramatic musical score.

Again Rodrigo is presented as the creature by revealing only his hand, and when his face is shown after Maria parks, his odd, slow reaction is matched by Mercouri's intense theatricality. The quick edits between their faces creates an expectation of romance (aided by the music) that is only met by her maternal hugging of him. Even this hugging under-

Judith (Isabel Maria Perez) is held by her mother, Maria (Melina Mercouri), in *10:30 P.M. Summer* (1966).

mines the idea of emotion, since it could simply be Maria attempting to use her body to warm Rodrigo, as does her giving him alcohol (although we know what alcohol means to Maria). As if again intended to undermine the idea of romance, Maria's stroking of Rodrigo's face results in his falling asleep, and Dassin keeps the camera on him to show the lighting transition from night to day.

The shower scene between Maria and Claire begins with a shot that recalls one in *Phaedra*, when Claire is seen in a mirrored reflection and Maria talks to her from off-camera, left of frame. Maria then joins Claire in the same mirrored reflection when Claire invites her to share the shower. Although there is no lesbian behavior, particularly once Claire moves away and sits down on the side of the shower stall, one has to admire Mercouri for letting herself be photographed with her face being showered upon.

Dassin does not show us what Paul sees when he finds Rodrigo dead, laying face down, and turns him over. Oddly, Paul tells Claire, "The sun, maybe," when she asks how he had died (though there is blood both on the ground and on his hand, and his gun lies next to him). The idea that Rodrigo has apparently killed himself, rather than believe that Maria will return to help him further, may be a sign of his lack of faith or an expression of the guilt he feels about the crimes he has committed. However, whatever the reason, Rodrigo's death is a blow to the narrative, since it returns Maria to her passive focus on Paul and Claire. The extended song that she sings with Judith on the car on the way back is an indication that Dassin is going to soften again, since the time he spends on it reads like an indulgence, with only the reaction shots he gives to Paul and Claire being of interest.

Dassin introduces Maria's "dream" by superimposing a record playing over the sex scene between Paul and Claire, and then superimposing Maria walking in the courtyard, shot in sepia or black and white, over more of the sex scene. Quick edits are used for Maria's supposedly awakened point-of-view shots of the courtyard, but the talking of Paul and Claire on the soundtrack suggest that their sex was not merely a dream, even though a shot of Paul sitting in the same chair where he was when Maria supposedly fell asleep may imply that he has never left it. (The idea that Paul and Claire only made love in Maria's dream is later reinforced when Paul tells Maria that they "walked in the woods behind the hotel" as she slept.) While ambiguity is not necessarily a bad thing in a film, in a narrative like this it just becomes frustrating and therefore impacts audience empathy.

The scene between Maria and Paul in their room, where it is implied that they will have sex, also implies that Claire has been hired by Maria to be Paul's new lover. We wonder why, if this is true. There has been repeated talk of their good time together in Verona, and it was after that that Maria had brought in Claire. We don't know where she was found or who she is otherwise, or if she even knew the married couple before. Nor do we know how Paul felt about Maria doing the hiring, if it is indeed true. We also wonder if the marriage is better with Claire attached, although obviously Maria's drinking cannot be a good thing. It might have been better had the treatment shown us the time in Verona, and shown us how Claire's presence came about, rather than make vague implications and suggestions, so that the viewer has to work out this puzzle backwards.

An abrupt cut from Paul, presumably about to make love to Maria, to clapping at the bar where the three are has Dassin using his quick edits, zooms and distorted imagery to generate a buildup of hysteria. A female dancer is seen through a wine glass, and Maria and Claire are laughing, with Paul apparently less amused. Maria placing her empty glass on a table seems to indicate her leaving, and her absence is cued by Paul and Claire calling for her in the daytime in the street. A bus is seen in a mirrored reflection, as is Paul and

Paul (Peter Finch) and his mistress, Claire (Romy Schneider), observe his alcoholic wife, Maria (Melina Mercouri, center), desperate for a drink in *10:30 P.M. Summer* (1966).

Claire in extreme long shot, and Dassin uses tilted angles, quick edits of buildings, and an extreme close-up of Paul calling at the side of the frame before pulling back to a view of the city. It seems we are to assume that either Maria has been swallowed up by the city, or that she has run away deliberately so that she cannot be found. Perhaps she has decided that Paul is better off now being with Claire. One can contemplate multiple theories and make differing interpretations. All we do know for sure is that the film is over, and it has left us unsatisfied and exhausted.

Since *Topkapi*, Melina Mercouri had played the lead in *The Uninhibited* (1965) and a dual supporting role in the comedy *A Man Could Get Killed* (1966). In *10:30 P.M. Summer*, her sixth title with Dassin, she is effective in her theatrical style of performance.

The sensual, Viennese-born Romy Schneider had entered films in Germany in 1953 at fifteen years of age and quickly became a star of Austrian titles. She played the leads in the historical romance *The Story of Vickie* (1954), the musical *A March for the Emperor* (1955), *Sissi* (1955), the comedy *Kitty and the Great Big World* (1956), *Sissi: The Young Empress* (1956), *The Girl and the Legend* (1957), the romance *Monpti* (1957), *Sissi: The Fateful Years of an Empress* (1957), the title role in the romantic comedy *Scampolo* (1958), the title role in the romance *Christine* (1958), the comedies *Die Halbzarte* (1959), *An Angel on Wheels* (1959) and *Die schone Lugnerin* (1959), and the French *Adorable Sinner* (1959). In the 1960s she made the last of her "Sissi" films, *Forever My Love* (1962), and attempted an international career. While she played a lot of supporting roles, including appearing with Mercouri in *The Victors*, she still scored leads in the French *Fire and Ice* (1962), the unfinished Henri-Georges Clouzot's *L'enfer* (1964), and *Chimney No. 4* (1966).

After *10:30 P.M. Summer*, Schneider alternated between supporting and leading roles.

In the 1970s she was the lead in *La califfa* (1970), *My Lover My Son* (1970), the thriller *Qui?* (1970), the romances *Un amour de pluie* (1974) and *That Most Important Thing: Love* (1975), the mystery *Dirty Hands* (1975), *Une femme à sa fenêtre* (1976), the war drama *Group Portrait with a Lady* (1977), and *A Simple Story* (1978). In the 1980s the actress had the lead in the science fiction title *Death Watch* (1980), *The Lady Banker* (1980), the horror *Fantasma d'amore* (1981), and a double lead role in her last film, *La passante du Sans-Souci* (1982), which was released a month before her death.

The rugged and husky, British-born Finch moved to Australia when he was a child, so is often considered Australian, and made his debut in the Australian comedy *Dad and Dave Come to Town* (1938). He played supporting roles in Australian films for a number of years; then, after being discovered by Laurence Olivier when the actor was touring Australia, was signed by Olivier to a contract which took Finch to England. There he continued as a supporting player, ironically playing an Australian in the war drama *The Wooden Horse* (1950). The actor's first Hollywood title was the adventure *Elephant Walk* (1954), and his first leading role was in the British comedy *Make Me an Offer* (1954). Finch played Simon in the comedy *Simon and Laura* (1955), and was the lead in *The Shiralee* (1957), the adventure *Robbery Under Arms* (1957), *Windom's Way* (1957), and the war drama *Operation Amsterdam* (1959). He supported Audrey Hepburn in his next major Hollywood feature, *The Nun's Story* (1959).

In the 1960s Finch played leads in the adventure *Kidnapped* (1960), the biography *The Trials of Oscar Wilde* (1960), *No Love for Johnnie* (1961), and the romances *In the Coll*

Maria (Melina Mercouri) wonders whether she and her husband, Paul (Peter Finch), should stay together in *10:30 P.M. Summer* (1966).

of the Day (1963) and *Girl with Green Eyes* (1964). After *10:30 P.M. Summer*, which seemed to take advantage of the actor's reputation as a womanizer, Finch continued the 1960s in supporting roles. In the 1970s the actor was involved in another love triangle in *Sunday Bloody Sunday* (1971), for which he was nominated for the Best Actor Academy Award. He starred in the crime thriller *Something to Hide* (1972) and the musical *Lost Horizon* (1973); played the title role (but was second-billed) in *The Nelson Affair* (1973); and took the lead in *England Made Me* (1973) and the historical drama *The Abdication* (1974). Although he was not top-billed in *Network* (1976), he would win the Best Actor Academy Award for his performance, and become the first actor to be so awarded posthumously.

Uncredited producer Anatole Litvak was a screenwriter, producer and director who had previously only produced and would go on to produce only his own directing titles. *10:30 P.M. Summer* would be the last credited title associate producer and editor Roger Dwyre would make with Dassin. The film would mark the only picture made for the production company Jorille. Marguerite Duras' novel would be filmed again as the crime drama *Half Past Ten* (2008), with different character names.

Release

October 24, 1966, with the tagline "Claire's body—I never looked at her naked without seeing her with Paul."

Reviews

"Torpid treatment of romantic trio makes for apathetic viewing. Talented cast chained to tedious script.... Dassin's direction is uncertain, frequently illogical, and for the most part, plodding. Miss Mercouri's thesping is in a similar vein."—*Variety*, October 19, 1966

"Dassin has filled the picture with a lot of bizarrerie but this sort of thing—and the performing—is as sodden and lacking in a sense of genuine human feeling as a rain-drenched electric sign."—Howard Thompson, *The New York Times*, November 12, 1960

"The family that plays together does not always make a *Never on Sunday*.... A Greek bearing gifts of a Mercourial nature can only squander them in this lurid, leaden adaptation of a novel by Marguerite Duras.... [It] hits the high mark of silliness."—*Time* magazine, November 4, 1966

"Overly pretentious.... Dassin was in danger of completely losing his audience."—Tony Crawley, *Films Illustrated*

"[A] farrago.... New Wave or Old Hat, it is a simply a dull story boringly told and indifferently acted."—Jay Robert Nash and Stanley Ralph Ross, *The Motion Picture Guide*

• •

Survival 1967 (1968)

[aka *Survival Hamilchama al Hashalom*]
Union Film Distributors

Credits: Producer/Director: Jules Dassin; Producer/Writer: Irwin Shaw; Photography: Christian Darraux, Daniel Vogel; Editors: Roger Dwyre, Michele Neny; Music: Irwin Bazelon; Color, 70 minutes. Filmed on location in Israel in June 1967.

Cast: Joseph Dassin (Narrator—English version); Claude Dauphin (Narrator—French version); David Ben-Gurion, Moshe Dayan, Levi Eshkol (Interviewees).

VHS/DVD: Not available in either format.

Synopsis

This is a documentary about the Six-Day War that was fought between Israel and Egypt, Jordan, Syria and surrounding Arab countries from June 5 to 10, 1967. We are shown the aftermath of the conflict, the story of refugees, interviews with Israeli leaders, and talks with the faculty and students of Chaim Weizman University. The film ends with questions about peace in the area in the future.

Notes

Since this documentary was not available to be viewed by the author of this book, the details of its content can only be deduced from sources like *The New York Times* review of the film by Renata Adler. The film seems to have a pro–Israeli bias, which is odd, since apparently the war was instigated and won by Israel. Adler claims that the producers, Dassin and Shaw, arrived after the war was over so that their coverage lacks immediate footage of the action, and that all those interviewed are Israeli. We do not know if the filmmakers were either disinterested in talking to participants from the Arab countries who were attacked or whether the losers of the conflict denied them access. The subject being the theater of war would seem to allow Dassin to further explore his favored theme of duplicity.

Described as a "paean to Israel," the film is characterized as an anti-war screed but is considered to have conflicting, alternating viewpoints and an overall lack of narrative focus. The narration, writes Adler, is "delivered by a series of persons who manage to sound simultaneously insincere, patronizing and indignant." She says it consists of "whole volleys of dud sarcasms" and "heady parallelisms [which have the effect of] an overstimulated presidential speechwriter." The lines Adler quotes include, "Do you expect peace here just because it is the second half of the 20th century?"—referring to the wars that have taken place in the Middle East throughout history. Other lines are: "Forgive us, ladies and gentlemen, we did not want to be exterminated," "They came for less romantic reasons [than to die here]; they came to live here," and, "Thou shalt not kill; they observe a new commandment—thou salt not perish."

Footage is shown of wounded men, Jews returning to the Western Wall, and monuments to Babi Yar and Buchenwald to present the tragedy of war, although again from the Jewish point of view (though non–Jews were also killed at Buchenwald). Adler labels the treatment as poor, reporting that it does not tell anything that is not already known, and what it does tell—in "fuzzy interviews"—about the Arab refugee problem, it tells unclearly. However, she praises one long sequence of a desert road, shot from the air, littered for miles with abandoned military equipment. Though she goes on to write that in this sequence there is a shot of a boy, "very reluctant to dive into a pool, who is quite evidently forced by a sense of the camera to do so."

Playwright and screenwriter Irwin Shaw had only previously produced, and would only produce one subsequent title, the romance *In the French Style* (1963), for which he was also the screenwriter. In his biography of Shaw, Michael Shnayerson claims that it was Shaw who approached Dassin in May 1967 to go to Israel to make a documentary. The director was an old friend of the writer's, and, claims Shnayerson, both felt strongly about the political situation and the war that seemed about to erupt. Dassin supposedly dropped the project he was working on (presumably the screenplay of the forthcoming *Up Tight!*) and recruited a five-man crew in Paris. Although Shaw had contacts with the Israeli forces, permission was not given to enter the country until June 11, the day after the end of the Six-Day War.

They travelled from the Sinai Desert through Israel to Syria and Jordan, filming the aftermath of the conflict and the peace negotiations between the Jews and the Arabs. In Jerusalem there was a festive air, with Jewish-American celebrities like Danny Kaye, Leon Uris, and Leonard Bernstein in attendance. Shnayerson quotes Leon Davidoff on Shaw and Dassin:

> Jules and Irwin were like fire and water. Jules was the aggressive one, trying to do everything at once. He wanted to rent helicopters, and wasted time going from general to general trying to procure them. He wanted to film 150,000 Jews going on a holy day to the Wailing Wall, but the authorities wouldn't let him.

So Dassin apparently used a hidden camera to get the shot.

Shnayerson describes the result as "fairly abortive," and says that Dassin retitled it *Rehearsal*, intercutting the footage he had with a ballet rehearsal to illustrate the film's new title and the idea that the Six-Day War could be a rehearsal for a bigger one. However, Dassin removed the ballet scenes before the film was released and changed the title back to what it is now. Shnayerson concludes that after Adler's savage review, the film "died a quick death."

This would be the last picture distributed by Union Film Distributors, who had been in operation since 1946 (though had not previously released any of Dassin's films).

Release

June 11, 1968

Reviews

"*SURVIVAL 1967* got to Israel on the seventh day of the six-day war and looks it.... Missing the action seems to have broken the spirit of Irwin Shaw, and Jules Dassin, entirely ... poor and ineffective propaganda ... a contrived, unmoving defensive travelogue, tacked on to a war.... Everything about it is off."—Renata Adler, *The New York Times*, June 12, 1968

....

Up Tight! (1968)

[aka *Betrayal/Uptight/Up Tight*]
Marlukin Productions

Credits: Producer/Director: Jules Dassin; Associate Producer: Jim Di Gangi; Co-producer (uncredited): Ruby Dee; Screenplay: Jules Dassin, Ruby Dee, Julian Maysfield, based on the novel *The Informer* by Liam O'Flaherty: Photography: Boris Kaufman; Editor:

Robert Lawrence; Music: Booker T. Jones; Production Design: Alexandre Trauner; Art Direction: Phillip Bennett; Set Decoration: Ray Moyer; Costumes: Theoni V. Aldredge; Makeup: Bob Sidell; Titles: John and Faith Hubley. Color, 104 minutes. Filmed on location in Cleveland, Ohio, and in Hollywood in June 1968.

Songs: "Johnny, I Love You" (Booker T. Jones), sung by Booker T. Jones and the MGs; "Children, Don't Get Weary" (Frank Williams), sung by Judy Clay, accompanied by Booker T. Jones and the MGs; "Blues in the Gutter" (Booker T. Jones), sung by Booker T. Jones; "Time Is Tight" (Al Jackson, Jr., Booker T. Jones, Donald "Duck" Dunn, Steve Cropper).

Cast: Raymond St. Jacques (B.G.); Ruby Dee (Laurie); Frank Silvera (Kyle Simpson); Roscoe Lee Browne (Clarence, aka Daisy Girl); Janet MacLachlan (Jeannie); Max Julien (Johnny Wells); Juanita Moore (Mama Wells); Richard Williams (Corbin); Michael Baseleon (Teddy); John Wesley Rodgers (Larry); Jitu Cumbuka (Rick); Ketty Lester (Alma); Robert DoQui (Street Speaker); James McEachin (Mello); Kirk Kirksey; Errol Jaye (Mr. Oakley); Isabelle Cooley; Alice Childress; Dick Williams; Van Kirksey; David Moody; Mello Alexandria; Julian Mayfield (Tank Williams). Uncredited: Vernett Allen (Ralph); Lovyss Bradley; Anthony Chisholm; Isabelle Cooley; Jules Dassin (Television Broadcast Host/Radio Announcer); Robert Foulk (Police Captain); Joel Fluellen (Kyle's Associate); Gavin MacLeod (White Man at Carnival); Alan Openheimmer (Unctuous Man in Arcade); Lonny Stevens; Bill Walker (Bartender).

VHS/DVD: Not available in either format.

Synopsis

Four days after the assassination of Martin Luther King, Tank Williams, an unemployed Negro steelworker, gets so drunk that he is unable to assist in the planned robbery of a Cleveland ammunition depot. His best friend, Johnny Wells, and Rick and Larry do it without him but are hampered by Tank's absence. During the robbery, Johnny kills a guard while the men make their getaway. Tank gets expelled from the militant committee led by B.G., who plans to use guns to fight their oppression, after being convinced that the murder of King has demonstrated the ineffectiveness of non-violence. Tank is approached by Clarence, a homosexual police informer, who reveals that there is a $1,000 reward offered for information leading to Johnny's capture. Needing the money, Tank reveals Johnny's whereabouts to the police.

The tenement where Johnny's mother has an apartment is raided, and Johnny is shot and killed. Tank spends his money drinking, although he has a small amount left to leave as a donation at Johnny's funeral. B.G. asks Tank to help him find out who the informer is, and Tank names Clarence, although Larry and Rick tell B.G. that they know the real informer is Tank. When Tank is brought in front of the committee, his lies about the money he has obtained are exposed, and he is sentenced to death. He escapes from Larry and Rick, who have been assigned to execute him, and hides in a hotel. He tells his girlfriend, Laurie, where he is, and she comes to him. When he tells Laurie that he is the informer, she tells him that he is dead. Found by Rick and Larry at the steel mill where he used to work, he climbs to the top of a steel bridge and is shot by Rick.

Notes

Although this racial drama continues the director's seeming interest in the theme of duplicity by making his protagonist an informer, Dassin once again errs in a bloated treatment that indulges in scenes of lesser interest. Ironically, it is the subplot of the revolution intended by black militants that is more interesting, exemplified in a bravura ten-minute sequence of moral complexity, though this film allows Dassin to occasionally display his visual virtuosity and to rein in his previous overuse of musical scoring for a greater dramatic effectiveness. Performances are pitched at an intense level that occasionally dips into unintentional humor, but credit must be given for the effort of a white man presenting the black man's point of view without it being crudely offensive. The film is the first for Dassin in eleven years that did not star Melina Mercouri, as it only features female characters in minor supporting roles. The narrative is unique in the director's canon for having his first openly gay character.

Animation under the opening credits shows a man running, prefiguring the plight of both Johnny and Tank; a man shot, prefiguring the use of guns; people in

Poster for *Up Tight!* (1968).

a park, suggesting the urban community; and two black men arm in arm, representing black brotherhood. The song "Johnny, I Love You" accompanies the images, sung by the male composer Booker T. Jones, with the idea of Johnny being loved by Tank. Title cards after the credits read "Martin Luther King was assassinated on April 4, 1968, in Memphis, Tennessee. He was buried in Atlanta, Georgia. Four days later." Under the song "Children, Don't Get Weary," Dassin uses color newsreel footage of the funeral of King, before another title locates us in Cleveland, Ohio, showing the steel mill setting of Tank's later drunken walk and death scene. The camera cuts to the poor reception of a television screen and pulls back to reveal people watching footage of King's "I Have a Dream" speech. The bad reception, which includes the picture rolling, indicates a poor neighborhood, as does the broadcast being pumped into the street via loudspeaker. The cheers for King in the footage transitions to a police siren; while Kyle's call for the neighborhood's agitated brothers to "Keep it cool" scores a laugh from the period use of slang (which will also include describing men as "cats").

Johnny, Rick and Larry standing around Tank as he sits naked in the bath recalls a similar scene of men around a naked man in *Rififi*; while the shower pouring water over Tank's face recalls the same effect on Melina Mercouri in *10:30 P.M. Summer*. The comment that "Memphis proves the answer is guns, more guns" follows the introduction of gunfire as the way King was killed, and prefigures the guns that will be stolen, the gunfire during the robbery, the gunfire between the police and Johnny at the tenement (resulting in Johnny's death), Tank at the shooting gallery, and Tank's own death.

The crime that the men plan qualify them as duplicitous criminals, although they're not in the same league as Tank will prove to be. The robbery sequence is shorter than Dassin's famous heist scenes in *Rififi* and *Topkapi*; it's only three minutes and uses dialogue after a brief period of dialogue-free action. Dassin zooms in on the hat Johnny has left behind during the gunfire exchange with the guard, which will allow the police to easily identify him as the culprit.

An exchange between a white police officer and Clarence as the King funeral footage is shown at the station introduces the repeated use of the word "nigger," which is now considered politically incorrect, something the police officer is sensitive about:

> POLICEMAN: Word of honor, I never thought that guy [King] was so important.
> CLARENCE: Because, my friend and white brother, you can't conceive of a nigger being important.
> POLICEMAN: Now that's a word I never use.
> CLARENCE: Please do. To thine own self be true.
> POLICEMAN: Oh, balls!

Clarence will go on to describe himself as a "nigger, stool pigeon, and faggot," although the only person he informs on is Tank to Larry and Rick, and even that is done indirectly.

The scene between B.G., Jeannie and Tank shows Jeannie's anger when she slaps Tank, blaming him for the botched robbery (since he was not part of the gang, as planned). It also offers an amusing line over the issue of Tank's drinking when B.G. says, "We're not running a rehabilitation center in this revolution—we don't have the time."

Tank and Clarence have an interesting exchange on the subject of him being a supposed stoolie. When Tank asks him, "How do you feel when you sell a man?" Clarence answers, "I don't care what happens to Johnny. Or to you. Or to my useless existence." Of course, it is prophetic that Tank should be so concerned about selling a man, since he will sell Johnny to the police. Even though Clarence does not sell anybody in the narrative, by talking to him in front of the street speaker and taking him home to show him the police photographs he has of Tank fighting with an officer (evidence that Clarence has the influence to make disappear), Clarence becomes an Iago figure of manipulation and instigation. The $1000 reward money recalls the reward money for Harry Fabian in *Night and the City*, and while the money appeals to Tank because he is unemployed, the next scene suggests that he can also use it for his girlfriend Laurie and her children. When Tank pushes Mr. Oakley into the path of an oncoming taxi, the scene plays as more comic than violent after the odious baiting Oakley has done to Tank beforehand, and because of the comic physicality Errol Jaye provides as Oakley.

The ten-minute scene of the committee's council is perhaps the best in the film, in spite of the film noir lighting used. Especially good is the appearance of the white man Teddy, who reveals himself in the following speech to Corbin as a caring ally to the black movement (though he denies being a "conscience-stricken liberal"):

> You remember me? We were together in Seoul. They threw us in the same jail. I remember you when we cried together in Mississippi. That's when we heard they killed those three kids. Two white, one black. I remember you when you read a pamphlet I wrote in Birmingham. You said that's good, Teddy. That's good.

The committee is willing to accept the money Teddy has brought, in spite of their no-whites policy. His rejection is clear when he says, "Here's something I wrote; if you don't want to read it you can use it for toilet paper," and B.G. tells him, "If you want to help us, send us some guns. You folks can buy them easier than we can." Kyle's associate is wise enough to respond to this with, "That's the way to win a war. Alienate your friends." He will object to the committee's desire to use guns with, "Violence is a self-defeating mother" (the last word being more jive slang).

Dassin uses the song "Blues in the Gutter" for Tank's depression over *his* rejection by the committee, who has told him that it was Johnny's idea to "cut him lose" because of his drinking. A hand-held camera films Tank literally walking in the gutter, which is full of water, and his entrance into the police station to inform is presented by Tank's subjective point of view. After Tank faces a policeman who appears with shaving cream on his face (presumably it's a slow night for crime), Dassin intercuts siren-blaring police cars with close-ups of Tank.

Teddy's attempt to warn B.G. and the committee about the police's knowledge of Johnny's location presents him as a man of conviction, despite the treatment he has received from them (even if the way he learns what he has is a plot contrivance—the bus he is in just happens to stop beside a police car in which a cop tells another, "We've got Johnny Wells"). The scene of the tenement assault by the police thankfully presents them as reasonable; it is the occupants who behave badly, throwing tin cans and bottles from their balconies in a shower of glass. Johnny's death is presented with a circular move of the camera in a subjective point of view that falls down to where Mama Wells and Jeannie stand, although his body is not seen to fall. Dassin will repeat this remarkable shot for Tank's death at the film's end.

Tank at the bar is one of the extended scenes that gets Dassin into trouble. The earlier scene between Tank and Johnny also suffers because of the lack of screen charisma of Max Julien as Johnny; while the later scenes of Tank wandering the streets, reminiscing at the steel mill, and Tank at the carnival all go on far too long to make their points and end up testing our patience.

Tank leaving money for the Wells (he is said to leave $20; but 20 out of $1000 either suggests his stinginess or the excess wastage of his drinking) is seen by B.G., which arouses his suspicion, since Tank rarely has any money. However, Larry and Rick following Tank gets an unexpected payoff when it is Tank who becomes the aggressor, strangling Rick, as an expression of Tank's guilt. B.G.'s request that Tank help them find the informer comes out of a belief that it is not Tank, although Rick and Larry believe that he *is* the informer, with the offer coming with a promise to return Tank to the committee that had rejected him. Tank's joy and relief is expressed in his hitting a wire that reaches over the rooftop where the scene takes place, and Dassin has the wire reverberate with sound for effect.

Tank naming Clarence as the informer is analogous to people naming names to HUAC, and perhaps easier for B.G. to believe because Clarence has admitted to being a "stool pigeon." Tank going to see Clarence to warn him isn't done as full disclosure, although Clarence's self-hating talk suggests that he wouldn't care if Tank fingered him even though it is a lie. Clarence is a pathetic figure because he has no self-esteem. He doesn't even attach any value to Claude, the boy he has in his apartment that we presume has been or is going to be his lover. The idea of gay men as sexual predators without feelings may apply to Clarence but not to Claude, who cares enough about Clarence to show concern for him when locked out of the room by Tank.

When Rick and Larry arrive at Clarence's, we hear examples of Clarence's wit. He describes the aggressive men with, "It's James Bond in colored time." After he is slapped by Rick, he says, "That's the trouble with every black man I know. He has no sense of the ridiculous."

Tank's questioning by B.G. and the committee is like the HUAC questioning. His slow answers were perhaps intended to create tortuous tension but actually comes off as little more than Dassin's further indulgence. However, Tank scores a laugh at Alma's outburst of calling him a liar by saying that he got his money from selling blood. Tank repeatedly lying, after also saying he won the money gambling, digs him into deeper trouble with both the committee and the audience. The scene picks up interest, as had the earlier committee scene, when Kyle voices his objection to Tank being found guilty of informing and being sentenced. Again, moral complexity is added to what appears to be a straightforward issue, with Kyle criticized for working within the "whitey's machine." The location where Tank is taken by Larry and Rick, which has flaming piles of tires, represents hell, and creates the expectation that Tank will be killed. However, a cut to Laurie undermines the expectation. Since we have seen Tank able to defeat the two other men when they followed him from the Wells funeral, his escape is not a surprise—though the surprise is that he uses his brains and not his brawn to do it by hiding behind a conveniently passing train.

When Tank tells Laurie that he is the informer, her repeated slapping of him is both the reaction of a moral person and a member of the neighborhood community. Although he doesn't tell her that he has named Clarence as the informant (and we don't see Clarence again in the narrative, so we assume he has not been harmed), perhaps to spare himself more slapping, he does make the existential but inexplicable statement that he doesn't know why he did it. *We* assume he did it for the money, and because he was told that it was Johnny who had made the committee reject him—both reasons being stronger than Tank's supposed love of Johnny. Like all good women of the movies, Laurie's anger turns to loving acceptance of her man, in spite of his selfish use of the reward money. (Laurie reduced to working as a prostitute after Tank's rough treatment of Mr. Oakely has ended her chances for welfare represents another of Dassin's recurring motifs: women as whores.)

Tank returning to the steel mill bridge for his suicidal death recalls the bridge of *The Naked City* and the suicidal leap in *Night and the City*. Dassin intercuts between Tank at the site and Rick and Larry in a car. We don't know how they have learned of Tank's whereabouts; perhaps Tank has told them, which is suggested by his calling and waving to them when they arrive. His calling recalls the call he made in the early scene, telling them to go away and then to come back. Interestingly, when faced with the task of shooting Tank (the final use of the gun motif), Larry can't do it, and Rick takes the gun to shoot. It is perhaps easier for Rick to kill Tank, seeing as how Tank nearly choked him to death earlier. Dassin repeats the circular camera move and subjective point of view for Tank's fall; while the dropping dirt which eventually covers the camera lens is like the dirt covering a coffin during a burial.

The film's pressbook mentions such items of curiosity as the set designer dumping new venetian blinds into a bathtub filled with coffee for an instant aging coloring; Dassin successfully pleading for rain, which came fifteen minutes after he was ready to shoot scenes outside an abandoned railroad station and continued throughout the night (when the weather prediction was for starry skies); Raymond St. Jacques arriving for the film wearing a beard and moustache that he had not warned the director about but which Dassin approved of; Melina Mercouri eating midnight suppers on the streets of Cleveland with Dassin when she visited; frustrated shoppers being unable to access the locked bargains in the "Famous Thrift Shop" which had been created in a vacant store by the production; and James McEachin using his real life experience of being a policeman for three years in New Jersey to add realism to his acting for his character's militant denouncing of policemen.

In his *Films & Filming* article, Gordon Gow claims the movie's best scenes were the Negro equivalent of the wake at Mama Wells', and the two scenes of the committee council. Dassin was particularly interested in the second committee scene, says Gow, who writes, "The formality of placements, and the spatial relationships between Tank and those that threatened him were dependent to a considerable degree upon Dassin's inspiration of the moment." Dassin is quoted as saying about the first committee scene:

> I did plan beforehand, how I would place the groups. But I drove my script clerk to complete madness by an enormous amount of cheating and recomposing, changing the positions of people quite arbitrarily on the floor. I wanted the character of Corbin, the real leader of the militants, to be always surrounded with African tonalities. And I didn't have those in the set, which was a bowling alley. So I just plucked actors who wore different clothes and grouped them around him all the time. The script clerk would say, "But *he* was *there* in the last shot, he *can't* be *here* in this one." I didn't pay any attention to that. So there was cheating and improvisation; and then as I went on, that entire sequence was "cut" as it was shot; there was not a single extra angle or added frame.
>
> In the trial scene, I knew broadly how I was going to place the people, but out of the rehearsal came the emphasis and the cutting and the close-ups. In other words, I plan the cutting continuity as I shoot.

Dassin also advises that the character of Teddy was his addition to the screenplay, as "a little editorializing [to not] alienate or exclude the white progressive from the [black militant] struggle." Dassin also explains his empathy with the militants:

> In America the black people have shown a patience and a behavior of non-violence that has lasted three hundred years. Very little explosion of revolt. And there was a willingness or hope or prayer that people would treat this another way, that racism in some way or another would die. But it just hasn't.

Gow interprets the distorted-mirror sequence in which Tank is forecasting a future in which Negroes will command as expressing two opposing viewpoints as extreme and therefore distorted. Dassin says that his intention was to imply that desire:

> The white people in the scene are well-intended, bemuddled liberals. They're having fun with Tank at first, but there is a patronizing demand on their part to be accepted. There's the wink of the eye that says, "We understand." And the whole thing adds up to such a distorted relationship, such a distorted sense of communication.
>
> The black people in America kept saying, up till a few years ago, "My God, why don't you listen to us? We are trying to tell you what the situation is. Why won't anybody listen? You appoint all kinds of investigation commissions to make a deep analysis of the obvious. Well, God, you know how we live. We can tell you about what we think has to be done. Listen to us." And there has either been a refusal of communication, or a distortion of what has been said and what has been heard. And this pretty much is what the scene is about.

In *I Was Born Greek*, Melina Mercouri described the film as a failure and writes of Dassin's disappointment:

> He put his heart into the film. He wanted so much for it. He believed it was needed, that it could contribute to America's understanding of the black man's agonizing struggle. He never let anyone see what failure did to him. But I live with him and I saw his heartbreak as a man and as an artist.

In the *Cineaste* interview Dassin himself calls the film a failure because his finger had fallen off the national pulse:

> I didn't trust myself. I cared deeply about the whole black condition in America. I wrote what I thought was a good screenplay but I questioned myself. Who are you to think you can write a screenplay about the black condition? First of all, you've been away so long. Secondly, your skin is white. So I called upon Julian Mayfield and Ruby Dee, who were to star in the film, to rework the script with me. Both of them are very gifted people whom I love, but I think they screwed up my screenplay. Not because of what they contributed but because it was no longer mine. I was writing in the lingo of the '40s. I changed that after listening to their counsel. Later, I came to believe that was a mistake. I should have stuck with my own version. It's a subtle point, but language conditioned a lot of the writing. I never regret having made the film, but it wasn't mine because I never trusted myself.

Dan Georgakas and Petros Anastasopoulos comment that Dassin was the only filmmaker to take on the subject when things were really hot. Dassin replies:

> I'm still trying to decide whether it was too early or too late. There are many good things in the film, and I'm still trying to work out all that went wrong. I wanted so much to do the subject that I accepted the condition imposed by the studio that it be a remake of *The Informer*. That was another unnecessary burden.

The Informer had originally been made by British International Pictures in 1929 as an early talkie, although it is said that the tale of the plight of Dublin rebels fighting the British occupation had been compromised by the casting of the Swedish Lars Hansen as the protagonist. The film was remade by John Ford in 1935, and it won Academy Awards for Best Picture and Best Actor (for Victor McLaglen, who played the informer Gypo Neal). The documentary *The Informer: Out of the Fog* on the DVD release describes the film as follows: "Called a visual masterpiece almost unparalleled in cinema history with its bold photography, dramatic lighting, and innovative effects, it was one of the first 'art house' films to be released by a major studio." A comparison of Ford's version with Dassin's remake serves to highlight Ford's superior treatment in his use of silence, humor, poetic touches, and subtle score. The Ford narrative benefits from occurring within a single night (which Dassin extends) and the use of fog to present the protagonist's supposedly foggy mental state (something which Dassin attempts to imitate with the use of rain). Dassin employs the same plot points of the Ford treatment to parallel American black activism with the 1922 Irish Sin n Fein rebellion, with a few alterations.

French movie card for *The Informer* (1935), which Jules Dassin remade as *Up Tight!* (1968).

The character of Gypo's girlfriend, Katie Madden, is much more significant to the original than Laurie is to the remake. Katie is clearly shown to be a prostitute in Ford's version, which is less apparent in Dassin's, and Gypo eventually gives her five of the twenty pounds reward money (whereas the Laurie character gets nothing). It is interesting how Katie throws away the five pounds even before she learns how Gypo got it, as if sensing it is blood money. Katie does not become angry the way Laurie does in the remake when told of the betrayal; and in the Ford version, Katie goes to the leader of the rebels to plead for forgiveness and tells them where Gypo is hiding. In a sense, Katie informs on Gypo, although it is shown that he is only pursued by Barteley and Tommy (the Larry and Rick characters in Dassin's version) when they eavesdrop to learn of Gypo's whereabouts. In Dassin's remake, Laurie does not go to the B.G. character, the equivalent of Ford's Dan Gallagher, nor does she inform on Tank, the revamped Gypo character.

In Ford's version, Gypo has been "court-martialed"—expelled from the rebels for a failure to execute a deserter—an action reflected later when Dennis draws the small straw and must execute Gypo for being an informer. (Dassin has Tank being drunk and unable to participate in the robbery as the reason he's thrown out of the "Committee.") Ford has an advertisement for travel to America for 10 pounds as Gypo's motivation for informing on Frankie McPhillip, although he wants Katie to go to America rather than himself; whereas Dassin implies that Tank informs on Johnny Wells for Laurie. Dassin never has Tank state his motivation, repeating Gypo's idea that "I don't know why I did it," with the motivations of both diluted by a fondness for alcohol. However, Gypo is shown to be the less weak of the two, since he still retains some control of the reward money. Gypo asks for and receives forgiveness from Frankie's mother in the film's climax, something Dassin does not allow for Tank.

However, Tank's sacrificial death is a reflection of Gypo's death in the church, where he falls in front of the church's altar when he is shot. The fact that in Ford's version Gypo is shot by Barteley and not Dennis, whose assignment it is, is reflected in Dassin's version—where it is the Barteley character, Rick, who shoots Tank (both Rick and Bartley were the first to believe that Tank/Gypo was the informer, despite his naming someone else). Ford provides a resonant image for the death of Frankie, with the attack on his mother's apartment smaller in scale than Dassin's, even if Ford's coverage of the scene reads as more hysterical than Dassin's due to the screaming of the women. Mary's placement in the scene as she tries to stop the British policemen getting to Frankie and thereby stopping him from getting a clear shot at them is a clever contradiction; and Ford uses a shot of Frankie's hand holding onto the staircase railing to convey his death, as Dassin will use the subjective camera for Johnny's supposed fall.

Another difference in the two treatments has Ford showing the appropriate disdain displayed by the British police when they give Gypo the reward money; Dassin does not. Ford's version also presents a character that is missing from Dassin's treatment—the blind beggar, who could represent Gypo's conscience and who is the first beneficiary of a portion of the reward money. At Frankie's wake, the coins accidently dropped by Gypo, and seen by all in attendance, is another touch not repeated by Dassin; and here Ford has Gypo directly give Frankie's mother some money directly, while Tank only anonymously leaves some at Johnny's wake. The person that Gypo names as the informer—the tailor Peter Mulligan—is a character previously unseen or identified in the narrative; Dassin, however, introduces Clarence early in *his* narrative. Dassin also adds the character element of Clarence being more morally ambiguous than Peter Mulligan; much more is made of Clarence's sexual orientation in Dassin's treatment.

Gypo being called a "king" by the crowd after he punches a presumably English toff and a policeman present him as more heroic than Tank. Both protagonists enjoy the false admiration of people using them for their money, with Gypo in particular receiving the attention of Terry (who, ironically, fails to secure any of his money). Dassin alters the timing of the Ford scenario in regards to the pleasurable use of the money. Dassin has Tank drinking in an extended sequence that parallels the one in Ford's version where Gypo orders fish and chips for the crowd rather than alcohol. Ford also never has Gypo warn Mulligan about how he has informed on him, as opposed to the way Dassin's Tank does. Ford's Aunt Betty sequence, which takes place at a presumed brothel, can be equated with Dassin's carnival sequence, because of the appearance of the British woman who is slumming. This figure, of a different class than the others, prefigures Dassin's use of the white middle-class crowd around Tank, who are also slumming. However, while Ford has Gypo give the woman money so that she can go back to London and pay her debts to Aunt Betty, Dassin's treatment lacks this generosity on the part of Tank, though an argument could be made that Tank warning Clarence is *his* form of generosity. Interestingly, both directors have trouble with these sequences of the protagonist enjoying his money. They both focus on them for too long and detract from the consequences we await. Perhaps these were designed to create the expectation that the informer will get away what he has done, though we sense that in neither scenario will that expectation be met.

A romance between Dan Gallagher and Frankie's sister, Mary, does not appear in Dassin's narrative, although the equivalent characters B.G. and Jeannie are seen together. B.G. certainly does not make a point of having Jeannie at Tank's committee trial, as Dan does with Mary. Mulligan's appearance at Ford's court of enquiry is different to Clarence's absence from Dassin's trial, since Dassin has shown Larry and Rick previously visit Clarence. The attendance of the blind beggar is also noteworthy, and perhaps helps Gypo to finally admit to his informing.

As opposed to Tank in Dassin's version, Gypo doesn't try to offer an alternative scenario as to how he got the money, which presents Tank as the more pathetic character; and Ford has Gypo put into a cell within the rebels' space before his execution, which Dassin does not. Gypo's escape from the cell by lifting off the ceiling is mirrored in Tank's escape from Rick and Larry, although Dassin doesn't repeat the idea of Gypo's second escape from the hotel room. Gypo finding Frankie's mother in the church may be a coincidence, but it does allow him to ask for forgiveness from her and God, which is paralleled by Dassin's version where Tank's suicidal sacrifice is a universal admission of his error but also a darker existential statement.

In the book *Tender Comrades*, Dassin says the company making the film in Cleveland was very much resented by the community, especially because they couldn't get black people for the crew. Filming after the assassination of Martin Luther King and the riots that followed, "We went into this atmosphere resented and not trusted and attacked—sometimes physically attacked. Then Bobby Kennedy was killed [June 5, 1968], and the mayor warned us to get out of town, saying he could not be responsible for our safety. So we had to finish the film in Los Angeles." Dassin also told Patrick McGilligan and Paul Buhle that James Earl Jones was supposed to have played the part of Tank, but at the last minute he changed his mind. "It all went haywire," Dassin says, "but I loved Ruby Dee and all those who worked on the film."

The film was the first (and last) major part for Julian Mayfield, who had previously played a band leader in the British romance *Our Virgin Island* (1958), which also featured Ruby Dee in a supporting role.

Shakespearean stage actor Raymond St. Jacques is said to have been the first black actor to have appeared in a regular role on television—in the western series *Rawhide*. He had made his film debut in a minor role in *Black Like Me* (1964) but would alternate between working in television and playing supporting film roles. After *Up Tight!*, the actor played the lead in the science fiction drama *Change of Mind* (1969) and the crime drama *Book of Numbers* (1973), which he also produced and directed, and essayed the supporting role of Martin Luther King in the biography *The Private Files of J. Edgar Hoover* (1977). After years of more television and supporting film roles he returned as the lead in the horror movie *Voodoo Dawn* (1991), which was released after his death in 1990.

Ruby Dee had made her film debut in a supporting role in the musical *That Man of Mine* (1946), and played in television and more supporting parts in film. After *Up Tight!*, she continued in supporting parts but scored rare leading roles in the African drama *Cool Red* (1976), *The Torture of Mothers* (1980), and the comedy *No. 2* (2006). She was nominated for the Best Supporting Actress Academy Award for her performance in the crime drama *American Gangster* (2007). *Up Tight!* would be the only film that Ruby Dee would (co)write and (co)produce.

The Jamaican born stage actor and director Frank Silvera made his film debut in a supporting role in the western *The Cimarron Kid* (1952), and was top-billed in two films for director Stanley Kubrick: the war drama *Fear and Desire* (1953), and the film noir *Killer's Kiss* (1955). Thereafter he played in television and supporting roles in film, with the actor's role as the political activist in *Up Tight!* reflecting how in real life Silvera founded a theater company for black actors called The Theatre of Being.

The mellifluous-voiced stage actor Roscoe Lee Browne made his film debut in *The Connection* (1962), and had worked in television and supporting roles in film before *Up Tight!* After *Up Tight!*, the actor played the title role (but was not top-billed) in the crime drama *The Liberation of L.B. Jones* (1970), and played his only leading feature role in the film version of his stage show *Behind the Broke Words* (2003).

Associate producer Jim Di Gangi had also been an assistant director, art director and production manager. His previous producer titles were the film noir *Edge of the City* (1957), which featured Ruby Dee in a supporting role, and the drug drama *The Connection*. *Up Tight!* was the only film to be made by Marlukin Productions.

Release

December 28, 1968, with the tagline "A man on the run. A life at stake. A people about to explode."

Reviews

"Heavy-handed use of *The Informer* to exploit current racial unrest.... Dassin chose to use old-fashioned Depression-era social commentary on an incomplete aspect of 1968 race relations, which resulted in showing only the 'preachy' side of the problem."—*Variety*, December 10, 1968

"An intense and furious movie ... [but it] misses a kind of cool in Dassin's direction, which has elements of a number of films made in the thirties, when to be socially aware was also to be convinced of simple rights and wrongs."—Bosley Crowther, *The New York Times*, December 19, 1968

"It occasionally rings true ... but it is impossible to respect."—*Time* magazine, January 3, 1969

"Everybody tries hard, but the material doesn't transfer successfully, and the movie lacks spirit.... Directed in a 1940s melodrama style."—Pauline Kael, *5001 Nights at the Movies*

"A forthright treatment of black militancy ... a good and interesting film, however, because of isolated elements. It has blunt and direct dialog; it has several powerful performances; It has moments of truth.... [But] Dassin's directing style is too impressionistic and arty for his subject matter."—*Chicago Sun-Times*, February 19, 1969

Promise at Dawn (1970)

[aka *La promesse de l'aube*]
Avco Embassy

Credits: Producer/Director: Jules Dassin; Executive Producer: Joseph E. Levine; Screenplay: Jules Dassin, based on the memoir by Romain Gary and the play *First Love* by Samuel Taylor; Photography: Jean Badal; Music: Georges Delerue; Editor: Robert Lawrence; Production Designer: Alexandre Trauner; Art Director: Auguste Capelier; Set Dressing: Charles Merangel; Sound: Jacques Lebreton; Costumes: Theoni V. Aldredge; Makeup: Otello Fava; Hairstyles: Renata Magnanti. Color, 101 minutes. Filmed at Studios de Bologne, Paris; Dole, France; Studios de la Victorine, Nice; and in the U.S.S.R.

Cast: Melina Mercouri (Nina Kacew); Assaf Dayan (Romain Kacew, age 25); François Raffoul (Romain Kacew, age 9); Didier Haudepin (Romain Kacew, age 15); Despo (Aniela); Jean Martin (Igor Igorevitch); Jacqueline Porel (Madame Mailer); Fernand Gravey (Jean-Michel Serusier); Maria Machado (Nathalie Lissenko); Elspeth March (Fat Woman); Carol Cole (Louison); Julie Dassin (Romain's Friend); Audrey Berindey (Valentine Mailer); Rene Clermont (Mr. Piekielny); Denis Berry (Belle Guele); Jacqueline Duc (Madame de Rare); Marina Nestora (Mariette). Uncredited: Muni (Angelique); Therese Thoreaux (Silent Film Heroine); Perlo Vita, aka Jules Dassin (Ivan Mosjukine); Romain Bouteille, Charles Milot (Film Directors); Philippe Castelli (Crew Member); Marcel Charvey, Van Doude (Officers); Christian de Tilliere (Russian Dance Teacher); Roland Dubillard (Teacher); Christian Duvaleix (Hotel Manager); Robert Lombard (Negresco Doorman); Rufus (Russian Violin Teacher); Jean Rupert (Buyer); Jacques Santi (Soldier); Katia Tchenko (Actress); Olga Valery; Dominique Zardi.

VHS/DVD: Not available in either format.

Synopsis

Nina Kacew is a flamboyant Russian actress who stars in silent films in Leningrad during the 1920s. She has grandiose ambitions for her 9-year-old son, Romain, who is the illegitimate son from her affair with actor Ivan Mosjoukine. Nina joins an acting troupe

Aniela (Despo), the nine-year-old Romain Kacew (François Raffoul), and his mother, Nina Kacewa (Melina Mercouri), in *Promise at Dawn* (1970).

but leaves them in Poland, where she pretends to represent a Paris designer and opens a dress shop. When her fraud is exposed, Nina takes Romain to Nice and befriends the jeweler Jean-Michel Serusier. To pay for Romain's education, Nina works a variety of jobs, but falling ill, is diagnosed as a diabetic.

In World War II Romain joins the French Air Force and later the R.A.F. in England. Wounded in action, he recuperates in a North African hospital. After the war, Romain returns to Nice and learns that his mother has died three and a half years before; she had arranged for Jean-Michel to post weekly one of the 250 letters she had written to him.

Notes

Dassin attempts to enliven this traditional and rather dull biography with a fractured narrative and the use of effects, like slow motion, soft-focus photography, expressionist angles, freeze frames, zooms and jump-cuts. However, the film only succeeds in its treatment of perversity and sadism, which occupy only minor plot points.

In her seventh title for the director, Melina Mercouri plays what might have been a tour de force for another actress. Although she remains likable and is willing to let herself look unattractive, Mercouri fails to reveal the range of emotion which might have generated greater empathy for the mother-son saga, which has decidedly tragic elements. An argument can be made that the character of Nina is duplicitous; however, this theme does not receive the extended exploration of Dassin's earlier films. Additionally, although it is pleasing to see the director return to a narrative that focuses on a female protagonist after the masculine-oriented *Up Tight!*, it is disappointing that the film fails to engage an audience in a dynamic drama.

A pre-credit sequence has Romain holding Nina's arm as they walk through the streets before running together, culminating in a "Russian kiss" (i.e., on the mouth), backlit by the sun, to make their silent promise. Dassin uses soft focus and slow motion to romanticize the relationship, with the promise later said that he will grow up to be famous. This promise is not realized over the course of the narrative, since it is only *after* the story ends that Romain becomes the supposedly world famous author. A second promise is attached to this moment by Nina promising to always be with her son, although his leaving her to join the Air Force in World War II will separate them (as will her death).

Under the opening credits Dassin uses footage of a female gorilla playing with her gorilla child in an enclosure, and we are presumably meant to parallel the apes with Nina and Romain. The story proper begins with letters exchanged between the 25-year-old Romain and Nina while she is in the hospital (where she will eventually die). The device of letters being read—a lazy style of storytelling—is one that will be repeated in the film as voiceover narration, and Dassin will employ flashbacks of the 9- and 15-year-old Romain as memories jogged by the letters. The screenwriter's jumbled narrative means that the tale is not presented chronologically, so that we only have the apparent age of Romain, and Nina's changing hairstyles, to locate us in time. Although it is a filmmaking contrivance, purists may still object to images and points of view given as Romain's when what we see could not possibly be such, given that one does not see oneself in memory or in life, and that Romain does not even appear in some scenes that are said to be taken from his memory.

Dassin frequently injects humor into the treatment. Slow motion is used to transition to the real-time scene of the 9-year-old Romain in dancing class, with the teacher miming hanging himself from a rope that dangles from the ceiling in response to the boy's ineptitude. While Nina seemingly calling the teacher "Comrade Faggot" would appear to be a setback after the non-stereotypical gay man Dassin featured in *Up Tight!* the violin teacher smashing the violin that Romain has attempted to play, though expected, is still funny.

Dassin transitions from Nina collapsed at Romain's victorious table tennis game to the 25-year-old Romain in an African sick bed behind mosquito netting. We are shown the nurse and doctor from Romain's point of view, from behind the netting, and then Romain's reflection in the pond of the hospital grounds. We also get Romain's upside-down point of view of an approaching nurse when he is lying down, whose image is turned around to the upright view when Romain sits up.

The extended scene at the film studio is entertaining for its peek into the behind-the-scenes mechanics of silent filmmaking, which includes the sinking of a ship and the director yelling instructions to the actors, one of which is amusingly dressed as a bear. The fact that multiple scenes are shot at the same time in different parts of the studio is acceptable since sound is not being recorded, and we gather that Romain is the illegitimate son of Ivan. The fact of Nina having had a child by a married man—Ivan's wife will appear in the silent film we see later—presents her character as being duplicitous, though surely Ivan is equally responsible for the affair. Dassin errs in using a too-obvious zoom for Nina's reaction to Igor's pants splitting during the stage show. Fortunately, Igor delivers a funny line in regards to the accident: "I did it on purpose. Always on closing night I tear my pants. It means the play's behind me."

The scene of the acting company singing goodbye to Nina teeters dangerously close to excess, and it is interesting that a character who has previously defined herself as an actress should decide to give it up so easily. Perhaps this is an expression of Nina's folly, her deluded belief that she can provide a better life for herself and Romain.

When she and Romain go to see Ivsan Mosjukine's (played by a deep-voiced, blonde Dassin) silent movie in a cinema, Dassin frames the screen by showing the audience at the bottom. He also uses quick edits for the scene's climax, intercutting the onscreen actress who wants to shoot Ivan (ironic, given the fact of the actor's apparent real-life affair) with Ivan and the black cat he holds.

One of the film's three best scenes features the 9-year-old Romain licking an ice cream while transfixed by the sight of the bosom of a partially undressed woman in the changing room of Nina's salon. The scene is interesting in the fixation of the boy, the woman's disturbed reaction, and his licking of the ice cream. Though it's amusing when one of his licks misses the ice cream because he is staring at the woman rather than the ice cream, his intense visual pursuit of her validates the violation the woman feels. The scene ends with Aniela's comment to Nina, "You're raising a sex maniac," and the close-up on Nina, which the narration tells us shows her pride in the boy. The issue of the boy being raised by a strong woman, yet turning out to be heterosexual and not homosexual, will be raised later in the narrative by a nurse that the 25-year-old Romain talks with.

The next scene is an extension of the former's perversity, when the 9-year-old Romain tries to look up the dress of the six-year-old Valentine, who stands on a table. This scene reverses the gender manipulation of the former by empowering Valentine, who demands

Romain Kacew (François Raffoul) and Valentine Mailer (Audrey Berindey) enjoy watching Nina Kacewa (Melina Mercouri) yell at Mariette's mother, Madame Mailer (Jacqueline Porel), in *Promise at Dawn* (1970).

that the boy eat things to earn the right to look up her dress. The humor of the scene comes from Romain's willingness to eat plant leaves, cigarettes, and other things (off-screen) that will eventually make him sick.

Dassin's use of freeze frames as dialogue plays for the salon party scene seems unnecessary, particularly when he abandons the device to let the scene play out normally. The expressionist angles, extreme close-ups, and jump-cuts used after Igor's pretence of being Nina's employer is exposed presents the party guests and Igor equally as grotesques, the former leaving in anger and the latter embarrassed by his deception. A woman putting out her cigarette in food recalls the same action in Alfred Hitchcock's *To Catch a Thief* (1955).

Brutality enters the scenario when the 9-year-old Romain is set upon by a group of anti-Semitic Polish school boys who taunt him for being Jewish, beating his face and stripping him of his pants. The scene is paid off by Nina's savage and surprising reaction to her son's injury and humiliation, when she slaps him and says the following:

> If ever again someone insults your mother in your presence, then they have to bring you home on a stretcher. I want them to bring you back bleeding with every bone in your body broken. You will defend your mother even if they kill you.

A train trip is used to show the narrative move from Russia to France, and slow motion and soft focus again comes into play for the transition of Romain from age 9 to 15. This transition recalls the opening scene in the way Nina and Romain walk hand in hand, another romantic take on their relationship, supported by the sunshine of Nice (as opposed to the winter of Russia). A montage reveals the jobs Nina takes on: beautician,

The 15-year-old Romain Kacew (Didier Haudepin) with his mother, Nina Kacew (Melina Mercouri), in *Promise at Dawn* (1970).

driver, painter, photographer, tour guide, dog walker and palm reader. Mercouri brings a sense of distaste and misery to all this work, suggesting that her unhappiness (perhaps because of her diagnosis of diabetes) feeds the eccentricity that will overwhelm Nina by the time Romain is 25. It also further suggests her character's duplicity, since she is not providing sincere service to those who have hired her. The idea of her duplicity is again explored in the scene of her attempted sale of family silver, since this is the silver we saw her retain from the depot men who came to empty the salon.

Dassin uses hysterical music for Nina's flight from the sight of the 15-year-old Romain caught in bed with Mariette; but the director's subsequent restraint and use of silence during Romain's chase of her, leading to a church, almost redeems his prior overuse of music. Soft focus and slow motion are inserted into the middle of the scene of the 25-year-old Romain leaving for duty, occurring after Nina gives him a glass jar of pickles, showing them holding hands (as the younger Romain had done). The exchange of letters is again used for narration, with colored newsreel footage showing the dropping of bombs. The mission during which Romain is a plane navigator and the pilot appears to be blinded would seem to be one pregnant with dramatic tension, but Dassin's treatment of the supposed twenty minutes where Romain must tell the pilot stories to keep him calm and then help him guide the plane to the ground is disappointingly devoid of tension. Ironically, it is the pilot, Arnaud, who receives the Red Cross medal for bravery and a street parade, with Romain's contribution going unrecognized, although he does sit in Arnaud's jeep during the parade.

Dassin even denies Mercouri's Nina her death scene, since the last time we see her she explains how she wants Jean-Michel to send the two-hundred-and-fifty letters she has written weekly to Romain, which he does three-and-a-half years after she has died. The film ends poignantly, more because of the beautiful music of Georges Delerue than the long shot of Romain sitting on the beach and leaning over, presumably crying for the loss of his mother.

In the *Films & Filming* article, Gordon Gow describes the film as "singularly clever in its balance of emotion and humor." In *I Was Born Greek*, Mercouri writes that while the company was filming in Nice, Dassin had a bad fall, breaking bones in both feet, and the film was shut down for five weeks. This delay meant that the planned shooting in Poland was cancelled, something which Mercouri claims was done because it was learned that the film had Jewish characters, and because Assaf Dayan, who played Romain at age 25, was the son of Israel's prime minister. Dayan had begun acting in Israeli films in 1967, and, after playing supporting parts, had starred in *Ha-Simla* (1970). He would go on to become a producer, screenwriter and director, and, after playing more supporting roles, returned as a lead in *Zimzum* (2001), *Odot Ha-Monitin* (2001), the comedy *The Gospel According to God* (2004), which he also directed, and *Things Behind the Sun* (2006). *Promise at Dawn* would be the only film role for François Raffoul, who played Romain at age 9, and the only one of her father's titles that Julie Dassin would appear in.

Scenes from the film appeared in the biographical documentary *From the Journals of Jean Seberg* (1995), since Seberg had been married to Romain Gary. *Promise at Dawn* is the only film made by the production company Nathalie Productions, although it is not credited in the print seen by the author. Executive producer Joseph E. Levine was the president of Avco Embassy, the company that would go on to distribute Dassin's future film *A Dream of Passion* (1978).

Release

January 21, 1971, in the U.S.A.

Reviews

"Dassin has added a lot of his own to what might otherwise be a rather conventional study of an unconventional woman.... Less than magnificent and far from brilliant, what [Mercouri] tries for in range and intensity [becomes] an ambitious program of caricature—which long before it is over has become a strenuous bore to watch."—Roger Greenspun, *The New York Times*, January 22, 1971

"In its own way, [Mercouri's] vital, uninhibited performance is mere makeup, covering the scenario's merchandised nostalgia. There is, of course, the melancholy possibility that the Dassins wished to construct a burlesque. Sadder still, they probably imagine that they have fashioned a eulogy."—Stefan Kanfer, *Time* magazine, February 8, 1971

"Dassin has tried to turn Gary's nostalgic celebration of his loving mother into a vehicle for Mercouri. But she seems to be playing a normal, hearty, hot nymphomaniac. The different parts of the past run together in a blur in this generally unsatisfying film, but there are a few good satirical sequences of a silent-movie idol."—Pauline Kael, *5001 Nights at the Movies*

"Scrappy star vehicle and unnecessary biopic in a variety of indulgent styles."—John Walker, *Halliwell's Film & Video Guide*

"It's mostly Mercouri's show, an uneven but well-acted chronicle of the life of writer Romain Gary and his resourceful actress mother. Dayan is good as the young adult Gary."—Leonard Maltin, *1997 Movie & Video Guide*

The Rehearsal (1974)

[aka *Drifting Cities*]
Melina Film/Nike Film

Credits: Director: Jules Dassin; Producer/Narrator: Melina Mercouri; Photography: Alan Metzger; Music: Mikis Theodorakis; Editor: Suzanne Bauman; Sound: Bill Daly; Production Manager: Ina Stathis. B&W, 84–92 minutes.

Filmed in New York City.
Songs: "Toubou Toubou" (Iannis Markopoulos); "Papadop" (Mitsos Kasulas, Iannis Markopoulos).
Cast: Melina Mercouri; Mikis Theodorakis; Renos Mandis; Stathis Giallelis; Robyn Goodman; Steve Inwood; Olympia Dukakis (Maria); Jerry Zafer; Yiannes Iordanidis; John Moratus; Dmitri Hadjis; John Randolph (George Papadopolous); Jerold Ziman (Doctor); Lou Zorich; Salem Ludwig; Steve Karp; Lou Tiano; Tom Eleopoulos; Phyllis MacBride; Phillip A.D.; Spiro Diakrousis; George Panousopoulos; Michael Hardstrark; Michael Mullins; Sarah Cunningham; James Dukas; Greg Antonacci; Elena Karam; Iannis Markopoulos; Brenda Currin; Vera Lockwood; Tom Aldredge; and Greek and American actors devoted to the restoration of democracy in Greece. And graciously: Arthur Miller; Rex Reed (credited and spoken of but not seen); Laurence Olivier (filmed appearance); Lillian Hellman; Maximillian Schell (filmed

appearance). Uncredited: Jules Dassin; Stephen Diacrussi (Singing Polytechnic Student); Philip DuVal (Theodorakis Choir Member); Barnard Hughes (Doctor).

VHS/DVD: Not available in either format.

Synopsis

This is a semi-documentary on the November 17, 1973, massacre of students by the Greek junta.

Notes

While this purports to be a studio-bound staging of the story of the 1973 uprising and murder of students and workers at the Polytechnic School of Athens, performed at the New York City ICamera Studios, Dassin presents it partly as a continuous narrative using standard lighting—and partly as a self-conscious rehearsal of a film using film noir lighting. It is telling that the film bears no screenplay credit, with a title card that advises that it is based on fact, with "actual dialogue reproduced and actual texts utilized." Given that it is claimed that the incident had no survivors, one has to wonder about the veracity of the given dialogue and texts. When the treatment stays with uninterrupted and edited narrative, the film is engrossing, if at times too padded with extended moments. However, it is when the film uses celebrity testimony readings, and the conceit of a filmed stage rehearsal, that Dassin becomes self-indulgent. He even gives himself an extended voice-over as we see him walking, with the rationale for making the film quickly turning into tedious polemic.

There is an assumption of context of the event on the part of the filmmakers, in spite of some expository narration, radio broadcasts and newsreel footage; and one also feels that an understanding of the Greek language would benefit a viewer, since all the songs are in Greek. However, Dassin does manage to sneak in a small subplot involving a police spy among the uprisers that allows the director to explore his theme of duplicity. There is also an act of violence that is both shocking and tame, given the nature of the unseen murders at the climax.

The camera follows Melina Mercouri (in her eighth performance for Dassin) into the rehearsal space, where she posts a sign that turns out to be the film's opening credits. The fact that the sign asks for volunteer and not paid artists suggests that perhaps Dassin could not raise the funds to make a proper feature, so that this film is the next best thing.

The use of songs in counterpoint to the uprising is rationalized in a cynical (though perhaps accurate) way by the idea that Greeks sing happy songs when things are bad. However, even when the director sometimes spends too much time on the songs, they do add flavor to the presentation.

Dassin himself is first seen via the back of his head when Mercouri arrives at the studio, and the phenomena of seeing him direct gets an added boost when we see his hands frame an image and the camera pulls back for the subsequent action. These initial scenes are interrupted by Dassin looking at a set design sketch, and archival photographs of the presumed real event highlights the artifice of filming a film rehearsal. (Another artifice is Greeks played by actors with American accents, although given that the rehearsal is being staged in New York, this is an acceptable convention. This recalls Dassin's *Reunion in France*, where the supposedly French Joan Crawford had an American accent.) The scene of the principals planning to occupy the school gets a funny line in "If three thousand Greeks can keep a secret we're making history"; and the information about how doctors are incorporated into the plan so that medical care can be provided for the students, with homes used as hospitals, is an indication of how well prepared the students are.

Not all the doctors are of a sympathetic nature, however; one doctor instructs torturers on the best body parts to inflict pain upon. This doctor tells them, "Those of you assigned to women's work, the ugliest will be chosen"; and his advice about sexually humiliating but not raping women is later expressed in the interrogation of Maria. The doctor's dialogue concerning rape includes a "joke": "Raping a woman can make a man soft in more ways than one. That's my standard joke. It gets a standard laugh."

Perhaps the film's most resonant moment, in terms of violence, comes during Maria's interrogation when her blouse is ripped open. Dassin allows the camera to stay on her for nearly one minute after he orders the rehearsal of the next scene, and we don't know whether the actress is still reacting to the moment as an actress or if she is meant to be Maria, with her suffering commented on by the sad music of the choir rehearsing for the next scene. Dassin eventually cuts away from Maria, but when he returns to her after another minute, she finally does up her blouse and walks away from the chair, with the suggestion being that she had remained in the chair, immobilized and reactive, for that second minute, even though the camera was not on her.

The uprising committee's discussion of the choice of a suitable slogan offers some humor. "Long Live Freedom" is said to be "too vague, too general," and "Down with the junta" (although it is seen later in the student headquarters) is passed over in favor of "Build the people's army." The uneasy alliance between students and the older workers is exemplified by a worker telling the students, "Your problem is education. Ours is bread." This concern is reflected in another slogan we see posted in the headquarters: "Bread, Freedom, Education."

Dassin returns to the scene of the students listening to the radio, which began the film, to start an extended portion of the film as an uninterrupted narrative. A portrait of the new dictator, Dimitri Ioannides, is altered so that his receding hairline and clean-shaven face resembles the bangs and moustache of Adolf Hitler.

The students' unreasonable reaction to the reasonable request by police to disperse suggests the rebellious lack of compromise of youth, and this misstep, as with a later refusal to disperse, is what leads to their deaths. The international interest in the siege is demonstrated by foreign reporters with cameras who conduct interviews, and it is during one of these filmed interviews that the guitarist intercedes.

The guitarist's behavior is commented upon because he breaks the uprising "discipline" of non-violent behavior. Like the interrogation of Maria, this scene supplies immediate dramatic conflict, with a body search revealing that the guitarist has a gun, which convinces the students that he is a police provocateur. While the conflict continues, with the group carrying the guitarist towards the gate, it dissipates when Dassin fails to show his ejection. Additionally, the discipline deprives them and us of a violent resolution to the problem, which is disappointing (though contextually apt).

The following downtime, when the students sleep, sing or sketch, is paralleled with nighttime, when the actors leave the studio, the latter reinforcing the idea that the actors are doing a job, even as volunteers. Dassin's appearance comes on what is presumably the morning after, his face finally seen. His voiceover intones:

> I've made some films I cared about but never, never like this one. Is it because I've lived in Greece and feel so close to the Greek people? Maybe. But Greece isn't different from Chile or all the other places where we set up dictators and fatten them and arm them against their own people. And all the other Americans who are contributing their work and their skills because they too hate what their government is doing. That their government supports regimes that murder their own children. That we have a hand in the making of such regimes. How many Chiles do we need before we learn? How many Vietnams? Are we going to turn Greece into the Vietnam of Europe?

Laurence Olivier's filmed appearance reading a Greek poem (photographed in London by Costa Gavras) in English is intercut with reaction shots and archival photographs.

We return to Maria being interrogated again, though this time she is naked. Dassin protects the actress' vulnerability by photographing her in long shot and in shadows. (In his interview with Tony Crawley in *Films Illustrated*, Dassin makes much of the "naked courage" of Dukakis, after her admission that she "didn't have an attractive body.")

When we see the dramatization of a recorded testimony of a mother whose son has been imprisoned, it scores a laugh. After a two-minute, one-take tirade by the actress, the sound recordist changes the tape. When he is ready to continue, she says, "What else can I tell you? Nothing."

An extended singing sequence is thankfully halted by banging noises on the soundtrack, said to be the police attack on the school. Dassin enhances the sound of tear gas bombs exploding by adding echoes, which seems an unnecessary contrivance, but the director convincingly conveys the crowd pandemonium for the camera. Newsreel footage, appearing to be from the students' point of view (though it could equally be from a helicopter), is intercut with the staged radio broadcasts. The negotiation between the police and demonstrates at the gate is interesting, since this is the second chance for escape that they refuse to take because of their unreasonable demands (they ask for the presence of foreign ambassadors and the Red Cross, a tactic clearly meant to further embarrass the police). The tank invasion is indicated by the scream of a female student in close-up (women are better screamers); and the newsreel footage of American Admiral Colbert reads as a further indictment of America's tolerance of the martial law that befell Greece.

Maximilian Schell (reappearing for the director after his role in Dassin's earlier *Topkapi*) provides the last bit of testimony, and, like Lillian Hellman, he is not interrupted. Dassin ends with bodies symbolically carried through the crowd, although this sequence goes on too long, to present the dead demonstrators; and a final credit dedicates the film to the students and workers who gave their lives on November 17, 1973, "for a free Greece."

In his *Cineaste* interview, Dassin said that the film was shot in 18 days with very little money, on a bare stage not much bigger than a hotel room. In *Tender Comrades*, Patrick McGilligan and Paul Buhle quote Dassin saying that the film represented for him the highest degree of creative freedom. "It was a moving experience," he said. Dassin also told Gordon Gow in his interview in *Films Illustrated* that *The Rehearsal* was the closest to him of all his movies. It would be the only film made by the Melina Film and Nike Film production companies. Melina Mercouri's prior title had been Dassin's biographical drama *Promise at Dawn* (1970), and she would be in his next, the drama *A Dream of Passion* (1978). John Randolph had previously worked for Dassin in a bit part in *The Naked City*.

Release

The film's delayed American release was due to the fact that even though the movie was completed by June 1974, it was considered irrelevant by the distributor after the fall of the dictatorship in July 1974. According to Dassin, the film was released in Greece (date unknown), but an eventual American release didn't come about until October 17, 2001. By then the film had becomes a curiosity rather than the protest piece Dassin had envisaged.

Reviews

"A powerful re-enactment."—World Film Directors
"A powerhouse cast!"—Time Out New York

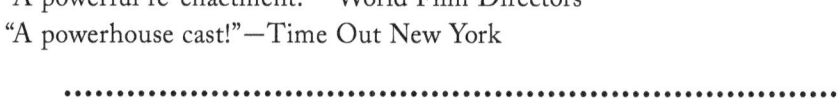

A Dream of Passion (1978)

[aka *Kravgi gynaikon*]
A Bren Film/MelinaFilm/Aries Enterprises/Avco Embassy Pictures Release

Credits: Producer/Director/Screenplay: Jules Dassin; Producer (uncredited)/Photography: Giorgos Arvanitis; Modern Greek Version of Medea: Minos Volonakis; Music: Yannis Markopoulos; Editor: Georges Klotz; Sets and Costumes: Dionyssis Fotopoulos; Sound: Thanassis Arvanitis; Makeup: Otello Fava. Color, 106–109 minutes, in English and Greek with English subtitles. Filmed in Paris Studio Cinema; Studio ERA, Athens; Polysound, Athens; and SIMQ, Boulogne.

Cast: Melina Mercouri (Maya/Medea); Ellen Burstyn (Brenda Collins); Andreas Voutsinas (Kostas); Despo (Maria); Yannis Voglis (Edward); Aleka Katselli; Andreas Philipidis (Stathis); Phaedon Georgitsis (Ronny); Betty Valassi (Margaret); Kostas Arzoglou (Bible Student); Irene Emirza (Diana); Panos Papaioannou (Manos); Nicos Galiatsos (Lighting Man); Olympia Papadouka (Attendant); Anna Thomaidou (Emma); Litsa Vaidou; Savvas Axiotis (Sound Man); Dimitri Papamichael (Jason); Manos Katrakis (Creon); Anthi Kariofili, Rea Fortuna, Olympia Tolika, Mary Chinari, Katerina Rourlou, Alexandra Pandelaki, Natasha Tsakarisianou, Sofia Sfiroera, Stella Yeromitsou, Eleni Georgiadou, Rita Lambrinou, Mariana Koutalou, Vicky Grammatica, Fotini Filosofou, Mina Negreponti (Medea Chorus). Uncredited: Freddie Germanos (Editor); Alexis Solomos; Stefanos Vlachos (Shopkeeper).

VHS/DVD: Video released by Nelson Entertainment on April 26, 1990. Not available on DVD.

Synopsis

Maya is a Greek movie actress returning to the stage, playing the title role of *Medea*, with rehearsals being filmed for the BBC television show *The Creative Program*. Maya decides to use the case of Brenda Collins, an American imprisoned in Greece for murdering her three children, for publicity. Brenda is known as the modern Medea, since she committed her murders to take revenge on her unfaithful husband. Maya visits Brenda, and a friendship forms between them. When Brenda finally agrees to tell Maya how she committed the murders, Maya uses this as the inspiration for her performance.

Notes

A continuation of the style of filmmaking Dassin employed for *The Rehearsal*, this attempt to parallel the story of the filmed rehearsal of a stage production of *Medea* with the star actress' friendship with a woman imprisoned for killing her children fails because the parallel does not include any resultant change. The director tests our indulgence with long excerpts from *Medea*, and the film only comes alive briefly during the six-minute set piece of the woman recalling her act of murder. The treatment's antagonism between the actress and the director has dramatic (and comic) potential that is not explored sufficiently; and while the screenplay offer the occasional humorous line, Dassin's gift for visual invention here seems thwarted. The narrative can be interpreted as exploring an act of duplicity—a recurring theme of the director in his prior titles—in the sense that the actress doesn't reveal her use of the prisoner to benefit her performance. In her ninth and last film appearance for the director, Mercouri delivers a monotonous performance (in an ironic counterpoint to her role in *Never on Sunday*, where she loves Medea), while Ellen Burstyn manages to supply some appealing and funny bursts of anger.

The film begins with a quote to explain the title: "...that this player here but in a fiction, in a dream of passion." We are told that the chorus we will see will speak in ancient, not modern, Greek, and another quote is shown: "I heard the cry of the anguished woman from Colchis and my heart suffers too." This quote prefigures the idea of Maya's supposed empathy for Brenda, although, interestingly, Brenda does not share the same empathy, which is one of the problems of the proposed transfer of personality (that ultimately does not occur). Narration takes the form of Maya speaking to her director, and shots of stone columns suggests the amphitheater the stage production will rehearse and finally perform in. After the credits, we go inside a theater (not a studio, since tiered seating is visible). It soon becomes apparent that the rehearsal is being filmed as a priority—as opposed to the filming being done merely as an observation of the rehearsal. This is troubling, and shows Dassin unsuccessfully attempting to mix the forms of stage and filmmaking. Although he shoots the television coverage in a traditional way, with no apparent editing, his camera still shows us the apparatus of the exercise, with lights, cameramen, and the television monitor. (Ironically, it is only when we see the black and white television coverage of the rehearsal, complete with rolling picture, that the performance has any resonance.)

Maya is first seen wearing a purple sheath, presumably presenting purple as passion, surrounded by the female chorus (all dressed in black), and Dassin plays the aural cue of the chorus rehearsing a song under an amusing comment made by Kostas about Maya, which also feeds into out knowledge of Mercouri as a political activist: "Look, if you're going to reduce this play—screw the poetry—shrink it down to current events because you read a copy of *Ms.* magazine, go ahead. Do it." This suggests that Maya is struggling within herself with her performance, and with Kostas' approval, although what we see seems fine. Maya also has a telling exchange with the costume designer when the woman shows Maya a sketch of Medea's proposed costume.

Actress Maya (Melina Mercouri, left) visits murderess Brenda Collins (Ellen Burstyn) in a Greek prison in *A Dream of Passion* (1978).

> MAYA: Why rags? The woman is a princess. Why rags?
> DESIGNER: They are not rags. The way I see Medea—
> MAYA: I care very much about how you see Medea, but I also care about how the audience sees me. Unfortunately, they want to see me young and beautiful, and I learned that by bitter experience. Try again darling.

Kostas makes another amusing observation when he voices his displeasure at Maya's performance and his disdain for the television crew's agenda. After the program director, Edward, tells him that "it's not just about Maya—it's about the entire making of *Medea*," Kostas replies, "That's why your cameras trail her all over Athens. If she would let you, you would follow her into the toilet."

The company's viewing of scenes from Ingmar Bergman's psychological drama *Persona* (1966; with Bergman thanked in the credits) seems odd, since at that point there is no reason for them to do so—apart from admiring the director's technique. The notion of the personality transformation, however, which is the Bergman film's plot, is introduced, but it receives no further expression in the narrative.

Another comment made by Maya seems to be autobiographical for Mercouri, when she says of Kostas, "He thinks I came back to the theater because I'm too old for the movies." At the time, Mercouri was approximately 58, and though she had been working in occasional supporting roles for directors other than Dassin (since *The Rehearsal*, Mercouri had played an international lesbian movie star in the 1975 romance *Once Is Not Enough*, and the Henry Kissinger counterpart in the 1977 Watergate comedy *Nasty Habits*), it was only her husband who was casting her as the lead. Even this film would prove to be her last, which makes Maya's comment perhaps self-fulfilling for Mercouri.

When Maya visits Brenda for the first time, Mercouri overdoes the shocked reaction to the sudden infiltration of the press into the visitor's room, and to Brenda's reaction of "God will punish you." The issue of Maya sleeping with the cameraman, Ronny (a younger man), and the domestic situation of her estranged husband using a room in her house as a photographer's studio, don't offer any plot payoffs. However, when Maya visits the library to research Brenda, she makes another seemingly Mercouri-esque autobiographical comment, this one about her globe-trotting years: "When I'm abroad, they ask, 'When are you going home?' Here they ask, 'When are you leaving?'" The idea that Brenda has killed her children on Father's Day is a ghoulishly funny touch, given a payoff in her climactic memory when we see a card left for him; though it is interesting how Maya is frightened out of Brenda's house in Glyfada when she sees the chalk outlines of the children's corpses. (The three outlines together will prove to be misleading, since in the flashback Brenda is shown to kill one boy separately.)

Maria the prompter makes a disparaging comment about Maya's continued struggle with her role when trying to run lines: "Your creative birth pains don't interest me. I've known you for 30 years. You bore me." It is when Maya returns to see Brenda—wearing heavy eye-liner and a severe scarf—that Brenda shows indications of her supposed schizophrenia by freezing mid-thought. Maya has to tap on the dividing glass to regain her attention. Explained as being a woman of little education, which may explain her religious fanaticism, Burstyn's casting seems right because of her limited vocal range and drab exterior. This is a woman, despite having borne three children, who presents as sexually repressed, with her schoolgirl hairdo almost suggesting a virgin (in opposition to Maya's overwhelming sensuality). However, Burstyn's anger comes as a surprise, though perhaps it shouldn't be, given Brenda's unhappiness and predicament. Burstyn also presents Brenda's physical awkwardness and loneliness, evidence that the religion she seeks as comfort doesn't satisfy and also doesn't absolve her of her murderous behavior—despite her claim that her religion justified her action.

Back at the rehearsals, Dassin shows Edward watching the television monitor rather than the live performance being filmed, which allows for three dimensions of activity. When Maya underplays, we assume that this is a result of Brenda's influence, and it is this level of playing that meets with Kostas' disapproval. His anger creates conflict and the suggestion that drama will occur, with the added touch of Ronny the cameraman filming Jason's reaction to Kosta. Kosta calling Maya's performance "self indulgent crap" is amusing, and his comment that she is playing Medea like a "whimpering shopgirl" seems an appropriate description of Brenda.

The celebratory party that follows the first rehearsal, has Maya and Jason singing a song (in another extended moment) with the repeated lyrics "We should never have met." This may be referring to a multitude of couples, though we presumably are meant to apply it to Maya and Brenda. The six-minute monologue that Maya delivers, supposedly inspired by the allegedly improvised monologue delivered by Marlon Brando in *Last Tango in Paris* (1972), fails to deliver anything exciting, apart from the minor information that Maya deliberately aborted the only child she had ever conceived. Dassin doesn't help things by intercutting reaction shots, including those of Brenda in prison, and changing the angle on Mercouri. However, the director's coverage of Brenda's memory of the killings is an improvement (although still flawed and not as impressive as set pieces from his previous titles).

Brenda's speech begins with a shot of the outside of the prison; then a subjective cam-

A Dream of Passion (1978)   231

Maya (Melina Mercouri) rehearses with Jason (Dimitri Papamichael) for a stage production of *Medea* in *A Dream of Passion* (1978).

era is used to transition from the prison corridor to the exterior of her house. The veracity of Brenda's memory is called into question by Brenda's point of view actually seeing herself, and also by Dassin cutting to shots of Maya, who we know was not there at the time. These time-travel effects allow Maya to be a witness (with the camera), and the impact the killings supposedly have on her are presented by the close-up of her eyes and a shot of her wearing red (the same color she wears in the end of her stage performance). Dassin's use of the musical score here—and the singing of the chorus—is less emphatic (and more effective) than in many of his prior films.

We are spared the sight of the children being murdered, with the act involving the first two merely suggested by Brenda raising a knife (which we have seen her, via subjective camera work, take from a kitchen drawer). Her chasing her son, the third child, is presented differently, since he is not a passive victim like the other two. His awareness of his mother's intention results in a brief chase. His death, too, occurs off-screen, confirmed by the sight of the knife in the kitchen sink surrounded by blood. Brenda then sitting at the table, where we see the Father's Day card for her husband, is perhaps a sign of resignation that she will be caught. In any case, it seems Brenda is waiting for her husband (a character who is never seen in the treatment, like the mistress) to see the killings, because she wants to see his reaction.

The film ends with an impressionistic collection of brief scenes around what we gather is the real stage performance (although since no audience is seen, it could also be a dress rehearsal). There follows shots of Brenda's cell door, Maya retrieving the knife we assume Medea will use to kill, the chorus singing, and an eyehole shot of Brenda in her cell on the floor praying. Images of Maya's Medea are intercut with Brenda as she screams at the same time as the chorus, and Brenda assumes a fetal position on the floor. The theater lights then go dark.

The idea of personality transformation is only one-sided (if that), if one is to believe that Maya's contact with Brenda has affected her portrayal. Brenda's psychic immobilization may only be temporary (as is Maya's, for that matter), so that it's hard to say for certain that Brenda has changed because of her contact with Maya. A nice touch, although perhaps impractical, might have been having Brenda attend the performance that Maya gives, so that she could see what the actress' interest in her was for, and also perhaps learn something about herself. Brenda could have just as easily watched it on television, since one would think that the making-of program would include the end result; but Dassin did not make these choices.

In the *Cineaste* interview by Dan Georgakas and Petros Anastasopoulos, Dassin denies that he represents the director character, and says that Maya was not close to Mercouri, although "because of living with [Mercouri], because of observing and spying on her—here and there [he] put something of her into Maya." He also says he wrote the part of Brenda for Burstyn, and that the two actresses formed a friendship from the moment they said hello (after he and Mercouri had gone to meet her at Athens airport). Dassin says it helped that Burstyn was practically living with them, and tells how he saw Burstyn wiping a spot from Mercouri's cheek before she went before the camera, and that Mercouri would sometimes adjust Burstyn's costume. When asked the implications of Brenda being a Christian fanatic, Dassin said, "That's a reflection of Euripides, when Medea calls upon the gods to witness that an oath is broken. It's a parallel."

Dassin rejects the idea of Kosta intended to be a homosexual character, although he wears a ponytail and seems effeminate. In the film, when Maya accuses him of being harsh on her because of his romantic feelings towards her, he denies it. Dassin claims that it was intended that they had had an "unsound" relationship; he now has a very deep affection for her, but "at the moment, he has his problems." Dassin further rejects this notion because he doesn't want to be seen as being anti-gay (although the alleged "Faggot" comment in *Promise at Dawn* comes to mind). He says, "I happen to have an affection for the man who played the part." The Sudanese-born Andreas Voutsinas' film career began spectacularly when he essayed the role of the flamboyantly gay valet Carmen Ghia in Mel Brooks' comedy *The Producers* (1968). However, it was otherwise unremarkable, apart from repeated appearances in Brooks' stock company and his playing the role of Dracula (though it was not the lead) in the French comedy *Les charlots contre Dracula* (1980).

In his *Film Criticism* article, Andrew Horton claims that "the complexity and sincerity of the relationship that develops between the two women in the film becomes representative of Dassin's fertile and rewarding fusing of his American past, his Greek present, and his need to express himself through his chosen art, film. Horton celebrates *A Dream of Passion* as the last example (since the article does not mention Dassin's final title, *Circle of Two*) of the director's desire to get out of the studio and onto the street, as he had begun doing with *The Naked City*, in an effort to "look at the world."

Horton continues:

> His move from the United States to Greece took him even further. In Greece Dassin learned to explore the reality of Greek myth and culture while maintaining many of his American narrative techniques and values. The films that resulted from these explorations have continued to prove of artistic, entertainment, and cultural interest to audiences on both sides of the Atlantic.

After working in television since 1960, Ellen Burstyn made her film debut in 1964 and was slow to become a star (in her efforts, it is said that she had used 25 different names), playing supporting roles and being nominated for the Best Supporting Actress Academy Award for *The Last Picture Show* (1971). She scored the lead in the cult horror title *The Exorcist* (1973), for which she was nominated for the Best Actress Academy Award. Burstyn would win the Oscar playing the title character in the romance *Alice Doesn't Live Here Anymore* (1974). After *A Dream of Passion*, she continued in leading roles in the romance *Same Time, Next Year* (1978), repeating her Tony winning stage role, and the fantasy *Resurrection* (1980), for both of which she was again nominated as Best Actress. Burstyn alternated between playing supporting roles in film, making made-for-television movies, and essaying the occasional lead, such as in the war biography *Hanna's War* (1988), the comedy *The Cemetery Club* (1993), *Cross the Line* (1996), the comedies *You Can Thank Me Later* (1998) and *Walking Across Egypt* (1999), and *Requiem for a Dream* (2000), for which she was Oscar nominated. The 2000s saw the actress play leads in the romance *The Elephant King* (2006) and *The Stone Angel* (2007), which featured her last leading role to date.

A Dream of Passion was the only picture made for the production companies Bren and Aries Enterprises, and was the last for Mercouri's company (which had made *Never on Sunday* and *Phaedra*). It was also the last title that Avco Embassy Pictures distributed for Dassin. *A Dream of Passion* was the first title co-produced by director of photography Giorgos Arvanitis, who would go on to also produce the Greek drama *Mia toso makryni apousia* (1985), which he also shot.

Release

August 1978, with the taglines "One played at being Medea—the other lived it," and "I heard the cry of an anguished woman and my heart cried too."

Reviews

"Awkward, pretentious and empty…. Burstyn's understated performance as a simple, Bible-spouting woman driven crazy by her husband's philandering is the movie's single redeeming feature. Otherwise there is nothing emotionally or intellectually involving here."—Richard Schickel, *Time* magazine, September 11, 1978

"[A] disastrous blend of Euripides, Bergman and sub–Cassavetes role-confusion … fails miserably in attempting to invoke 'Persona-l' correspondences between them. A hammer-blow insistence on the 'relevance' of Greek tragedy, a modish 'distancing' of the creative process, and a token exploration of feminist implications conspire to produce a nightmare of pretension."—*Time Out Film Guide*

"Weird and ineffective character drama which badly needs discipline."—John Walker, *Halliwell's Film & Video Guide*

"Aside from Burstyn's powerhouse performance as an American jailed in Greece for killing her three children, this attempt to parallel her story with Medea's is the kind of idea that should never have left the story conference. Mercouri is typically hammy as the actress who takes up her cause."—Leonard Maltin, *1997 Movie & Video Guide*

"A curious film that suffers from a lack of directorial path, still worth a look because of the talents of the actresses involved.... Some goriness [but] Dassin does leave something to the imagination, and creates even more horror than might have been photographed."—Jay Robert Nash and Stanley Ralph Ross, *The Motion Picture Guide*

Circle of Two (1981)

[aka *Obsession*]
Film Consortium of Canada/Jerome Simon and Milton Zyrman Productions

Credits: Director: Jules Dassin; Producer: Henk Van Der Kolk; Executive Producer: William Marshall; Associate Producer: Bob Rodgers; Screenplay: Thomas Hedley, from the novel *A Lesson in Love* by Marie-Terese Baird; Photography: Laszlo George; Editor: David Nicholson; Music: Bernard Hoffer; Production Design: Claude Bonniere, François De Lucy; Creative Consultant: Fima Noveck; Sound: Owen Sound; Ashley's Paintings: Harold Town; Set Dressers: Joyce Liggett, Don McQueen; Costume Designer: Theoni V. Aldredge; Mr. Burton's Makeup: Ron Berkeley; Makeup: Barbara Palmer; Hairstylist: Adrian Hofman. Color, 98–105 minutes. Filmed in New York City; Toronto, Canada; and Antigua, Barbuda, from August 27, 1979, to November 3, 1979.

Song: "Circle of Two" (Bernard Hoffer, Stanley Jay Gelber), sung by Kacey Cisyk; "Carmina Burana" (Carl Orfi), sung by Bishop Strachan Girls Choir.

Cast: Richard Burton (Ashley St. Clair); Tatum O'Neal (Sarah Norton); Nuala Fitzgerald (Claudia Aldrich); Robin Gammell (Mr. Michael Norton); Patricia Collins (Mrs. Philipa Norton); Donann Cavin (Smitty); Norma Dell'Agnese (Ruspoli); Michael Wincott (Paul); Kate Reid (Dr. Emily Reed); Elan Ross Gibson (Gym Mistress); Maggie Morris (Music Teacher); Larry Ewashen (Man in Cinema); Daisy White (School Secretary); George Bourne Sr. (Old Man); Bibi Caspari (Mime); Gordon Jocelyn (Antique Shop Proprietor); Brendan McKane, A. Frank Ruffo, Morison Bock (Men at Outdoor Café); Yanka Van Der Kolk (Gallery Receptionist); Mack Dolgy (Art Gallery Client); Leo Leyden (Harold Bodel); Les Carlson (Doctor at Hospital); Patrick Patterson (Mover); Pamela Hyatt (Mrs. Smyth); Doug Smith (Mr. Smyth); Grace Stevens (Mrs. Ruspoli); Jimmy Leone (Mr. Ruspoli); Elias Zarou (Doorman); Roslyn Forsyth (Stand-in for Ms. O'Neal); George Cunningham (Stand-in for Mr. Burton). Un-credited: Jules Dassin (Man in Subway Crowd).

VHS/DVD: DVD released by Tango Entertainment on May 4, 2006.

Synopsis

Fifteen-year-old Sarah Norton skips school to attend an X-rated movie, which is also attended by 60-year-old artist Ashley St. Claire. They meet again when Ashley witnesses Sarah's break-up with her boyfriend, Paul, at a Toronto patisserie. Sarah is intrigued by Ashley, and gives him her prose to read. After praising her writing talent, Ashley invites Sarah to visit his country art studio. Saddened by the fact that Ashley has not created any new work for ten years, Sarah asks him to paint a portrait of her. He agrees, although he is unhappy with the result. However, with Sarah's encouragement, Ashely paints portraits of a man who works at the local curio shop.

Sarah finds a nude painting that Ashley had done of his former lover, Claudia, and offers to pose nude for Ashley. He declines, but the nude Sarah is seen by Paul, who is spying on the duo. On the way home from the studio, Sarah is confronted by Paul in a cornfield. Overcome with jealousy, Paul tries to rape her. Sarah hits him with a rock and fractures his skull. The attack on Paul makes the relationship between Sarah and Ashley public, and her parents lock her in her room when she refuses to stop visiting Ashley. After receiving advice from Dr. Reed, the parents throw a party for Sarah's sixteenth birthday, but she uses her new freedom to go to New York, where, she has learned, Ashley has gone. Ashley tells Sarah that although he loves her, they cannot be together, and he watches Sarah leave on the subway to go back to Toronto.

Notes

Dassin's last movie is a shockingly prosaic May-December romance featuring unsatisfying performances, an overdone score and little visual invention. The theme of duplicity occurs in a narrative of forbidden love between a 60-year-old man and a 15-year-old girl, although their love remains unconsummated. Duplicity is also expressed in the behavior of the girl's scorned boyfriend, whose attempted rape of her is a sequence of implied brutality that references similar scenes of violence in the director's prior work. Occasionally the screenplay features humorous lines, but these are not enough to redeem the treatment, which mostly fails to rise above the level of soap opera. However, its presentation of the anachronistic artist can be paralleled with Dassin himself (although this is presumably unintentional), prefiguring his failed future as a filmmaker.

The opening scene in the schoolgirls' locker room presents an all-femme environment inhabited by cruelty in the way we see a fat girl being tormented by her clothes being withheld from her. Interestingly, Sarah is presented as separate from this world; she is not one of the tormenters, yet is also unaware of the torment of another. This will reinforce the idea of her being an unusual person, one who leads a life of solitary reflection as a writer (although we also see that she has friends). Sarah skipping school to go to the movies is the first representation of her as a duplicitous character, with the fact that she goes to see a dirty movie more an expression of her curiosity than her sexuality (since later she will reveal that she has refused to have sex with her boyfriend, Paul). Dassin does not show any of the movie, with its nature only indicated by its soundtrack.

Ashley being in the same cinema at the same time as Sarah is a romantic comedy meet-cute scenario, after she has moved away from a younger man who has offered to light her cigarette. The meeting of the couple is redeemed by the fact of his being asleep—perhaps a comment on his age, given that even a dirty move can't sustain his interest. Thankfully, Sarah hitting his head with her bag as she leaves the cinema does not allow for a meaningful introduction.

It is when Ashley sees Sarah with Paul at the patisserie that we get their proper introduction. The narrative has him observing her breaking up with Paul, and Sarah hiding to avoid him, which is more duplicitous behavior on her part. The fact that Ashley is again at the same location at the same time as Sarah is more contrivance, as is the idea that she hides from Paul behind the pillar next to Ashley's table. Paul's return after his failure to locate Sarah demonstrates his determined nature, which will be paid off later in his apparent stalking of her, and the jealousy that will motivate it and the attempted rape. However,

Poster for *Circle of Two* (1980).

Sarah giving Ashley her prose to read, after only having met him once, we presume is meant to show the soulful connection they share, with Sarah's gift being doubly resonant in light of the anxiety of the situation she is in. Ashley advising her after Paul has left is a sign of his empathy with her as much as presenting the character as a wise counsel.

As an artist who has not painted in ten years, Ashley is a character in crisis, and we figure that the universe has placed Sarah in his path so that she can help him overcome it. However, this requires that she be extraordinary, and although the treatment works to make Sarah eccentric, O'Neal fails to make Sarah as captivating as she should be. Part of the problem may be that the actress is in transition from child to adult roles, and, like Shirley Temple before her, the natural aging process makes the adult performer less appealing than her former child-self. O'Neal's childhood spunk, which read as more adult than a child, is reversed here in the actress' passive persona, which recalls the passive earnestness of her father, actor Ryan O'Neal. While Sarah does encourage Ashley to paint and is responsible for his renewed interest, she seems to lacks the quality that would inspire obsession in a man four times her age. (This undermines Ashley's telling Sarah, "You are the most perplexing, intriguing girl," as he raises her on an artwork frame as if on a literal pedestal.) It's not that she's unattractive, since O'Neal is pretty; it's just that she is not the "woman" that her doctor will later describe her as. (Her virginal white blouses and knee-length skirts clue us in to the fact that she isn't a Lolita-type nymphet (although it is said that O'Neal had to keep her legs covered throughout the entire movie because she had been involved in a terrible car accident shortly before filming, and her legs had suffered second and third-degree burns from skidding on the pavement). The actress doesn't give a bad performance, but she's still "uncooked." She's a vague and ephemeral presence, and what she fails to bring to Sarah affects Burton. Without given much to react to, he ends up staring at her—but not in a good way, since it seems he is more somnambulist than obsessed.

The plot point of Sarah's writing is soon abandoned after Ashley comments that she has "a natural talent," with the assumption that if he had not thought so, their relationship would not have continued. Her discussion with Ashley about *Hamlet* has an added frisson, since Burton had played the part on stage to much acclaim in his early career, and had made a filmed version in 1964. Sarah's repeated asides to Columbo, introduced by the poster of Peter Falk on her bedroom wall, is another attempt to make Sarah odd, but they read more as arch (with matters not helped by the fact of Ashley not knowing who Columbo is—revealing him to be a non-populist aesthete). Her spying on Ashley jogging is more duplicity, and his initial interest in the disfigured man in the park who cuts up and eats potatoes suggests that Ashley aligns himself with the man. The scene in which Sarah and Ashley watch people dancing is interesting in how she leaves to dance with the others, but he does not offer to dance with her. In spite of Sarah resting against Ashley as a sign of them being a romantic couple, the difference in their ages, or of Ashley's fear of public exposure, seems an issue.

Dassin supplies a potentially arresting visual in the flower image that Ashley paints with a candle flame under a canvas, while the following body shape he paints with a blowtorch is an indication of the cubist-style abstract form that Ashley's later portraits take. However, his initial painting of Sarah—at her suggestion—is shown via a montage. After Sarah reveals that she lies to her parents about where she goes when she sits for Ashley—another sign of her duplicity—he is shown wearing the artist's clichéd wardrobe of paint-spattered overalls. Sarah looking at her portrait, painted in a realistic style, dressed in the same outfit she wears in the portrait, is another visual with potential that Dassin fails to fully utilize as mirrored imagery. Although the portrait looks good to us, Ashley's unhappiness with it is met with no response from Sarah. We don't know if she likes it or not; rather she replies, "Do it again," since it is *his* opinion that matters and not hers, apparently. His pleasure at her further encouragement allows them to hug—but not kiss—which seems to express the parameters of their relationship.

It is Ashley seeing the same disfigured man in the curio shop—while a cacophony of music plays, recalling *Topkapi*—that is the first payoff to seeing him earlier, when Ashley asks if he can paint him. Ashley's fascination with the man, perhaps the artist's appreciation, is prefigured by Sarah saying, "He gives me the creeps," and Ashley replying, "Me too." Paul seen outside the shop as Ashley and Sarah walk past is the first sign that Paul may be stalking Sarah, unless it is an incredible coincidence.

The relationship parameters are reviewed and further defined when Sarah asks Ashley to make love to her, and he rejects her advance with anger. (Burton's bursts of anger partially redeems his otherwise lackluster performance.) Ashley's concern over the age difference, although he admits to *wanting* to have sex with her, inspires a funny line when Sarah says, "I wouldn't care if you were in a wheelchair." And the couple's resolution to not have sex but to kiss is a compromise of increased and cautious intimacy.

Sarah finding the nude portrait of Claudia, and Claudia's arrival, creates the first interesting narrative complication. We see that Ashley has redone Sarah's portrait as an abstract, and is presumably happier with it, since it is this (and his abstract portraits of the disfigured man) that he will take to New York to try and sell. However, it is Claudia's response to the news of Ashley's relationship with Sarah, rather than his renewed ability to work, that inspires her funny response. After he tells her he has known Sarah for a month, Claudia says, "You goddamn fool. You're a perfect age to play the horse's ass." Claudia's swift return to New York is disappointing, but her visit does inspire Sarah to want to be painted nude by Ashley. His response is just as angry as his response to her request to make love; but it is Paul seeing Sarah nude through the studio door keyhole, and his misinterpretation, that results in the attempted rape. (Dassin gives Paul an extreme close-up for his voyeurism.)

Naturally Paul's behavior is duplicitous, but it is interesting that Sarah is punished for simply appearing nude before Ashley, rather than for making love to him, which Paul assumes has happened. Paul's anger is based on jealousy over what he thinks Sarah has denied him but has given Ashley, and their confrontation in the cornfields evokes the dangerous cornfields of Alfred Hitchcock's *North by Northwest*. Sarah's empathy for Paul changes when she hears his accusation, and her slapping him in response can be seen as a provocation. Dassin uses a subjective camera for mutual points of view during the struggle. The director spares us an impact shot when Sarah hits Paul with the rock in self-defense, and switches to the subjective camera again for what at first appears to be Sarah's point of view when she runs back to Ashley's studio, but then isn't when Sarah appears in front of the camera.

The idea of locking Sarah in her room to keep her away from Ashley is ludicrous, so the expectation is created—and met—that when her parents open her door to talk to her she fights to escape. Her father slapping Sarah is the violent expression of his frustration, and Dassin relies on the cliché of repeated shots of Sarah's mother hanging up the telephone on Ashley calling, and her bringing back the tray of untouched food in light of Sarah's hunger strike, to represent the passage of time. Sarah's mother receives a noteworthy reaction to Ashley coming to the Norton house door, which is superior to Sarah's father's "Get the hell out":

> You may be older than we are, but we don't need your advice. Now it's obvious we can't appeal to your sense of decency, but maybe, just maybe, you have a sense of the ridiculous, because you are ridiculous, Mr. St. Clair.

The introduction of Dr. Reed provides us with the odd information that Paul was "mainlining methadrin" as a reason (drugs) for his attempted rape. Dr. Reed also gets the howler, "I supervised your entrance into this world, and I'll be damned if I'm going to supervise your exit." When the doctor suggests that they should treat Sarah like "a woman deeply in love," Sarah's mother comments, "Doctor, you need a doctor," and sarcastically asks, "Would you like us to reserve them a suite at the Plaza?" This funny rejoinder is topped by Reed's reply, "I don't like the Plaza."

The idea of a party for Sarah's sixteenth birthday to lure her out of her room, and as a sign of good faith, seems a bizarre one. Dr. Reed gets a funny "Jesus" reaction upon seeing that Sarah has climbed from her window onto a tree branch—just after Sarah's mother has asked her how the doctor thinks the party is going. Sarah's response is amusing, showing an awareness of the trick her parents are attempting: "Did any of you ever hear of someone committing suicide by diving into a birthday cake?"

Naturally, Sarah goes after Ashley, as predicted, and Dassin makes a cameo appearance as a man in the crowded subway, gesturing to someone unseen to draw attention to himself. Sarah is seen in separate medium and long shots in the security monitors of Claudia's apartment as the doorman rings for Ashley; while Ashley being unable to sell his paintings is an indication of himself as a failed artist out of step with what sells in these times. This might seem a cruel blow after his being able to overcome his painter's block, and Burton reacts angrily yet again at the idea of him conducting a retrospective. Sarah's attack on Ashley for leaving her in Toronto finally allows for a display of passion on her part, but Dassin inexplicably swamps Ashley's three-minute monologue of apology to her with a sea of music, perhaps to try to cover up the stiff blocking of Ashley's movements. Dassin presents the separation of the couple back at the subway by having both of them separately swallowed up by the crowd.

In his article for *Films Illustrated*, Tony Crawley calls the film one of Dassin's "lightest—if not the slightest since *Two Smart People*. It could be the sheer surprise of seeing Burton working for once, though not even Dassin can draw much out of the unctuous O'Neal horror show, but the film does work, and rather agreeably so." Crawley claims that Ryan O'Neal and Lee Majors make uncredited cameos in the x-rated film sequence, though the author of this book could not spot them. Dassin faced the problem that the scenario invites—that the slightest wrong shading could lead the older man into the dirty old man trap, something which Crawley claims Billy Wilder tumbled into with his *Love in the Afternoon* (1957), in which a fifty-six-year-old Gary Copper romanced a teenage-looking (but twenty-eight-year-old) Audrey Hepburn. (Burton is said to have been fifty-five to O'Neal's seventeen.) Said Dassin:

> I wouldn't care for that. So we meet the situation head-on. She amusingly refers to him as the dirty old man. But there's nothing titillating or anything. We don't play that game. Its two people who are really mad about each other. It's not about age, but about love.

Crawley claims that the age gap cannot be dismissed because it's there in every frame, in every Burton wrinkle. Dassin replies: "But that's it! That's the point. That's the saving grace. She has more courage than he does. He's forever trying to send her away. But she won't have it."

Crawley reports that Dassin did not cast Burton, but rather Burton chose Dassin. Said the director:

> I had nothing to do with the casting. The producer came to me and asked would I make a film with Burton and O'Neal. One recoils at these ready-made packages, but on studying it, I thought it was perfect casting. Richard is a very good performer. He's just had a long down period.

This last claim is questionable because Burton's last "down period" in terms of film-making would have been from 1975 to 1976, when he had no titles released.

Dassin said that when he was in London making *Night and the City* he had seen Burton in the stage play *The Lady's Not for Burning* in 1949. Apparently, Dassin wired Darryl F. Zanuck and told him about the actor, but Zanuck had heard that Burton had skin that didn't photograph well; but a few years later he would make his first film for Twentieth Century–Fox, being the mystery romance *My Cousin Rachel* (1952).

Dassin would say that Burton was a joy to work with, and he particularly liked the sound of the actor's voice:

> There is a moment that's very nice in the film, where he's going to be called to the telephone. He's just leafing through a book as I made the shot. "Hey, look at this page here," I said. It was just a list, the names of flowers. I love the sound of flower's names. I said, "Read them." And he did, and it's so lovely, I put it in the film.

The director was also enchanted by O'Neal:

> Nothing fazes Tatum! I don't know whether she is like her character or whether it's the part that took over. Her character was in conflict with her whole little cosmos. And whether that went into the way she behaved on the set, the way she remained unfazed by Richard or anybody else, I don't know. She holds her own, though. Very, very disciplined. She wants to be perfectly clear about everything. She doesn't bring anything to the part that isn't in the script, she hasn't really learned about that yet. But she comes entirely open and says: Take me. Which is not a small offering.

Dassin says it was the girl's role that attracted him to the script. The outsider, Crawley theorizes, is a recurring character in the director's films and symptomatic of the younger generation, which Dassin admitted had him completely confounded.

In *Tender Comrades*, Dassin said he did the film for the money, and his opinion of the casting had apparently changed:

> When you cast Tatum O'Neal in the role of a magical young creature who enchants an oldish man, you're dead. The producers were under the impression that she was a huge star. I remembered her from a child's performance and was dumb enough not to ask what had become of her. I signed to do the film and then I went to California to meet her, at which point I said to the guys, "Don't make the movie!" But I was bound. Well, it was a disaster.... In order to do something to help the film, I cut it in such a way that she would be least objectionable. [But the producers] got their hands on it and turned it around, and I sued and asked to have my name removed [unsuccessfully].

In Tatum O'Neal's autobiography, *A Paper Life*, she confirms the story of her being in a car accident before filming began. She says that her father Ryan had given her the script to read, although he was less than enthusiastic about its quality. O'Neal writes that she was uncomfortable about being "forced" to do the seminude scene where her breasts were exposed, but "even when I had my clothes on I felt ill at ease making the movie. I was still limping from the accident. I'd gained weight, so I look different, and my voice sounds a bit artificial because I'm just not present—my essence as an actress is missing." However, O'Neal claims to have enjoyed working with Burton, who used to say that he was Dante and would call her Beatrice (which is her middle name), and "a divine enchanting creature." The actress also reports that although Burton's doctor had given orders for him not to drink, the actor still drank beer and wine, and snuck shots of liquor. When Burton was drunk, the "divine enchanting creature," writes O'Neal, was described by him as "the most divine enchanting fucking little cunt I have ever seen." Burton would also ask her to sit on his lap; she declined.

In his book *My Brother*, Graham Jenkins quotes Burton's grumble about the film: "At my age they should have paid me danger money." In *Richard Burton: Prince of Players*, Michael Munn quotes the actor on how he enjoyed working with Tatum O'Neal. "She has terrific vitality and enthusiasm. It's so much better than working with someone who knows it all and is very blasé about it." Burton is also said to have commented to Dassin about the issue of him playing older than his real age. "Here I am looking fitter and younger than I have in years and everybody's going to say *Look how he's gone to the dogs again*." The actor described the film as a "delicately balanced story [since] the two personalities have to complement each other very much and be totally believable or they run the risk of being just a dirty old man with a beautiful young girl. It's a tremendous job for the director."

Burton had made his film debut in a supporting role in the British *Women of Dolwyn* (1949). After playing more supporting roles in British titles, he broke into American films with *My Cousin Rachel* (1952), for which he earned a Best Supporting Actor Academy Award nomination. The actor scored his first leading role in the war drama *The Desert Rats* (1953), and continued as the lead in *The Robe* (1953), for which he was nominated for the Best Actor Academy Award. He starred in the biographies *Prince of Players* (1955) and *Alexander the Great* (1956), the historical actioner *Bitter Victory* (1957), and the British drama *Look Back in Anger* (1959). Burton began the 1960s with leads in *Ice Palace* (1960) and *The Bramble Bush* (1960), but his association with wife Elizabeth Taylor meant that his screen billing fell below hers in six of the eight films they made together during this decade, the exceptions being *Doctor Faustus* (1967), which he co-directed, and *The Comedians* (1967).

One of his Taylor titles would be *Who's Afraid of Virginia Woolf?* (1966), for which he would earn another Best Actor Academy Award nomination. He played the title character in the biography *Becket* (1964), again receiving a Best Actor Academy Award nomination, and starred in *The Night of the Iguana* (1964), a filmed version of his stage triumph *Hamlet* (1964), the thriller *The Spy Who Came in from the Cold* (1965), earning him another Best Actor nomination, the war adventure *Where Eagles Dare* (1968), and the historical drama *Anne of the Thousand Days* (1969), for which he was again nominated as Best Actor. In the 1970s Burton assayed the lead in the war drama *Raid on Rommel* (1971), starred in the crime drama *Villain* (1971), was top-billed over Taylor in the comedy *Under Milk Wood* (1972), played the title characters in the biography *The Assassination of Trotsky* (1972) and the crime drama *Bluebeard* (1972), and starred in the war dramas *The Battle of Sutjeska* (1973) and *Massacre in Rome* (1973). After a break, Burton returned as the leads in the mysteries *Equus* (1977), for which he was nominated for the Best Actor Academy Award, *The Medusa Touch* (1978), the war adventure *The Wild Geese* (1978), the mystery *Absolution* (1978), and the war drama *Breakthrough* (1979). After *Circle of Two*, the actor played the lead in *Lovespell* (1981), but lost top-billing to John Hurt in the science fiction thriller *Nineteen Eighty-Four* (1984), Burton's final film.

Tatum O'Neal made her film debut at the age of ten in the comedy *Paper Moon* (1973), for which she won the Best Supporting Actress Academy Award, making her the youngest competitive winner. She followed this with more supporting roles and then scored the lead in the family drama *International Velvet* (1978), which was her title prior to *Circle of Two*. After *Circle of Two* the actress would go on to appear in the comedy *Little Darlings* (1980), *Prisoners* (1981), the action drama *Certain Fury* (1985), the comedy *Little Noises* (1992), the romance *The Scoundrel's Wife* (2002), and the thriller *Saving Grace B. Jones* (2009) in which she played the title character (but was not top-billed).

Circle of Two was the third feature by the production company Film Consortium of Canada, which had begun with the cross-dressing comedy *Outrageous!* (1977) and would go on to make two more titles, ending with the music drama *Hank Williams: The Show He Never Gave* (1981). Producer Henk Van Der Kolk was the producer of all the titles made by the Film Consortium of Canada, as was executive producer William Marshall. Marshall was also a screenwriter of his first producing title, the horror film *Dr. Frankenstein on Campus* (1970), and would continue to executive produce titles up to 2009. Associate producer Bob Rodgers had previously produced and directed the documentary short *The Fiddlers of James Bay* (1980), and would only associate produce one other title after *Circle of One*— Film Consortium of Canada's *Mr. Patman* (1980).

Release

May 1980, with the taglines "Their lives would always be entwined...," "Theirs' was a love against all odds," "True love knows no bounds," and "Love makes it right."

Reviews

"A charming, earnest movie which promises but does not deliver a grand, emotional statement.... Burton gives one of his best performances. O'Neal, however, is never convincing as the catalyst for his new-found strength. She has a tendency to posture and smile and comes off prettier than she is inspiring."—*Variety*, May 28, 1980

"Preposterous.... Tatum O'Neal and a dissipated Richard Burton as lovers so mismatched they could be in the Guinness Book."—Richard Corliss, *Time* magazine, April 6, 2008

"Dassin does not go for the cheap thrill, but the result is slight and forgettable."—Leonard Maltin, *1997 Movie & Video Guide*

"Pedestrian and rather unsavory."—Jay Robert Nash and Stanley Ralph Ross, *The Motion Picture Guide*

"Terribly tastefully done, and pretty boring with it. Dassin is so afraid that the story will veer into smut that he reins it back with neurotic severity. And O'Neal, it must be said, is no teenage seductress—in fact, she seems to be reading most of her lines off cue cards."—*Channel 4 Film*

Bibliography

Aachen, George. *Memorable Films of the Forties.* Sydney: Rastar Press, 1997.
Alleman, Richard. *New York: The Movie Lover's Guide—the Ultimate Insider Tour of Movie New York.* New York: Broadway, 2005.
Andrews, Bart, Thomas J. Watson, and Gale Gordon. *Loving Lucy: An Illustrated Tribute to Lucille Ball.* New York: St. Martin's Griffin, 1982.
Askin, Peter. *Trumbo.* Samuel Goldwyn Films/Red Envelope Entertainment/Safehouse Pictures/Filbert Steps Productions/Reno Productions, 2007.
Astor, Mary. *A Life on Film.* New York: Delacorte Press, 1971.
Ball, Lucille. *Love, Lucy.* Berkley, 1997.
Ballinger, Alex, and Danny Graydon. *The Rough Guide to Film Noir.* Rough Guides, 2007.
Barranger, Milly S. *Jessica Tandy: A Bio-Bibliography.* Greenwood Press, 1991.
_____. *Unfriendly Witnesses: Gender, Theater, and Film in the McCarthy Era.* Carbondale: Southern Illinois University Press, 2008.
Barzman, Norma. *The Red and the Blacklist: The Intimate Memoir of a Hollywood Expatriate.* Nation Books, 2004.
Basinger, Jeanine. *The Star Machine.* New York: Alfred A. Knopf, 2007.
Bennett, Bruce. "A Tale of Two Careers: The Theatrical Realism of Jules Dassin." Retrieved September 1, 2010, from http: www.movingimagesource.us.
Bergan, Ronald. *Anthony Perkins: A Haunted Life.* Little, Brown, 1995.
_____. *The United Artists Story.* London: Octopus Books, 1986.
Berry, John. *The Hollywood Ten* (1950). Released on the Criterion DVD of Spartacus on April 24, 2001.
Biesen, Sheri Chinen. *Blackout: World War II and the Origins of Film Noir.* John Hopkins University Press, 2005.
Bishop, Jim. *The Mark Hellinger Story: A Biography of Broadway and Hollywood.* New York: Appleton-Century-Crofts, 1952.
Borde, Raymond, Etienne Chaumeton, and Paul Hammond. *A Panorama of American Film Noir (1941–1953).* City Lights, 2002.
Bordman, Gerald. *American Musical Theater: A Chronicle.* Oxford University Press, 2001.
Bould, Mark. *Film Noir: From Berlin to Sin City.* London, New York: Wallflower, 2005.
Brady, Kathleen. *Lucille: The Life of Lucille Ball.* Billboard Books, 2001.
Bret, David. *Joan Crawford: Hollywood Martyr.* New York: Da Capo Press, 2008.
Brunetta, Gian Piero, and Jeremy Parzen. *The History of Italian Cinema: A Guide to Italian Films from Its Origins to the Twenty-First Century.* Princeton University Press, 2009.
Buford, Kate. *Burt Lancaster: An American Life.* New York: Da Capo Press, 2001.
Buhle, Paul, and Dave Wagner. *Hide in Plain Sight: The Hollywood Blacklistees in Film and Television, 1950–2002.* Palgrave Macmillan, 2004.
Burstyn, Ellen. *Lessons in Becoming Myself.* Riverhead Trade, 2007.
Callow, Simon. *Charles Laughton: A Difficult Actor.* London: Methuen, 1987.
Canales, Luis. *Imperial Gina: The Strictly Unauthorized Biography of Gina Lollobrigida.* Branden Books, 1990.
Casty, Alan. *Communism in Hollywood: The Moral Paradoxes of Testimony, Silence and Betrayal.* Lanham, Toronto, Plymouth, U.K.: Scarecrow Press, 2009.
Caute, David. *Joseph Losey: A Revenge on Life.* London, Boston: Faber & Faber, 1997.
Celli, Carlo, and Marga Cottino-Jones. *A New Guide to Italian Cinema.* Palgrave Macmillan, 2007.
Ceplair, Larry. *The Inquisition in Hollywood: Politics in the Film Community, 1930–1960.* University of Illinois Press, 2003.

Chandler, Charlotte. *It's Only a Movie: Alfred Hitchcock, a Personal Biography*. Applause Books, 2006.
_____. *Not the Girl Next Door: Joan Crawford, a Personal Biography*. Applause Books, 2009.
Christopher, Nicholas. *Somewhere in the Night: Film Noir and the American City*. Counterpoint, 2006.
Clarke, Roger. "You'll Never Work in This Town Again," interview with Jules Dassin. *The Independent*, August 9, 2002. Retrieved March, 5, 2010, from http:www.independent.co.uk.
Clooney, George. *Good Night, and Good Luck*. Warner Independent Pictures//2929 Entertainment/Participant Productions/Davis Films/Redbus Pictures/Tohokushinsha/Section 8, 2005. DVD released by Warner Home Video, 2006.
Clurman, Harold. *The Fervent Years: The Group Theatre and the '30s*. New York: Da Capo Press, 1983.
Cogley, John. *Report on Blacklisting: 1. Movies*. New York: Arno Press and the *New York Times*, 1972.
Conrad, Christine. *Jerome Robbins: That Broadway Man*. Booth-Clibborn, 2000.
Considine, Shaun. *Bette and Joan: The Divine Feud*. New York: E.P. Dutton, 1989.
Corliss, Richard. "Master of the Heist." *Time* Magazine, April 6, 2008.
Crawley, Tony. "Greece Is the Word." *Film Illustrated* 10, no. 116 (May 1981): 307–312.
Cripps, Thomas. *Making Movies Black: The Hollywood Message Movie from World War II to the Civil Rights Era*. Oxford University Press, 1993.
Crivello, Kirk. *Fallen Angels: The Lives and Untimely Deaths of 14 Hollywood Beauties*. Secaucus, NJ: Citadel Press, 1988.
Cronyn, Hugh. *A Terrible Liar: A Memoir*. New York: William Morrow, 1991.
Custen, George F. *Twentieth Century's Fox: Darryl F. Zanuck and the Culture of Hollywood*. New York: Basic Books, 1997.
Dassin, Jules. 2004 interview at the Los Angeles County Museum of Art (LACMA) on DVD of *The Naked City*. Criterion Collection, 2007.
_____. Interview on DVD of *Night and the City*. Criterion Collection, 2005.
_____. Interview on DVD of *Rififi*. Criterion Collection, 2001.
_____. Interview on DVD of *Thieves' Highway*. Criterion Collection, 2005.
Dauth, Brian. *Joseph L. Mankiewicz Interviews* (Conversations with Filmmakers). University Press of Mississippi, 2008.
Davis, Ossie, and Ruby Dee. *With Ossie and Ruby: In This Life Together*. It Books, 2000.
Davis, Ronald L. *Duke: The Life and Image of John Wayne*. Norman: University of Oklahoma Press, 1998.
De Carlo, Yvonne, and Doug Warren. *Yvonne: An Autobiography*. St. Martins Press, 1987.
Deutelbaum, Marshall, and Leland Poague. *A Hitchcock Reader*. Wiley-Blackwell, 2009.
Dickos, Andrew. *Street with No Name: A History of the Classic American Film Noir*. University Press of Kentucky, 2002.
Dmytryk, Edward. *Odd Man Out: A memoir of the Hollywood Ten*. Carbondale, Edwardsville: Southern Illinois University Press, 1996.
Douglas, Gordon. *I Was a Communist for the F.B.I*. Warner Bros. Pictures, 1951. DVD released by Warner Bros., 2009.
_____. *Walk a Crooked Mile*. Edward Small Productions for Columbia Pictures, 1948.
Duke, Patty. *Call Me Anna: The Autobiography of Patty Duke*. Bantam, 1988.
Dundy, Elaine. *Finch, Bloody, Finch: A Biography of Peter Finch*. London: Michael Joseph, 1980.
Eames, John Douglas. *The Paramount Story: The Complete History of the Studio and Its 2,805 Films*. Crown, 1985.
Eberly, Stephen L. *Patty Duke: A Bio-Bibliography*. Greenwood Press, 1998.
Ellenberger, Allan R. *Margaret O'Brien: A Career Chronicle and Biography*. McFarland, 2004.
Enns, Chris, and Howard Kazanjian. *The Young Duke: The Early Life of John Wayne*. Globe Pequot, 2009.
Epstein, Michael. *Arthur Miller, Elia Kazan and the Blacklist: None Without Sin*. Thirteen/WNET New York American Masters, 2002.
Erickson, Glenn. Audio commentary on DVD of *Night and the City*. Criterion Collection, 2005.
Eyman, Scott. *Lion of Hollywood: The Life and Legend of Louis B. Mayer*. Simon & Schuster, 2005.
Faulkner, Trader. *Peter Finch: A Biography*. London: Angus & Robertson, 1979.
Ford, John. *The Informer*. RKO Radio Pictures, 1935. DVD released by Warner Home Video, 2006.
Francis, Karl. *One of the Hollywood Ten*. Alibi Films International/Morena Films/Bloom Street Productions/Saltire Entertainment, 2000.
Freedland, Michael. *Hollywood on Trial: McCarthyism's War Against the Movies*. Anova Books, 2008.
Friedgen, Bud, and Michael J. Sheridan. *That's Entertainment III*. MGM, Turner Entertainment Co., 1994. DVD released by Warner Home Video, 2004.
Geist, Kenneth L. *Pictures Will Talk: The Life and Films of Joseph L. Mankiewicz*. New York: Da Capo Press, 1978.

Georgakas, Dan, and Anastasopoulos. "A Dream of Passion: An interview with Jules Dassin." *Cineaste* IX, no. 1 (1978): 20–24.
Gonthier, David, Jr. *American Prison Films Since 1930*. Lewiston, Queenston, Lapeter: Edwin Mellen Press, 2006.
Gordon, Bernard. *Hollywood Exile or How I Learned to Love the Blacklist*. Austin: University of Texas Press, 1999.
Gottlieb, Sidney. *Hitchcock on Hitchcock: Selected Writings and Interviews*. University of California Press, 1997.
Gow, Gordon. "Style and Instinct: Interviews with Jules Dassin." *Films and Filming*, Part 1: vol. 16, no. 4 (February 1970): 22–26; Part 2: vol. 16, no. 6 (March 1970): 66–70.
Green, Alfred E. *Invasion USA*. American Pictures, 1952. DVD released by Synapse Films, 2002
Griffin, Fariella. *Red Scare: Memories of the American Inquisition*. W.W. Norton, 1980.
Guerrero, Ed. *Framing Blackness: The African American Image in Film*. Temple University Press, 1993.
Hannsberry, Karen Burroughs. *Bad Boys: The Actors of Film Noir*. Jefferson, NC: McFarland, 2003.
_____. *Femme Noir: Bad Girls of Film*. Jefferson, NC: McFarland, 1998.
Hardy, Phil. *The BFI Companion to Crime*. London: Cassell, 1997.
Harvey, James. *Movie Love in the Fifties*. New York: Alfred A. Knopf, 2001.
Helpern, David. *Hollywood on Trial*. Cinema Associates, 1976.
Higham, Charles. *Charles Laughton: An Intimate Biography*. London: W.H. Allen, 1976.
Higham, Charles, and Joel Greenberg. *Hollywood in the Forties*. London and New York: A. Zwemmer, A.S. Barnes, 1968.
Hirsch, Foster. *The Dark Side of the Screen: Film Noir*. New York: Da Capo Press, 2001.
_____. *Joseph Losey*. Boston: Twayne Publishers, 1980.
Hirschhorn, Clive. *The Universal Story*. London: Octopus Books, 1983.
Hoberman, J. "An Expatriate at Home Among Stark Images." *The New York Times*, March 22, 2009. Retrieved September 2, 2010, from http: www.nytimes.com.
Hopper, Jerry. *The Atomic City*. Paramount Pictures, 1952. VHS released by Paramount, 1998.
Horton, Andrew. "Jules Dassin: A Multi-National Filmmaker Considered." *Film Criticism* viii, no. 3 (Spring 1984): 21–35.
Hughes, Lloyd. *The Rough Guide to Gangster Movies*. Rough Guide, 2005.
Humphries, Reynold. *Hollywood's Blacklists*. Edinburgh University Press, 2010.
Husted, Christopher. Interview on DVD of *Night and the City*. Criterion Collection, 2005.
Huston, John. *The Asphalt Jungle*. MGM, 1950. DVD released by Warner Home Video, 2004.
Jenkins, David, with Sue Rogers. *Richard Burton, a Brother Remembered*. London: Century, 1993.
Jenkins, Graham, with Barry Turner. *Richard Burton, My Brother*. London: Sphere Books, 1988.
Johnson, Lamont. *Fear on Trial*. Alan Landsburg Productions, 1975.
Jones, Dorothy B. *Communism and the Movies: A Study of Film Content*. A subsidiary project of The Fund for the Republic, 1956.
Kael, Pauline. *5001 Nights at the Movies*. New York: Holt, Rinehart, and Winston, 1984.
_____. *Reeling*. Boston and Toronto: Little, Brown, 1976.
Kahn, Henry. "It's an Outrage." *Picturegoer*, July 9, 1955.
Karol, Michael. *Lucy A to Z: The Lucille Ball Encyclopedia*. iUniverse Star, 2004.
Kashner, Sam, and Nancy Schoenberger. *Furious Love: Elizabeth Taylor, Richard Burton and the Marriage of the Century*. Harper, 2010.
Katz, Chuck. *Manhattan on Film: Walking Tours of Hollywoods' Fabled Front Lot*. Limelight, 2005.
Kazan, Elia. *Elia Kazan: A Life*. New York: Da Capo Press, 1977.
Keaney, Michael F. *British Film Noir Guide*. Jefferson, NC: McFarland, 2008.
Koch, Christopher. *Blacklist: Hollywood on Trial*. American Movie Classics/Koch TV Productions, 1996.
Kolin, Philip C. *A Streetcar Named Desire*. Cambridge: Cambridge University Press, 2000.
Krutnik, Frank. *In a Lonely Street: Film Noir, Genre, Masculinity*. Routledge, 1991.
Lanzoni, Remi Fournier. *French Cinema: From Its Beginnings to the Present*. New York: Continuum, 2002.
Lawrence, Greg. *Dance with Demons: The Life of Jerome Robbins*. Berkley Trade, 2002.
Leitch, Thomas. *Crime Films*. Cambridge: Cambridge University Press, 2002.
Lellios, Fay Efrosini. *The Long Haul of A. I. Bezzerides*. 21/31 Productions, 2004.
Leon, Masha. "On the Go: A Tribute to Jules Dassin." *The Jewish Daily Forward*, April 11, 2008. Retrieved on September 1, 2010, from http: www.forward.com.
Leverich, Lyle. *Tom: The Unknown Tennessee Williams*. W.W. Norton, 1997.
Ludwig, Edward. *Big Jim McLain*. Warner Bros. Pictures in association with Wayne-Fellows Productions, 1952. DVD released by Warner Home Video, 2007.

Lumet, Sidney. *Daniel*. Paramount/John Heyman Production, 1983. DVD released by Legend Films on July 1, 2008.
Maltin, Leonard. *1997 Movie & Video Guide*. New York: Plume, 1996.
Mason, Paul. Interview on DVD of *Brute Force*. Criteria Collection, 2007.
May, John R., and Michael Bird. *Religion in Film*. Knoxville: University of Tennessee Press, 1982.
Mayer, Geoff, and Brian McDonnell. *Encyclopedia of Film Noir*. Greenwood, 2007.
McCarey, Leo. *My Son John*. Rainbow Productions in association with Paramount Pictures, 1952.
McGilligan, Patrick. *Alfred Hitchcock: A Life in Darkness and Light*. HarperPerennial, 2004.
McGilligan, Patrick, and Paul Behle. *Tender Comrades: A Backstory of the Hollywood Blacklist*. New York: St. Martin's Griffin, 1999.
Menzies, William Cameron. *The Whip Hand*. RKO Radio Pictures, 1951.
Mercouri, Melina. *I Was Born Greek*. New York: Doubleday, 1971.
Miller, John. *Peter Ustinov: The Gift of Laughter*. Orion Publishing, 2003.
Montand, Yves, with Herve Hamon and Patrick Rotman, translated from the French by Jeremy Leggatt. *You See, I Haven't Forgotten*. New York: Alfred A. Knopf, 1992.
Mordden, Ethan. *Beautiful Mornin': The Broadway Musical in the 1940s*. Oxford University Press, 1999.
_____. *Open a New Window: The Broadway Musical in the 1960s*. Palgrave Macmillan, 2001.
Morella, Joe, and Edward Z. Epstein. *Loretta Young: An Extraordinary Life*. Santa Barbara, CA: Landmark Books, 1986.
Morley, Margaret. *Larger Than Life: The Biography of Robert Morley*. London: Robson Books, 1979.
Moseley, Roy. *Bette Davis*. University of Kentucky Press, 2003.
Moser, Laura. *Bette Davis (Life and Times)*. Haus Publishing, 2004.
Muller, Eddie. *Dark City: The Lost World of Film Noir*. St. Martin's Griffin, 1998.
Munby, Jonathan. *Public Enemies, Public Heroes: Screening the Gangster from Little Caesar to Touch of Evil*. University of Chicago Press, 1999.
Munn, Michael. *John Wayne: The Man Behind the Myth*. NAL Trade, 2005.
_____. *Richard Burton: Prince of Players*. Skyhorse Publishing, 2008.
Murphy, Brenda. *Congressional Theatre: Dramatizing McCarthyism on Stage, Film and Television*. Cambridge University Press, 2003.
_____. *Tennessee Williams and Elia Kazan: A Collaboration*. Cambridge: Cambridge University Press, 1992
Naremore, James. *More Than Night: Film Noir in Its Contexts*. University of California Press, 2008.
Nash, Jay Robert, Stanley Ralph Ross. *The Motion Picture Guide*. Chicago: Cinebooks, 1987.
Navasky, Victor S. *Naming Names*. New York: Penguin, 1980.
Newquist, Roy. *Conversations with Joan Crawford*. Secaucus, NJ: Citadel Press, 1980.
Nochimson, Martha P. *Dying to Belong: Gangster Movies in Hollywood and Hong Kong*. Wiley-Blackwell, 2007.
O'Neal, Tatum. *A Paper Life*. New York: HarperEntertainment, 2004.
O'Sullivan, Sean, and David Wilson. *Images of Incarceration: Representations of Prison in Film and Television*. Waterside Press, 2004.
Palmer, James. *The Films of Joseph Losey*. Cambridge: Cambridge University Press, 1993.
Palmer, Laura Kay. *Osgood and Anthony Perkins: A Comprehensive History of Their Work in Theatre, Film, and Other Media, with Credits and an Annotated Bibliography*. Jefferson, NC: McFarland, 1991.
Parish, James Robert. *The Fox Girls*. New Rochelle, NY: Arlington House, 1972.
_____. *Great Child Stars*. New York: Ace Books, 1976.
_____. *Prison Pictures from Hollywood: Plots, Critiques, Casts and Credits for 293 Theatrical and Made-for-Television Releases*. Jefferson, NC: McFarland, 2000.
Parish, James Robert, and Ronald L. Bowers. *The MGM Stock Company: The Golden Era*. London: Ian Allen, 1973.
Pettey, Homer B. *Topographic Economics in Dassin's Thieves' Highway*. Film Criticism, Winter 2008. Retrieved May 15, 2010, from www.FindArticles.com.
Polan, Dana. Interview on DVD of *The Naked City*. Criterion Collection, 2007.
Pollack, Sydney. *The Way We Were*. Columbia Pictures Corporation/Rastar Productions, 1973. Special Edition DVD released by Sony Pictures, 1999.
Powrie, Phil. *The Cinema of France*. New York: Wallflowers Press, 2006.
Preminger, Otto. *Advise and Consent*. Sigma Productions, 1962. DVD released by Warner Home Video, 2005.
Quirk, Lawrence J., and William Schoell. *Joan Crawford: The Essential Biography*. University Press of Kentucky, 2002.

Radosh, Ronald. *Red Star Over Hollywood: The Film Colony's Long Romance with the Left*. Encounter Books, 2005.
Rappaport, Mark. *From the Journals of Jean Seberg*. Waterbearer Films/Couch Potato Productions, 1995. DVD released by Image Entertainment, 1999.
Reid, Gordon. "Dassin and the New Touch." *Continental Film Review*, October 1957.
Ricci, Mark. *The Films of John Wayne*. New York: Citadel Press, 1970.
Rich, Nathaniel. *San Francisco Noir*. Little Bookroom, 2005.
Ritt, Martin. *The Front*. Columbia Pictures/Persky-Bright Productions/Devon Company/Rollins-Joffe Productions, 1976. DVD released by Sony Pictures on February 17, 2004.
Roberts, Randy, and James S. Olson. *John Wayne: American*. Bison Books, 1997.
Robinson, Harlow. *Russians in Hollywood, Hollywood Russians: Biography of an Image*. Northeastern, 2007.
Robson, Mark. *Trial*. MGM, 1955.
Rolls, Alistair, and Deborah Walker. *French and American Noir: Dark Crossings (Crime Files)*. Palgrave Macmillan, 2009.
Rouse, Russell. *The Thief*. Harry M. Popkins Productions, 1952. DVD released by Image Entertainment, 2002.
Sanders, James. *Celluloid Skyline: New York and the Movies*. Knopf, 2003.
_____. Interview on DVD of *The Naked City*. Criterion Collection, 2007.
Sarris, Andrew. *You Ain't Heard Nothin' Yet: The American Talking Film History and Memory, 1927–1949*. New York: Oxford University Press, 1998.
Schickel, Richard. *Elia Kazan: A Biography*. HarperPerennial, 2006.
Schildkraut, Joseph. *My Father and I*. New York: Viking Press, 1959.
Schneider, Steven Jay. *101 Gangster Movies You Must See Before You Die*. Cassell Illustrated, 2009.
Schon, Jeffrey. *"Film Noir": Episode of American Cinema*. A New York Center for Visual History production in co-production with KCET and the BBC, 1994.
Schoolcraft, Ralph. *Romain Gary: The Man Who Sold His Shadow*. University of Pennsylvania Press, 2002.
Server, Lee. *Ava Gardner: Love Is Nothing*. St. Martin's Griffin, 2007.
Severo, Richard. "Jules Dassin, Filmmaker, Dies at 96." *The New York Times*, 1 April 2008. Retrieved August 15, 2010, from http:www.nytimes.com.
Shepherd, Donald, Robert Slatzer and Dave Grayson. *Duke: The Life and Times of John Wayne*. Citadel, 2002.
Shnayerson, Michael. *Irwin Shaw: A Biography*. New York: Putnam's, 1989.
Sikov, Ed. *Dark Victory: The Life of Bette Davis*. Holt Paperbacks, 2008.
Silver, Alain. Audio commentary on DVD of *Thieves' Highway*. Criterion Collection, 2005.
Silver, Alain, and James Ursini. Audio commentary on DVD of *Brute Force*. Criteria Collection, 2007.
_____, and _____. *Film Noir Reader*. Limelight Editions, 2004.
Silver, Alain, James Ursini, and Elizabeth Ward. *Film Noir*. London: Secker & Warburg, 1979.
Singer, Kurt. *The Charles Laughton Story*. London: Robert Hale, 1954.
Smith, Steven. *Gene Tierney: A Shattered Portrait*. Van Ness Films in association with Foxstar Productions and A&E Network, 1999.
Smith, Valerie. *Representing Blackness: Issues in Film and Video*. London: Athlone Press, 1997.
Spicer, Andrew. *Historical Dictionary of Film Noir*. Scarecrow Press, 2010.
Spoto, Donald. *The Art of Alfred Hitchcock: Fifty Years of His Motion Pictures*. Anchor, 1991
_____. *The Dark Side of Genius: The Life of Alfred Hitchcock*. New York: Da Capo Press, 1999.
_____. *The Kindness of Strangers: The Life of Tennessee Williams*. New York: Da Capo Press, 1997.
_____. *Spellbound by Beauty*. London: Arrow, 2009.
Springsteen, R.G. *The Red Menace*. Republic Pictures, 1949. VHS released by Republic Pictures, 1998.
Sragow, Michael. "Jules Dassin: The Early Years." Retrieved September 1, 2010, from http: www.salon.com.
Stanfield, Peter, Frank Krutnik and Steve Neale. *"Un-American Hollywood": Politics and Film in the Blacklist Era*. Rutgers University Press, 2007.
Stephens, Michael L. *Gangster Films: A Comprehensive, Illustrated Reference to People, Films and Terms*. Jefferson, NC: McFarland, 1996.
Stevens, Matthew. *Jewish Film Directory: A Guide to More Than 1200 Films of Jewish Interest from 32 Countries Over 85 Years*. Wiltsire, UK: Flicks Books, 1992.
Stevenson, Robert. *Woman on Pier 13*. RKO Radio Pictures, 1949. DVD released by Warner Bros., 2009.
Stine, Whitney, with Bette Davis. *Mother Goddam: The Story of the Career of Bette Davis*. Hawthorn Books, 1974.
Suskin, Steven. *Second Act Trouble: Behind the Scenes at Broadways' Big Musical Bombs*. Applause Books, 2006.
Tellotte, J. P. *Voices in the Dark: The Narrative Patterns of Film Noir*. University of Illinois Press, 1998.

Testa, Carlo. *Italian Cinema and Modern European Literatures: 1945–2000*. Praeger, 2002.
Thomas, Bob. *Joan Crawford: A Biography*. New York: Simon & Schuster, 1978.
Thomas, Tony. *Ustinov in Focus*. Oak Tree Publications, 1971.
Thomas, Tony, and Aubrey Solomon. *The Films of 20th Century–Fox*. Secaucus, NJ: Citadel Press, 1979.
Thomson, David. *Bette Davis (Great Stars)*. Faber & Faber, 2010.
_____. *The New Biographical Dictionary of Film*. New York: Alfred A Knopf, 2004.
Tierney, Gene, with Mickey Herskowitz. *Self-Portrait*. New York: Berkley Books, 1979.
Truffaut, François. *The Films in My Life*. London: Allen Lane, 1975.
Truffaut, François, and Helen G. Scott. *Hitchcock* (revised edition). Simon & Schuster, 1985.
Tzeirani, Pauline. "Jules Dassin Biography." Melina Mercouri Foundation, 2007. Retrieved 5 March 2010 from http:www.melinamercourifoundation.org.
Ustinov, Peter. *Dear Me*. London: Heinemann, 1977.
Vaill, Amanda. *Somewhere: The Life of Jerome Robbins*. Broadway, 2008.
Vaughan, Robert. *Only Victims: A Study of Show Business Blacklisting*. New York: Putnam's, 1972.
Vermilye, Jerry. *Bette Davis*. London: W.H. Allen, 1973.
Vogel, Michelle. *Gene Tierney: A Biography*. Jefferson, NC: McFarland, 2005.
Waggner, George. *Red Nightmare*. Warner Bros. Pictures for the U.S. Department of Defense Information and Education Division, 1962. Available as a special feature on the DVD release of *Invasion U.S.A.*, Synapse Films, 2002.
Wagner, Dave, and Paul Buhle. *Blacklisted: The Film Lover's Guide to the Hollywood Blacklist*. Palgrave Macmillan, 2003.
Wagstaff, Christopher. *Italian Neorealist Cinema: An Aesthetic Approach*. University of Toronto Press, 2008.
Wald, Malvin. Audio commentary on DVD of *The Naked City*. Criterion Collection, 2007.
Walker, John. *Halliwell's Film and Video Guide 2000*. London: HarperCollins Entertainment, 1999.
Walker, Michael. *Hitchcock's Motifs*. Amsterdam University Press, 2006.
Wayne, Jane Ellen. *The Golden Girls of MGM: Greta Garbo, Joan Crawford, Lana Turner, Judy Garland, Ava Gardner, Grace Kelly, and Others*. New York: Da Capo Press, 2003.
Weaver, Tom. *John Carradine: The Films*. Jefferson, NC: McFarland, 1999.
Wellman, William A. *The Iron Curtain*. 20th Century–Fox, 1948.
Werker, Alfred. *Walk East on Beacon!* Columbia Pictures, 1952.
Williams, Tennessee. *Memoirs*. New Directions, 2006.
_____. *Notebooks*. Yale University Press, 2007.
_____. *Plays 1937–1955*. Library of America, 2000.
_____. *Selected Letters: Volume II, 1945–1957*. New Directions, 2007.
Wills, Gary. *John Wayne's America*. Simon & Schuster, 1998.
Winch, Arden. "The Persecution of Jules Dassin." *Picture Post* 69, no. 10 (1955): 14–16.
Winecoff, Charles. *Split Image: The Life of Anthony Perkins*. New York: Dutton, 1996.
Winkler, Irwin. *Guilty by Suspicion*. Warner Bros./Arnon Milchan Productions, 1990.
_____. *Night and the City*. Penta Entertainment/A Tribeca Production, 1992.
Wood, Robin. *Hitchcock's Films Revisited*. Columbia University Press, 2002.
Wyman, Ric B. *For the Love of Lucy: The Complete Guide for Collectors and Fans*. New York: Abbeville Press, 1995.
Yates, Peter. *The House on Carroll Street*. Orion Pictures, 1988. DVD released by MGM (Video & DVD), 2003.
Young, Loretta, with Helen Ferguson. *The Things I Had to Learn*. Kingswood, Surrey: World's Work, 1961.
Zmijewsky, Boris, Steven Zmijewsky, and Mark Ricci. *The Complete Films of John Wayne*. Citadel, 2000.
Zolotow, Maurice. *John Wayne: Shooting Star*. New York: W.H. Allen, 1974.

Index

The Affairs of Martha 7, 9, 11, 58–63, 93
Astor, Mary 8, 74, 75, 76–77

Ball, Lucille 9, 96, 97, 98, 99, 100, 101, 141
Bohnen, Roman 7, 8, 10, 51, 111
Brasseur, Pierre 25, 162–163
Browne, Roscoe Lee 41, 216
Brute Force 10, 11, 12, 26, 48, 94, 101–112, 114, 115, 118, 124, 126, 135, 137, 143, 146, 156, 170, 192
Burstyn, Ellen 44, 228, 229, 230, 232, 233
Burton, Richard 44, 193, 237, 238, 239, 240, 241–242

The Canterville Ghost 6, 8, 77–86
Carlson, Richard 7, 59, 62, 76
Carroll, John 9, 89, 90, 94
Celui qui doit mourir see *He Who Must Die*
Circle of Two 44, 232, 234–242
Cobb, Lee J. 12, 126, 130, 131
Conte, Richard 12, 129
Cortesa, Valentina 12, 129
Crawford, Joan 1, 7, 64, 65, 66, 67, 68, 69
Cronyn, Hume 8, 9, 10, 89, 90, 91, 92, 94, 103, 107, 110–111, 112

Davis, Bette 20–21, 76, 131
Dayan, Assaf 42, 222, 223
Dee, Ruby 41, 212, 215, 216
Despo 27, 33, 218
Dorn, Philip 64, 68, 69
A Dream of Passion 44, 48, 222, 227–234
Du rififi chez les hommes see *Rififi*
Duff, Howard 11, 111, 118, 121
Dymtryk, Edward 11, 13, 15, 19, 45, 46

Finch, Peter 32, 201, 202–203
Fitzgerald, Barry 11, 115, 120

Half Angel 18
Hart, Dorothy 11, 121
He Who Must Die 3, 24, 25, 45, 48, 149, 150–157, 159, 168, 170, 194
Hellinger, Mark 10, 11, 12, 109, 110, 114, 118, 119, 121
Hodiak, John 9, 97, 99, 100
House Un-American Activities Committee (HUAC) 1, 2, 3, 8, 10, 12, 13, 14, 16, 17, 19, 20, 21, 62, 79, 93, 108, 111, 120, 130, 131, 136, 141, 146, 188, 210
Hunt, Marsha 1, 7, 9, 11, 12, 13, 59, 60, 61, 62, 63, 89, 90, 92, 93, 94

I Was a Communist for the FBI 13
Illya Darling 31, 33–36, 37, 40, 166
The Informer 212–215
The Iron Curtain 13

Jacques, Raymond St. 41, 211, 216

Kazan, Elia 130, 141, 146
Kelly, Gene 22, 23, 25, 183

Lancaster, Burt 10, 106, 109, 110
Laughton, Charles 6, 8, 79, 80, 83, 84, 85, 86
The Law see *Where the Hot Wind Blows*
Lawrence, Barbara 12, 131
Lemmon, Jack 27, 28
A Letter for Evie 9, 10, 11, 62, 86–95, 110
Lollobrigida, Gina 25, 158, 160, 161–162, 163, 164

Maltz, Albert 13, 17, 119–120
Manuel, Robert 22
Marshall, Herbert 8, 72, 74, 75, 76
Mastroianni, Marcello 25, 160, 161, 163, 164

Mayer, Louis B. 6, 9–10, 12, 67, 69, 83
Mayfield, Julian 41, 212, 215–216
Mercouri, Melina 1, 22, 23, 24, 25, 26, 27, 28, 29, 30, 31, 32, 33, 34, 35, 36, 37, 38, 39, 40, 41, 42, 43, 44, 45, 46, 47, 48, 127, 151, 153, 154, 155, 156, 158, 161, 164, 165, 166, 169, 170, 171, 172, 173, 174, 175, 176, 177, 178, 179, 180, 181, 182, 183, 184, 185, 186, 188, 189, 192, 194, 195, 197, 198, 199, 200, 201, 203, 207, 208, 211, 212, 218, 220, 221, 222, 223, 224, 226, 228, 229, 230, 231, 232, 233
Mohner, Carl 22, 24
Montand, Yves 25, 39, 160, 163, 164
Morley, Robert 31, 189, 190, 193–194

The Naked City 11, 13, 48, 110, 111, 112–122, 124, 126, 134, 135, 137, 143, 159, 210, 226, 232
Nazi Agent 6, 7, 48, 52–58
Never on Sunday 1, 26–28, 31, 48, 127, 156, 164–173, 181, 182, 185, 188, 192, 194, 197, 203, 228, 233
Night and the City 1, 5, 8, 10, 17, 24, 48, 67, 70, 114, 118, 128, 130, 132–141, 143, 146, 147, 159, 189, 197, 209, 210, 240
Night and the City (1992 remake) 140
Nolan, Lloyd 9, 97, 100–101

O'Brien, Margaret 6, 8, 80, 81, 84, 86
O'Neal, Tatum 44, 237, 239, 240–241, 242

Perkins, Anthony 27, 29–30, 175, 176, 177, 179, 180, 181, 182, 183, 184, 185

Index

Peters, Susan 8, 76, 77
Phaedra 28–30, 48, 156, 171, 173–185, 189, 192, 194, 196, 197, 198, 200, 233
Promise at Dawn 42, 43, 217–223, 232

The Rehearsal 43, 48, 154, 170, 193, 223–227, 228, 229
Reunion in France 1, 7, 14, 48, 63–70, 97, 105, 224–225
Rififi 1, 3, 16, 17, 18, 19, 22, 24, 26, 47, 48, 131, 141–150, 156, 159, 167, 179, 186, 189, 190, 194, 195, 196, 208

Schell, Maximilian 31, 189, 191, 193, 194, 226
Schildkraut, Joseph 7, 51
Schneider, Romy 32, 201–202
Servais, Jean 22, 24, 143, 148

Silvera, Frank 41, 216
Survival 67 2, 38, 40, 45, 203–205

Tamiroff, Akim 31, 194
The Tell-Tale Heart 3, 7, 8, 10, 49–52
10:30 P.M. Summer 32, 48, 192, 194, 195–203, 208
Thieves' Highway 3, 12, 17, 24, 48, 111, 122–132, 135, 143, 159
Tierney, Gene 17, 135, 137, 139
Topkapi 31, 45, 48, 183, 185–195, 199, 208, 226, 238
Trial 14, 15
Two Smart People 9, 95–101, 105, 159, 174, 198, 239
Two's Company 20–21, 33

Up Tight! 3, 41, 48, 205–217, 219

Ustinov, Peter 31, 47, 188, 189, 191, 192–193, 194, 195

Vallone, Raf 30, 176, 178, 179, 183, 184–185
Veidt, Conrad 7, 54, 56, 57, 58
Vita, Perlo 22, 143, 149

Walk a Crooked Mile 13
Walk East on Beacon! 14, 15
Wayne, John 7, 14, 67, 68, 69, 94
Where the Hot Wind Blows 2, 25, 45, 157–164, 165, 194
Widmark, Richard 17, 134, 139
The Woman on Pier 13 13, 14

Young, Loretta 18, 19
Young, Robert 8, 84, 85, 86
Young Ideas 8, 10, 46, 62, 68, 70–77

www.ingramcontent.com/pod-product-compliance
Lightning Source LLC
Chambersburg PA
CBHW081549300426
44116CB00015B/2816